MW01009400

Get started with your **Connected eBook**

Redeem your code below to access the **ebook** with search, highlighting, and note-taking capabilities; **case briefing** and **outlining** tools to support efficient learning; and more.

1. Go to www.casebookconnect.com
2. Enter your access code in the box and click **Register**
3. Follow the steps to complete your registration and verify your email address

ACCESS CODE:

Scratch off with care.

If you have already registered at CasebookConnect.com, simply log into your account and redeem additional access codes from your Dashboard.

Is this a used book? Access code already redeemed? Purchase a digital version at **CasebookConnect.com/catalog**.

If you purchased a digital bundle with additional components, your additional access codes will appear below.

"I liked being able to search quickly while in class."

"Being able to highlight and easily create case briefs was a fantastic resource and time saver for me!"

"I loved it! I was able to study on the go and create a more effective outline."

For technical support, please visit https://support.aspenpublishing.com

10094990-0001

ASPEN CASEBOOK SERIES

ARBITRATION

PRACTICE, POLICY, AND LAW

THOMAS J. STIPANOWICH
WILLIAM H. WEBSTER CHAIR IN DISPUTE RESOLUTION AND
PROFESSOR OF LAW
PEPPERDINE UNIVERSITY/CARUSO SCHOOL OF LAW

AMY J. SCHMITZ
THE JOHN DEAVER DRINKO/BAKER & HOSTETLER CHAIR IN LAW
THE OHIO STATE UNIVERSITY MORITZ COLLEGE OF LAW AND
PROGRAM ON DISPUTE RESOLUTION

ASPEN
PUBLISHING

To contact Customer Service, e-mail customer.service@aspenpublishing.com, call 1-800-950-5259, or mail correspondence to:

> Aspen Publishing
> Attn: Order Department
> PO Box 990
> Frederick, MD 21705

Printed in the United States of America.

1 2 3 4 5 6 7 8 9 0

ISBN 978-1-5438-5918-8

Library of Congress Cataloging-in-Publication Data

Library of Congress Cataloging-in-Publication Data application is in process.

About Aspen Publishing

Aspen Publishing is a leading provider of educational content and digital learning solutions to law schools in the U.S. and around the world. Aspen provides best-in-class solutions for legal education through authoritative textbooks, written by renowned authors, and breakthrough products such as Connected eBooks, Connected Quizzing, and PracticePerfect.

The Aspen Casebook Series (famously known among law faculty and students as the "red and black" casebooks) encompasses hundreds of highly regarded textbooks in more than eighty disciplines, from large enrollment courses, such as Torts and Contracts to emerging electives such as Sustainability and the Law of Policing. Study aids such as the *Examples & Explanations* and the *Emanuel Law Outlines* series, both highly popular collections, help law students master complex subject matter.

Major products, programs, and initiatives include:

- **Connected eBooks** are enhanced digital textbooks and study aids that come with a suite of online content and learning tools designed to maximize student success. Designed in collaboration with hundreds of faculty and students, the Connected eBook is a significant leap forward in the legal education learning tools available to students.

- **Connected Quizzing** is an easy-to-use formative assessment tool that tests law students' understanding and provides timely feedback to improve learning outcomes. Delivered through CasebookConnect.com, the learning platform already used by students to access their Aspen casebooks, Connected Quizzing is simple to implement and integrates seamlessly with law school course curricula.

- **PracticePerfect** is a visually engaging, interactive study aid to explain commonly encountered legal doctrines through easy-to-understand animated videos, illustrative examples, and numerous practice questions. Developed by a team of experts, PracticePerfect is the ideal study companion for today's law students.

- The **Aspen Learning Library** enables law schools to provide their students with access to the most popular study aids on the market across all of their courses. Available through an annual subscription, the online library consists of study aids in e-book, audio, and video formats with full text search, note-taking, and highlighting capabilities.

- Aspen's **Digital Bookshelf** is an institutional-level online education bookshelf, consolidating everything students and professors need to ensure success. This program ensures that every student has access to affordable course materials from day one.

- **Leading Edge** is a community centered on thinking differently about legal education and putting those thoughts into actionable strategies. At the core of the program is the Leading Edge Conference, an annual gathering of legal education thought leaders looking to pool ideas and identify promising directions of exploration.

To my mother, Mary Stipanowich, my wife, Sky, and my children, Laura, Tom, Nick, and Sarah—all of whom have taught me lessons about managing conflict

—T.S.

To my Dad, Larry Schmitz, for care and encouragement through the years

—A.J.S.

Summary of Contents

CONTENTS

The title of this book and accompanying materials, *Arbitration: Practice, Policy, and Law,* reflects a unique focus that places primary emphasis on practice and problem-solving for counselors, advocates, and arbitrators. The authors, two prominent leaders in the ADR and arbitration fields, brought to the effort not only decades of teaching, but also broad practical experience as advocates, arbitrators, expert witnesses, and active participants in the development of statutes, arbitration procedures, ethics standards, and practice guidelines, and even as leaders of or advisors to arbitration institutions.

Instead of simply addressing arbitration law and doctrine (the strong emphasis of most arbitration texts), we begin by introducing the broad range of processes that fall within the rubric of "arbitration" and how arbitration fits in a landscape that includes negotiation, mediation, and litigation. We then explore the practical opportunities and challenges presented by arbitration; our sequential treatment ranges from crafting arbitration agreements to selecting arbitrators to conducting the pre-hearing process, managing hearings, and dealing with arbitrator decisions, or awards. Only then do we move to discussion of the extensive legal framework supporting these out-of-court processes. We intend that this approach will provide students (including both neophytes and experienced practitioners) with a more complete and useful picture that allows users to see arbitration as a special set of tools in their toolbox for managing and resolving disputes and not simply another source of work for courts.

Our book also offers a multi-perspective approach that should translate well in a variety of arbitration courses — for law students as well as for masters' programs that also serve non-lawyers. We wrote the book primarily from the perspective of lawyers representing clients, but it is equally useful for would-be neutrals from a variety of backgrounds — which is entirely appropriate, since not all arbitrators are lawyers. We also took pains to carefully distinguish practice, policy, and law commonly associated with commercial (business-to-business) arbitration, well-established for generations, and arbitration under contracts between consumers or employees and various companies, which has been the focus of considerable controversy and political debate in recent decades. Our treatment of the history of arbitration includes nods to two of our country's greatest presidents, while our analysis of contemporary trends includes recent "soft-law" guidelines, key court decisions, and up-to-the-minute statutory developments, including the brand-new "#MeToo"-inspired law that limits enforcement of pre-dispute arbitration clauses in sexual harassment cases. The discussion is punctuated by accounts of actual disputes and literary examples that vividly illustrate key points.

Nowhere is the currency and uniqueness of this book more evident than in our attention to technology and its expanding impact on dispute resolution — a trend dramatically accelerated by the recent pandemic. Professor Schmitz, one of the most visible experts and thinkers about online dispute resolution (ODR) and online arbitration (or, to use a term she coined, "OArb"), developed new questions and problems that allow students to actively engage with the technological changes now being embraced in practice. Indeed, a great strength of our book and materials is the strong emphasis placed on questions and interactive problems, many of which were inspired by real-life experiences of the authors or colleagues. Along with extensive practical exercises (including "The Arbitration Game") and role-plays in the Teachers Manual, these elements bring the readings and other materials to life. They afford students opportunities to develop practice skills (counseling, negotiating, drafting, advocacy, managing prehearing preparation, conducting hearings, and rendering arbitration awards); to engender familiarity with various leading arbitration rules (AAA, JAMS, CPR), ethical standards, and legal doctrine; and to provoke critical thinking about the readings and other class materials.

At the same time, those interested in engaging students in the application of relevant legal doctrine will find ample coverage in this book. Our primary emphasis is on the Federal Arbitration Act (FAA), the body of federal law which has expanded exponentially in recent decades to play a critical role in state as well as federal courts. The evolution of the law is traced through carefully edited excerpts of cases and accompanying questions and problems. The discussion then shifts focus to explore the impact of arbitration provisions in standardized contracts of adhesion affecting employees and consumers. Importantly, the materials do not take any sort of political stance on these issues. Instead, they supplement an extensive discussion of developments in the courts, in legislatures, through "community protocols," and other approaches.

The book concludes with two chapters highlighting important developments in dispute resolution that may be relevant to students of arbitration. Chapter 9 offers a fresh and important discussion around "mixing and matching" in dispute resolution, either in multifaceted court programs or "mixed-mode" approaches that include stepped dispute resolution processes and hybrid roles for neutrals (such as single-neutral med-arb or arb-med). Chapter 10 explores three expanding directions in ADR practice: dispute systems design (DSD), online dispute resolution (ODR), and human rights applications. These emergent areas are shaping the field in exciting ways, and it is our hope that students who are interested in ADR continue studying these and other areas.

Instructors using this book should be aware of the many supplemental materials available on this book's website, including an extensive library of PowerPoint presentations covering the topics of the course. The website also offers links to 100 "Arbitration Conversations"—Professor Schmitz's interviews with arbitration practitioners, arbitrators, and scholars that provide expert guidance on critical issues in arbitration practice and law.

A note about form: In order to focus discussion and conserve space, we have substantially edited the readings and have converted all in-line citations of articles to endnotes. Deletions of material are shown by three dots, but omitted footnotes and other references are not indicated.

This book, a culmination of our combined decades of teaching, practicing, and shaping dispute resolution in legal contexts, could not have been developed without the efforts and input of the many students (and practicing lawyers) we have had the pleasure of teaching, or with whom we co-taught. They were instrumental in the preparation of a book and materials that we hope will have a significant impact on the next generation of lawyers and arbitrators.

June 2022

ARBITRATION

CHAPTER 1

ARBITRATION—THE BIG PICTURE

There is a good chance that if you are a student reading this book for a course, you know little or nothing about arbitration. Yet arbitration processes have become a critical part of the landscape of dispute resolution. Today, whether they know it or not, the great majority of U.S. citizens are currently bound by an agreement to arbitrate disputes in lieu of going to court. Arbitration may come into play not just in our business relationships but also in our place of work, our investments, and even the apps on our cell phones.

Knowledgeable attorneys understand the term "arbitration" to refer to any process in which a private third-party neutral renders a judgment, or "award," regarding a dispute after hearing evidence and argument like a judge. "Arbitration" comprehends a wide variety of procedures, similar in varying degrees to litigation and usually intended as a partial or complete substitute for court trial.

Look at the "Dispute Resolution Spectrum" below. Several forms of arbitration are referenced in the chart—but most types are listed on the right side of the spectrum, among "Adjudicative Processes/Binding." This arrangement emphasizes two essential characteristics of most arbitration procedures: They are adversary *adjudicative* procedures analogous to court trial, and they result in a judgment (award) that is *binding*.

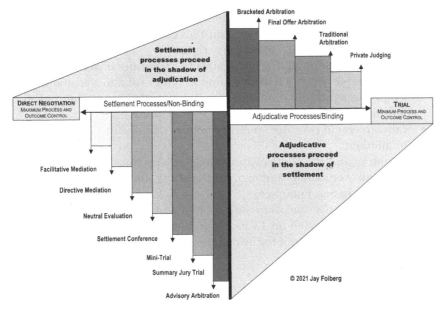

Dispute Resolution Spectrum

When lawyers are involved in arbitration, they act as advocates for parties in much the same way they do in court trial. They make oral arguments at hearings, present documentary and testimonial evidence, and prepare briefs for the arbitrators, who act as neutral decision makers. When the lawyers' work is done, the parties and lawyers await an award from the arbitrators. Arbitration awards are generally more difficult to overturn than court judgments. Although arbitration procedures and practice vary in detail and may differ significantly from court trial, arbitration processes are of a fundamentally different character from negotiation, mediation, and other processes on the left side of the Dispute Resolution Spectrum.

One form of arbitration, "Advisory Arbitration," is included on the left side of the Dispute Resolution Spectrum. This refers to a kind of process where an arbitrator or arbitration panel renders a nonbinding advisory award. Such processes are sometimes utilized in state or federal courts prior to trial of a case. The advisory award is not enforceable in court, but it may stimulate voluntary settlement of a dispute before trial. Advisory arbitration is not, however, the primary focus of the next eight chapters. Instead, we concentrate on binding arbitration pursuant to agreement of the parties.

In the United States, lawyers are most often involved with arbitration pursuant to a private agreement between two or more parties. The agreement usually provides that the arbitration award will be mutually binding and enforceable in a court of law. An extensive body of rules, practices, case decisions, and ethical standards has grown up around forms of contract-based, binding arbitration. This will be the chief emphasis of Chapters 1 through 8.

What kinds of disputes may find their way into binding arbitration under the terms of an agreement? The answers may surprise you. Consider the following examples of disputes that have been the subject of arbitration[1]:

- A dispute involving the design and construction of a Major League Baseball stadium;
- A controversy between U.S. financial institutions and the government of Iran;
- A claim for employment discrimination and intentional infliction of emotional distress by an employee against his employer;
- A dispute over intellectual property rights;
- A claim of fraud by an investor against her securities broker;
- A controversy between a bank issuing a credit card and a customer;
- A fight over the valuation and distribution of assets among entities and individuals in the wake of a corporate dissolution;
- A disagreement over the quality of textiles manufactured by one company for another;
- A claim against the company providing an "app" on your cell phone;
- A dispute over liability and damages resulting from delays in the arrival of a cargo ship in San Francisco;
- A controversy over the disqualification of an Olympic skater;
- A dispute adjudicated on TV as entertainment, à la "Judge Judy"; and
- An issue of punishment for infractions of National Football League rules.

A.   *BRIEF HISTORY OF ARBITRATION*

Arbitration has a long and venerable history, having been used by many cultures in a variety of contexts over the centuries. In Biblical times, King Solomon was famous for his wisdom as an arbitrator. Archaeologists have found papyrus documenting arbitration among Phoenician grain traders. The Roman Law Digesto refers to the figure of *arbiter*, an elder of the community who would settle private disputes. References to arbitration may be found in the Quran and the ethical teachings of the Mahabharata. In England, arbitration was recognized as part of the judicial system as early as 1281. Many Native American tribes turned to wise elders to resolve disputes.

Binding arbitration has long been an attractive alternative for commercial parties, for whom courts were often too slow and cumbersome, too expensive, too inflexible in remedy making, and lacking in familiarity with business practices. In medieval times, merchant courts dispensed speedy justice for traders at commercial fairs. Similarly, in the American colonies, arbitration among merchants was common since it proved more efficient and effective than the courts. Our first president, George Washington, served as an arbiter of private disputes before the Revolution, and incorporated the following provision in his will:

> I hope and trust, that no disputes will arise concerning [the devises in this will]; but if, contrary to expectation, of the usual technical terms, or because too much or too little has been said on any of the Devises to be consonant with law, My Will and direction expressly is, that all disputes (if unhappily any should arise) shall be decided by three impartial and intelligent men, known for their probity and understanding, two to be chosen by the disputants — each having a choice of one — and the third by those two. Which three men thus chosen, shall, unfettered by Law, or legal constructions; declare their Sense of the Testator's intention; and such decision is, to all intents and purposes to be as binding on the Parties as if it had been given in the Supreme Court of the United States.[2]

The New York Chamber of Commerce has provided for the use of arbitration beginning with its inception in 1768, and the New York Stock Exchange established arbitration as a dispute resolution mechanism in its 1817 constitution. In many places, private arbitration offered an alternative form of justice for communities in the long periods between visits of circuit courts. Indeed, arbitration provided the only means for international merchants from Great Britain and the United States to resolve disputes while they continued to engage in trade during the American Revolutionary War. As a lawyer in frontier Illinois, Abraham Lincoln represented clients in arbitration and, as an arbitrator, determined a boundary line between disputants' properties.

By the middle of the twentieth century, dozens of industry and trade associations were sponsoring private arbitration programs for business-to-business disputes. Binding arbitration also became a fixture in arbitration of rights and interests under collective bargaining agreements between unions and employers.

Today, arbitration remains an important alternative to court litigation of business disputes, and many organizations in the United States and other countries offer a variety of services to parties who wish to arbitrate, including lists of potential arbitrators, arbitration procedures, and administrative services. Use of arbitration is widespread among Fortune 1000 corporations.[3] In international trade and business relationships, binding arbitration provides a critical substitute for litigation in national courts. Leading institutions providing international arbitration have reported growing caseloads; a recent tabulation found more than 120 international arbitrations in which a billion dollars or more was at issue.[4]

In recent years, binding arbitration agreements have become a feature of many contracts between employers and individual employees, as well as contracts for consumer goods and services. These developments reflected, among other things, an important shift in prevailing judicial attitudes toward arbitration—the courts that were once skeptical of binding arbitration now tend to embrace it as an effective dispute resolution option. The United States Supreme Court has spearheaded this evolution by liberally interpreting the Federal Arbitration Act (FAA), which provides for the enforcement of arbitration agreements and awards.

As you will see in our survey of arbitration practice in Chapters 2 through 4, arbitration procedures are in many respects analogous to litigation, and have become even more similar as a result of the dramatic expansion of arbitration into what has been called an "all-purpose surrogate" for court trial. A substantial body of case law has evolved around arbitration, as explored in Chapters 5 and 6. Not surprisingly, business users of arbitration often complain that their experiences have become more and more like going to court. Paradoxically, concerns about the relative non-reviewability of arbitration awards have led some attorneys to draft contract provisions for judicial review of the legal or factual merits of arbitration awards. The same concerns have led some major providers of arbitration services to offer parties the option of an appellate arbitration panel.

Meanwhile, the appearance of provisions for binding arbitration in credit card, cell phone, and other consumer contracts, as well as individual employment contracts, has raised legitimate and strong concerns regarding the fairness of particular arbitration procedures and outcomes in these settings. These concerns have produced a variety of responses—including the creation of special protocols and standards, judicial decisions, and state and federal legislation. In a related vein, the growing use of arbitration to resolve international investment disputes between multinational corporations and the governments in developing countries has come under fire. These concerns and related responses are the subject of Chapters 7 and 8.

Today, forms of arbitration are often employed as part of multi-faceted systems for management and resolution of conflict, as explored in Chapter 9. Chapter 10 examines aspects of systems design as well as rapidly developing technological innovations affecting arbitration and dispute resolution.

B. *ARBITRATION vs. LITIGATION*

According to one study of conflict resolution among leading corporations, business lawyers choose arbitration over litigation in a public forum for a variety of reasons: to achieve a speedy resolution; to avoid the costs and delays of litigation; to forgo extensive discovery; to escape the glare of a public proceeding; to avoid the publication of a legal precedent; to choose a decision maker with pertinent business or legal expertise; or to achieve a more satisfactory or more durable resolution. Arbitration may or may not achieve these anticipated benefits. Much hinges on key choices made by parties and their attorneys at the time of drafting and during the course of the arbitration process—choices that should be informed by the particular needs and goals of the parties.

1. *Relative Speed and Economy*

As compared to litigation, arbitration has traditionally been touted as a more efficient, speedy, and inexpensive path to justice. There is empirical evidence indicating that in some categories of cases, especially those that do not involve high stakes, arbitration is often speedier than court trial.[5] Arbitration sometimes avoids, and often limits, time-consuming (and costly) procedural steps such as pretrial motion practice and discovery. And due to relatively strict limits on judicial review of arbitration awards, the likelihood of lengthy post-arbitration appellate practice is relatively low.

However, depending on the scope or complexity of the issues, the nature of agreed-upon procedures, the orientation of legal counsel, and the process management skills of the arbitrator(s), arbitration may end up being just as lengthy or as costly as litigation. Lawyers are often inclined to introduce more extensive procedural elements into the process, including discovery and motion practice analogous to those available in court, and to require the services of multiple arbitrators whose often busy schedules must be coordinated. Appellate arbitration procedures are also available under some arbitral rules. Indeed, many business attorneys now say that arbitration has become too "judicialized." This seems to defeat arbitration's fairness, efficiency (including speed and cost), and certainty goals.[6]

In recent years, mounting concerns about the perceived lack of efficiency and excessive cost in U.S. and international arbitration inspired the publication of a variety of guidelines for stakeholders in arbitration. These include the International Chamber of Commerce (ICC) Commission Report on *Techniques for Controlling Time and Costs in Arbitration* (2009) and the U.S. *College of Commercial Arbitrators Protocols for Expeditious, Cost-Effective Commercial Arbitration* (2010). Among other things, these standards highlight the variety of factors that affect the cost and length of arbitration and tend to put particular emphasis on the importance of proper planning and case management at all stages of the arbitration process, including the period prior to hearings when parties exchange information and present motions asking the arbitrators to make decisions about many different aspects of the case. These influential "soft-law" guidelines and related developments in commercial arbitration procedures are discussed in Chapter 4.

At the same time, the introduction of technology into arbitration has helped make arbitration cheaper and easier for parties and arbitrators. The use of virtual hearings saves the time and cost of traveling to hearings. Computer-mediated communications also allow for easy exchange of documents from the comfort of parties' homes, with the participants wearing their pajamas if they so desire. Asynchronous communications also enhance convenience. For example, company personnel handling disputes presumably prefer to respond to work-related communications during the workday. However, consumer complainants may be working or caring for children during the day and therefore only have the time to deal with their personal or home-related claims in the evening or during other off-work hours. Asynchronous communication therefore addresses these different scheduling needs. More will be said about online arbitration throughout the book.[7]

2.   *Privacy and the Avoidance of Precedent*

Arbitration typically involves proceedings that are not open to the public, which makes them "private." However, they are not necessarily confidential unless the parties sign a confidentiality agreement. Such agreements are common, however, because confidentiality is a major concern for many parties who utilize the arbitration process. Extremely sensitive business and personal documents, including those detailing financial information, are foreclosed from the public, and witnesses are also shielded from public scrutiny during arbitration. At a time when many business users' primary assets include tightly guarded intellectual property, confidentiality surrounding dispute resolution processes is more important than ever. At the same time, arbitration awards are not normally made public, although there are significant exceptions, including situations in which a motion is made before a court to confirm, vacate, or modify an award. Moreover, the law places major obstacles in the way of parties seeking court testimony by arbitrators regarding the process or their decision.

Privacy and confidentiality of arbitration has created controversy in some cases. For example, private arbitration proceedings have been under fire for keeping information regarding sexual harassment and police brutality out of the public eye. On the other hand, the privacy of arbitration has been particularly valuable in intellectual property disputes.[8]

Unlike court judgments, arbitration awards do not typically establish precedents for other cases that do not involve the same parties and dispute. This principle is sometimes reinforced by practical limitations such as the absence of a public decision and the lack of a published rationale accompanying the award. As discussed below, arbitrators traditionally have issued written decisions that are publicly available only in special areas such as labor law and domain name disputes. Even there, however, the awards do not function as a strict form of precedent. Thus, arbitration is a desirable dispute resolution option if one party wants to avoid a precedent. If, on the other hand, a party seeks to establish a new precedent affecting other pending or future disputes, arbitration may be less attractive.

Finally, because one is usually not bound to participate in arbitration or to accept the legal consequences of an arbitration award unless one is a party to an agreement to arbitrate, lawyers who craft business arrangements involving several parties and multiple contracts need to pay particular attention to the functioning of arbitration in multiparty disputes. Otherwise, a party may find itself engaged in multiple proceedings, facing the prospect of inconsistent results.

3. Choice of Expert Decision Maker(s)

Arbitration allows parties to select their own decision maker(s); they have the freedom to choose experts in pertinent fields, including law, business and finance, accounting, engineering, technology, and other areas. In some cases, a panel of arbitrators may bring to the table complementary knowledge, skill, and experience. For example, an arbitration panel selected to resolve a complex construction dispute might consist of a lawyer familiar with construction contracts and disputes, an architect or engineer, and a contractor or construction manager. Likewise, it is especially important to have an arbitrator well versed in blockchain technology decide a dispute around cryptocurrencies. Moreover, the ability of an arbitrator (or chair of an arbitration panel) to manage the dispute resolution process may be of paramount significance—especially in large or complex cases.

Of course, the practice of choosing decision makers with related professional background and expertise enhances the likelihood that those chosen will have connections to the parties or will already have formed perspectives on issues at the heart of the dispute. While some arbitrating parties may view such relationships as positive qualifications for arbitrators, others may take the opposite view.

The important thing is for parties to have sufficient information to make an informed judgment about the background and connections of prospective arbitrators. For this reason, as explored later, arbitration agreements, statutes, and ethical codes routinely require arbitrators to disclose relationships to the parties and their counsel, as well as other information that might indicate a conflict of interest.

4. Informality and Flexibility

Another trademark of arbitration is its informality. The atmosphere tends to be less formal and intimidating than a court proceeding; arbitrations frequently take place in a conference room, hotel, the office of the organization providing arbitration services, or other suitable meeting space. Moreover, the rules of evidence and procedure are usually somewhat flexible, allowing the parties to submit certain kinds of evidence that would not be considered in court. For clients frustrated by the rigidity and cost of formal rules of evidence and court procedures, this can be a benefit. However, attorneys must make their clients aware that this relaxation of the rules also means that parties in an arbitration process may not receive all of the formal procedural opportunities and protections of litigation. For example, hearsay may be more widely admitted than in court, even if arbitrators give it less weight. Arbitrators generally have discretion in running the proceedings, which may mean more truncated proceedings in some cases, or more expansive consideration of evidence where arbitrators fear that their refusal to hear material evidence will provide grounds for reversal of an award under federal or state law. Again, much hinges on the choice of arbitrator(s) and other decisions made by attorneys and the parties in defining the process.

Notably, arbitrators know that their awards generally will not be measured against judicial precedent, and courts have sometimes spoken of the ability of arbitrators to rely on their own notions of fairness and equity to tailor a remedy appropriate to the circumstances. On the one hand, in some forms of arbitration, including in some commercial and labor arbitration, the emphasis was and is on "fact-dominated rough justice. Equity, not law, is the order of the day. . . ."[9]

At the same time, in some contexts, lawyers often dominate the process and may judicialize the proceedings. Many advocates and arbitrators place considerable emphasis on legal issues and legal precedents, and anticipate a result that comports with applicable law. In any event, parties bargain for the determination of the arbitrator and not the court, and modern law places stringent limits on judicial review of arbitral awards. It is very difficult for parties to overturn awards on the basis of errors of fact or law.

5. Finality

Arbitration awards are, in fact, more ironclad than jury verdicts or trial court judgments, since appeal is limited to very narrow grounds. Courts give great deference to arbitrators and allow very few avenues of redress. This finality may be one of the greatest advantages of arbitration for many clients who want to get a dispute behind them and move on with new business. It can, however, be a serious disadvantage for parties who are displeased with a ruling or believe that the integrity of the process was compromised, or where a dispute presents important or novel legal issues.

Lawyers sometimes express concern about the possibility that arbitral awards will be undisciplined by legal or other norms, resulting in unpredictable and unforeseeable outcomes. A survey of Fortune 1000 corporate counsel indicates that the leading concern of many lawyers representing business clients is that arbitrators will not properly apply legal standards.[10] The complaint is often made, with some justification, that some arbitrators "split the baby" to avoid hard decisions on the merits. But in modern, lawyer-dominated arbitration practice, law is increasingly likely to play an important role throughout the arbitration proceeding—and an award of 40 to 60 percent of the amount claimed may be fully justified on legal or factual grounds. A recent survey of experienced U.S. arbitrators provides strong evidence that in the absence of a contrary agreement, arbitrators work hard to understand and follow applicable law and "carefully read and reflect upon legal arguments and briefs presented by counsel"; however, about one-quarter of the group also said that sometimes they "feel free to follow [their] own sense of equity and fairness even if the result would be contrary to applicable law."[11]

Again, this makes arbitration's finality a serious consideration for practitioners entering into an arbitration agreement. If they are concerned regarding rigorous application of precedent and the danger of an extreme or seemingly irrational award, arbitration may be an unacceptable option for a particular dispute. Alternatively, attorneys may use arbitrator selection, along with guidelines and standards, to reduce the risk of a "knucklehead" award. As we will see in Chapter 6, some attorneys have attempted to alter arbitration agreements to allow courts to review arbitration awards on their merits. Although the Supreme Court has quashed this attempt to expand judicial scrutiny of awards under the Federal Arbitration Act, some state courts have enforced such provisions.[12]

6. Arbitration as a Choice-Based Process

When all is said and done, it may be that the greatest potential benefit of arbitration is the flexibility afforded to participants in crafting a private system of justice tailored to fit the needs of their specific dispute. However, this places a premium on the ability of legal counsel to provide effective guidance in making process choices. Parties often choose an administered process where arbitral institutions help with the various stages of arbitration. Forms of administrative support include electing arbitrators, scheduling, and handling fees and expenses. Some parties forgo administrative support, opting instead for a non-administered arbitration to minimize costs. Sometimes parties take a purely ad hoc approach to arbitration, although (as discussed in Chapter 2) relying totally on one-off drafting sometimes produces unforeseen and unpleasant consequences.

PROBLEM: CHOOSING ARBITRATION: A DIGITAL DOWNLOAD CONTRACT

Your client, MDM, is an entertainment production company based in Los Angeles. One of the many television shows the company produces is a popular series entitled "Starscape." The series is shown exclusively on a cable network, which airs the show in an expanding number of U.S. markets. "Starscape" has enjoyed relatively high ratings and has a strong following of loyal and enthusiastic fans.

The Fandom Company (Fandom) of Chicago, Illinois, owns and administers a Web site called "ScapePlace.com." On this site, visitors can find transcripts of interviews with "Starscape" cast members as well as airdates and other things of interest to fans of the show. Users can log on to the site after a brief, and free, registration process.

Now that "Starscape" is about to enter its third season, MDM is negotiating a contract with Fandom allowing Fandom to host video files of "Starscape" episodes on its "ScapePlace" site. Fandom is interested in hosting the files, as it would mean a huge increase in traffic to the ScapePlace site. ScapePlace, like many other such sites, makes its profit by providing advertising space. The more visitors, the more money advertisers will be willing to pay to place their banners on the site.

MDM also anticipates benefits from the arrangement. Its marketing people believe that allowing Fandom to distribute episodes of "Starscape" to people who access the ScapePlace site would increase the show's following beyond that of the limited cable market. MDM hopes the increased interest in the show will put pressure on the network to expand the number of markets airing the series, as well as increase the interest in the season boxed DVD sets of "Starscape" MDM plans to release early next year.

MDM plans to include in the contract numerous limitations and conditions relating to the quality of the video files Fandom can provide. For example, the contract will prohibit Fandom from hosting video files of seasons one and two of "Starscape" that are larger than 80 MB. The clarity of an 80 MB video file would be enough for a viewer to enjoy the episode in a two-inch box on their computer monitor, but would not be of a high enough quality to compete with the soon-to-be-released DVDs.

Suppose you are discussing with your client, MDM, the possibility of including an arbitration provision in the dispute resolution clause of the proposed contract with Fandom. What, if any, aspects of this scenario suggest that MDM may want to propose an arbitration provision? What aspects might make arbitration less appealing than litigation? In addition to the foregoing reading in Section B, "Arbitration vs. Litigation," use the "Simple Checklist on the Suitability of Arbitration" to help you develop your answers.

A Simple Checklist on the Suitability of Arbitration

Some years ago, the International Institute for Conflict Prevention & Resolution (CPR), a New York–based nonprofit organization that brings together leading lawyers and scholars to discuss, develop, and promote effective approaches to business conflict, published an ADR Suitability Screen for the guidance of lawyers and clients considering the use of mediation, arbitration, and other ADR options. The following checklist, loosely based on that document, provides a starting point for counsel advising clients about whether to agree to arbitrate disputes with another party, or instead to litigate controversies in court. A "Yes" answer to a question would tend to support a choice of arbitration, while a "No" answer would support using traditional litigation.

A. Is the ability to be able to choose the decision maker(s) likely to be an important objective?

B. Are the disputes likely to require an understanding of complex or technical factual issues?

C. Might it be important to have an expedited adjudication process?

D. Might the privacy of the hearing or the confidentiality of information shared in the process be important?

E. Is there likely to be little or no concern regarding the establishment of precedent or articulation of public policy?

F. Will it be satisfactory to employ something less than the full discovery procedures contemplated by court rules?

G. Is there unlikely to be a vital corporate interest or "bet the company" dispute that will require the full panoply of procedural protections afforded by a court, including full appellate rights?

C. FAIRNESS CONCERNS

As stated above, effective use of and satisfactory experiences with arbitration usually hinge on users' ability to make appropriate procedural choices. For this reason, serious issues of substantive fairness and unequal bargaining power sometimes arise with respect to arbitration of disputes under some kinds of standardized contracts. Individuals may be surprised to find themselves bound by pre-dispute arbitration provisions after having purchased consumer goods and services. There are concerns over the elimination of an aggrieved party's right to a trial by a judge or jury, the potential loss of related procedural protections and, in particular, concern about an accompanying waiver of that party's right to bring a claim in the form of a class action.

Fairness issues also arise in employment disputes, when employees find they are bound to assert any claims against an employer through arbitration because of the individual employment agreement they signed before any disputes arose. Sometimes, consumers or employees assert that they are in a "take it or leave it" position because all jobs in a given industry or all similar products can only be obtained by signing nearly identical arbitration clauses. Such contracts can be said to contain elements of "adhesion." In such circumstances, the secrecy provided by the arbitral process, plus participants' real or perceived lack of control over designing the dispute resolution process and choosing the arbitration provider or arbitrator(s), can foster suspicion, anger, and less incentive to comply with an arbitral award. Besides inspiring a number of efforts by stakeholders to create due process standards for consumer or employment arbitration, these concerns have prompted some courts to more carefully scrutinize arbitration agreements and awards. State legislatures have also sought to place restrictions on arbitration agreements in adhesion settings. Such efforts have often faltered in the face of strong federal pro-arbitration policy, including a series of Supreme Court decisions that strongly support the enforceability of class action waivers and other provisions in agreements to arbitrate. In recent years, these issues have become highly politicized, and various efforts have been made in the U.S. Congress to restrict the use of arbitration in consumer and employment transactions. These subjects are explored in more detail in Chapters 7 and 8.

QUESTIONS

1. The checklist may prove to be a useful tool in acquainting a client with fundamentals that affect a choice to arbitrate, but it doesn't offer a nuanced introduction to the choices arbitration offers participants. As noted above, it is sometimes said that for commercial relationships, the greatest single conceptual advantage of using arbitration is *choice*—the ability to tailor the dispute resolution process to suit the dispute. These may include choices regarding the expertise of arbitrators, the number of and selection methods for arbitrators, the kind of proceeding (including "streamlined" or "expedited"), the desired level of privacy and confidentiality, the nature of the award, and other elements. It is also said that such choices are often ignored, or made by default. What factors might prevent parties and their attorneys from focusing on choice making about their arbitration agreement?

2. Why are arbitration agreements usually made at the time the parties enter into a contract, before any disputes actually arise? Would it be better to only enforce post-dispute arbitration agreements? Why or why not?

3. In what contexts might parties have different views regarding the utility of arbitration?

4. Also, how much time do you expect that parties entering into a contract actually spend on the subject of arbitration and dispute resolution?

5. A number of jurisdictions feature commercial courts that offer a level of expertise regarding commercial matters and, sometimes, expedited case processing. Might the availability of such an alternative influence your advice to a client regarding the choice between arbitration and litigation?

D. ARBITRATION vs. NEGOTIATION AND MEDIATION

In this course or other courses, you may have become familiar with the role negotiation and mediation may play in resolving disputes outside the courtroom. Parties have the opportunity to forge their own paths to a resolution in ways that take into account personal or business priorities and interests that no court judgment can address, and tailoring solutions beyond the scope of judicial relief. Party-centered, informal, and flexible approaches can enhance the possibility of preserving or improving important continuing relationships and improving communication and understanding among participants.

While binding arbitration is often perceived as preferable to going to court, it is nearly always more formal, time consuming, and expensive than unassisted negotiation or mediation—and cedes final decision-making authority to a third party. And although it is sometimes said that arbitration may help reduce friction between the parties and lay the groundwork for future relations, its impact is often as negative as litigation's. Arbitration processes are, after all, typically backward-looking, adversarial proceedings in which the parties take a back seat to their lawyers and to a third-party decision maker who will impose a judgment.

For these reasons, lawyers and parties increasingly view arbitration as a last resort among ADR processes, to be employed only after negotiation and/or mediation have failed. Today, business lawyers often advise clients to attempt negotiation and mediation even after they have agreed to arbitrate and, if appropriate, to continue such settlement attempts during the arbitral process. Where other methods are unavailing, of course, binding arbitration may be the most appropriate "backstop" form of third-party adjudication.

QUESTION

6. Take another look at the facts set out in the Problem above. If you were proposing a dispute resolution provision for a contract between MDM and Fandom, would you include terms calling for the parties to negotiate or mediate before turning to arbitration? Why or why not?

E. THE MANY FACES OF ARBITRATION

To make the most of the opportunities afforded by arbitration, you will need to appreciate the wide diversity of arbitration processes and the range of choices available to parties in arbitration. The following summaries provide a glimpse into a spectrum of different applications of arbitration and encourage you to think about underlying process choices and policy questions.

After reading each summary, consider and try to answer the following general questions, along with any other questions posed:

- How would you briefly characterize the arbitration procedure(s) discussed? (Court-like or informal? Law-oriented or focused on something else? Lengthy or expedited?)

- What policies or practical concerns do you suppose led responsible decision makers to develop the current system? What are the pros and cons of the approach(es), and why was the balance struck in the way it was?
- Who are the arbitrators, and what kind of background or experience do they bring to the table?

1.   Construction/Commercial Arbitration: "Mainstream" Arbitration

As a U.S. lawyer or party, you are most likely to have an experience with binding arbitration in the course of disputes arising under a commercial or construction contract. The construction industry is an example of a commercial sector that places strong emphasis on resolving grievances and disputes informally, efficiently, and outside the court system. Motivated by the desire to achieve a profit and to maintain good working relations with clients and other project participants, most successful design and construction businesses generally seek to avoid trial if at all possible. Going to court can ruin business relationships, destroy morale, and derail a construction project.

Arbitration has long been a favored alternative to going to court to resolve engineering and construction disputes. A mid-1980s survey of construction attorneys demonstrated that arbitration was generally perceived as a fair alternative to trial before a judge or jury.[13] On average, moreover, arbitration was a speedier means of dispute resolution than either jury or bench trial, and somewhat less costly overall. Perceptions and experiences varied significantly; however, there was a strong impetus for trying to improve arbitration.

In the late 1990s, the American Arbitration Association (AAA), which has long been one of the leaders in the field of commercial and construction dispute resolution, developed new Construction Industry Arbitration Rules. These rules have been updated over time but essentially allow three alternative paths for cases of different sizes. These included a "Fast Track" scheme for cases involving claims of relatively low value (originally, under $50,000); a "Regular Track" aimed at cases involving claims up to $1 million; and a "Large and Complex Track" for cases involving more than $1 million. Each scheme represents a different prioritization of various process attributes. Fast Track procedures emphasize speed and simplicity: Procedures include abbreviated timetables, limited extensions of time, expedited arbitrator appointment, limited information exchange, and streamlined hearings.

Regular Track procedures updated traditional arbitration procedures in order to provide arbitrators with construction law or industry expertise, clarified arbitrator authority, and enhanced speed. Revisions to standard forms permitted parties' input regarding desired arbitrator qualifications. The new rules made clear the arbitrator's authority to control discovery "consistent with the expedited nature of arbitration"; and included a more explicit statement of arbitral authority to control hearings and to take interim protective measures, "including measures for the conservation of property." The new rules also require arbitrators to provide a "concise, written breakdown of the award" and a "written explanation" if requested by all parties or if the arbitrator believes it to be appropriate.

Large and Complex Track procedures feature an elite panel of neutrals and special supplementary pre-hearing procedures, including arbitrator-supervised discovery; they may be further tailored to the specific needs of the case by agreement of the parties. The process commences with an administrative conference with an AAA case manager to discuss the parties' needs, including views on arbitrator qualifications, and to consider the use of mediation. A later "preliminary hearing conference" is conducted by the arbitrators to discuss discovery and other preparations for arbitration and, once again, to explore the possibility of mediation and other alternatives. In addition to directing the production of documents, the rules make clear that arbitrators control the amount of discovery afforded the parties in accordance with the expedited nature of arbitration.

The AAA thus sought to maximize the flexibility of its arbitration procedures and permit a tailoring of the process to the particular needs of different cases. Ultimately, however, the best-crafted procedures may mean little in comparison to the capabilities of arbitrators in whom so much discretion is placed. For this reason, the AAA's most important reform was to pare down its large national rosters of construction arbitrators in an attempt to enhance the quality of neutrals. The AAA has made a major effort to develop and maintain a multidisciplinary list of potential arbitrators made up of legal, design/engineering, and construction professionals, and to ensure that all receive regular skills training.

The AAA's reforms in the construction arbitration arena paved the way for almost identical changes to the AAA Commercial Arbitration Rules and commercial arbitration panels. The "three-track" approach, pared-down panels, and enhanced training became common elements of AAA administration.

More recently, competition for commercial arbitration business has arisen in other organizations such as JAMS (which originally stood for "Judicial Arbitration and Mediation Services") and various other national and regional provider organizations. They do not, however, typically follow the "three-track" approach of the AAA; some organizations list only lawyers and former judges, and not professionals from other disciplines, on their panel of prospective arbitrators. Administrative options for arbitration, recent changes to leading procedures, and new procedural options (such as "streamlined" procedures) are discussed in Chapter 4.

QUESTIONS

7. What do you think of the AAA's response to concerns about construction arbitration? Could you imagine using some form of expedited or streamlined procedures for cases involving something larger than a $75,000 claim? How would use of technology in the proceedings possibly address concerns about economy and efficiency in arbitration?

8. There appears to be a trend in the direction of employing tribunals composed entirely of arbitrators with legal backgrounds.[14] What are the relative pros and cons of using an arbitration panel made up of three lawyers instead of a multidisciplinary panel for a construction or business dispute? Explain.

9. Although arbitration is still an important option for resolving construction disputes, in the last decade some standard construction industry contract documents have been modified to place greater emphasis on mediation and at processes aimed on resolving disputes in early stages. Why do you suppose this is true?[15]

2. *Labor Arbitration Under Collective Bargaining Agreements*

Labor arbitration arises under the collective bargaining agreements between employers and the unions representing employees. This area of the law is one in which the federal government predominates due to a history of congressional involvement designed to keep the economy running as smoothly as possible, while parties to labor agreements resolve disputes. Additionally, both management and union leaders sought systems for addressing inevitable disputes safely and efficiently. Labor disputes were among the most common subjects for arbitration for much of the twentieth century, and arbitration has played a central role in the sphere of labor-management relations. Labor arbitration is statutorily mandated, chiefly under §301(a) of the Labor Management Relations Act. Procedures for dispute resolution are set out in federal law and contractual agreements between unionized employees and management.

Arbitration procedures under collective bargaining agreements vary with needs and circumstances. Some parties agree to conduct labor arbitration under the pertinent rules of an institution, such as the AAA, while others use an ad hoc process. Parties usually employ a single arbitrator selected by mutual agreement; however, depending on the industry and the nature and size of the dispute, a three-member "tripartite" arbitration board may be appointed. In this instance, the board will consist of one member chosen by management, one selected by the labor union, and a neutral who will serve as chair.[16] It is then up to the parties to decide what qualifications they require the arbitrators to possess. Generally speaking, labor arbitrators need not be specialists in the subject matter, but a background in social or economic study is desirable; they are frequently non-lawyers. Labor arbitrators are typically required to issue published awards, although the awards are not regarded as binding precedents. Like other arbitral awards, labor arbitration awards are difficult to overturn. However, a court may vacate an award if the award does not draw its "essence" from the collective bargaining agreement, from which the claim arises. See the Supreme Court's 1960 *Steelworkers Trilogy*, 363 U.S. 564, 363 U.S. 574, 363 U.S. 593.

Labor cases under collective bargaining agreements tend to divide into two modes of adjudication: *rights-based* arbitration and *interest* arbitration. In rights-based arbitration, parties look for an interpretation or application of the laws, agreements, and practices that exist within the "four corners" of the collective bargaining agreement. A party may dispute the meaning or application of one or more of the provisions that are already in existence. In interest arbitration (which is more prevalent in the public sector), the arbitrator must determine what *should* or *could* have been in the terms and conditions of employment; the arbitrator must look outside the preexisting contract, considering fairness, policy, and expediency to make a determination.[17]

QUESTION

10. Why do you suppose management and labor often use "tripartite" arbitration panels?

3. Securities Arbitration

Ever since the seminal Supreme Court decision in *Shearson/American Express v. McMahon*, 482 U.S. 270 (1987) (holding that claims under the Racketeer Influenced and Corrupt Organizations Act and the Securities and Exchange Act of 1934 are subject to arbitration), investors have been required by contract to arbitrate their disputes with brokerage firms. With the oversight and approval of the Securities and Exchange Commission (SEC), a quasi-governmental but essentially private administrative body now known as The Financial Industry Regulatory Association, Inc. (FINRA) was established to administer arbitrations. Securities arbitration case filings vary with the markets: they generally spike during economic downturns and dwindle in periods of relative stability.[18]

Judicial encouragement of securities arbitration is partly founded on the perceived benefits for both industry members and customers, including reduced costs and speedier results. The arbitration system has made it possible to try smaller cases that might never have seen the inside of a courtroom. At the same time, the costs associated with arbitration hearings, including administrative costs and arbitrator fees, can in some cases be an obstacle.

The number of arbitrators appointed depends on the amount and type of relief sought by the investor. For claims of $50,000 or less, FINRA appoints one arbitrator and the claim is subject to simplified arbitration procedures.[19] For claims between $50,000 and $100,000, FINRA appoints one arbitrator, unless the parties agree in writing to three arbitrators.[20] For claims over $100,000, FINRA appoints three arbitrators; traditionally this panel includes a chairperson that is "public" (i.e., not affiliated with the securities industry), another public arbitrator, and a non-public arbitrator, affiliated with the securities industry, typically a broker or manager.[21]

As investors are compelled to arbitrate their disputes, there has been much controversy over investors giving up their right to trial by jury in court. Critics long complained that fairness in the process is compromised when a member of the securities industry (non-public arbitrator) has the authority to pass judgment on his/her peers. After years of concern by investor-advocates, FINRA gave investors the option to have a three-member panel made up of arbitrators without experience in the securities industry.[22] This means that any involvement by non-public arbitrators is solely at the election of investors.

To ensure due process for investors, high-value securities arbitration procedures have become increasingly similar to court procedures. There is, for example, document discovery,[23] and arbitrators have the authority to award punitive or exemplary damages in appropriate cases.[24] However, there are usually no pre-hearing depositions, pre-hearing substantive motions, contention interrogatories, or requests for admissions.[25]

Investor/broker arbitration and mediation are regulated more extensively than any other form of out-of-court dispute resolution. The SEC has long overseen the practices and policies of FINRA and other self-regulatory organization arbitration programs, conducting periodic audits and passing on changes to arbitration procedures; the U.S. Government Accountability Office also conducts occasional reviews. There is also a well-established body of experienced lawyers who regularly represent investors in arbitration.

However, concerns remain about the extent to which securities arbitration may in some ways favor brokers and brokerage houses. There have been efforts in Congress to prevent contract terms requiring arbitration of securities brokerage disputes. The Dodd-Frank Wall Street Reform and Consumer Protection Act (2010) empowered the SEC to study and prepare a report to Congress on securities arbitration and "prohibit or impose conditions or limitations on" securities arbitration agreements. This and other related developments are discussed in Chapter 8.

QUESTIONS

11. Why is investor/broker arbitration subject to government agency regulation, unlike construction industry and commercial arbitration?

12. If you were an investor, would you prefer to go to arbitration or to court? Explain your choice. Consider the statement of a successful investor advocate based in Los Angeles:

> Given the tremendous time and expense of pursuing any civil case in today's reduced staff, overworked and lengthy[-]delay court system, I believe that almost every case that seeks actual damages of less than $1,000,000 can be more efficiently pursued in arbitration using a fair forum. By the time one pursues a claim for less than $1,000,000 against, for instance, a large well-financed public corporation, by successfully defending motions to dismiss based on the pleadings and thereafter engaging in discovery involving depositions, contention interrogatories, requests for admissions and successfully defending summary motions and fending off any appeals, the average civil plaintiff may well have his or her $1,000,000 recovery significantly reduced by the expense of the court process. . . . [A]rbitration of a claim for less than $1,000,000 in a fair forum takes substantially less time and hence less expense because it involves significantly less discovery. . . . Finally, petitions to vacate an award, the only avenue of appealing an adverse arbitration award, are much more limited than typical appeals of a court issued judgment.

---

4. *International Commercial Arbitration and Investment Arbitration*

Arbitration has become the preferred method of dispute resolution for international commercial disputes. The term "international" marks a distinction between arbitrations that are purely domestic and those that go beyond national boundaries because of the nature of the dispute, the nationality of the parties, or a selection of a neutral place to conduct proceedings — *the seat of arbitration*. The term "commercial" relates to the "business" nature of the dispute. Note that the addition of this international element adds significant complexity to the settlement of disputes, such as different languages, currencies, legal systems, and political and economic backgrounds, to list a few.

One may speculate that there are many reasons for why arbitration has developed so intensely in the settlement of international disputes. It is possible to list: (1) neutrality of the arbitrators, as opposed to one of the parties "playing at home"; (2) international enforceability of decisions, as guaranteed by international treaties and conventions; (3) flexibility and adaptability of procedures; (4) enhanced confidentiality and privacy; (5) decision makers chosen for their expertise and availability; and (6) continuity (as the arbitrator typically oversees a dispute from start to finish).

Scenario #1

Imagine you are an attorney working for O'Deal, a surfing goods manufacturing company, conducting business out of southern California. In your first year, O'Deal starts to get involved with the Brazilian market, selling goods and buying raw materials. Would you be comfortable in resolving eventual disputes in Portuguese? Under Brazilian contract law? Before Brazilian courts with Brazilian procedural rules? With Brazilian attorneys? If the situation were reversed, would your Brazilian counterpart feel comfortable resolving disputes in English, in California, under California contract law, with Californian procedural rules, and with U.S. attorneys? Wouldn't both parties feel more comfortable with a more flexible proceeding in which their needs and concerns could be addressed? What might that look like?

As with domestic arbitration, "international commercial arbitration" is a mechanism (1) for the settlement of disputes, (2) based on consent, (3) which is private, and (4) which leads to a final and binding determination of the rights and obligations of the parties. If the power of national judges derives from their investiture, the power of arbitrators derives from parties' agreement to arbitrate, expressing their *consent*. Arbitration is detached from the court system of any country (State); it is a *private* form of adjudication by third parties—arbitrators. And this source of power—*consent*—is what provides greater flexibility, allowing the disputants to agree on a choice for the procedural rules, the substantive law, the seat of arbitration, the arbitrators, and several other issues they might find relevant.

One additional and extremely relevant aspect is the decision—*the arbitral award*—in which the arbitrator(s) allocate the rights and duties between the parties. The *award* shall be (1) final, that is, subject to strictly limited grounds of appeal; and (2) binding upon the parties, which enforceability shall be assured by an international treaty. The preeminent international arbitration treaty is the 1958 New York Convention on the Recognition and Enforcement of Arbitral Awards (the "New York Convention").[26] By entering into the New York Convention—which today has 156 signatory nations—countries undertake an obligation to enforce foreign arbitral awards. There is no similar treaty for the enforcement of foreign judicial decisions.

Another area of international arbitration pertains to the resolution of foreign direct investment disputes. Investment arbitration is treated as a separate area of international arbitration, distinct from commercial arbitration, because of the nature of the parties and the substantive nature of the dispute. In investment arbitration, the dispute is not between private parties (e.g., between individuals and corporations) but instead involves public parties (with individuals and corporations on one side and States on the other). The involvement of sovereign States in investment arbitration often raises issues of politics and policy that do not arise in commercial arbitration.

Foreign direct investments (FDIs) are extremely relevant for economic development. FDIs include capital investments in another State, transfer of technology and know-how, development aid, and the transfer of goods to another State. These investments are based on bilateral agreements — *between the investor's home State and the investment host State* — or multilateral agreements — *between several nations, including the investor's home State and the investment host State.*

If there is no other arrangement, a dispute between a host State and a foreign investor will have to be settled by the domestic courts of the host State. From the investor's point of view, this raises several concerns, particularly the potential lack of impartiality of the courts, the procedural rules that will apply, the relevant substantive law, and even whether the courts have the knowledge and expertise necessary for such a complex dispute.

Scenario #2

Imagine now that O'Deal is investing in Indonesia, Malaysia, and Papua New Guinea. The reasons vary but certainly include the marketing benefits of being present in places with "epic" waves; the tax benefits of production in a place with a cheap labor force; and the desire of Mr. O'Deal, the owner, to increase profits while doing some good for the community, because of fond memories of a surfing trip to Indonesia when he was younger. What if the government of Indonesia retains your company's goods? Would you feel comfortable resolving your disputes with the government of Malaysia in Malaysian courts? In Malay (the official Malaysian language)? Under Malaysian contract law? With Malaysian procedural rules? With Malaysian attorneys? Wouldn't you rather resolve your disputes with Papua New Guinea in a neutral setting, before neutral arbitrators, and neutral procedural rules and relevant substantive law?

In order to overcome these difficulties, an initiative from the World Bank in the 1960s led to the creation of the 1965 Convention on the Settlement of Investment Disputes between States and Nationals of Other States, which created the International Centre for Settlement of Investment Disputes (ICSID). At the time of writing, 159 States are parties to the ICSID Convention, undertaking an obligation to resolve investment disputes under the ICSID Rules and waiving sovereign immunity for the enforcement of the awards.

Although it is not without problems or concerns, many believe that international arbitration, whether for resolving commercial or investment disputes, is the most reliable and predictable way to resolve international disputes.

5.   *Arbitration at the Olympics*

The Court of Arbitration for Sport (CAS) was established in 1984 to address various international sporting disputes. The CAS created a special ad hoc program for arbitration of urgent sports-related disputes at the Olympic Games (including doping, issues of nationality, and judging matters).

During the 2002 Olympic Winter Games in Salt Lake City, Utah, a major controversy erupted in the final of the men's 1,500-meter short-track speed-skating race. Many Americans cheered for Apolo Anton Ohno, an aggressive young skater who had qualified for the final despite sustaining an injury requiring six stitches in an earlier race during the games. He competed against a strong field, including Korea's most acclaimed short-track skater, Kim Dong-Sung. The skaters raced around the track at incredible speeds. Heading into the final lap, Kim was the only skater Ohno needed to pass to win gold. Kim cut off Ohno and crossed the finish line just ahead of him. The referee ruled immediately, however, that Kim was disqualified because he had illegally blocked Ohno during the final lap. While many American fans rejoiced and the Salt Lake City crowd cheered, a "firestorm of protest" was set off around the globe. Ohno received death threats, and an Italian skater declared he should be shot. The U.S. Olympic Committee's server crashed after it received more than 16,000 emails protesting the disqualification.

Korean officials immediately protested, but Chief Referee James Hewish of Australia refused to overturn the disqualification. The next day, Korean officials pursued their claims within speed-skating's governing body. When that group confirmed the referee's decision as final, the Korean Olympic Committee appealed to the CAS, the final and exclusive dispute resolution board for the Olympic Games. As a condition of participating in the games, all athletes and organizations must sign entry forms agreeing to binding arbitration before the CAS. Two days after the race, the CAS held a hearing. Judge R. S. Pathak of India headed the Salt Lake arbitral pool, which involved nine arbitrators, each from a different country. The International Council of Arbitration for Sport had selected the arbitrators before the start of the games for their expertise in arbitration and sports law. Each arbitrator signed a declaration attesting to his independence before the games began.

Late that evening, Kim's disqualification appeal was heard by a panel of three arbitrators; a British lawyer served as president and the other members were from Switzerland and Finland. During the arbitration proceeding, panelists called the referee and his four assistants as witnesses. Other interested parties were summoned, including the Korean Skating Union and the Olympic Committees of the United States, Canada, China, Italy, and France. An American attorney represented the Korean committee, which had to establish that the referees acted with bad faith or arbitrarily. All parties agreed that the panelists could not attempt to "second guess" decisions made by the referee on technical "field of play" issues. The grievant's attorney cited the controversy surrounding the earlier men's 1,000-meter race when Ohno, who was leading, wiped out in the final turn and brought down three other skaters with him. Additionally, counsel argued that U.S. media pressure and local audience pressure in Ohno's favor influenced the referee.

The arbitrators could review a videotape of the race, even though the head referee did not have instant replay review at the time of the race, but declined to do so because this would be closer to a technical "field of play" review than an examination of bad faith or illegitimate decision making. Instead, the arbitrators heard from three assistant referees (from the United States, Norway, and England) that they had independently observed the Korean skater's "cross-tracking" infraction, noted that disqualification was the appropriate penalty, and reported this to the head referee at the conclusion of the race. The arbitrators, finding the witnesses honest and straightforward, ruled in favor of Ohno retaining the gold medal. On February 23, only three days after the race, the arbitrators issued a nine-page "Final Award" upholding the disqualification.

QUESTIONS AND NOTE

13. Is the fact that we are dealing with an *international* sporting event relevant to the discussion?

14. Why do you suppose this kind of expedited arbitration process was selected for the Olympics? If arbitration were not an available alternative, how would problems of this kind be resolved?

15. During the Beijing Olympics in February 2022, a CAS ad hoc panel of three arbitrators was called upon to conduct a hearing and rule upon whether a provisional suspension against 15-year-old Russian figure skater Kamila Valieva should be reinstated. The suspension had been levied by the Russia Anti-Doping Agency (RUSADA) after tests by a doping control lab revealed traces of a prohibited substance in a sample provided by Valieva the previous December; the suspension was subsequently lifted after a hearing before RUSADA's Disciplinary Anti-Doping Committee (DADC). The DADC ruling was appealed to CAS by the International Olympic Committee (IOC), the World Anti-Doping Agency (WADA), and the International Skating Union (ISU). In a controversial decision, the CAS arbitration panel rejected the appeal, thus permitting Valieva to continue competing in the Olympics. The 41-page decision by the tribunal reflects the potential procedural complexities with which sports arbitrators must grapple, including multi-party proceedings, jurisdictional issues, different standards of proof, and the challenge of interpreting and applying rules that in the panel's view were flawed by internal inconsistencies.[27]

---

6.   *Writers Guild Arbitration*

The matter of who gets credit for writing a screenplay is of critical importance to the reputation and economic well-being of writers (whose residual income from long-term exploitation of a film usually depends on being credited), and the question is often laden with controversy. In the United States, the Writers Guild of America (Guild) determines who receives credit for writing screenplays or developing an original story or character(s) on which a screenplay is based. Any production company that signs the Guild Minimum Basic Agreement is bound by the Guild rules, including the procedure for determining credit. When a film is completed, the producer is required to present proposed screenwriting credits to the Guild and send copies of the final script to all writers who worked on the script. Upon objection by any writer to the producer's proposal, the matter is submitted to arbitration. Arbitration is also required in any circumstance where a director or producer of the film is proposed for credit. This arbitration process is frequently triggered; between 1993 and 1997, for example, there were 415 Guild arbitrations representing around one-third of all films whose credits were submitted.

During arbitration, members of the Guild review all drafts of the screenplay by each writer and follow a set of arcane formulae for determining the credits. For example, an "original writer" must contribute at least one-third of the final screenplay to receive credit. Subsequent "script doctors" must author more than half of the final screenplay to receive credit, as must a production executive. A maximum of three writers may receive screenplay credit if they worked in collaboration, and a maximum of three teams of three writers may be credited, no matter how many actually worked on it. Often, many more individuals are actually involved; for example, it is said that the film adaptation of *The Flintstones* (1994) had approximately 35 writers.

Arbitrators may also be required to address the permissible use of requested pseudonyms. One memorable case involved a writer who was so angry over changes made to his work by the production company that he sought to take his name off the credits and substitute "Eiben Scrood" in protest. His request was denied.

In screenwriting credit arbitration, the identities of the arbitrators are secret, and parties sometimes complain about the fact that they have no opportunity to object to the lack of qualifications or the possible lack of impartiality of their judges. Moreover, parties are not given the opportunity for an oral hearing, nor is a rationale provided for the decision of the arbitrators. (While there is a panel to address appeals from arbitration, it is limited to considering procedural objections.) The secrecy of the arbitration process and the formulae governing decisions have led to strong criticisms by some Guild members. For example, after arbitrating credits for the 1998 film adaptation of Hunter Thompson's *Fear and Loathing in Las Vegas*, Terry Gilliam resigned from the Guild in protest. He described the arbitration process as a "Star Chamber" and claimed he spent more effort on the credit battle than he did on the screenplay itself. However, the Writers Guild of America, West membership upheld the arbitration procedures in 2002.

QUESTION

16. Can a process that does not involve a face-to-face hearing be "arbitration"? (In Chapter 5 we will see that whether something qualifies as "arbitration" under applicable statutes may make a difference.)

---

7.   *Uniform Dispute Resolution Procedures*

Some evaluative but nonbinding online arbitration programs have developed in certain contexts. For example, a non-final online administrative resolution process under the Uniform Dispute Resolution Procedures (UDRP) through Internet Corporation for Assigned Names and Numbers (ICANN) has shown some success.[28] The UDRP was adopted on August 26, 1999, and the implementation documents were approved on October 24, 1999.[29] Parties have used the UDRP online procedure to obtain a relatively quick and cheap determination of who may use a contested domain name. These UDRP procedures allow parties to present their cases online to a panel that must provide each party "a fair opportunity to present its case." The panel consists of one or three "arbitrators" at the election of either party. Panelists must be impartial and independent, and all communications between panelists and the parties must be made through a case administrator appointed by the dispute resolution provider. The panel then produces a written nonbinding decision on the parties' claims within 14 days of the panel's appointment. *See Virtual Countries, Inc. v. S. Afr.*, 148 F. Supp. 2d 256, 259-261, 265 n.10 (S.D.N.Y. 2001).

Although the procedure flows like AAA and other usual arbitration processes, the court in *Parisi v. Netlearning, Inc.*, 139 F. Supp. 2d 745, 751-753 (E.D. Va. 2001), held that the UDRP proceedings do not constitute binding arbitration under the FAA. *See also Lockheed Martin Corp. v. Network Solutions, Inc.*, 141 F. Supp. 2d 648, 651-652 (N.D. Tex. 2001); *Barcelona.com, Inc. v. Excelentisimo Ayuntamiento De Barcelona*, 330 F.3d 617, 624 (4th Cir. 2003). The UDRP itself allows for judicial intervention, which can occur before, during, or after the UDRP's dispute-resolution process, and thus it is not "arbitration" under federal and state law. At the same time, the UDRP is different from traditional arbitration because proceedings must be online unless the panel specifically determines that it is "an exceptional matter" and therefore an in-person, telephonic, or teleconferenced hearing is necessary. UDRP Rules, at 959. In addition, proceedings only cover cancellation and transfer of the domain names abusively registered and not claims for damages or injunctive relief other than return of a domain name. Any judicial determination of a respondent's appeal will trump the panel's decision, provided that ICANN receives documentation regarding the lawsuit within ten days after it is notified of the decision.

QUESTION

17. Why do you suppose the UDRP uses an arbitration process that results in a decision or award that is not legally binding? Also, why do you think this is an online process? Do you think the online aspect or finality issue (or both) provided foundation for courts holding this process was not the type of arbitration governed by the FAA?

8. Court-Connected Arbitration

In recent decades, court-connected pretrial arbitration became popular as a perceived remedy for backlogs and delays experienced in some court systems. Hence, court rules or statutes sometimes require advisory arbitration or nonbinding arbitration of certain types of disputes, such as lawsuits involving medical malpractice claims and civil claims filed in courts of a lesser monetary amount (e.g., suits involving less than $25,000 or $50,000 in damages). Typically, volunteer lawyers serve as neutrals in these proceedings. The arbitrations are "mandatory" only in the sense that arbitration is a precondition to litigation. The arbitral awards issued are usually not binding in such situations, and indeed they often cannot be, since both the United States Constitution and most state constitutions guarantee access to the courts and juries for most civil controversies.[30] However, court-annexed arbitration tends to be quite different from private arbitration pursuant to party agreement.

Notably, court-connected arbitration programs have become much less popular in recent years, eclipsed by court-connected mediation. Furthermore, online dispute resolution (ODR) programs are growing in popularity as means for expanding access to justice and remedies in the courts. Many courts now have stepped online processes for parties to negotiate, mediate, and sometimes arbitrate online as a precursor to, or replacement of, litigation. This can save the time, travel, cost, and stress of in-person procedures.[31]

QUESTION

18. Why has ODR in the courts grown in recent years? What are the pros and cons of such court-connected online processes?

---

9. "Judge Judy" Contexts

You may have seen TV "syndicourt judges" like Judge Judy and wondered whether they were just actors or "real" court judges under state authority. In fact, they are usually arbitrators per party agreement. For example, a court ruled that an arbitration led by Mayor Ed Koch on "The People's Court" TV show constituted an arbitration, defined as "a process of dispute resolution in which a neutral third party renders a decision after a hearing at which both parties have an opportunity to be heard." *Kabia v. Koch*, 713 N.Y.S.2d 250, 254 (Civ. Ct. 2000). This was the case even though the TV format meant that the arbitration award was paid by producers, rather than the parties themselves. *Id.*

Judge Richard Posner has referenced Judge Judy's arbitral power as an example of how parties may give up procedural rights by consenting to an arbitration. *Roughneck Concrete Drilling & Sawing Co. v. Plumbers' Pension Fund, Loc. 130, UA (United Ass'n)*, 640 F.3d 761, 766 (7th Cir. 2011). He notes that parties are free to submit disputes to Judge Judy, although her awards may be overturned under arbitration law. The Brooklyn Family Court overturned an award granted by Judge Judy relating to child support, because it was not an issue that was submitted to her for arbitration. *B.M. v. D.L.* n.o.r. N.Y.L.J. 3/20/2000, p.30, cols. 4-6 (Family Court, Kings County 2000). However, the court did not question the validity of the agreement itself or Judge Judy's role as an arbitrator.

F. THE FRAMEWORK OF ARBITRATION: CONTRACTUAL AND LEGAL STANDARDS

Arbitration practice involves a lot of rules, and effective counselors, advocates, and arbitrators need to have a working knowledge of these standards. They reflect both the private contractual foundation of arbitration as well as public laws, and include the following:

1. The Agreement to Arbitrate

Because binding arbitration is usually a creature of contract, the clause(s) by which parties bind themselves to arbitrate are usually the primary source of rules for the process. An arbitration clause will probably incorporate, by reference, the applicable arbitration procedures and related administrative framework, if any. It may also indicate what law should control the arbitration agreement and any resulting award, as well as the separate issue of what law should be applied by the arbitrators. Chapter 2 will examine key elements of agreements to arbitrate, as well as guidelines for drafting.

2.   *Arbitration Procedural Rules*

Agreements to arbitrate frequently incorporate procedural rules covering everything from the filing of an arbitration demand and the selection of arbitrators to the rendition of an arbitration award (e.g., "All disputes arising under the contract or the breach thereof . . . shall be resolved under the ACME Commercial Arbitration Rules and Procedures"). Such rules are often developed and published by organizations that provide services to arbitrating parties in the form of administrative support for arbitration and lists of prospective arbitrators.

3.   *Arbitration Statutes*

Today, federal and state statutes, along with a vast and growing body of related case law, play an important role in U.S. arbitration practice. The most important source of public law governing arbitration is the Federal Arbitration Act (FAA), 9 U.S.C. §§1-16 (2000). State arbitration laws, generally in line with the Uniform Arbitration Act (mimicking the FAA) or its revised version, may also figure prominently in some circumstances. Although these statutes are mainly addressed to courts enforcing arbitration agreements and awards, they may have a direct or indirect impact on arbitration proceedings. Arbitration statutes and related judicial decisions will be explored in Chapters 5 and 6 as well as portions of Chapters 7 and 8.

4.   *International Conventions*

Arbitration plays an indispensable role in international business transactions, in part because the great majority of sovereign nations have signed key conventions that provide for arbitration of private disputes. As noted above, the leading international convention is the New York Convention. The great majority of the world's nations are signatories to the New York Convention, which establishes a platform for the enforcement of international arbitration agreements and awards rendered in other countries. The New York Convention is said to make arbitration awards more enforceable than court judgments in international cases.

5.   *Substantive Law Applicable to the Merits of an Arbitrated Dispute*

Although it will be discussed only briefly in this volume, it is common for contracting parties to provide that their agreement will be interpreted in accordance with the law of a particular jurisdiction. Such provisions are likely to control the law that arbitrators apply in the course of deciding issues before them.

6. Ethics Rules

The parties' agreement or organizations providing arbitration services may require arbitrators to abide by certain ethical standards in the course of their service. In the United States, the most widely used set of arbitrator ethics standards is the *Code of Ethics for Arbitrators in Commercial Disputes*. In Chapter 3, we will examine and apply ethical rules touching on the important topics of arbitrator conflict of interest, disclosure, and disqualification.

7. "Soft Law" Providing Guidance for Participants in Arbitration

An established array of "protocols," "guidelines," "checklists," and other documents have been published for the purpose of giving advice and counsel to parties, attorneys, arbitrators, and other stakeholders in U.S. and international arbitration. These forms of "soft law" are not binding on participants in arbitration (although some are amenable to being incorporated in the parties' agreement to arbitrate), but they are typically designed to influence the choices made before and during arbitration. In the materials associated with Chapter 4, you will have a chance to apply guidelines aimed at making arbitration more expeditious and cost-effective.

G. LOOKING AHEAD

Chapters 2 through 4 provide an introduction to the fundamentals of arbitration practice in its most prevalent form: business-to-business arbitration. We will explore, among other things, the various routes by which parties arrive at arbitration; basic considerations for attorneys drafting arbitration agreements; the selection of qualified arbitrators; arbitration procedures, including the management of information exchange and discovery; and arbitral awards and remedies. Along the way, you will become familiar with some leading arbitration procedures and the organizations that sponsor them, as well as important ethical standards governing the activities of arbitrators.

Chapters 5 and 6 treat the expanding legal framework of American arbitration and address current legal issues confronting practitioners, including the scope and functions of arbitration statutes, judicial enforcement and facilitation of arbitration agreements, and judicial treatment of arbitration awards. Attention is given to Supreme Court jurisprudence expansively interpreting and enforcing arbitration agreements under the FAA, and you will be exposed to key underlying principles, including:

- Judicial respect for the autonomy of parties who have agreed to arbitrate;
- The concept that agreements to arbitrate are *separable* (or *severable*) from the contracts of which they are a part, and may be enforceable even if the entire "container" contract is not; and

- The doctrine of *federal preemption*, under which FAA policies supporting the enforceability of agreements to arbitrate preempt contrary state law (whether the product of legislation or judicial declaration).

We also briefly touch upon and compare international arbitration theory and legal doctrine.

Chapters 7 and 8 examine arbitration under the terms of standardized contracts, including transactions involving consumer goods and services and individual employment contracts, the special concerns associated with arbitration in these contexts, and the evolution of the surrounding legal and regulatory framework. We review Supreme Court precedents that have redefined the landscape of employment and consumer disputes as well as concurrent efforts by Congress in response.

Chapter 9 examines arbitration against the backdrop of multi-step or mixed-mode dispute resolution systems. Chapter 10 takes us to the cutting edge of process design and technological change.

Endnotes

1. For a compendium of arbitration and dispute resolution approaches, see Stipanowich, Thomas J. (2001) *Contracts Symposium: Contract and Conflict Management*, 2001 Wis. L. Rev. 831.
2. Nordham, George W. (1982) *George Washington and Money*.
3. Stipanowich, Thomas J. & Lamare, J.R. (2014) *Living with "ADR": Evolving Perceptions and Use of Mediation, Arbitration and Conflict Management in Fortune 1,000 Corporations*, 19 Harv. Negot. L. Rev. 1.
4. Stipanowich, Thomas J. (2014) *Reflections on the State and Future of Commercial Arbitration: Challenges, Opportunities, Proposals*, 25 Colum. Am. Rev. Int'l Arb.
5. Weinstein, Roy. (2017) *Arbitration Offers Efficiency and Economic Benefits Compared to Court Proceedings*, N.Y. Disp. Resol. Law.
6. Schroeder, Roland & McIlwrath, Michael. (2011) *The View from an International Arbitration Customer: In Dire Need of Early Resolution*, Int'l In-House Counsel J.
7. Schmitz, Amy J. (2010) *"Drive-Thru" Arbitration in the Digital Age: Empowering Consumers Through Regulated ODR*, 62 Baylor L. Rev. 178-244.
8. Schmitz, Amy J. (2006) *Untangling the Privacy Paradox in Arbitration*, 54 Kan. L. Rev. 101-144 (2006).
9. Brunet, Edward. (2002) *Defending Commerce's Contract Delegation of Power to ICANN*, 6 J. S. Emerg. Bus. L. 1.
10. Stipanowich, Thomas J. & Lamare, J.R., *supra* note 3.
11. Stipanowich, Thomas J., *supra* note 4.
12. Schmitz, Amy J. (2002) *Ending a Mud Bowl: Defining Arbitration's Finality Through Functional Analysis*, 37 Ga. L. Rev. 123-204.
13. Stipanowich, Thomas J. (1988) *Rethinking American Arbitration*, 63 Ind. L.J. 425.
14. Stipanowich, Thomas J., *supra* note 4.
15. Stipanowich, Thomas J. (2010) *Arbitration: The "New Litigation,"* 2010 U. Ill. L. Rev. 1 (January).

16. Zumbolo, Anthony. (2018) *The Acceleration and Decline of Discord: Collective Bargaining Impasses in New York State*, 36 Hofstra Lab. & Emp. L.J. 163.

17. Ruben, Alan M. (2003) *Elkouri & Elkouri: How Arbitration Works*.

18. https://www.finra.org/arbitration-mediation/dispute-resolution-statistics.

19. *12000 Code of Arbitration Procedure for Customer Disputes*, FINRA at 12401(a), finra.org/12000 (last visited July 10, 2020).

20. *Id.* at 12401(b).

21. *Id.* at 12401(c).

22. *Id.*

23. *Id.* at 12506-12507.

24. *13000 Code of Arbitration Procedure for Industry Disputes*, FINRA at 13802(e), finra.org/13000 (last visited July 10, 2020).

25. *12000 Code of Arbitration Procedure for Customer Disputes*, FINRA at 1245(a), finra.org/12000 (last visited July 10, 2020).

26. https://www.uncitral.org/uncitral/en/uncitral_texts/arbitration/NYConvention.html.

27. *Read the Full Ruling from the Court of Arbitration for Sport on Kamila Valieva*, N.Y. Times, Feb. 17, 2022, https://www.nytimes.com/interactive/2022/02/17/sports/olympics/court-of-arbitration-for-sport-ruling-on-kamila-valieva.html?auth=link-dismiss-google1tap.

28. Osborn, Jason M. (2000) *Note: Effective and Complementary Solutions to Domain Name Disputes: ICANN'S Uniform Domain Name Dispute Resolution Policy and the Federal Anticybersquatting Consumer Protection Act of 1999*, 76 Notre Dame L. Rev. 209, 214.

29. Internet Corp. for Assigned Names and Numbers (ICANN): Rules for Uniform Domain Name Dispute Resolution Policy, 39 I.L.M. 952 (2000) [hereinafter UDRP Rules]; World Intellectual Property Organization (WIPO), Arbitration Rules, http://www.wipo.int/amc/en/arbitration/rules/index.html (last visited July 8, 2020).

30. Schmitz, Amy J. (2009) *Nonconsensual + Nonbinding = Nonsensical? Reconsidering Court-Connected Arbitration Programs*, 10 Cardozo J. Conflict Resol. 587-625.

31. Schmitz, Amy J. (2019) *Expanding Access to Remedies Through E-Court Initiatives*, 67 Buff. L. Rev. 101-173.

CHAPTER 2

ARBITRATION AGREEMENTS

A. INTRODUCTION

In the modern environment, arbitration deals with a much broader range of conflict, from simple consumer disputes to big cases involving complex legal issues. While parties may see the virtues of a private substitute for court trial in many different kinds of cases, the nature of that private alternative will vary with the circumstances. Arbitration may mean anything from a rudimentary, expedited, non-lawyered process involving a quality determination by a technical or commercial expert to a much more formal proceeding with many of the trappings of court trial.

As an attorney, you will need to carefully tailor arbitration processes to the varying needs and expectations of parties — and legal counselors and advocates should be well informed regarding the many choices that arbitration presents. By introducing you to key issues surrounding arbitration, we hope to provide you with the knowledge and skills you will need to fulfill the promise, and avoid the pitfalls, of arbitration for your clients. We will place considerable emphasis on various standards that govern or provide guidance for arbitration proceedings, arbitrators, and advocates. These include procedures, policies, and guidelines of national and international institutions supporting or sponsoring arbitration.

Arbitration is generally a creature of contract, and businesses often participate in private arbitration processes and comply with the decisions of arbitrators without any resort to courts of law; indeed, avoidance of court processes is often an important goal of parties choosing arbitration. We devote this chapter and Chapters 3 and 4 to a start-to-finish consideration of arbitration processes and procedures, as well as some pertinent ethical considerations for arbitrators and lawyers, and defer extensive treatment of the legal "backdrop" to Chapters 5 and 6.

Nevertheless, it is critical to have a framework for the judicial enforcement of agreements to arbitrate and of arbitration awards. In the last few decades, this legal framework has assumed an ever-increasing role in the practice of arbitration, directly or indirectly affecting virtually every aspect of arbitration. Lawyers must therefore understand the interplay of federal arbitration law and state statutes on arbitration in the United States, and the role of international treaties in arbitration of cross-border disputes. Hence, while the legal framework of arbitration is primarily addressed in Chapters 5 and 6, with discussion of court decisions associated primarily with arbitration agreements and awards relating to consumer or employment contracts in Chapters 7 and 8, we make brief references to arbitration law and its impact throughout this chapter.

B. THE CONTRACTUAL FOUNDATIONS OF ARBITRATION

Parties usually end up in arbitration because they have entered into a contractual agreement to arbitrate. Occasionally, parties agree to submit a dispute to arbitration after it has arisen. These post-dispute agreements are called *submission agreements*. Much more commonly, however, parties commit themselves to arbitrate long before any dispute arises through a clause that binds them to arbitrate some or all future disputes that arise out of the relationship. Such clauses, known as *pre-dispute agreements to arbitrate*, have long been a standard feature of collective bargaining agreements between unions and employers, as well as construction and other kinds of commercial contracts. In recent years, they have been included in contracts relating to employment, insurance, health care, retail sales, banking, professional services (including legal services), real estate agreements, repair services, utility services, and myriad other transactions.

You may be the attorney responsible for considering whether to incorporate an arbitration provision in a client's contract. That decision is often complicated by the fact that no disputes have actually arisen, and decisions about arbitration must be based on prior experience and educated guesses. Today, a contract drafter should also consider whether arbitration should be preceded by other strategies for resolving disputes, such as stepped negotiation or mediation. These options, and the growing use of multistep or "hybrid" approaches, will be explored in Chapters 4.K and 9. Other choices remain. How broad should the arbitration agreement be? Is it necessary to have the administrative support (including arbitration procedures, a list of arbitrators, and case managers) of a third-party institution? How should arbitrators be selected? What level of procedural "due process"—discovery, pre-hearing practice, evidentiary rules—is appropriate? What remedies may an arbitrator grant? Will the award include findings of fact or conclusions of law, or will it be a "bare" award? These and other considerations for drafters are treated in the following pages, as are issues confronting lawyers who serve as advocates for parties in the arbitration process.

Increasingly, businesses are placing arbitration clauses in "boilerplate" contracts with employees and consumers. (Do you have a credit card? A cell phone? Are you required to arbitrate with anyone?) Because such terms are not usually subject to negotiation and typically purport to waive the right to go to court, they raise legitimate concerns about the fairness of the alternative system. We return to these intriguing issues in Chapters 7 and 8. First, however, it is important to gain an appreciation of how arbitration works, and how it may be most effectively employed, in the broad run of business-to-business arrangements.

QUESTIONS

1. *Basic pre-dispute provisions.* Arbitration provisions come in all shapes and sizes. Most, however, tend to be relatively concise and straightforward. Consider the following model arbitration clause, which is recommended by a major provider of arbitration services for inclusion in contracts:

    Any controversy or claim arising out of or relating to this contract, or the breach thereof, shall be settled by arbitration

> administered by the American Arbitration Association in accordance with its [insert type of rules] Arbitration Rules [including the Emergency Interim Relief Procedures], and judgment on the award rendered by the arbitrator(s) may be entered in any court having jurisdiction thereof.

Can you identify five functions served by this provision? Notice that the parties can select from arbitration rules for various types of disputes (e.g., commercial, construction, labor, patent, financial planning, and wireless Internet).

2. *Submission agreements.* As noted above, sometimes parties agree to submit existing disputes to arbitration. A basic template for such an agreement would look something like this:

> We, the undersigned parties, hereby agree to submit to arbitration the following controversy: _____. The arbitration will be conducted in accordance with the Commercial Arbitration Procedures of the ACME Dispute Resolution Association, as modified below. A judgment of any court having jurisdiction may be entered upon the award.

What are the potential advantages of making the decision to arbitrate after disputes have arisen? Why do you suppose that many fewer arbitrations are conducted pursuant to the terms of submission agreements as compared to pre-dispute agreements in contracts?

C. MAKING EFFECTIVE CHOICES REGARDING ARBITRATION

Because parties seek different things from arbitration, and because business goals and needs vary by company, transaction, and dispute, no one form of arbitration is always appropriate. For this reason, the central value of arbitration is not speed, or economy, or privacy, or neutral expertise, but rather the ability of parties to make key process choices to suit their particular needs.

A report by the American College of Trial Lawyers linked the disappearance of civil trials with high cost and delay; the report called for an end to the "one-size-fits-all" approach of current federal and state litigation procedures and for the development of alternatives that offer quicker, less expensive resolution. Such choices are readily available in arbitration, as it is based on the agreement of those involved. If parties truly desire an expedited procedure in which speed and economy are the preeminent goals, it is possible to structure and implement a "lean" arbitration process. If, on the other hand, cost savings and a quick result are much less important than having a controlled, private version of litigation with extensive legal due process and a tribunal made up of three high-profile decision makers that results in a highly "authoritative" decision, that, too, is an option. The key is fitting the process to the problem.

Unfortunately, contract planners and drafters usually "drop" arbitration and dispute resolution provisions into commercial contracts without much reflection or discussion. While experienced arbitrators and thoughtful advocates may function effectively within this kind of framework, all too often, arbitration under standard one-size-fits-all procedures takes on many of the trappings of litigation, with commensurate costs and delays.[1] The result is frustration and disappointment for those coming to arbitration expecting it to be more efficient and economical than trial.

If you have the opportunity to counsel clients regarding arbitration and dispute resolution, therefore, take to heart these key practice pointers.

1. Don't Wait Until You Are in the Middle of Negotiating to Consider and Discuss Dispute Resolution Options

At some point before negotiating or drafting a contract, discuss your client's goals and priorities in managing conflict, including (1) flexibility; (2) low cost or cost efficiencies; (3) a speedy outcome and avoidance of undue delay; (4) "fairness" and "justice"; (5) legal due process; (6) results comporting with commercial, technical, or professional standards; (7) predictability and consistency in result; (8) a final and binding resolution; (9) privacy and confidentiality; and (10) preservation of a relationship plus continuing performance. The identified goals and priorities become touchstones for process selection. If, for example, your client places a high priority on getting disputes resolved relatively quickly, it may be appropriate to incorporate a streamlined procedure in the arbitration clause, at least for some disputes. If there is a significant need for protection of trade secrets or other information likely to be relevant to disputes, special attention should be paid to the crafting of language protecting the confidentiality of such information.

2. Make Sure the Arbitration Procedures (and Administering Organizations) You Choose Support Your Client's Goals

Don't simply adopt the same old arbitration boilerplate, but instead make deliberate selections based on client goals and needs. Today, arbitration counsel should know about choices in the arbitration marketplace and make a knowledgeable selection among procedures and among organizations sponsoring arbitration. For example, you should be aware that some organizations publish or emphasize a single one-size-fits-all set of arbitration rules, whereas others offer a range of procedures designed for different kinds of cases or disputes of different sizes or levels of complexity. Some institutions specialize in arbitrators who are lawyers or retired judges, and others offer a choice among arbitrators with different professional backgrounds. Some organizations have rules that offer much more protection for confidential information (as will be discussed in Chapter 4.G.2).

3. Employ Arbitration as Part of a Conscientiously Developed Program for Managing Conflict

As discussed in Chapter 1, arbitration is rarely the appropriate starting point for resolving disputes. More and more contractual dispute resolution provisions include arbitration as the final stage in (and backdrop for) other approaches to resolve disputes, such as negotiation and mediation. See Chapter 4.K.

4. Choose Outside Counsel and Arbitrators on the Basis of Client Goals

There are two other early "choice points" for users of arbitration—the selection of legal counsel to represent a client's interests in the resolution of disputes, and the selection of arbitrators to resolve those disputes. In both cases, the choices parties make are just as critical as process choices, if not more so. Indeed, effective advocates and arbitrators may overcome the deficiencies of inadequate procedures; poor advocates and arbitrators may undermine the best-crafted procedural program.

Thoughtful and sophisticated lawyers may navigate through the arbitration process in a way that most effectively promotes client goals, and may even collaborate with opposing counsel to develop integrative process solutions that promote mutual benefits. Similarly, well-equipped arbitrators may make effective use of their discretion to strike an appropriate balance between efficiency and fairness—or, as necessary, to address other party needs, such as confidentiality.

QUESTIONS

3. Under what circumstances might clients and counsel be most likely to devote time and attention to planning and drafting dispute resolution provisions in business contracts?

4. What might be done to overcome the problem that in negotiating contracts, parties usually spend little or no time addressing dispute resolution provisions?

The remainder of this chapter is intended to provide you with basic guidance regarding choices made by lawyers and clients during the course of arbitration, and to help develop the skills you will need to provide effective counseling and advocacy in arbitration.

D. DRAFTING ARBITRATION AGREEMENTS: ARBITRATION PROCEDURES AND ARBITRATION INSTITUTIONS

1. Standard Institutional Procedures

Today, arbitrations are commonly conducted under stipulated rules or procedures that regulate the process in roughly the same way that judicial rules of procedure regulate litigation in court. The following discussion will remind law students of aspects of a first-year course in Civil Procedure.

Arbitration rules and procedures are developed and published by various for-profit or nonprofit institutions that provide guidance or support for arbitration proceedings. Such institutions promote their services in the dispute resolution marketplace and actively encourage parties to "choose them" by incorporating their rules in agreements to arbitrate. Leading institutions in the United States include the nonprofits American Arbitration Association (AAA) and the International Institute for Conflict Prevention & Resolution (CPR), and the for-profit JAMS (which originally stood for "Judicial Arbitration and Mediation Services"), as well as other national and regional organizations. Global arbitration institutions include the International Chamber of Commerce (ICC), the London Court of International Arbitration (LCIA), the AAA's International Centre for Dispute Resolution (ICDR), and many other national or regional bodies in countries throughout the world.

These institutions have developed arbitration rules that tend to be lengthy and thus are typically incorporated only by reference in the agreement to arbitrate. Arbitration procedures vary among institutions, and by subject matter. In the United States, there are a wide variety of arbitration rules for different trade groups or practice areas, including securities disputes, construction matters, commercial disputes, and intellectual property disputes. Some organizations publish different sets of rules to handle cases of varying size or complexity. You can usually find and download these arbitration rules on organization Web sites.

Arbitration procedures usually address most or all of the following: how to file an arbitration demand (or joint submission) and other pleadings; what constitutes "notice" for procedural purposes; methods for choosing arbitrators (including disclosure requirements for would-be arbitrators and procedures for challenging appointees); pre-hearing conferences (preliminary hearings); information exchange; motion practice; the conduct of hearings; arbitral awards and remedies; and procedures for publication or clarification of awards.

In addition to publishing arbitration procedures, arbitration institutions also (1) maintain lists or panels of arbitrators, (2) provide administrative support for arbitration proceedings, and (3) in some cases, support mediation and other processes as well as arbitration. When it comes to arbitration, therefore, familiarity with applicable rules, and with the organizations that publish them, is as essential for drafters and advocates as familiarity with the procedural and evidentiary rules in court trial.

2. *Panels of Arbitrators: Ethical Standards*

By incorporating an institution's arbitral procedures in their agreement, parties have probably indicated their mutual intent to utilize certain services of the "provider" institution (although they usually can alter provider rules by agreement). These services include, among other things, help in appointing arbitrators. For this purpose, most providers sponsor panels of prospective arbitrators. The makeup of these lists varies considerably from institution to institution and offers a critical point of comparison. For example, some institutions include only arbitrators with legal or judicial backgrounds on their panels, while others sponsor much more diverse panels.

In a particular case, the institutional role may involve providing names of candidates from which the parties may choose arbitrators, helping with the appointment process, administering a process for determining and resolving conflicts of interest, and replacing arbitrators if necessary. Some arbitration organizations operate as an intermediary between the parties and the arbitrators in regard to collecting arbitrator fees and expenses from the parties.

Some arbitral institutions also publish or adhere to ethical rules for the guidance of arbitrators. The leading U.S. standard is the *Code of Ethics for Arbitrators in Commercial Disputes*. Originally developed in 1977, the Code was updated by a joint effort of the American Bar Association (ABA), the AAA, and CPR and reissued in 2004. The Code of Ethics is used extensively by commercial arbitrators in the United States, and has been adopted as a standard of practice by the AAA, CPR, and other institutions for arbitrators operating under their rules. Some ethical precepts, including principles governing arbitrator disclosure of conflicts of interest, may parallel legal principles under federal and state arbitration law or provisions of institutional arbitration procedures. However, the Code is not intended to have legal consequences, but only to guide the behavior of the arbitrator(s). And, unlike rules of professional conduct for lawyers, there is no general mechanism for policing infractions of the Code by arbitrators.[2]

3. *Ad Hoc Arbitration vs. Arbitration Supported by an Institution*

The AAA and JAMS are two of the most visible arbitration "provider" institutions in the United States. Although there are important differences between the two organizations, both publish a variety of arbitration procedures, sponsor panels of individuals who may act as arbitrators, and offer administrative support for arbitrations. Both assess fees for these services. JAMS also usually takes a percentage of its arbitrators' fees.

At the same time, there are other institutions in the United States and abroad, and they offer various levels of administrative support. They also may offer mediation and other services, which become important when implementing a "stepped" or mixed-mode conflict resolution program. Institutions can also be very helpful in transmitting communications between parties and arbitrators, handling fees and expenses, scheduling and setting locations for hearings, putting arbitration awards in final form, and even conducting a substantive review of the award before publication.

By way of contrast, the CPR offers a system aimed at non-administered or "minimally administered" arbitration. The *CPR Rules for Non-Administered Arbitration* are designed to allow parties to arbitrate with no administrative support from an outside organization; "administrative" functions are instead performed by the parties and/or the arbitrator(s). Under these CPR Rules, CPR's only potential role is to help with arbitrator selection upon the request of the parties; then and only then does CPR charge an administrative fee. In international commercial arbitration, the *United Nations Commission on International Trade Law (UNCITRAL) Arbitration Rules* are the well-established counterpart to the *CPR Rules for Non-Administered Arbitration*.

Should parties incorporate institutional rules or develop purely ad hoc arrangements under which the parties conduct arbitration without institutional support? The answer depends on the circumstances.

Using established procedures reduces the possibility that disputes will arise regarding *the procedures themselves*. An experienced, independent organization may be able to help the parties avoid common problems that they did not anticipate when drafting the arbitration agreement. In cases where counsel or clients lack experience with the arbitration process, an administrative structure may provide comfort and guidance. Where hostility or lack of trust hinders the working relationship between parties or between counsel, the administrative structure may be necessary to promote a smoother and more efficient process. For example, it is important in most cases to have a default procedure for arbitrator selection and other functions in the event that a party fails to comply with procedures. Finally, consistent with the consensual character of arbitration, institutional procedures may be modified in important ways by agreement of the parties where necessary.

However, institutional involvement usually entails costs that should be weighed against benefits provided. In some cases, moreover, there may be questions about the quality of an institution's administrative services, or delays resulting from institutional efforts.

A non-administered or "self-administered" arbitration avoids or minimizes the administrative fees and offers potential flexibility in the structuring and management of the arbitration process, but it must be approached with care. The sophistication and working relationship of parties and their counsel are the primary factors to consider in choosing administered or non-administered arbitration. Parties with more experience may choose little or no administration on the grounds that some or all of those functions may be unnecessary or will be assumed by the arbitrators. Parties opting for non-administered arbitration need to put great importance on selecting an experienced arbitrator (or chair for a multi-arbitrator panel) because this individual will often assume administrative responsibilities. Thus, one factor in deciding whether to use non-administered arbitration is the availability of an experienced, efficient arbitrator who can shepherd the parties through the process. Parties should ideally also rely on appropriate published models in structuring their rules for non-administered arbitration, such as the CPR Rules (either U.S. or international versions) or the UNCITRAL Arbitration Rules in the international sphere.

QUESTIONS

5. Where parties elect not to adopt any organization's arbitration procedures and instead follow an ad hoc approach to arbitration, it has been said that the failure to consult institutional rules or other models for guidance is done at the parties' peril. Why would this be so?

6. What kinds of administrative services might be most important to parties and arbitrators?

7. Should it ever make a difference to users of arbitration that, in addition to charging an administrative fee directly to the parties for their own services, some organizations providing arbitration services take a share of the arbitrators' fees—perhaps as much as 50 percent? Why or why not?

PROBLEM 1: SELECTING ARBITRATION PROCEDURES AND ARBITRATION INSTITUTIONS

Review the hypothetical scenario of Problem 1 in Chapter 1, which involves a planned contractual arrangement between your client, Los Angeles–based entertainment company MDM, and Chicago-based "dot-com" Fandom for the Internet posting of video files. Assume that after discussing the matter with your client (MDM), there is a strong inclination to incorporate an arbitration agreement in the contract currently being negotiated between MDM and Fandom. Your client informs you that the parties have no prior relationship, and that the Fandom people are, in the opinion of your client's businesspeople, "really smart but typical dot-com types, crossed with obsessive TV fan types"—not your typical business partners. Their lawyer is a relatively sophisticated corporate lawyer but probably knows little about arbitration or other forms of ADR. If disputes arise under the agreement, they are most likely to involve questions of contract interpretation and breach, intellectual property law (copyright, licensing, etc.), as well as technical factual issues involving software and electronic transmission.

To help you in rendering advice to the client, your senior partner has encouraged you to engage in some online research. She says you can learn a lot by carefully examining the Web sites of arbitration provider organizations, looking carefully at their arbitration rules, and reviewing their administrative services and fee structures. She asks you to look at the Web site of either (a) the AAA or (b) JAMS. She suggests that you attempt to answer each of the following questions with respect to the organization you choose.

A. Taking into account the nature of the contract and the parties, does the organization publish arbitration rules, including specialized rules, which might be useful in resolving disputes between MDM and Fandom? Are there different procedures for cases of different size or complexity?
B. What kinds of administrative services does the organization provide? What are the administrative fees, if any?
C. Does the organization list arbitrators with pertinent backgrounds or expertise? Where are they located? What are their fees?
D. Where are the organization's administrative offices? Can arbitration hearings be held at convenient locations?
E. Compare and contrast the rules and services of AAA or JAMS with CPR, which publishes "non-administered" procedures. Which organization/rules do you believe are most appropriate to use in the MDM/Fandom contract, and why?

E. SCOPE OF THE ARBITRATION AGREEMENT AND OTHER DRAFTING ISSUES

1. Scope of the Arbitration Agreement

An important issue for every drafter is the *scope* of the arbitration agreement—in other words, what disputes related to the contract and the parties' relationship will be subject to arbitration? This question is key because, as is explained more fully in Chapter 5, parties are legally required to arbitrate only those disputes that are contemplated by their arbitration agreement. One of the most common grounds for setting aside an arbitration award—and the ground most likely to result in an overturned award—is that the arbitrators "exceeded their power" under the arbitration agreement.

As noted earlier, it is common practice for drafters to use extremely broad language in describing the scope of the agreement. Broad provisions can minimize the likelihood of court disputes over what is "arbitrable," especially since courts enforcing arbitration agreements under the Federal Arbitration Act (FAA) and similar state statutes interpret these now-familiar, essentially ubiquitous terms with a presumption *in favor of arbitration.*

For instance, in *Scherk v. Alberto-Culver,* 417 U.S. 506 (1974), the U.S. Supreme Court held that "any controversy or claim" was held to be a broad term including statutory claims under the Securities Exchange Act of 1934. Moreover, phrases such as "arising out of," "relating to," "with respect to," and "in connection with" broaden the scope of the arbitration clause combined with the aforementioned "any controversy or claim" or "any disputes" to the extent of contractual claims, torts, and statutory claims. *See Pennzoil Exploration & Production Co. v. Ramco Energy Ltd.,* 139 F.3d 1061, 1068 (5th Cir. 1998) (characterizing as "broad" an arbitration clause covering "any dispute, controversy or claim arising out of or in relation to or in connection with the agreement"). In response to the judgments of the courts, leading arbitral institutions such as AAA, JAMS, and CPR provide the sample clauses for different types of arbitration, which all include the phase "any disputes (or any controversy or claims) arising out of or relating to." Therefore, such forms of words are to be considered when drafting the arbitration clause to validate the jurisdiction of the arbitral tribunal.

Sometimes, however, attorneys may believe they have sound reasons for limiting what is arbitrable to specific issues. They may wish to reserve issues of particular size, complexity, or subject matter for the public forum, either because they are uncomfortable with the perceived risks of arbitration or because they believe a court may provide more suitable relief, such as a preliminary injunction or temporary restraining order. Attorneys must take care in drafting arbitration provisions, as any errors, inconsistencies, or ambiguities may result in controversies about whether the dispute that has arisen is arbitrable.

2.   *Other Drafting Issues*

❖ John Townsend

Drafting Arbitration Clauses: Avoiding the 7 Deadly Sins[3]

From time to time, someone tries to define what a perfect arbitration clause would look like. Efforts to do so usually founder on one of the strengths of arbitration, which is its adaptability to the particular circumstances of the parties and the dispute. Therefore, while it is difficult to generalize about what would make a "perfect" clause, it is not nearly as difficult to identify some of the features that make for a bad one. This article identifies seven of the most damning "sins" that plague arbitration clauses and offers suggestions for addressing the most important issues drafters face.

EQUIVOCATION

. . . The essence of this sin is the failure to state clearly that the parties have agreed to binding arbitration. Because arbitration is a creature of contract, if there is no contract, there is no agreement to arbitrate. . . . [The author offers the following example:]

> In case of dispute, the parties undertake to submit to arbitration, but in case of litigation the Tribunal de la Seine shall have exclusive jurisdiction.

What this clause commits the parties to is nothing other than years of litigation about how to resolve any dispute that may arise. That is the sulfur and brimstone that threatens the drafter who puts such a clause in the client's contract: The client will spend what will seem like an eternity, and a great deal of money, trying to resolve the dispute.

The overriding goal of the drafter of an arbitration clause should be to draft a provision that, if a dispute arises, will help the parties obtain an arbitration award without a detour through the court system. First and foremost, that means that the drafter must produce an enforceable agreement to arbitrate. For an American lawyer drafting an agreement that will involve a transaction in interstate commerce, that means an agreement that a court will recognize as coming within the meaning of Section 2 of the FAA. This provision states:

> A written provision in . . . a contract evidencing a transaction involving commerce to settle by arbitration a controversy thereafter arising out of such contract or transaction, or the refusal to perform the whole or any part thereof, . . . shall be valid, irrevocable, and enforceable, save upon such grounds as exist at law or in equity for the revocation of any contract. . . .

INATTENTION

Anyone who regularly deals with arbitration has no doubt heard someone say, "No one really paid any attention to the arbitration clause," explaining that the drafters decided at around 2:00 A.M. in the morning on the day of the closing that they should provide for arbitration and pasted in a copy of the nearest clause available.

What this describes is the sin of inattention: drafting an arbitration clause with insufficient attention to the transaction to which it relates. This is far from the ideal approach. An arbitration clause should be designed to fit the circumstances of the transaction and the parties' needs. The drafter may well select a standard "off-the-shelf" clause prepared by one of the well-known arbitration institutions — one can do far worse — but the off-the-shelf clause should only be selected because it is right for the deal. "The key is to pay sufficient attention to the underlying transaction so that the arbitration clause can be tailored to the client's particular requirements and to possible disputes that may reasonably be anticipated."

When advising a client about dispute resolution options and deciding on the type of clause to use, the drafter, at a minimum, should ask the following questions:

- *What type of dispute resolution process is best suited to the client and the transaction?*

Arbitration is not the only option. There are many alternative dispute resolution processes and there is always litigation. In particular circumstances it may be preferable to litigate in court, provided that the parties can agree on which court to designate and whether that court will have jurisdiction. Litigation, however, may not be an option in an international agreement.

- *If arbitration is selected, does the client understand that the arbitration clause will commit the client to a binding process that involves certain trade-offs?*

Arbitration has advantages, prominent among them privacy, as well as the possibility of crafting a process that will be speedier and more economical than litigation. It also provides the opportunity for the parties to choose a fair and neutral forum—and to participate in the selection of the decision maker and the rules that will be applied.

On the trade-off side, the client should understand that it is giving up some rights provided by law to litigants. These may include the right to a jury trial, the right to an appeal and, under certain [mainly international] institutional arbitration rules . . . the right to claim punitive damages, unless the contract provides otherwise.

The drafter should be especially cautious about giving in to the temptation to advise the client to agree to arbitrate some types of disputes and go to court for others. This may be inevitable in some countries that do not allow certain types of disputes to be arbitrated (e.g., patent disputes) — but dividing jurisdiction should be the subject of an advanced course in drafting. Do not try it at home.

- *Have the parties considered providing for steps preceding arbitration, especially if the relationship between the parties is an ongoing one?*

It may be that, in light of their prior relationship, the parties should agree to mediate or negotiate before heading into arbitration. They can always arbitrate if less adversarial techniques are unsuccessful. A "step clause" can be drafted with as many steps preceding arbitration as the parties desire.

OMISSION

A drafter who omits a crucial (or even a useful) element from an arbitration clause commits the sin of omission. This can result in a clause that expresses an agreement to arbitrate, but fails to provide guidance as to how or where to do so. Here is an extreme example:

> *Any disputes arising out of this Agreement will be finally resolved by binding arbitration.*

This clause is probably enforceable because it clearly requires the parties to arbitrate disputes. However, it does not achieve the goal of an arbitration clause, which is to stay out of court. Unless the parties can agree on the details concerning their arbitration, they will have to go to court to have an arbitrator or arbitral institution selected for them. . . .

In the arbitration, the parties will still have to resolve disputes about when, where and how to conduct the arbitration. It is far better to provide in the arbitration clause for the minimum fundamentals needed to get an arbitration under way without the intervention of a court. . . .

OVER-SPECIFICITY

The opposite of the sin of omission is the sin of over-specificity. Rather than providing insufficient detail, the drafter provides too much. Drafters occasionally take the job of crafting an arbitration clause as a challenge to show how many terms they can invent. This can produce a clause that is extremely difficult to put into practice. For example:

> *The Arbitration shall be conducted by three arbitrators, each of whom shall be fluent in Hungarian and shall have twenty or more years of experience in the design of buggy whips, and one of whom, who shall act as chairman, shall be an expert on the law of the Hapsburg Empire.*

This may seem like a comic exaggeration, but if you substitute computer chips for buggy whips, with appropriate adjustment of the language and law in question, you will find this example chillingly similar to many that make their way to arbitration.

Basically, it is a big mistake to over-draft an arbitration clause. When the arbitration clause is excessively detailed, those layers of detail can make it difficult or impossible to arbitrate a dispute when one arises. The standard clauses recommended by the major arbitral institutions are used by many knowledgeable people because they have been tested by the courts and they do the job.

UNREALISTIC EXPECTATIONS

A companion sin to over-specificity is the sin of unrealistic expectations. We have all encountered arbitration clauses along the following lines:

> *The claimant will name its arbitrator when it commences the proceeding. The respondent will then name its arbitrator within seven (7) days, and the two so named will name the third arbitrator, who will act as chair, within seven (7) days of the selection of the second arbitrator. Hearings will commence within fifteen (15) days of the selection of the third arbitrator, and will conclude no more than three (3) days later. The arbitrators will issue their award within seven (7) days of the conclusion of the hearings.*

There are circumstances that may justify, indeed even require, tight time limits. It may be reasonable to provide for accelerated resolution of an urgent matter, such as the need for provisional relief of a dispute involving the use of a trademark or one that would delay a major construction project. But most commercial arbitration proceeds at a more stately pace. While clients and their attorneys understandably become impatient with that pace, they should be aware that too tight a timeframe for an arbitration can cripple the process before it gets started. The risk is, as usual, collateral litigation. American courts have been less rigid than their European counterparts in finding that a failure to meet a deadline in an arbitration agreement deprives an arbitrator of jurisdiction to proceed with the arbitration. However, drafters should not invite a challenge on that basis by imposing unrealistic deadlines on the parties, the case administrator, or the arbitrator.

LITIGATION ENVY

Sometimes the drafter of an arbitration clause cannot be reconciled to the thought of letting go of the familiar security blanket of litigation. What sometimes results is a clause that calls for the arbitration to follow court rules. This is the sin of litigation envy. Take the following clause, which the author once had to deal with as the chair of an ad hoc arbitration panel:

> *The arbitration will be conducted in accordance with the Federal Rules of Civil Procedure applicable in the United States District Court for the Southern District of New York, and the arbitrators shall follow the Federal Rules of Evidence.*

Trying to conduct the arbitration under rules designed for an entirely different kind of proceeding produced predictable and needlessly expensive wheel-spinning. The arbitrators had to decide whether and how to apply the local rules of the Southern District, whether a pre-trial order was required, whether the parties were obligated to make the mandatory disclosures required by the Federal Rules, and other controversies about discovery of the sort that people resort to arbitration to escape.

Whether administered or non-administered arbitration is desired, there are many good sets of procedural rules available that can be incorporated in an arbitration clause. Any one of them is preferable to requiring an arbitration to be conducted according to the rules governing litigation. . . .

OVERREACHING

Sometimes the drafter of an arbitration clause cannot resist the temptation to tilt the arbitration process in favor of his or her client. This is the sin of overreaching. . . . The temptation to overreach in drafting the arbitration clause should be strongly resisted. It is not only wrong, but it is also counterproductive. [The author uses as an example the notorious arbitration provision included in Hooters' individual employment contracts, which we will read about in Chapter 7.]

DOING IT RIGHT

If one knows what to avoid in drafting the arbitration clause, how does the drafter go about drafting it correctly? The beginning drafter is well advised to begin with a standard clause by one of the many respected arbitral institutions. The websites of the principal arbitral institutions provide recommended provisions for both administered and non-administered arbitration that have been tested by the courts and that work. . . . [It is wise to begin with the following steps:]

Step 1: Define what is arbitrable.
Step 2: Commit the parties to arbitration.
Step 3: Pick a set of rules (and, in this case, an arbitration institution to administer the case).

Step 4: Provide for entry of judgment. This is essential to enforcement in the United States.

PROBLEM 2: HOW NOT TO DRAFT AN ARBITRATION CLAUSE!

Building on the fact pattern set out in the Problem in Chapter 1, assume MDM and Fandom included in their contract the following arbitration provision:

> Any controversy arising out of any of the terms or conditions of the contract and involving more than $1,000,000 may be submitted to arbitration administered by the AAA. Said arbitration will commence within five days of the dispute arising and will be completed within ten days.

Once the contract was in place, Fandom began uploading 80 MB video files of seasons one and two "Starscape" episodes on ScapePlace.com. Six months into the contract, MDM discovered that Fandom had begun uploading high-quality 450 MB videos of season three episodes to ScapePlace.com. In total, seven such video files of "Starscape" had been made available on the site. Outraged, MDM asked you, its attorney, to initiate immediate legal action.

You immediately notified Fandom of MDM's intention to arbitrate. One week later you filed a demand with the AAA on behalf of MDM, alleging that Fandom had frustrated the contract's purpose, and that Fandom had distributed the season three video files without MDM's permission and in violation of MDM's copyright as well as the specific terms of the parties' contract. On behalf of MDM, you requested compensatory damages for copyright violations and breach of contract totaling $900,000 for each third season episode of "Starscape" uploaded to ScapePlace.com, as well as $5 million in punitive damages. You also sought interim relief in the form of a preliminary injunction to prevent Fandom from continuing to display the season three episodes.

A. Do you see any potential procedural defenses that Fandom might raise in response to your arbitration demand? If you were counseling MDM with regard to other contracts, would you advise your client to use different language in its arbitration clauses? If so, what language would you suggest adding or removing?

B. Assume for the sake of discussion that the agreement called for the application of the *AAA Commercial Arbitration Rules and Mediation Procedures* (including Procedures for Large, Complex Commercial Disputes). (Reminder: These rules may be found on the AAA Web site.) If Fandom decides not to submit voluntarily to arbitration, what do these Rules say about who would decide the question of whether certain issues are within the scope of the arbitration clause — the court or the arbitrator(s)?

Endnotes

1. Stipanowich, Thomas J. (2010) *Arbitration: The "New Litigation,"* 2010 U. Ill. L. Rev. 1 (January); Stipanowich, Thomas J. (2014) *Reflections on the State and Future of Commercial Arbitration: Challenges, Opportunities, Proposals,* 25 Colum. Am. Rev. Int'l Arb.

2. Sabin, Cameron L. (2002) *Adjudicatory Boat Without a Keel: Private Arbitration and the Need for Public Oversight of Arbitrators,* 87 Iowa L. Rev. 1337.

3. Townsend, John. (2003) *Drafting Arbitration Clauses: Avoiding the 7 Deadly Sins,* 58 Disp. Resol. J. 28.

CHAPTER 3

SELECTING ARBITRATORS

A. SELECTING THE ARBITRATOR(S)

1. Key Attributes of Arbitrators

It has been said that the selection of the arbitrator(s) is the single most important decision confronting parties in arbitration, since in many respects "the arbitrator *is* the process." The choice of arbitrators is critical for two reasons: Arbitrators have primary control over the arbitration proceedings, and their decisions on the merits of a case are unlikely to be disturbed since, as we will see in Chapter 6, judicial review of arbitral awards tends to be extremely limited.

The necessary attributes of arbitrators will vary according to particular circumstances and a party's interests, needs, and priorities. In selecting their own decision maker(s), parties to arbitration frequently seek out those with specialized commercial, legal, or technical knowledge, training, and experience. The assumption is that such grounding reduces the amount of time that will be required to explain issues in dispute to the arbitrators and enhances the likelihood that the outcomes will be more in keeping with pertinent business, legal, or technical standards. This approach contrasts with the realities of most public tribunals: Judges tend to be generalists, steeped in legal traditions and focused on application of legal standards; jurors may be chosen precisely because they *lack* pertinent expertise.

Fairness and open-mindedness are deemed critical to the reality and perception of due process, and standard arbitration procedures are designed from the vantage point of promoting even-handedness in the process. Of course, there is frequently a tension between expertise and impartiality. Besides the fact that arbitrators may bring to the hearing room a point of view that is conditioned by their experience, they are often of the same business or professional community as the parties. While this may only enhance their acceptability as arbitrators, such relationships might also give rise to potential conflicts of interest. For this reason, standard arbitration procedures provide a mechanism for disclosure of potential conflicts of interest by prospective and sitting arbitrators. See Section B below.

Particularly in large or complex cases, arbitrators must have strong case management skills. They, or at least the designated chair of the tribunal, should be able to run arbitration proceedings efficiently and attentively, and act decisively when necessary. Foresight, planning, diligence, and dedication are normally required to achieve a quick and efficient resolution — which is what arbitrating parties should expect in the absence of a mutual agreement to the contrary. Unfortunately, judging by the experiences of arbitrating parties, such expectations are sometimes frustrated, particularly in large, complex cases. In addition to emphasizing the importance of proactive case management, organizations sponsoring arbitration services have taken steps to ensure that arbitrators have sufficient time in their schedule to conduct a case. AAA Commercial Arbitration Rule R-18 provides that an arbitrator "shall be subject to disqualification for . . . inability or refusal to perform his or her duties with diligence. . . ."

2.   Diversity Issues

The gender and racial or ethnic background of arbitrators are issues that have attracted much more attention in recent years, both in terms of the diversity of panels maintained by organizations providing arbitration services and representation on arbitration tribunals. Recent studies indicate that women and minorities are underrepresented among experienced arbitrators.[1]

This can have important ramifications. For example, studies suggest that many, if not most, lower-paid employees are subject to arbitration clauses in their employment cases, including disputes arising from discriminatory treatment in the workplace. However, the arbitrators deciding their cases are largely older white men.[2] Providers AAA, JAMS, and CPR all have taken steps to increase arbitrator diversity; recently an unsuccessful suit by Jay-Z drew attention to the subject.[3] AAA has a diversity fellowship program designed to provide mentoring to diverse ADR professionals. JAMS provides a sample diversity and inclusion arbitration clause that parties may incorporate that states a diverse arbitrator will be appointed "wherever practicable." CPR has a diversity task force, created in 2006, and includes a "diversity statement" when providing a panel of arbitrators for consideration that asks the parties to select more diverse individual panelists. Nonetheless, some have called for more direct actions that should be taken to promote diversity among arbitrators.[4]

QUESTION

1. In what ways might the gender and racial or ethnic background of arbitrators have a real or perceived impact on arbitration process and outcomes? How might greater diversity be attained in actual practice?

---

3.   Sources of Information About Arbitrators

It is imperative for counsel to conduct a thorough, independent investigation of potential arbitrators; this may mean examining their professional qualifications, education, training, arbitration experience, fees, and even published awards and writings. Most sponsoring organizations offer updated arbitrators' biographies, as well as information on the identification, training, and evaluation of listed arbitrators. They may also provide information on potential arbitrators' possible conflicts of interest, availability, and fee schedules.

In important cases, counsel sometimes seek to arrange a joint interview with the arbitrator in which both sides ask questions of the arbitrator in person or by telephone. Candidates may be asked about their background, relevant professional experience, including experience with the issues of the particular dispute, the availability of the candidate to oversee the dispute, and the candidate's personal expertise and style in handling disputes. Moreover, the parties and their counsel often clear up potential conflicts of interest during this interview.

Sometimes, a party or its lawyer may contact a prospective arbitrator without involving the other party or counsel. Such ex parte communications raise potential concerns about exactly what was discussed, since arbitrators, like judges, are normally expected to be independent and impartial, and to avoid communicating separately with individual parties or counsel. For this reason, Canon III of the *Code of Ethics for Arbitrators in Commercial Disputes* (2004), the most widely used ethics rules applicable to arbitrators in U.S. cases, provides:

> B. An arbitrator or prospective arbitrator should not discuss a proceeding with any party in the absence of any other party, except in any of the following circumstances:
> (1) When the appointment of a prospective arbitrator is being considered, the prospective arbitrator:
> (a) may ask about the identities of the parties, counsel, or witnesses and the general nature of the case; and
> (b) may respond to inquiries from a party or its counsel designed to determine his or her suitability and availability for the appointment. In any such dialogue, the prospective arbitrator may receive information from a party or its counsel disclosing the general nature of the dispute but should not permit them to discuss the merits of the case.

Paragraph 8(a) of the *International Bar Association (IBA) Guidelines on Party Representation in International Arbitration* mentions that it is not improper for a party representative to have ex parte communications when a party representative communicates with a prospective party arbitrator to determine his expertise, experience, ability, availability, willingness, and the existence of potential conflicts of interest. On the other hand, Article 1 of the *International Arbitration Practice Guideline on Interviews for Prospective Arbitrators*, produced by Chartered Institute of Arbitrators, admonishes prospective arbitrators for international arbitration to be aware whether the national law applicable to international arbitration proceedings in which they are involved prohibits certain kinds of ex parte communications prior to appointment.

One fast and efficient means of accumulating information about candidates is through the use of the Internet. Some professional, trade, and Internet groups provide arbitrator biographies and links to their publications. Public, private, and governmental ADR organizations and alternative dispute resolution resources can also be accessed. In some cases, awards that have been written by arbitrators may be found by using an arbitrator's name, company, or firm to search LexisNexis, Westlaw, and other search engines. Attorneys also frequently make queries of colleagues on popular arbitration and dispute resolution listservs.

4.   Number of Arbitrators

Another consideration for parties is the number of arbitrators who will be employed to adjudicate the dispute. The most common scenarios involve using a single arbitrator or a panel of three arbitrators to issue a decision.

Generally, arbitration procedures establish guidelines for the use of arbitration panels. As a rule, for relatively low-dollar disputes, or where it is vital to limit the cost of the arbitration, a single arbitrator is preferable. Sole arbitrators may also be utilized in bigger cases, avoiding the additional costs and scheduling difficulties associated with a multi-member panel. A 2013 survey of members of the College of Commercial Arbitrators (CCA), an organization of leading U.S. arbitrators, indicated that nearly nine-tenths of respondents had served as a sole arbitrator in cases involving up to $1 million, and nearly one-third had done so in cases involving $50 million or more.[5]

If cost is less of a factor, then a panel of three arbitrators can offer distinct advantages. Some lawyers advance the rationale that the decision of a three-member panel is more authoritative, especially if the award is unanimous. Furthermore, it is thought, a panel of three arbitrators is less likely to hand down irrational or arbitrary awards because the arbitrators can "check" each other. Finally, a three-member panel can provide a unique mix of experience and perspectives. Differing expertise may be complementary. For instance, an arbitrator familiar with construction disputes states:

> I've appreciated the way arbitrators with different backgrounds complement each other. Construction professionals understand the way things go together, the dynamics of the job site, and relevant cost implications. Experienced construction lawyers place these realities in the legal framework of statute, common law and contract. In the best case, each arbitrator brings something to the table, and relies on the other arbitrators.

When choosing a panel, measures must be taken to identify the panel's chair. Sometimes the panel chair is selected by the arbitration organization; other times, the arbitrators or the parties agree on a chair. The chair normally acts as the panel's voice and is primarily responsible for managing the arbitration proceedings. Chairs may have to arrange the meeting times and locations for the parties. Sometimes, they solely run several or all of the pre-hearing conferences. They should be counted on to facilitate a sense of teamwork and effective communication among panel members. In addition to supervising the work of the panelists, the chair is expected to keep in close contact with the appropriate arbitration organization. Under AAA rules, for instance, the chair should coordinate with the AAA case administrator regarding issues such as fee deposits, scheduling, hearing location, physical surroundings, availability of equipment, and storage of documents. Under the *Code of Ethics for Arbitrators in Commercial Disputes* (2004), the chair is also responsible for reassuring the arbitration organization that all panelists are conforming their behavior to the Code. As an efficiency measure, parties sometimes agree that discovery issues will be handled by the panel chair instead of engaging the entire arbitration tribunal.

5. Selection Processes

There are several different methods of selecting arbitrators. In some cases, the parties identify the arbitrator(s) by name in the agreement or set forth experiential or professional qualifications in the arbitration provision. Most commonly, however, selection occurs after a dispute has arisen. The parties may jointly agree on the arbitrator(s), or delegate an arbitration institution or other third party to make the selection(s) for them. Many institutional arbitration procedures contemplate a "list selection" process, in which parties identify and rank suitable candidates from lists provided by the institution; the latter selects those mutually acceptable candidates based on the highest overall rankings. In some cases, the failure of the parties to agree upon one or more arbitrators requires the institution to select an arbitrator.

One other popular approach in the United States and in international arbitration is the "tripartite panel"—a panel of three arbitrators in which each party designates one panelist, and the two party-designees (or "party arbitrators") agree upon a third, who then chairs the panel. This seemingly straightforward and balanced approach appears to have much to recommend it. As we will see, however, there has been considerable concern regarding the role of party arbitrators and their relationships with those who appointed them. In U.S. practice, party arbitrators are sometimes expected to forsake independence and impartiality and instead advocate the cause of the party that appointed them; such expectations conflict with conventional international practice and may produce confusion and disarray.

PROBLEM 1: ARBITRATOR SELECTION METHODS
Suppose you are representing ECOPLAZA, an owner/developer that intends to construct a vast new "green" (environmentally sustainable) shopping center/office complex. You are negotiating a contract with Biggtel, Inc., one of the world's largest engineering and construction companies, to design and build the project. You expect the project to take at least two and perhaps as many as three years to complete and believe it may cost $500 million or more.

A. Consider the pros and cons of each of the following approaches:
   a. Identifying a mutually acceptable retired judge (by name) as the sole arbitrator of disputes under the ECOPLAZA/Biggtel contract;
   b. Identifying some other mutually acceptable person (by name) as the sole arbitrator;
   c. Setting out experiential, professional, or other qualifications for one or more arbitrators in the contract;
   d. Agreeing to have each party pick an arbitrator after a dispute arises, resulting in a two-member arbitration tribunal;
   e. The same as the last approach, except that the panel has three members, and the party-appointed arbitrators (or the parties themselves) pick the third arbitrator.
B. Suppose the parties elected to arbitrate under the auspices of the most relevant AAA arbitration rules and did not specify any method for

selecting arbitrators. (Does the AAA have rules specifically designed for construction disputes? If you can't recall, check the Web site.)

  a. Would there be a single arbitrator or arbitration panel? (Does the answer depend on the circumstances?)
  b. How would the selection process work, assuming the parties had no other selection agreement?
  c. How are the arbitrators' fees paid, and how are communications between the parties and the arbitrators handled?
  d. What are the relative merits or demerits of the AAA "list selection" process as compared to the alternatives set out in part "a" above? Could you agree to use the AAA lists of arbitrators but utilize a different arbitrator selection process?

B.   ARBITRATOR DISCLOSURE AND CHALLENGES

As discussed above, the selection of private decision makers with ties to the same business or professional community as the parties or their counsel involves a tension between two principles: party autonomy in selecting arbitrators of their choice, on the one hand, and concepts of judicial fairness, independence, and impartiality, on the other. To reconcile the potential conflict between these principles, arbitrators are expected to make a timely disclosure of facts that may raise "conflict of interest" concerns, including relationships with counsel, the parties, witnesses, or the issues in dispute. Armed with this information, parties may make a knowledgeable choice about a candidate's suitability for the role of arbitrator, and accede to or, alternatively, deny or challenge their appointment. The concept of arbitrator disclosure—and related guidelines for arbitrators, parties and counsel, arbitral institutions, and courts—are embodied in institutional arbitration procedures, ethical guidelines for arbitrators, and federal and state arbitration law. The advent of the Internet has introduced an added layer of complexity to arbitrators' disclosure obligations in relation to arbitrators' online activities, communications, and relationships. As there is currently no case law specifically on this area, arbitrators must apply (and expand) the principles set out in relevant ethics codes, arbitration rules, and case law on arbitration disclosure generally.[6]

We will emphasize institutional procedures and ethical standards below and address related legal issues in Chapter 6.C.

1.   Institutional Procedures for Disclosure and Challenge

A key element of most institutional arbitration procedures is the procedure for arbitrator disclosure and challenge. Under the AAA Commercial Arbitration Rules, for example, upon appointment arbitrators must "disclose to the AAA any circumstance likely to give rise to justifiable doubt as to the arbitrator's impartiality or independence, including any bias or any financial or personal interest in the result of the arbitration or any past or present relationship with the parties or their representatives" (R-17). Upon a showing of arbitrator partiality, the AAA will inform the parties of the situation, and conclusively rule on any objections the parties make to the continued appointment of the allegedly biased arbitrator.

2. *Ethical Standards*

The *Code of Ethics for Arbitrators in Commercial Disputes* (2004) is the most widely used of standards setting out ethical responsibilities for U.S. arbitrators, including obligations to uphold the fairness and integrity of the arbitration process. It is utilized in arbitrations sponsored by the AAA and some other provider organizations, or other places where parties agree to its use.

Canon I of the Code begins with a checklist for prospective arbitrators:

One should accept appointment as an arbitrator only if fully satisfied:

(1) that he or she *can serve impartially*;
(2) that he or she *can serve independently from the parties, potential witnesses, and the other arbitrators*;
(3) that he or she *is competent to serve*; and
(4) that he or she can be available to commence the arbitration in accordance with the requirements of the proceeding and thereafter to *devote the time and attention to its completion that the parties are reasonably entitled to expect* [emphasis added].

Canon II requires arbitrators, before they accept appointment, to "disclose any interest or relationship likely to affect impartiality or which might create an appearance of partiality or bias." The obligation is a continuing one, and requires disclosure to all parties and to other appointed arbitrators. The Canon proceeds to identify courses of action for an arbitrator, including withdrawal in appropriate circumstances.[7] What other obligations does the Code place on arbitrators?

PROBLEM 2A: ARBITRATOR DISCLOSURE AND CHALLENGE: ETHICAL ISSUES

A. You represent the Carmin Co., a manufacturer of high-tech GPS units used in automobiles, in a dispute with SamCo, Inc., a national "buying club" with stores all over the country. The parties have a long-term contract under which SamCo is obligated to buy certain amounts of various Carmin products each month. In recent months SamCo has refused to accept the required number of these Carmin products, citing various alleged defects. After efforts to negotiate were unavailing, Carmin demanded arbitration under the terms of the contract, and three arbitrators were mutually selected for the arbitration panel through a list selection process. The parties have been preparing for hearings for several months, and have just exchanged lists of the witnesses they plan to present in the arbitration hearing. The chair of the arbitration panel now reveals that she has current business dealings with a key witness for SamCo. You and your client are very concerned about the connection. Select a set of published commercial arbitration procedures (e.g., AAA, JAMS, CPR) and ascertain what your client should expect to happen, and what course of action it should pursue, under those procedures. Be prepared to cite sections that address the relevant obligations of the arbitrators and pertinent administrative procedures.

B. If, instead, you are the chair of the arbitration panel in this proceeding and have just become aware that one of the key witnesses will be an individual with whom you have business dealings, what would your ethical responsibilities be under the current version of the *Code of Ethics for Arbitrators in Commercial Disputes*?

a. What if, instead of a current business connection, your relationship with the witness was common membership in a state bar association committee? A country club?

b. What if a partner in your law firm represents the witness's company in a separate legal action?

3. *Disclosures Required by Statutes Governing Arbitration*

Although our primary discussion of the law surrounding arbitration will be presented in later chapters, it is important to note that some state arbitration statutes establish affirmative disclosure requirements for arbitrators. Section 12 of the Revised Uniform Arbitration Act (2000), upon which the arbitration law of many states is based, states:

> Before accepting appointment, an individual who is requested to serve as an arbitrator, after making a reasonable inquiry, shall disclose to all parties to the agreement to arbitrate and arbitration proceeding and to any other arbitrators any known facts that a reasonable person would consider likely to affect the impartiality of the arbitrator in the arbitration proceeding, including:
>
> (1) a financial or personal interest in the outcome of the arbitration proceeding; and
> (2) an existing or past relationship with any of the parties to the agreement to arbitrate or the arbitration proceeding, their counsel or representatives, a witness, or another arbitrator.

The obligation to disclose is a continuing one, and it applies to all arbitrators, however appointed. The RUAA also establishes an explicit connection between undisclosed conflicts of interest and possible vacatur (overturning) of arbitration awards under §23 of the Act.

The Federal Arbitration Act (FAA), which applies to written arbitration provisions in transactions evidencing interstate commerce or maritime transactions, does not include affirmative disclosure requirements. However, as discussed in

Chapter 6, an arbitrator's failure to disclose certain conflicts of interest may furnish grounds for a motion to vacate an award under the FAA, although strong policies supporting the finality of arbitration awards make courts hesitant to order vacatur on such grounds.[8]

The state of California has established mandatory arbitrator disclosure requirements that are the most stringent in the United States. California Ethics Standards for Neutral Arbitrators in Contractual Arbitration, Standard 7 (2006); Cal. Civ. Proc. Code §§1281.85, 1281.9 (West 2015). Under California law, prospective arbitrators are required to assess their ability to be impartial and to decline an appointment if they are unable to be so "notwithstanding any contrary request, consent or waiver by the parties." They are also required to disclose "all matters that could cause a person aware of the facts to reasonably entertain a doubt that the proposed neutral arbitrator would be able to be impartial." Cal. Civ. Proc. Code §1281.9(a). Included within those disclosure obligations are six specific disclosures concerning relationships the arbitrator or any member of his or her immediate family has or had with any party or lawyer for a party in the current arbitration proceeding. Arbitrators must recuse themselves if any party objects to their continued service on the basis of the disclosures. It is possible, moreover, that a timely party objection may serve as the basis for vacatur of an arbitration award even if an administering organization has previously refused to remove an arbitrator on the same grounds. *See Azteca Construction, Inc. v. ADR Consulting*, 2004 WL 1895135 (Cal. Ct. App. 2004).

4. *"Party Arbitrators" on Tripartite Panels*

Tripartite arbitration panels are a common feature of the landscape. The concept—each party picks an arbitrator, and the two "party arbitrators" agree on a third arbitrator (who usually is made the chair)—is seemingly straightforward and inherently fair. As illustrated in Problem 2B, under leading U.S. arbitration procedures and ethical rules the expectation is that party arbitrators selected by individual parties, like other arbitrators, will act *independently and impartially*.

Such arrangements, however, sometimes produce unanticipated results and may result in litigation. This is due to the fact that, although it is by no means common practice, there are sometimes circumstances in the United States where wing arbitrators selected by the individual parties are expected to be predisposed toward "their" party, or even overtly partisan. This reality creates potential pitfalls for unwary clients, counsel, and arbitrators.

PROBLEM 2B: ARBITRATOR DISCLOSURE AND CHALLENGE: "PARTY ARBITRATORS"

As in Problem 2A, you represent Carmin Co. in arbitration proceedings with SamCo., Inc. Now, however, assume that their arbitration agreement called for a tripartite arbitration panel. Accordingly, Carmin appointed Craft as its arbitrator and SamCo appointed Silver; Craft and Silver jointly selected Professor Perfect as the third arbitrator. You and your client have been very careful not to communicate with arbitrator Craft, but now, midway through the hearings, you find out that arbitrator Silver has been actively working with and assisting SamCo in the preparation of its case. You and your client are truly alarmed and are considering your next steps.

A. What procedural options does your client possess if the parties agreed to arbitrate under the *JAMS Comprehensive Arbitration Rules & Procedures* (2021)? Would the result be the same under the AAA Commercial Arbitration Rules?

B. Would it make any difference if the parties incorporated the AAA Rules in their agreement but specified that the arbitrators appointed by individual parties would not be independent and impartial but could be "predisposed toward the party that appointed them"? In such a case, would the California Ethics Standards require mandatory disclosures by the party-appointed arbitrators? *See* Standard 2.

C. What does the *Code of Ethics for Arbitrators in Commercial Disputes* provide with respect to the standards applicable to the "party arbitrators" that are each appointed unilaterally by one of the parties? Canon III.B.2, 3, and 4 address interactions and communications between party arbitrators and parties during the appointment process. Look carefully at Canon X, which establishes special rules for those circumstances in which it is expected that party arbitrators will be non-neutral, as well as Canon IX, which requires party arbitrators to take steps to ascertain as early as possible the nature of their role and to make a joint report to the parties. Do you believe these are workable responses to concerns about the roles of party arbitrators, and concerns about non-neutrality?

D. Suppose the parties' arbitration provision calls for a tripartite panel (in which each party picks one of the arbitrators and they jointly pick a third arbitrator), but the provision does not incorporate the AAA Rules or any other arbitration procedures. How would you know whether party arbitrators have to be independent and impartial, what disclosures they would be required to make, if any, and so on? *See, e.g., Certain Underwriting Members of Lloyds of London v. Ins. Co. of Am.*, 2019 WL 4686584, No. 17-1137 (2d Cir. June 7, 2018) (distinguishing between party-appointed and neutral arbitrators in considering evident partiality).

QUESTION

2. Although leading arbitration rules typically call upon party arbitrators on tripartite panels to serve in an independent and impartial capacity, there is ongoing discussion and debate among arbitrators and practitioners regarding the precise — and proper — functions of party arbitrators in U.S. and international arbitration. For example, the CCA/

Straus Institute Survey of experienced U.S. arbitrators suggests that although tripartite tribunals tend to work very well, the great majority of respondents believe party arbitrators are at least sometimes perceived as being "predisposed toward the party that appointed them," and are something other than independent and impartial even when the procedures require the latter. A similar majority believed that party arbitrators at least sometimes decide close questions in favor of the party that appointed them.[9]

Is there a problem with party arbitrators being predisposed toward their appointing party? Should party arbitrators perform in all respects like arbitrators selected by both parties or by a third party, or could you imagine benefits from their acting somewhat differently? How would you deal with these kinds of issues if you were an attorney representing a party in an arbitration involving a tripartite panel that includes wing arbitrators appointed by individual parties?

5. Can a Party, or a Party Employee or Official, Be the Arbitrator?

Whatever concerns are raised by tripartite panels involving partisan wing arbitrators, such arrangements offer a modicum of fairness since there is a degree of balance on the tribunal. But what if the parties' contract provides that disputes will be arbitrated by one of the parties, or someone employed by or an official of a party? This question creates tension between two principles of arbitration: (1) party choice (leaving parties free to choose/allow a non-neutral arbitrator as part of their contract), and (2) upholding arbitration's legitimacy as a fair, neutral, quasi-judicial process.

The international arbitration community overwhelmingly rejects the notion that a party to a dispute can serve as arbitrator in its own case, as reflected in the International Bar Association Rules on Conflicts of Interests (2014). The IBA justifies this stance on the legal maxim that "no man can be his own judge" (first articulated in the Justinian Codex, circa 535 A.D.). The same principle has underpinned a number of U.S. court decisions. *See, e.g., McConnell v. Howard University*, 818 F.2d 58 n.12 (D.C. Cir. 1987); *Astoria Med. Group v. Health Ins. Plan of Greater N.Y.*, 11 N.Y.2d 128, n.1 (1962). There are, however, a number of U.S. decisions upholding arbitration awards rendered by individuals employed by or closely associated with parties.

You do not need to be a New England Patriots fan or even an aficionado of professional football to have heard about the so-called Deflategate episode, in which NFL Commissioner Roger Goodell suspended Patriots quarterback Tom Brady for four games on the basis of his "role in the use of underinflated footballs by the Patriots" during the AFC Championship Game in January 2015, and his failure to cooperate with the subsequent NFL investigation. What you may not know is that the relevant procedure is a kind of arbitration. Cases of this kind are governed by Article 46 of the collective bargaining agreement between the NFL and the players' union, the NFL Players Association (NFLPA). Goodell's initial disciplinary decision was pursuant to Section 1(a), which provides:

> All disputes involving a fine or suspension imposed upon a player for conduct on the playing field (other than as described in Subsection (b) below) or involving action taken against a player by the Commissioner for conduct detrimental to the integrity of, or public confidence in, the game of professional football, will be processed exclusively as follows: the Commissioner will promptly send written notice of his action to the player, with a copy to the NFLPA. Within three (3) business days following such written notification, the player affected thereby, or the NFLPA with the player's approval, may appeal in writing to the Commissioner.

Brady, through the NFLPA, appealed the suspension in accordance with Section 2(a), which provides:

> For appeals under Section 1(a) above, the Commissioner shall, after consultation with the Executive Director of the NFLPA, appoint one or more designees to serve as hearing officers. . . . Notwithstanding the foregoing, the Commissioner may serve as hearing officer in any appeal under Section 1(a) of this Article at his discretion.

Goodell designated himself as hearing officer (arbitrator). The NFLPA filed a motion seeking Goodell's recusal from arbitrating Brady's appeal since he could not lawfully arbitrate a matter involving his own alleged commission of a violation of the collective bargaining agreement, and regarding which he was a central witness. Goodell refused to recuse himself and eventually upheld the suspension. Goodell's decision was eventually upheld by the Second Circuit. *See Nat'l Football League Mgmt. Council v. Nat'l Football League Players Ass'n*, 820 F.3d 527, 531-532 (2d Cir. 2016); *Nat'l Football League Mgmt. Council v. Nat'l Football League Players Ass'n*, 125 F. Supp. 3d 449, 452-453 (S.D.N.Y. 2015), *rev'd*, 820 F.3d 527 (2d Cir. 2016). We will more fully explore the legal issues raised by these decisions in Chapter 6.C, in the context of a general discussion regarding overturning arbitration awards for "evident partiality."

Endnotes

1. Stipanowich, Thomas J. (2017) *Living the Dream of ADR: Reflections on Four Decades of the Quiet Revolution in Dispute Resolution*, 18 Cardozo J. Conf. Resol. 513, 525-530; *"Are We Getting There?" International Arbitration Survey: Diversity on Arbitral Tribunals* (2017), at https://www.bclplaw.com/en-US/insights/diversity-on-arbitral-tribunals-are-we-getting-there.html. *See also* Bjorklund, Andrea K. (2020) *The Diversity Deficit in International Investment Arbitration*, J. World Inv. & Trade.
2. Green, Michael Z. (2020) *Arbitrarily Selecting Black Arbitrators*, 88 Fordham L. Rev. 2255.
3. *Jay-Z Has 99 Problems, and . . . Lack of Diversity is One*, JDSupra, https://www.jdsupra.com/legalnews/jaj-z-has-99-problems-and-of-92312/.
4. *Id.*

5. Stipanowich, Thomas J. & Ulrich, Zachary. (2014) *Arbitration in Evolution: Current Practices and Perspectives of Experienced Commercial Arbitrators*, Colum. Am. Rev. Int'l Arb., Vol. 25.

6. Bedoya, Alonso. (2018) *Arbitration, Social Media and Networking Technologies: Latent Existing Conflicts*, Kluwer Arbitration Blog.

7. Cole, Sarah R. (2004) *Updating Arbitrator Ethics*, 10 Disp. Res. Mag. 24.

8. Mills, Lawrence R. & Brewer, Thomas J. (2005) *A Courtroom Lawyer's Guide to Arbitration*, 31 Litigation 42.

9. Stipanowich, Thomas J. & Ulrich, Zachary, *supra* note 5.

CHAPTER 4

ARBITRATION PROCEDURES AND AWARDS

A. *OVERVIEW OF THE ARBITRATION PROCESS*

1. *Stages of Arbitration*

Arbitration typically involves several procedural stages, although specific features will depend on the parties' agreement and incorporated arbitration rules. The process nearly always begins with the filing of a demand and other pleadings and the appointment of arbitrators. Arbitrators usually begin preliminary planning for the process by means of a pre-hearing conference or phone call to develop a tentative timetable, flesh out procedures, and set the stage for all that follows.

What follows depends on the nature and complexity of the case, but modern commercial arbitration usually involves weeks or months of pre-hearing preparation. Counsel may be engaged in filing and arguing motions, exchanging information, engaging in discovery, identifying and preparing witnesses (including experts), assembling documents to be presented at the hearing, and preparing pre-hearing briefs. During this stage, arbitrators often play an active oversight role, addressing motions, discovery disputes, and other procedural issues.

Then comes some form of hearing. Although in some cases arbitration hearings may be a far cry from a court trial, they typically embody basic rudiments of due process. Commercial cases involving lawyers may bear a number of the hallmarks of a court trial—with some important differences. See Section G below.

Arbitration concludes with arbitrator deliberations leading to the rendition of an award. The form of the award will vary depending on the parties' agreement and applicable rules; there may or may not be a published rationale or opinion along with the award. The issuance of a "bare" award, limited to a straightforward declaration of the panel's grant or denial of relief, was traditionally viewed as a bulwark against judicial intrusion into the award because it made it nearly impossible to decipher, and critique, the reasoning behind the arbitrator's decision. However, especially in larger cases, parties usually require arbitrators to provide a statement of reasons for their decisions.

With the rise in consumer and employment arbitration, we see more informal arbitration proceedings in these cases, usually involving less money. For example, a consumer arbitration may take place in less than ten days from filing to award. Hearings may be online or by telephone in many cases, cutting down on time and cost.

2. Roles of Attorneys

The attorney's role during the arbitration process depends on the type of case. In simple consumer cases or in "trade" arbitrations involving the quality of goods, there may not even be attorneys, or the attorney's role may be minimal. In contrast, in complex commercial cases, attorneys in arbitration are active in preparing and presenting a case, similar to litigation. These attorneys usually file pleadings, conduct interviews, prepare witnesses, prepare exhibits, create trial notebooks, and perhaps engage in extensive information exchange and discovery. Attorneys in arbitration normally make opening and closing arguments, prepare briefs on factual or legal issues, and may even file dispositive motions, as well as motions to confirm or vacate an arbitration award.

This is not to say, however, that arbitration advocacy is the same as trial advocacy. Pre-hearing practice in arbitration, motion practice and discovery, may be more abbreviated and attenuated—perhaps much more so—than in litigation. Experienced lawyers and arbitrators warn that arbitration is not a forum for the strutting and posturing employed by some lawyers in civil trials. Many arbitrators place great emphasis on legal counsel working cooperatively with respect to information exchange and the preparation of the case for arbitration, and may themselves play an active role in supervising this effort. Moreover, attorneys should remember that because their panel of adjudicators may bring significant expertise to the table, the latter may find extensive explication or foundation-laying unnecessary or even offensive. Perhaps most importantly, rather than act as passive recipients of the evidence adduced by counsel, arbitrators may join in the questioning of witnesses. Arbitrator's questions of witnesses may offer clues as to what arbitrators think is important; occasionally, the arbitrators' interrogation surfaces critical facts.

PROBLEM 1: THE ARBITRATION PROCESS

Assume you have been appointed chair of a panel of three arbitrators to arbitrate the dispute involving Carmin Co., manufacturer of the "Nügi" high-tech GPS units used in automobiles, and SamCo, Inc., a national "buying club" with stores all over the country. The parties have a long-term contract under which SamCo is obligated to buy certain amounts of various Carmin products each month. In recent months, SamCo has refused to accept the required number of various Carmin products, citing various alleged defects. Carmin's demand for arbitration includes a claim for more than $5 million in damages. For the purpose of answering the questions below and in the following sections (B-E), assume the AAA Commercial Arbitration Rules are applicable.

A. Just after the arbitrators have been appointed, the defendant, SamCo, seeks to file a counterclaim for damages against Carmin. Who determines whether the counterclaim should be heard?

B. After reviewing the initial pleadings of the parties, you realize that you have very little information on the factual and legal issues. How might you go about getting more information about the parties' positions? What other information might you seek, how, and when?

If you were an attorney for one of the parties in this arbitration, how might you make the most of the arbitration process? In what ways might your preparation and presentation be different from your efforts in litigation?

B. *LAYING THE GROUNDWORK: THE PRE-HEARING CONFERENCE*

No set of commercial arbitration procedures provides a precise blueprint for conducting an arbitration. Even if such detail were possible, it would not be desirable in light of the wide range of claims, controversies, and circumstances with which arbitrators are presented. It is during the pre-hearing process that the often-sketchy procedural framework established by the arbitration agreement is refined. It is here that the participants may have the opportunity to determine the precise nature of their arbitration experience.

In "fleshing out" the bare bones of the arbitration agreement, arbitrators typically enjoy considerable leeway. Leading commercial arbitration rules reinforce the well-recognized broad discretion of arbitrators to manage virtually all aspects of the arbitration. At the same time, effective arbitrators recognize that participants are usually best served by striving for party consensus, and by reserving unilateral arbitrator rulings for when consensus cannot be achieved.

In the simplest commercial arbitrations, there may be little or no need for active pre-hearing management by the arbitrator. Standard "fast-track" rules place a premium on getting the dispute resolved with minimal process. (*See, e.g.*, AAA Commercial Arbitration Rules, Expedited Procedures.) As the stakes grow or the issues become more complex, it becomes increasingly important for the arbitrator to take a more active role in managing the process with the involvement and, it is to be hoped, the cooperation of the parties.

In light of the variety of management issues that may arise in the course of arbitration, participants are well advised to consult appropriate guidelines. Applicable arbitration procedures may provide guidelines for the pre-hearing stage. For example, the CPR Non-Administered Arbitration Rules direct arbitrators to hold a "pre-hearing conference for the planning and scheduling of the proceeding." The purpose of the conference is "to discuss all elements of the arbitration with a view to planning for its future conduct." The pre-hearing conference (or in AAA parlance, "preliminary hearing") provides an opportunity to address the full range of procedural matters, including (1) clarifying the contractual basis of the arbitration and the issues presented, the rules governing arbitration, and the location of hearings; (2) specifying approved methods of communication; (3) identifying jurisdictional issues; (4) establishing a framework for addressing motions for interim or provisional relief, and for dispositive motions; (5) establishing a timetable or schedule for the process; (6) developing a framework for information exchange and discovery; (7) setting specific ground rules for the hearings; (8) considering protections for confidential information; and (9) setting parameters for the arbitration award. Additional conferences may be scheduled from time to time as the arbitrators deem necessary for effective management of the process.

Arbitrators often issue an initial procedural order (or "case management order") after a pre-hearing conference. This document, which sets forth a timetable and many other elements of the "arbitration plan," is usually submitted to the parties for their review and comment before final issuance. Keep in mind that this initial planning document, which in international arbitration is often referred to as the "terms of reference," is not intended as an inflexible limitation but as an adaptable and dynamic template that is likely to evolve or change to some extent as the case progresses.

QUESTIONS

1. As chair of the arbitration tribunal for the Carmin/SamCo arbitration in Problem 1, what kinds of things would you hope to accomplish at an initial pre-hearing conference? Can you find one or more useful templates for subjects to be addressed in a pre-hearing conference? Some arbitration procedures offer lists of potential topics. An excellent example designed for use in international proceedings is the *UNCITRAL Notes on Organizing Arbitral Proceedings* (2016).[1] It is sometimes used as a set of guidelines in U.S. commercial arbitration.

2. Might it make sense to have the parties' representatives try to see what procedural matters they can agree on before the pre-hearing conference? Should business executives representing Carmin and SamCo be present in the pre-hearing conference? Why or why not?

3. If you were the attorney for Carmin in this arbitration, what should you do in preparation for, during, and after the preliminary hearing?

C. JURISDICTIONAL ISSUES

Because arbitration is a creature of contract, a valid and enforceable agreement to arbitrate is a fundamental prerequisite to an arbitrator's jurisdiction. When a party challenges an arbitrator's jurisdiction on the basis that it is not bound by a valid arbitration agreement, or that the arbitration agreement does not cover the matters at issue, there may be a question as to whether the jurisdictional issue should be resolved by the arbitrator or by a court. This is often referred to as a question of "arbitrability." The answer on who decides the question depends on the agreement of the parties.

If the parties have agreed that arbitration shall be governed by any of the leading standard arbitration procedures, the authority of arbitrators to decide jurisdictional issues will probably be clear. For example, the JAMS Comprehensive Arbitration Rules provide:

> Once appointed, the Arbitrator shall resolve disputes about the interpretation and applicability of these Rules and conduct of the Arbitration

hearing. The resolution of the issue by the Arbitrator shall be final. . . . Jurisdictional and arbitrability disputes, including disputes over the formation, existence, validity, interpretation or scope of the agreement under which Arbitration is sought, and who are proper Parties to the Arbitration, shall be submitted to and ruled on by the Arbitrator. The Arbitrator has the authority to determine jurisdiction and arbitrability issues as a preliminary matter.

Under this provision, parties to a contract that incorporates the JAMS procedures (or similar rule of the AAA or others) agree to consign virtually all questions touching upon the arbitrator's authority to the arbitrator. This is sometimes referred to as a delegation clause. The policy behind such provisions is to discourage resort to the courts and avoid related delays and disruptions to the arbitration process.

The goals of speed and efficiency are further served by provisions that require those asserting jurisdictional challenges to act promptly or run the risk of being deemed to have waived the right to challenge. For example, the AAA Commercial Arbitration Rules provide:

> A party must object to the jurisdiction of the arbitrator or to the arbitrability of a claim or counterclaim no later than the filing of the answering statement to the claim or counterclaim that gives rise to the objection.

Note on Arbitration Law.   As we will see, in the absence of a clear provision delegating to the arbitrator the authority to decide whether an agreement to arbitrate is valid and enforceable, or whether a controversy falls within the scope of the agreement to arbitrate, U.S. federal arbitration law and prevailing state arbitration law put those matters in the hands of the courts. However, an arbitration provision that incorporates language such as that above has been held to provide "clear and unmistakable" evidence that the parties want the arbitrators to determine such "jurisdictional" questions and overcomes the usual presumption in favor of having a court do so. Indeed, Supreme Court jurisprudence has strongly endorsed enforcement of such delegation clauses. See Chapter 5.C.2 and Chapter 8.B.1.

QUESTION

4. Carmin and SamCo are parties to a long-term contract; they agreed to arbitrate disputes "arising under or relating to their contract or the breach or termination thereof." Midway through the term of their contractual relationship, the parties have a serious disagreement about the requirements relating to Carmin's performance under the contract. Carmin's demand for arbitration with SamCo includes a request that the arbitrators render a decision declaring its rights under the contract with SamCo—what is commonly referred to as a "declaratory judgment." In its answering statement, SamCo states that Carmin's claim is outside the jurisdiction of the arbitrators under the AAA Commercial Arbitration Rules. As chair of the arbitration panel, your fellow arbitrators look to you to offer guidance on a course of action. Based on your reading of the AAA Rules, how should the arbitrators handle this matter?

D.   INTERIM MEASURES AND EMERGENCY RELIEF

Imagine that your client and her joint venture partner have come into serious conflict. You have filed an arbitration demand on behalf of your client to obtain damages and other relief from her partner under the parties' agreement. Meanwhile, your client informs you that she has credible information that her joint venture partner is planning to leave the country with key business assets, thereby undermining the entire purpose of the arbitration. What can you do to deal with this emergency? To address such situations, many arbitration rules specifically authorize arbitrators to grant interim remedies equivalent to a preliminary injunction from a court, such as preserving the condition of perishable goods or taking appropriate security measures or even monetary relief. (Moreover, the FAA and state arbitration statutes grant implied power to arbitrators to provide interim remedies.) Most broad-form commercial arbitration agreements allow arbitrators the authority, for instance, to direct a posting of a bond as security for claims or order the creation of an escrow account. On the other hand, only a court is able to exercise a contempt power to enforce the preservation of assets or to ensure continuing performance. Arbitrators lack such a contempt power, even though they are able to issue non-criminal sanctions against one or more parties. Therefore, if a party secures interim relief, an arbitrator's order may have to be enforced by a court as an interim award subject to confirmation under the relevant state or federal arbitration law.

What if the threat of irreparable harm emerges before the arbitrator or arbitration tribunal has been appointed? There are a couple of possibilities. First of all, arbitration rules often provide that in such circumstances, turning directly to a court for emergency relief will not be deemed incompatible with the agreement to arbitrate. That is, parties can seek an appropriate court order without fear that the other party will be able to successfully argue that the resort to court amounts to a waiver of the right to arbitrate. Courts, however, are sometimes hesitant to interfere if the parties have an arbitral agreement. For example, in *DHL Info. Services (Americas). Inc. v. Infinite Software Corp.*, 502 F. Supp. 2d 1082, 1083 (C.D. Cal. 2007), the district court looked at whether a request for a preliminary injunction should be reviewed by the court or by the arbitrator. The court ruled that the arbitrator should review the matter, because the parties had agreed to arbitrate "any controversy or claim arising out of or relating to the Agreement, or the breach thereof" under AAA arbitration rules. Despite the fact that the AAA rules stated that judicially granted interim relief was permissible in such circumstances, the court "decline[d] to rush in where the arbitrator is free to tread." *Id.* In contrast, the court in *Toyo Tire Holdings of Americas Inc. v. Cont'l Tire N.A., Inc.*, 609 F.3d 975, 977 (9th Cir. 2010), reversed and remanded a district court's finding that they could not grant injunctive relief when the parties have agreed to arbitrate and the arbitrator has the power to grant that relief. In this case, the parties' arbitration was governed by the Rules of Conciliation and Arbitration of the International Chamber of Commerce, which allows judicially imposed interim relief. *Id.* The opinion noted that in this instance, a party was seeking an injunction to preserve the status quo, and thus allowing a court to issue interim relief could be important for preserving the integrity of the arbitral process. *Id.*

Another possibility contemplated by leading arbitration rules is the appointment of a special emergency arbitrator who is empowered for the limited purpose of rapidly addressing the request for emergency relief pending the formation of an arbitration panel.

Note on Arbitration Law. As indicated above, the roles of arbitrators and courts in circumstances of this kind may not be fully understood without a consideration of statutory or decisional law, which will be treated in Chapter 5.E.3.

QUESTIONS

5. What guidance do the AAA Commercial Rules provide regarding arbitrators' granting of preliminary relief in circumstances like that described above? This issue will be revisited during our discussion of pre-award judicial support of arbitration in Chapter 5.E.3.
6. If the arbitrators have not yet been appointed, do the AAA Commercial Rules contemplate the possibility that a party might seek relief from a court?
7. If arbitrators have not yet been appointed, what other option is there?

E. DISPOSITIVE MOTIONS

Arbitration usually begins with very general pleadings offering little detail regarding the issues in dispute or the positions of the parties. As a rule, therefore, a dismissal of claims on the pleadings is inappropriate in arbitration. As the parties exchange information and develop more detailed positions, however, there may be some point at which issues have ripened sufficiently for arbitrators to act knowledgeably upon a motion for summary disposition — that is, the equivalent of a motion for summary judgment in court. It may then be possible for arbitrators to determine that a party will be unable to bear the burden of proving a case in the arbitration hearing and render an award in favor of the opposing party.

Dispositive motions in arbitration are a double-edged sword. Excessive, inappropriate, or mismanaged motion practice is regarded as one of the primary contributors to increased costs and delays in arbitration. The problem is that, as in court, motion practice often contributes significantly to arbitration cost and cycle time without clear benefits. The filing of motions leads to the establishment of schedules for briefing and argument. This entails considerable effort by advocates, which may be for naught if the arbitrators postpone a decision until the close of hearings because of the existence of unresolved factual disputes. If prudently employed, however, such motions are a potentially useful tool for narrowing arbitral issues prior to hearings and limiting discovery, thus avoiding unnecessary preparation and hearing time. Sometimes, an arbitrator's ruling on such a motion will stimulate early settlement of the case.

The arbitration rules of leading providers contain provisions specifically authorizing arbitrators to address dispositive motions. The American Arbitration Association's Commercial Arbitration Rules and Mediation Procedures grant arbitrators the power to rule on preliminary dispositive motions.[2] It states: "The arbitrator may allow the filing of and make rulings upon a dispositive motion only if the arbitrator determines that the moving party has shown that the motion is likely to succeed and dispose of or narrow the issues in the case." Similarly, JAMS also allows arbitrators to receive and rule on preliminary motions for summary disposition.[3] The rule states: "The Arbitrator may permit any Party to file a Motion for Summary Disposition of a particular claim or issue, either by agreement of all interested Parties or at the request of one Party, provided other interested Parties have reasonable notice to respond to the request."

In contrast, FINRA's Code of Arbitration Procedure for Customer Disputes discourages motions to dismiss a claim prior to the conclusion of a party's case.[4] When such a motion is made, it must be in writing, separate from the answer, and filed after the answer is filed. If the arbitration is before a panel of arbitrators, the motion must be decided by the full panel, and a decision to grant the motion must be unanimous. Furthermore, the rules put additional parameters on hearings, and the arbitrator(s) can only grant such a motion if they find that (1) the non-moving party previously released the claim in dispute by a signed settlement or written release; (2) the moving party was not associated with the account, security, or conduct at issue in the claim; or (3) the non-moving party previously brought a claim regarding the same dispute against the same party that was fully adjudicated on the merits and a final order, judgment, decision, or award was issued.[5]

Note on Arbitration Law.   In practice, some arbitrators have been reluctant to make preliminary rulings disposing of all or part of a case because they are fearful of having their award vacated by a court on the basis that they failed to hear material or relevant evidence. See Chapter 6.D. Nonetheless, even in the absence of rules allowing for motions, such actions will probably be deemed to fall within the broad discretion of arbitrators in managing hearings and fashioning relief. The key is to allow for opportunity to present one's case. *See, e.g., Global Reinsurance Co. v. TIG Ins. Co.*, 2009 U.S. Dist. LEXIS 7697 (S.D.N.Y. Jan. 20, 2009); *Schlessinger v. Rosenfeld, Meyer & Susman*, 47 Cal. Rptr. 2d 650 (Ct. App. 1995).

QUESTION

8. Suppose that, in the early stages of arbitration, SamCo moves to dismiss Carmin's claim on the basis that the contract provides:

   > No claim may be brought more than one (1) year after the transaction, occurrence, or event on which it is based.

   SamCo argues that Carmin did not file its original demand for arbitration until 14 months after SamCo first refused to take some of Carmin's goods, and therefore Carmin's claim should be barred by this contractual "statute of limitations." How should you as an arbitrator respond to this motion? What information might be relevant to resolving this on a preliminary basis? Assume the parties agreed to arbitrate under the AAA Commercial Arbitration Rules.

F.   INFORMATION EXCHANGE/DISCOVERY

It used to be that a major difference between U.S. arbitration procedures and court litigation was the relative absence of discovery—that is, the obtaining of evidence from the other party through requests for answers to interrogatories, requests for production of documents, requests for admissions, and sworn depositions—in arbitration. But U.S. arbitration practice has changed dramatically, and today some amount of discovery is normal. Most would agree that in arbitration, as in court trial, fundamental fairness often requires a sharing of information, and it is generally fairer and more efficient to have a consensual or supervised information exchange prior to hearings. The problem is that discovery has traditionally accounted for the bulk of costs and time spent in litigation. The expansion of discovery stands out as the primary contributor to greater expense and longer cycle time in arbitration, as affirmed by a poll of participants at the 2009 National Summit on the Future of Commercial Arbitration:

If you believe arbitration fails to meet the desires of business users regarding speed, efficiency, and economy, to what extent does excessive discovery tend to contribute to that result?

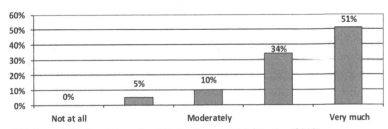

CCA Protocols for Expeditious, Cost-Effective Commercial Arbitration (2010).

Today, it is not unusual for legal advocates to agree to extensive discovery in advance of arbitration, and even to use standard civil procedural rules as a template. That said, many arbitrators and some arbitration rules aim to hold the line on excessive discovery, and discovery in U.S. arbitration is usually more limited than in litigation. This reflects the normal or conventional expectation that arbitration offers a speedier and more efficient path to resolution, and that cost-benefit considerations will temper the normal broad relevance standard in litigation. For example, the CPR Non-Administered Arbitration Rules state that

> the Tribunal may require and facilitate such discovery as it shall determine is appropriate in the circumstances, taking into account the needs of the parties and the desirability of making discovery expeditious and cost-effective.

The accompanying commentary explains that as contemplated by the CPR procedures, "[a]rbitration is not for the litigator who will 'leave no stone unturned.'" Most often, arbitrators will seek to restrict discovery to categories of information, such as documents, that speak to the primary issues in dispute. The AAA Commercial Arbitration Rules, for example, place heavy emphasis on exchange of documents. Requests for admission and interrogatories are relatively rare, and, unless the parties have otherwise agreed, arbitrators often demand justification for the taking of depositions. For example, the *AAA Procedures for Large, Complex Commercial Disputes* (a part of the AAA Commercial Arbitration Rules), L-2(f) (Oct. 1, 2013), provide:

> In exceptional cases, at the discretion of the arbitrator, upon good cause shown and consistent with the expedited nature of arbitration, the arbitrator may order depositions to obtain the testimony of a person who may possess information determined by the arbitrator to be relevant and material to the outcome of the case.[6]

Arbitrators in larger or high-stakes disputes often permit depositions to preserve testimony or save time at the hearing.

The CCA/Straus Institute Survey of experienced U.S. arbitrators reveals that the great majority play a relatively proactive role regarding discovery. They respond promptly to party motions regarding discovery, encourage parties to limit the scope of discovery, and work with counsel to limit or streamline discovery. When discovery issues arise, they first usually try to address the issues informally, perhaps through a conference call, and may "mediate" a mutually satisfactory resolution. More often than not, they actively monitor discovery and remain attuned to conflicts.[7] Competent arbitrators help set and enforce strict time limits for information exchange. An arbitrator may draw an adverse inference if a party refuses to comply with a discovery order.

Note on Arbitration Law. The FAA and most state arbitration statutes do not specifically address the subject of arbitration-related discovery. However, the FAA and corresponding state laws give arbitrators authority to issue subpoenas to parties or nonparties and provide for their judicial enforcement. FAA Section 7, for example, states that arbitrators may "summon in writing any person to attend before them or any of them as a witness and in a proper case to bring with him or them any book, record, document, or paper which may be deemed material as evidence in the case." As we will see in Chapter 5.E.2, however, courts have reached different conclusions about whether the FAA language supports judicial enforcement of subpoenas for a deposition or pre-hearing discovery. Revisions to the Uniform Arbitration Act (UAA) have attempted to directly address these and other concerns through specific provisions for arbitrator-supervised discovery, including depositions.

In the United States, moreover, the courts may order non-parties in the United States to provide testimony or to produce documents to assist in foreign proceedings pursuant to 28 U.S.C. §1782 when such evidence is "for use in a proceeding in a foreign or international tribunal . . . when a request made, by a foreign or international tribunal or upon the application of any interested person." In *Intel Corp. v. Advanced Micro Devices, Inc.*, 542 U.S. 241, 258 (2004), the U.S. Supreme Court appeared to adopt an expansive interpretation of the scope of §1782 by concluding that the European Commission was a "foreign or international tribunal"—a conclusion that some interpreted to open the door to applying §1782 to international arbitration proceedings. However, courts remain divided on the issue. Although *In re Application of Republic of Ecuador v. Douglas*, 153 F. Supp. 3d 484, 487 (D. Mass. 2015), held that that investment arbitration tribunal constituted under bilateral investment treaties was an "international tribunal" under §1782, courts differ respecting the application of the section to international commercial arbitration tribunal. *See In re Dubey*, 949 F. Supp. 2d 990, 992 (C.D. Cal. 2013) (private arbitrations do not fall within §1782); *In re Babcock Borsig AG*, 583 F. Supp. 2d 233 (D. Mass. 2008) (private arbitrations fall within §1782).

QUESTIONS

9. Suppose you have been appointed to arbitrate disputes between Carmin and SamCo under the JAMS Comprehensive Arbitration Rules. You review the parties' arbitration agreement and discover that it provides that "discovery in this proceeding will be conducted in accordance with the Federal Rules of Civil Procedure." You believe that, as a rule, it is not necessary or appropriate for parties to engage in full-blown, court-like discovery in commercial arbitration. At this point, could you, and should you, announce to the parties that you will not permit this breadth of discovery and limit it in various ways with an arbitrator order? If not, how should you handle the situation?

10. Consider another kind of factual situation. Suppose that at the time Carmin filed an arbitration demand, it was discovered that SamCo's CEO, Barbara Bates, is severely ill. If Ms. Bates's testimony is considered essential to Carmin's case, what steps might be undertaken to preserve Ms. Bates's testimony in arbitration? Assume the JAMS Comprehensive Arbitration Rules apply.

11. The *IBA Rules on the Taking of Evidence in International Arbitration* (2010) were designed as a way of accommodating the differing expectations of discovery-focused U.S. lawyers and advocates with civil law backgrounds in international arbitration. Take a look at the *IBA Rules*, and see if you can figure out what kinds of differences inspired the Rules. Also, do you think it would ever be appropriate for U.S. parties and counsel to adopt the *IBA Rules* in a domestic arbitration proceeding in the United States?

G.   THE HEARING

1.   General Structure of Hearings

Arbitration hearings are generally less formal than court trial and may be held around a conference table. However, commercial arbitrations typically feature some of the basic elements of trial. Usually, each side will present an opening statement, followed by introductory evidence, examination and cross-examination of witnesses, testimony under oath, and closing statements and arguments. Unless otherwise agreed, the formal rules of evidence and civil procedure do not apply, and thus hearsay or other testimony inadmissible in court may be considered by arbitrators. Arbitrators normally have wide discretion on whether to allow in various evidence. Experienced arbitrators now utilize a wide variety of techniques to actively manage hearings.[8]

Depending on the complexity of the matter and number of parties involved, a hearing could last less than a day or could extend over a long period of time, at the convenience of parties and arbitrators. Scheduling hearings in complex cases can sometimes delay arbitral proceedings, particularly with a panel of highly sought-after neutrals.

Note on Arbitration Law.   Many arbitrators err on the side of admitting evidence, at least partly because they are aware that an award may be overturned (vacated) by a court where an arbitrator is "guilty of misconduct . . . in refusing to hear evidence pertinent and material to the controversy" or "guilty of misconduct in refusing to postpone the hearing, upon sufficient cause shown," FAA, 9 U.S.C. §10(a)(3) (Supp. 1994). See Chapter 6.D.

QUESTIONS

Consult the AAA Commercial Rules in addressing these questions.

12. Suppose one party to arbitration seeks to avoid the expense and inconvenience of an oral hearing and to rely entirely on submissions of written documents, briefs, and so on. Is it within the arbitrators' authority to direct a "paper hearing"?

13. You would like to have the statements of several witnesses that are redundant to other testimony to be introduced by affidavit. Is this permissible?

14. The night before the first day of four consecutive days of scheduled hearings, an attorney for one of the parties sends a fax and email to inform opposing counsel and the arbitrators that she and her client will be unable to attend the proceedings that week. The explanation is that the client has been called away "on personal business." You learn of the communication the following morning, right before the hearing is scheduled to begin. Meanwhile, the other party has appeared for the hearing. What is the appropriate course of action for the arbitrators?

15. The case centers on a valuation question, and each of the parties has hired an accountant to address the key issues. Can the arbitrators put them on the stand at the same time, ask them questions simultaneously, and even permit them to question one another? Can the arbitrators appoint their own expert and have the parties pay the cost?

16. After several days of hearings, the plaintiff announces that it has concluded the presentation of its case. It is fairly clear that the plaintiff has not proved its case, but the arbitrators believe that it is likely that the information exists to support its case. Is it appropriate, and within the arbitrators' authority, to direct the parties to provide additional information on the key issues?

17. If your client seeks a cost-effective and expeditious arbitration process, what process choices might help to realize these goals? Before consulting and comparing current arbitration procedures, you may want to consult

> the *CCA Protocols for Expeditious, Cost-Effective Commercial Arbitration* (2010) or, for international arbitration, the *ICC Techniques for Controlling Time and Costs in Arbitration* (2018). (Note: In lieu of this Question, your teacher may assign a related exercise, *Negotiating and Drafting a Dispute Resolution Agreement.*)

2. *Privacy and Confidentiality*

Arbitration hearings offer a greater degree of privacy than the courthouse. There is often no official record, and arbitrators can bar nonessential persons from the hearing room. In some cases, additional confidentiality protections are established by the agreement of the parties or by arbitral order.

Arbitrators and arbitral institutions have obligations to preserve the privacy of the process under applicable procedural rules and ethical standards, and public policies protect arbitrators from having to testify. However, absent a specific agreement, parties and their agents have no obligation to preserve the confidentiality of exchanged documents or arbitration-related communications or events.[9] They can even disclose the latter to third parties, like the media.

This lesson was brought home in one memorable case involving the Los Angeles–based J. Paul Getty Museum and its former curator of European drawings, Nicholas Turner. Turner had sued the Getty Museum for fraud, alleging that the Museum had failed to reveal that several drawings in its collection were forged. The matter went to arbitration. Getty lawyers filed a motion with the arbitrator for an order preventing Turner from sharing any information discovered during the case with the media; they argued that arbitration is an "inherently confidential proceeding." Denying the motion, the arbitrator reportedly observed, "*Erin Brockovich* [a legal action depicted in detail in a well-known film] was an arbitration."[10] Thus, parties must take special *additional* steps to protect confidentiality if they want to ensure that arbitration proceedings remain confidential.

Third parties engaged in legal action against one of the parties to the arbitration may also seek information shared in the arbitration. They may be able to get that information through discovery if it has not been established as confidential. Therefore, parties seeking to protect sensitive or proprietary information usually request that the arbitrators issue appropriate protective orders or, if mutually acceptable, enter into a post-dispute confidentiality agreement. In transactions involving key intellectual property or other sensitive proprietary information, however, the best course is to ensure confidentiality in arbitration as a part of initial contract planning.[11]

Note on Arbitration Law. Neither the Federal Arbitration Act nor the Uniform Arbitration Act (the widely used template for state arbitration laws) includes a provision protecting the confidentiality of arbitral proceedings. As held in *Industrotech Constructors Inc. v. Duke University*, 67 NC App. 741, 314 S.E.2d 272 (1984), unless the parties' agreement or incorporated arbitration rules offer explicit protections for the confidentiality of communications (including testimony or shared exhibits) in arbitration, U.S. law recognizes no such protections. In the *United States v. Pan-handle Eastern Corp.*, 118 F.R.D. 346 (1988), the court held that there is no existence of an implied obligation emanating from the agreement between the parties in the absence of express contractual agreement concerning confidentiality. *See also Contship Containerlines, Ltd. v. PPG Industries, Inc.*, 00 Civ. 0194 (RCC) (HBP), 99 Civ. 10545 (RCC) (HBP) (S.D.N.Y. Apr. 17, 2003).

QUESTION

18. Suppose your client is concerned about protecting trade secrets in arbitration. What level of protection will standard rules (such as those of AAA or JAMS) offer for trade secrets? *See A. T. v. State Farm Mut. Auto. Ins. Co.*, 989 P.2d 219 (Colo. Ct. App. 1999) (holding that records disclosed at an arbitration hearing were permitted to be used at a later, unrelated trial because the party did not request a protective order and did not enter into a confidentiality agreement with insurance company); *but see Group Health Plan, Inc. v. BJC Health Sys., Inc.*, 30 S.W.3d 198 (Mo. Ct. App. 2000) (holding that confidentiality agreement signed by parties in an earlier arbitration proceeding was enough to prevent documents from being disclosed in a new arbitration proceeding). What additional protections might be included in the arbitration agreement or incorporated rules?[12] (Note: In lieu of this Question, your teacher may assign a related exercise, *Negotiating and Drafting a Dispute Resolution Agreement.*)

---

3. Virtual Hearings

Over time, there has been an increase in the use of online communications and hearings in arbitration. Online arbitration ("OArb") includes asynchronous as well as synchronous communications, text-only proceedings as well as virtual hearings, and mixtures thereof. OArb's use of technology eliminates the costs and stress of travel and in-person processes, perhaps creating better or more attainable access to remedies in some cases. Imagine parties in Chicago and London providing evidence and statements at times that fit their schedules and time zones. Eliminating travel saves the need for arranging childcare or missing work, as well as the stress that often comes with in-person processes.

OArb is just one example of online dispute resolution (ODR), which more generally encompasses use of technology to assist prevention and resolution of disputes. Most ODR, however, is not OArb because it involves facilitation of communications aimed to spark voluntary settlement.[13] For example, ODR may operate more like online mediation that does not settle the dispute without the parties' mutual agreement. OArb is a distinct subset of ODR because it generally culminates in a final and binding award under the FAA. This binding nature has caused many to shy away from OArb in the past out of concern that one needs an in-person hearing—especially where large dollar amounts are at stake or they otherwise fear the consequences of a binding award.

Nonetheless, interest in OArb has spiked during the course of the Covid-19 pandemic. Virtual meeting technologies such as Skype, Google Meet, WebEx, and Zoom have made virtual hearings relatively cheap and easy, and individuals have become accustomed to online communication in the lock down. Indeed, in larger dollar claims and areas traditionally wed to arbitration such as labor and construction, in-person arbitration has long been the norm, and there was not great movement toward OArb until Covid-19 forced wider adoption. Even in the beginning of the pandemic, most parties were stating an intention to wait to arbitrate until they could do so in person because of inexperience with using virtual platforms or long-held beliefs that in-person hearings are always the best method for resolution. Furthermore, parties who benefit from delay presumably benefitted from the "Covid excuse" for putting off litigation or arbitration. As the pandemic continued, however, parties grew eager to resolve their disputes and arbitrators warmed up to virtual arbitration. Disputes have accumulated as the pandemic has raged on, and parties have increasingly embraced virtual platforms as their best and safest means for moving forward—especially with most courts still closed and uncertainty as to when courts will reopen or function in an efficient manner.

Notably, some arbitrators who have now used OArb state that they will not likely return to in-person hearings. This is even true with respect to larger dollar claims. Many parties have likewise voiced favor for online hearings. The cost savings is no doubt contributing toward this shift. It will be interesting to see OArb develops in a post-pandemic world.[14]

NOTE AND QUESTIONS: LEVERAGING TECHNOLOGY FOR FAIR, EFFECTIVE AND EFFICIENT ARBITRATION

Leveraging Technology for Fair, Effective and Efficient International Arbitration Proceedings,[15] developed by a commission of the International Chamber of Commerce, was designed to assist parties and arbitral tribunals in using technology in a fair, cost-effective, and efficient way. It examines certain technologies being used on the international arbitration stage, addresses technological features and functionalities that can enhance arbitrations, and identifies useful procedural practices and pitfalls to avoid. The Report also contains guidelines and exemplary provisions for incorporating technology in arbitration as well as helpful checklists for conducting virtual hearings. Because the Report reflects, and represents, critical developments in arbitration practice both internationally and in the United States, it is well worth reviewing. While you are reviewing the Report, consider the following questions.

19. Section 2 of the Report indicates that arbitral institutions and other professional bodies are changing their expectations regarding the technological competence of arbitrators, and basic technological understanding is increasingly a factor in the evaluation of proposed arbitrators. How would you rate your own level of technological competence? As you ponder that question, consider the following ways in which technology may be transforming the arbitration experience, and related issues.

20. Section 4 discusses the electronic exchange of communications, exhibits, and other submissions. The Report notes the prevalence of electronic

communication via email and other messaging services during arbitration. What are some of the potential security concerns associated with email? What about using "chat" in online video platforms? What suggestions does the Report make about how electronic documents can best be organized, authenticated, served, signed, and submitted?

21. Section 5 considers the usefulness of e-briefs (briefs with embedded electronic hyperlinks to cited exhibits and testimony). What are some of the considerations associated with e-briefs? Also, how might data analytics and/or artificial intelligence (AI) be used in predictive coding to assess the merits of a party's case and to identify responsive documents?

22. Section 6 identifies issues that emerge when using technology in evidentiary hearings. What are some of these issues? Moreover, what are some of the key factors that parties and arbitrators should consider in determining whether a virtual or hybrid hearing is appropriate for the case? What are some of the issues associated with witness testimony in the new technological environment?

23. Section 3 of the Report suggests that the use of technology in arbitration should be subjected to cost analysis to ensure that technology used is appropriate for the size and nature of the dispute, party and arbitrator competencies, data security, and efficiency. The Report suggests that parties take time before or during the case management conference to discuss and agree on how technology will factor in the arbitration. Having reviewed the Report, how should counsel address these issues? Should they work in concert? Why or why not?

H. ARBITRATION AND MULTIPARTY DISPUTES

Imagine you are an attorney who is contacted by a company that just moved into its newly built headquarters building and discovered a major problem with the roof. Your client is uncertain whether the problem results from the architect's design, the builder's workmanship, or some combination of the two. When you consult the contract documents, you discover that your client has separate contracts with the architect and the builder and both include arbitration agreements, but neither agreement says anything about how you might arrange for a single arbitration in which all parties are present. You end up having to file for arbitration separately under each of the contracts, and all too often you may find out that there is no method for joining all the parties in one proceeding. Because arbitration is a creature of contract and no party may be bound to arbitrate with another party in the absence of agreement, a party "in the middle" of a multiparty dispute with multiple contracts may find itself in the awkward position of pressing a case in multiple forums.

Although some arbitration rules (such as the *AAA Construction Industry Arbitration Rules* (2015)) contemplate that there may be multiple claims or defendants, or that someone might seek to join other parties or consolidate arbitration proceedings in a single hearing, there is usually no substitute for careful drafting by parties wishing to effectively accommodate multiparty disputes in arbitration.

QUESTION

24. Suppose you are approached by a corporate client who wants to build a building and enter into separate contracts with a design architect and a builder. The client prefers arbitration to litigation for a variety of reasons but is aware of the problem of trying to bring all parties into a single proceeding. Assuming you have the agreement of the architect and builder not to resist an approach that permits the building owner (your client) to join everyone in a single arbitration, how might you draft such a provision?

Note on Arbitration Law. Questions surrounding the arbitration of multiparty disputes have been the focus of court decisions in the United States and abroad. In recent years, several United States Supreme Court decisions have addressed issues associated with the arbitration of class actions, including allowance of class arbitrations and the enforceability of arbitration clauses waiving a party's right to join in a class action. The Supreme Court also has weighed in on application of estoppel in arbitration. These developments are discussed in Chapter 8.B.2.

I.   ARBITRATION AWARDS AND REMEDIES

1.   Arbitrator Discretion and Finality of Arbitration Awards

One reason many parties choose arbitration is to avoid the risk of facing an unpredictable or unreasonable jury verdict. They repose trust, instead, in the decision-making abilities of legal professionals, former judges, or subject matter experts that are selected by agreement of the parties. Although arbitration awards tend to be straightforward decisions granting damages and allocating various costs, arbitration rules often emphasize the wide discretion of arbitrators in determining awards; for example, the AAA Commercial Arbitration Rules allow for "any remedy or relief that the arbitrator deems just and equitable and within the scope of the agreement, including, but not limited to, specific performance of a contract."

Binding arbitration is founded on the premise that when parties agree to allocate responsibility for adjudication to an identified private third party, respect for party autonomy dictates that that decision should not ordinarily be disturbed or second-guessed. To ensure the finality of arbitral awards, consistent with the agreement of the parties, while promoting fundamental fairness of process, the FAA and corresponding state arbitration statutes contemplate very limited avenues of appeal and forms of redress from arbitral awards. See Chapter 6. Judicial scrutiny is restricted to generally procedural aspects, or determining whether the arbitrator's award was within the grant of authority agreed to by the parties. This is laid out in Section 10 of the FAA and does not allow a court to vacate an award for errors of law or fact. One court suggested that the process under the FAA "ought not to be called review at all." *UHC Mgmt. Co. v. Computer Servs. Corp.*, 148 F.3d 992 (8th Cir. 1998).

Thus, arbitrating parties can count on awards being accorded a relatively high degree of finality—a result that many perceive as a benefit. But many other

U.S. attorneys, far from focusing on the potential benefits of this arrangement, concentrate on what arbitration is *not*—litigation with *de novo* review appeal on errors of law and more limited review of factual errors. In a survey of Fortune 1000 corporate counsel, the difficulty of appeal was the most-cited reason why companies do not choose arbitration.[16] This perspective is most understandable in the context of high-stakes cases, many of which now find their way into commercial arbitration. In addition to discouraging some business parties from arbitrating, these concerns have fueled attempts to contract for expanded judicial review of arbitration awards, which the U.S. Supreme Court has quashed as a matter of federal arbitration law.

Unease about limitations on appeal in commercial arbitration is closely intertwined with expressed fears that arbitrators might fail to follow, or to properly apply, pertinent legal standards. In the international arena, this uncertainty is compounded by issues of choice of law and potential cultural conflicts. There is also concern that arbitrators tend to "split the baby," or engage in inappropriate compromise, as a way of avoiding hard decisions or encouraging repeat business by arbitrating parties. The source and factual basis of the perception that arbitrators tend to "compromise" are little understood, and the AAA has taken pains to rebut the notion.

NOTE AND QUESTION: WHAT PRICE HISTORY?

On November 22, 1963, Abraham Zapruder stood on top of a concrete pillar and filmed President and Mrs. John F. Kennedy as their motorcade travelled through Dallas's Dealey Plaza. What Zapruder captured with his camera was the horrific assassination of a President—26 seconds that shook the world. It was ultimately determined that the film should be taken by the U.S. government and placed in the National Archives, and that just compensation should be paid to the Zapruder family.

In October 1998, a company established by the Zapruder family to handle financial matters relating to the film and the U.S. government entered into an agreement for binding arbitration to assess just compensation for the in-camera original of the Zapruder film. The agreement provided that each side would pick an arbitrator, and the parties would jointly pick a third arbitrator who would serve as chair. A two-day hearing was set for May 1999. The Zapruder interests had selected well-known dispute resolution professional Kenneth Feinberg as arbitrator; the government selected Walter Dellinger, former solicitor general. Retired federal circuit court judge Arlin Adams was chosen to be chair. Their task: to assess the fair market value of the Zapruder film.

At the hearing, both sides submitted testimony from expert appraisers, but the very uniqueness of this historical and cultural artifact presented both sides with a considerable challenge. One of Zapruder's experts asserted that the film was more valuable than paintings by Van Gogh or Renoir, or Leonardo da Vinci's illustrated *Codex Leicester*—objects that had commanded $26 to $80 million on the market. In light of these conclusions, Zapruder's counsel argued for the highest possible award permitted by the parties' earlier agreement—$30 million.

Some government experts took an entirely different approach, comparing the Zapruder film to other camera-original films. They pointed out that by these standards, the six-foot-long film comprised less than half a minute of screen time, had several frames missing, and had shrunk slightly. They also argued that it was the copyright for the film, and not the film itself, which was of greatest value. Another government expert drew comparisons between the film and other artifacts of U.S. history, such as Lincoln's handwritten notes for the "House Divided" speech, which sold for $1.5 million at auction. The government concluded that, all things considered, the appropriate value for the film was $750,000.

In a 2-1 decision, the arbitration panel awarded the Zapruder family $16 million for the film. Arbitrators Feinberg and Adams wrote the decision, and Arbitrator Dellinger filed a dissent. A thorough and thoughtful description of the entire arbitration, from the dynamics of arbitrator selection to the negotiations preceding the final award, may be found in Alexandra Zapruder's book *Twenty-Six Seconds: A Personal History of the Zapruder Film* 380-412 (2016).

25. Why do you think the panel majority made the award it did? Why did Dellinger dissent?

NOTE AND QUESTIONS: ARBITRATORS APPLYING THE LAW

In the College of Commercial Arbitrators/Straus Institute Survey of veteran U.S. arbitrators, all respondents asserted that they always (or usually) "carefully read and reflect upon legal arguments and briefs presented by counsel." Nearly all indicated that in the absence of an agreement to the contrary, they "do [their] best to ascertain and follow applicable law in rendering an award." There was also a strong tendency to "invite counsel to brief legal issues in the case."[17]

Award Deliberation and Rendering
CCA/Straus Institute Survey of Experienced Arbitrators (2013)
Q: *As an arbitrator, how often do you do the following in rendering a final award?*

	Always	Usually	About half the time	Sometimes	Never
In the absence of a contrary agreement between the parties, I do my best to ascertain and follow applicable law in rendering an award.	86.7% (111)	11.7% (15)	0.0% (0)	1.6% (2)	0.0% (0)
I invite counsel to brief legal issues in the case.	54.7% (70)	35.2% (45)	3.9% (5)	6.3% (8)	0.0% (0)

I carefully read and reflect upon legal arguments and briefs presented by counsel.	97.7% (125)	2.3% (3)	0.0% (0)	0.0% (0)	0.0% (0)
I feel free to follow my own sense of equity and fairness in rendering an award even if the result would be contrary to applicable law.	0.8% (1)	0.0% (0)	0.0% (0)	25.0% (32)	74.2% (95)

26. Notice that although arbitrators generally appear to place great emphasis on understanding and following applicable law, around one-quarter of responding arbitrators indicated that they "feel free to follow [their] own sense of equity and fairness . . . even if the result would be contrary to applicable law." What are the implications of this?

27. If you were concerned about arbitrators "following their conscience" in lieu of applicable law, what might you do to address the matter? Is there a difference in the language of leading arbitration procedures? Compare, for example, the AAA Commercial Arbitration Rules with international standards such as the UNCITRAL Arbitration Rules. Do they make reference to application of law in arbitral awards?[18]

2. *Punitive or Exemplary Damages*

Notes on Arbitration Law.   In the United States, courts levy civil "punitive" or "exemplary" damages for the purpose of punishing and deterring certain kinds of egregious behavior. The authority may be derived from statutes or from common law. As we will see in Chapter 6.E, the authority of arbitrators to entertain and to honor claims for punitive or exemplary damages under the broad provisions of standard arbitration procedures is well established under U.S. federal arbitration law and the law of most states. Thus, arbitrators have considered and on occasion awarded relief in the nature of "common law" punitive damages as well as exemplary damages pursuant to statutes like the Racketeer Influenced and Corrupt Organizations Act (1970). This in turn raises questions regarding the ability of courts to police punitive arbitral awards under limited standards for judicial vacatur of awards.

QUESTION

28. If you were drafting an arbitration provision in a commercial contract, would you favor or disfavor denying arbitrators the authority to award punitive and exemplary damages? Why or why not? What if the contract involved an international business transaction? A consumer or employment contract? With regard to the last situation, please note that limits on remedies that would be available in court may furnish grounds for a judicial finding that an arbitration agreement is unconscionable. See Chapter 7.E.

3. *Final Offer Arbitration*

Options exist for parties to create their own arbitration rules, and to limit the scope of arbitral remedies. One popular variant that parties have adopted is "final offer arbitration," often termed "baseball arbitration" because of its importance in Major League Baseball salary dispute resolution. Final offer arbitration requires that each party submit its "final offer" to the arbitrator after making appropriate submissions on the merits of the dispute. The arbitrator then chooses the most fair and reasonable offer, considering all of the facts and arguments presented. The arbitrator is not permitted to compromise, to split the difference, or to compose what they regard as a better or more just solution. The arbitrator must select one final offer or the other as the basis of the award.[19]

A "final offer arbitration" procedure has been used in Major League Baseball salary arbitrations with great success for nearly 40 years and has become a familiar example of arbitration for baseball fans.[20] The concept was implemented to eliminate the risk that an arbitrator would split the difference between a player and team's offers.[21] Some surmise, however, that final offer arbitration has actually encouraged parties to settle before the arbitration panel reaches a decision.[22] The result has been that while the percentage of eligible Major League Baseball salary disputes actually filed to arbitration has increased considerably over time, the percentage of disputes actually decided by an arbitration panel has decreased from 9 percent of cases between 1974-1993 to 2 percent of cases in 2011 and 4 percent of cases in 2012.[23] The hope in "final offer arbitration" is that the parties will partake in good faith negotiations to facilitate a reasonable settlement. The risk of a complete loss if the arbitrator chooses the other party's offer encourages both parties to engage in pre-arbitration negotiations and to produce final offers closer to the other party's final offer.

Procedures differ on whether they are "blind" — that is, whether or not the arbitrator is ignorant of the parties' proposals. If the arbitrator has been informed of the parties' proposals, the arbitrator chooses between the parties' proposals for the award, selecting the proposal that the arbitrator finds most reasonable and appropriate. If the arbitrator has not been informed of the parties' proposals, the arbitrator renders the award, and the award is then corrected to conform to the party proposal that is closest to the arbitrator's award. The award, as corrected, becomes the final award.

Typically, the parties may exchange revised written proposals at any time before the close of the hearing. A party's revised proposal supersedes any prior proposal by that party.[24]

QUESTIONS

29. Consider the following conclusion:

> Baseball's salary arbitration saves time and money over conventional negotiations by providing structure to salary negotiations and imposing strict timing requirements for filing, submission of final offers, the hearing, and the arbitrator's decision. Because

the arbitrator does not issue a written decision, further costs are
eliminated.[25]

Do you tend to agree or disagree with this conclusion? Why?
30. Can you think of a situation where you would use final offer arbitration?
     Why do you suppose it is not more widely used?[26]

J. FORMS OF AWARD

Not so long ago in the United States, it was common for arbitration awards to
be issued without an accompanying rationale or explanation. Under this approach,
an arbitrator in the case of Carmin, Inc. and SamCo, Inc. (Problem 1) might review
papers and hold hearings over several days, and a few days or weeks later issue a
single-sentence award:

SamCo shall pay Carmin $125,000 in damages.
                                        /s/ Arbitrator

As Carmin's lawyer, you might be terribly disappointed in the amount of the
award, reasoning that if the arbitrator ruled in Carmin's favor, damages so far below
the amount claimed make no sense as a matter of contract law or in terms of fairness.
SamCo's lawyer might also be upset because the award does not acknowledge its counterclaims. Nevertheless, both parties have little recourse. Even if courts were willing to
scrutinize arbitral awards closely, the lack of explanation leaves little to scrutinize.

The AAA traditionally advised commercial arbitrators not to explain their
awards because written reasoning gives parties possible grounds for appeal based
on their dissatisfaction with the outcome, undermining the advantage of arbitration as a prompt and final method of dispute resolution. Writing a rationale may
also take time and complicate the deliberation process, especially when there are
three arbitrators. The process may also be more difficult for non-lawyer arbitrators.

If parties to a dispute agree that some statement of explanation is appropriate, however, it is their prerogative to so direct the arbitrators. Written awards
explaining in detail the rationale behind an arbitrator's decision have been standard for many years in the areas of labor relations and international commercial
arbitration. Today, commercial arbitration agreements in business contracts often
call for arbitrators to reveal their reasoning. Under AAA Rules, the arbitrator(s)
are advised to accommodate such a request. On the other hand, the CPR Rules
for non-administered arbitration and JAMS Comprehensive Arbitration Rules
make written opinion the default option for arbitrators, unless the parties agree
otherwise.[27]

While the drawbacks to written, reasoned awards mentioned above are valid,
their benefits are becoming more apparent—especially in high-stakes cases. For
one thing, obvious errors can be brought to the arbitrator's attention rapidly.
Moreover, requiring arbitrators to write out their thought process can lead to a
more complete analysis of the issues involved. Parties are more likely to feel that

they were, if not "victorious," at least heard on the matter. The commentary accompanying the CPR Rules states:

> [Requiring arbitrators to include a statement of reasons with their award] gives rise to second thought as to the soundness of the result. . . . [A]ny tendency on the part of arbitrators to reach compromise awards should be restrained by the requirement of a reasoned award. . . . In CPR's view, the risk that a reasoned award will be successfully challenged normally is small and outweighed by the other considerations mentioned above.[28]

While written opinions by arbitrators do not function as broad judicial precedent, they may in some cases provide insight into an arbitrator's leanings, experience, and qualifications. Of course, the outcome and reasoning in one arbitral decision might be limited by the factual circumstances and evidence presented, providing little indication of how that arbitrator would rule in the next situation, or with a different panel of arbitrators.

Although it is becoming more common for parties and administering organizations to require written opinions, lawyers are less likely to advise clients to seek written opinions in disputes where the stakes are smaller because parties typically bear the expense of the additional time arbitrators devote to rendering more detailed written opinions. Written opinions may be most valuable where a novel issue is presented, where a case is quite complex, where significant amounts of money are at stake, or where there is a special need for the adjudicator's rationale—such as, for example, a dispute where an award may serve as a basis for damages in a separate adjudication involving a third party.

Notes on Arbitration Law.   Although leading arbitration rules do not provide specific guidance on what constitutes a "reasoned award," U.S. courts have occasionally rendered decisions addressing such requirements. In *Cat Charter, LLC v. Schurtenberger*, 646 F.3d 836 (11th Cir. 2011), the Eleventh Circuit took a very flexible, or lenient, approach to the issue. In that case, the parties had agreed to require the arbitrators to issue a "reasoned award"; after five days of hearing and extensive briefing, the arbitrators produced an award supported by a two-sentence statement on prevailing claims without any factual or legal analysis. The trial court vacated the award on the basis that in failing to provide a more fulsome statement of reasons to support their award, the arbitrators exceeded their power. However, the Eleventh Circuit reinstated the award on the basis that the requirement of a "reasoned award" could be met by statements that went beyond a mere declaration of award to a particular party. Should the parties have desired a more extensive treatment of the issues, "they could have requested that the Panel provide findings of fact and conclusions of law." The same approach has been followed in other decisions. *See Leeward Construction Co. v. American University of Antigua (AUA)-College of Medicine*, 826 F.3d 634 (2d Cir. 2016); *Olson v. Harland Clarke Corp.*, 676 Fed. Appx. 635 (9th Cir. 2017).

1. *Private Appellate Processes*

In light of concerns regarding the lack of oversight of arbitration awards, some attorneys have counseled clients to opt for an appellate arbitration process. CPR,

JAMS, and the AAA all offer optional appellate arbitration procedures. The JAMS appellate procedure is adopted as a part of consensual arbitration procedures in a small percentage of filed cases, although it is seldom actually used. Those favoring private appeal may view it as a salutary alternative to judicial review, both in terms of cost and time saving, while providing meaningful oversight of the arbitral award. Some believe private procedures can alleviate the need to challenge an award in court, while enhancing confidence in the arbitration process. Others argue that appeal to a private panel may only add to the time and expense of finally resolving a dispute. Better, some say, to concentrate on the first arbitral proceeding and "getting it right the first time around."

QUESTION

31. Suppose your business client, Micron, is in the process of forming a contract with Dall Computers to install Micron 2021 software in every computer Dall makes. Micron is inclined to include an arbitration provision in the contract but is concerned about the risk of an extreme or irrational award in arbitration. This contract is of critical importance to Micron's business, and there could well be a dispute with "bet-the-company" stakes. Advise Micron regarding the pros and cons of each of the following options:
   A. Employ a panel of three arbitrators for disputes involving larger stakes;
   B. Direct the arbitrators to follow certain legal standards in reaching a decision;
   C. Direct the arbitrators to provide a written rationale for their award;
   D. Agree that the parties will attempt to establish a range (a minimum and a maximum) for the arbitrators' award;
   E. Agree that the arbitrators will not be empowered to consider claims for punitive or exemplary damages, or to make such awards;
   F. Agree to appellate arbitration.

K.   ARBITRATION AND SETTLEMENT

1.   Arbitration in Multi-Step Agreements; Impact of Mediation

As discussed in Chapter 1, although binding arbitration is often a favorable alternative to the litigation process, it is ill-suited to be the primary process option for serving the day-to-day needs of businesses. In seeking to fulfill client goals and priorities through effective conflict management, counsel should not consider arbitration in isolation. Rather, the logical first step is negotiation, followed in many commercial dispute resolution procedures by mediation. As explained in the *CCA Protocols for Cost-Effective, Expeditious Commercial Arbitration* (2010):

> Resolving conflict through negotiation or mediation usually affords parties a superior opportunity to avoid significant cost or delay, and offers several other potential benefits, including greater control over outcome,

enhanced privacy and confidentiality, preservation or improvement of business relationships, and better communications.

Although opinions may vary regarding the desirability of a contractual provision for mediation, the option should normally be considered.[29]

Sixty percent of respondents to the CCA/Straus Institute Survey observed that the growth of "mediation and other conflict management approaches" was having a significant or moderate impact on their arbitration practice. The large majority of respondents (82.8 percent) expected the use of mediation to increase in the future. Just as mediation has played an important role in the dramatic drop-off in the rate of trial in federal and state courts, it is very likely to be having an impact on the usage of arbitration. Mediation appears to be contributing to the increased percentage of cases in arbitration that are settled prior to the rendition of an award. It is also perceived as having an impact on some arbitrators' caseloads.

In those cases where they are unable to fully resolve disputes, mediators with arbitration experience should be particularly adept at helping to facilitate agreement on the details of an arbitration process tailored to the circumstances. Creative, experienced mediators have long understood that even in the absence of an all-around substantive settlement, mediators may nevertheless facilitate the creation of a blueprint for customized arbitration.[30]

Once the decision is made to incorporate multiple steps or stages, however, a good deal of care must be given to the practical efficacy of the provisions to be employed. Careless drafting can result in confusion and unintended consequences—including the intervention of a court.

2. Arbitrators Setting the Stage for Settlement?

As with litigation in court, the arbitrator's management of the pre-hearing and hearing stages is juxtaposed against not one but two potential eventualities: Although the parties are on the road to adjudication, there is always the possibility—even the probability—of a negotiated settlement. The results of the CCA/Straus Institute Survey indicate that in recent years experienced arbitrators have tended to observe higher rates of settlement in the cases they arbitrate. However, the data also indicate that the experienced rates of settlement vary widely, raising a number of questions.

Today, arbitrators (like judges) must be constantly attuned to the possibility that their managerial activities will not only create opportunities for settlement, but may leverage the settlement posture of one or the other of the parties. In the United States, arbitrators have in various ways been discouraged from overtly encouraging settlement. But as arbitration processes have come to resemble litigation with its extensive emphasis on pre-hearing process and arbitrators have become more actively involved in case management, it is only natural that advocates and arbitrators reflect on the role arbitrators might play in creating an environment for settlement. Today, cases in the arbitration process very often settle at the pre-hearing stage, usually at one of the key decision points when counsel must open the file and make choices regarding disposition of the case. Experienced arbitrators know that in certain circumstances the very act of engaging the parties in preliminary discussions at or immediately prior to the pre-hearing conference may promote settlement.

Arbitrators may help set the stage for settlement by taking steps to accommodate mediation during the course of arbitration proceedings. For example, the *Center for Effective Dispute Resolution (CEDR) Rules for the Facilitation of Settlement in International Arbitration* (2009) require arbitrators to "insert a [m]ediation [w]indow in the arbitral proceedings when requested to do so by all [p]arties in order to enable settlement discussions," and, moreover, to "adjourn the arbitral proceedings for a specified period so as to enable mediation to take place" in certain circumstances.

Note that "mixed-mode" and "stepped" processes will be further explored in Chapter 9. Indeed, lawyers, as problem solvers, must consider a wide range of options when designing a dispute resolution process to meet their clients' needs. Arbitration, mediation, negotiation, litigation, and other processes should not be viewed in isolation. Moreover, proper dispute system design should be intentional in light of goals, stakeholder, context and culture, processes and structure, resources, success, accountability, and learning—all to be considered at the end of this book.

Endnotes

1. https://uncitral.un.org/sites/uncitral.un.org/files/media-documents/uncitral/en/arb-notes-2016-e.pdf.
2. *Commercial Arbitration Rules and Mediation Procedures*, Am. Arbitration Ass'n at R-33 (Oct. 1, 2013), https://adr.org/sites/default/files/Commercial%20Rules.pdf.
3. Comprehensive Arbitration Rules & Procedures, JAMS at Rule 18 (July 1, 2014), https://www.jamsadr.com/rules-comprehensive-arbitration/.
4. *12000 Code of Arbitration Procedure for Customer Disputes*, FINRA at 12504(a), finra.org/12000 (last visited July 10, 2020).
5. *Id.*
6. https://www.adr.org/sites/default/files/CommercialRules_Web.pdf.
7. Stipanowich, Thomas J. (2014) *Reflections on the State and Future of Commercial Arbitration: Challenges, Opportunities, Proposals*, 25 Colum. Am. Rev. Int'l Arb.
8. Stipanowich, Thomas J. & Ulrich, Zachary. (2014) *Arbitration in Evolution: Current Practices and Perspectives of Experienced Commercial Arbitrators*, Colum. Am. Rev. Int'l Arb., Vol. 25.
9. Poorooye, Ayinash & Feehily, Ronan. (2017) *Confidentiality and Transparency in International Commercial Arbitration: Finding the Right Balance*, 22 Harv. Negot. L. Rev. 275, 279 ("The arbitrators have an obligation to observe a general duty of confidentiality, while the parties' obligations often depend on a confidentiality agreement.").
10. Landesman, Peter. (2001) *A Crisis of Fakes: The Getty Forgeries*, N.Y. Times.
11. Stipanowich, Thomas J. (2009) *Arbitration and Choice: Taking Charge of the "New Litigation,"* 7 DePaul Bus. & Comm. L.J.
12. Schmitz, Amy J. (2006) *Untangling the Privacy Paradox in Arbitration*, 54 Kan. L. Rev. 101.

13. Schmitz, Amy J. & Rule, Colin. (2017) *The New Handshake: Online Dispute Resolution and the Future of Consumer Protection*; Schmitz, Amy J. (2018) *Building on OArb Attributes in Pursuit of Justice, in Arbitration in the Digital Age: The Brave New World of Arbitration* (Maud Piers & Christian Aschauer, eds.).

14. Amy J. Schmitz, The Arbitration Conversation, at https://arbitrate.com/the-arbitration-conversation/ (interviewing many arbitrators supporting these notions).

15. *Leveraging Technology for Fair, Effective and Efficient International Arbitration Proceedings*, Int'l. Chamber of Com. (Feb. 2022), https://iccwbo.org/content/uploads/sites/3/2022/02/icc-arbitration-and-adr-commission-report-on-leveraging-technology-for-fair-effective-and-efficient-international-arbitration-proceedings.pdf. *See* Schmitz, Amy J (2021) *Arbitration in the Age of Covid: Examining Arbitration's Move Online*, 22 Cardozo J. Conflict Resol. 245-92. Schmitz, Amy J. and Mendes, Claire, *Online Arbitration Protocols* (July 28, 2021). University of Missouri School of Law Legal Studies Research Paper No. 2021-13, Available at SSRN: https://ssrn.com/abstract=3894707.

16. Stipanowich, Thomas J. & Lamare, J.R. (2014) *Living with "ADR": Evolving Perceptions and Use of Mediation, Arbitration and Conflict Management in Fortune 1,000 Corporations*, 19 Harv. Negot. L. Rev. 1.

17. Stipanowich, *supra* note 7

18. *Id.*

19. *Final Offer Arbitration Supplementary Rules*, Am. Arbitration Ass'n (January 2015), https://www.adr.org/sites/default/files/Final%20Offer%20Supplementary%20Arbitration%20Procedures.pdf.

20. Abrams, Roger. (1998) *Legal Bases: Baseball and the Law.*

21. Gleason, Erin & Sussman, Edna. (2019) *Final Offer/Baseball Arbitration: The History, The Practice, and Future Design*, 37 Alternatives to High Cost Litig. 1.

22. Pauwelyn, Joost. (2018) *Baseball Arbitration to Resolve International Law Disputes: Hit or Miss?*, 22 Fla. Tax Rev.

23. *Id.*

24. *JAMS Employment Arbitration: A Step-by-Step Guide*, Practical Law Practice Note w-001-9398 (effective July 1, 2014).

25. Meth, Elissa M. (1999) *Final Offer Arbitration: A Model for Dispute Resolution in Domestic and International Disputes*, 10 Colum. Am. Rev. Int'l Arb.

26. *Avoiding Unpredictable Results in Gas Price Disputes: Helping Tribunals to Spot the Best Outcome*, Practical Law UK Articles w-007-5745 (Apr. 12, 2017).

27. *Commercial Arbitration Rules and Mediation Procedures*, Am. Arbitration Ass'n at R-46(b) (Oct. 1, 2013), http://www.adr.org/sites/default/files/CommercialRules_Web.pdf; 2019 Administered Arbitration Rules, Int'l Inst. for Conf. Prevention & Resol. at Rule 15.2 (Mar. 1, 2019), https://www.cpradr.org/resource-center/rules/arbitration/administered-arbitration-rules-2019.

28. 2018 CPR Non-Administered Arbitration Rules, Commentary, Rule 15: The Award.

29. Stipanowich, Thomas J. (2010) *Arbitration: The "New Litigation,"* 2010 U. Ill. L. Rev. 1; Schmitz, Amy J. (2006) *Confronting ADR Agreements' Contract/No-Contract Conundrum with Good Faith,* 56 DePaul L. Rev. 55.
30. Stipanowich, Thomas J. & Ulrich, Zachary P. (2014) *Commercial Arbitration and Settlement: Empirical Insights into the Roles Arbitrators Play,* 6 Y.B. Arb. & Mediation 1.

CHAPTER 5

THE LAW OF ARBITRATION; JUDICIAL ENFORCEMENT OF ARBITRATION AGREEMENTS

A. *INTRODUCTION: HISTORICAL SHIFTS IN JUDICIAL AND LEGISLATIVE SUPPORT FOR ARBITRATION*

As discussed in Chapters 1 and 2, arbitration has been a popular dispute resolution choice throughout history in many cultures. But its use has waxed and waned over time in the United States, reflecting power struggles between advocates of arbitration and those who were suspicious of its potential to supplant court adjudication and interfere with the law governing contractual relations. On the one hand, English and American colonial courts guarded their power "jealously" and were quite hostile to arbitration agreements, readily allowing parties to evade their agreements to arbitrate. On the other hand, merchants favored arbitration because they could select their own decision makers and rules. At the behest of increasingly powerful business interests, state legislatures actively attempted to reverse judicial hostility and encourage arbitration in the twentieth century. In 1925, Congress enacted the Federal Arbitration Act (FAA) — a "modern" arbitration statute in the sense that it provided for the specific enforcement of pre-dispute arbitration provisions in contracts. Business-to-business disputes were a most common subject of arbitration in the decades following enactment of the FAA; after World War II, arbitration became an increasingly popular method of resolving labor disputes, an arena for which Congress had developed a specified framework for arbitration to prevent violence, the delayed resolution of problems, and the resultant disruption of business.

Until the 1980s, however, the use of arbitration was limited by judicial decisions refusing to allow statute-based claims to be arbitrated. Judges were suspicious that arbitration would be too different from court adjudication and arbitrators less willing to follow or capable of following the law. They recalled, perhaps, that Aristotle once explained that "the arbitrator sees equity, the juror the law; indeed that is why an arbitrator is found—that equity might prevail."[1] The Supreme Court viewed public judgments rendered by federal trial courts as desirable mechanisms of social regulation on statutory matters, emphasizing their effect in shaping the conduct of nonparties. Moreover, judges were skeptical that parties had knowingly and voluntarily waived their rights to the judicial forum for statutory claims like those under federal securities laws. *See, e.g., Wilko v. Swan,* 346 U.S. 427 (1953).[2]

During the 1980s, however, the Supreme Court reinterpreted congressional intent, finding that the FAA created a broad national policy favoring arbitration when parties choose it. In a number of cases, the Court emphasized that, "[b]y agreeing to arbitrate a statutory claim, a party does not forgo the substantive rights afforded by the statute; it only submits to their resolution in an arbitral, rather than judicial, forum." *Mitsubishi Motors Corp. v. Soler Chrysler-Plymouth, Inc.,* 473 U.S. 614, 628 (1985). The Court reasoned that the arbitral forum provided distinct advantages for many parties. In the words of the Court: "[Arbitration] trades the procedures and opportunity for review of the courtroom for the simplicity, informality, and expedition of arbitration."

Following the Supreme Court's lead, many other federal and state courts have been highly respectful of arbitration as a dispute resolution option, even for statutory claims founded on alleged employment discrimination, consumer fraud, or securities law violations. Although fairness concerns surrounding the use of pre-dispute arbitration agreements in standardized consumer and employment contracts have generated great controversy, as discussed in Chapters 7 and 8, most courts have heartily endorsed arbitration as a general alternative to litigation of civil disputes; they have also shown great deference to arbitrators and their decisions (awards). One federal judge's remarks about why courts should welcome arbitration, rather than be suspicious of it, typified the tone and sentiments of many American jurists at the close of the twentieth century:

> Access to the courts now is neither affordable nor expeditious. In many federal district courts and state courts, years pass before an aggrieved party can even have the proverbial day in court. In the meantime, the process grinds along, inflicting staggering legal expenses on the parties. Except for the very rich (and very poor, in some circumstances), we have simply priced the court system beyond the reach of most citizens, because the cost of litigation far exceeds the value of the decision itself. Indeed, even the most resourceful parties often decline to pursue legal rights, simply because quickly accepting or paying a sum of money in settlement of any claim often costs far less than determining in court the merit of that claim. In short, our current legal system for resolving disputes is losing the respect of the public and is rapidly approaching failure.

Bright v. Norshipco & Norfolk Shipbuilding & Drydock Corp., 951 F. Supp. 95, 98 (E.D. Va. 1997). *See also Gilmer v. Interstate/Johnson Lane Corp.,* 500 U.S. 20 (1991).

This chapter traces the evolution and expansion of arbitration under court decisions during the past four decades. It details the legal framework developed by courts as they interpret federal and state statutes governing arbitration. In general, modern courts, relying in large part on the FAA, have developed a legal framework that respects and undergirds the role of arbitrators as decision makers and honors the apparent mutual intent of parties to use arbitration rather than the courts. These decisions also tend to give effect to important arbitration attributes, including efficiency and finality. (Not until Chapters 7 and 8 do we directly address the fairness concerns that have caused courts, legislatures, and other groups to seek to limit the use of arbitration clauses in consumer and employment contracts and other "adhesion contract" settings.)

B. ELEMENTS OF MODERN ARBITRATION LAW

1. The Federal Arbitration Act

Common law developed in England and early colonial practice in the United States supplied two doctrines that courts used frequently to undermine parties' agreements to arbitrate: *revocation* and *unenforceability.* Although arbitration has been used throughout American history, courts might, for example, allow a party to revoke its earlier consent to arbitrate once a dispute arose. To counter these doctrines when parties had clearly agreed to arbitrate, Congress in the FAA instructed judges to treat written agreements to arbitrate like other valid contracts—and to provide for their specific enforcement. Although this bare-bones Act is short, it has become a powerful tool to support agreements to arbitrate, allowing courts to compel parties to proceed with arbitration and stay (i.e., put on hold) related litigation, enforce subpoenas issued by arbitrators, and enforce arbitration awards. After Congress adopted the FAA, most states also adopted statutes giving courts specific authority to support arbitration agreements and enforce arbitral awards. Because the Supreme Court has construed the FAA so broadly in recent decades, however, the role of state arbitration statutes has been limited to some extent in comparison to the role of the FAA. This will become clear as you read Section D, which explains how the law regarding enforcement of arbitration agreements under the FAA *preempts* contrary state law. Today, judicial decisions under the FAA make agreements to arbitrate fully enforceable in both federal and state courts. As the Second Circuit 'observed, "it is difficult to overstate' the strong federal policy in favor of arbitration, and it is a policy we 'have often and emphatically applied.'" *Arciniaga v. Gen. Motors Corp.,* 460 F.3d 231, 234 (2d Cir. 2006) (quoting *Leadertex, Inc. v. Morganton Dyeing & Finishing Corp.,* 67 F.3d 20, 25 (2d Cir. 1995)).

You should read the FAA in its entirety, but the following road map examines its major provisions. It illustrates the different ways courts are called on to enforce and facilitate arbitration agreements and awards. Courts must assist parties by enforcing agreements to arbitrate, support the arbitrators in exercising the powers granted to them by Congress and the parties' agreements, and enforce duly issued arbitration awards.

A Quick Tour of the Federal Arbitration Act

- **Section 2** of the FAA states that written agreements to arbitrate "in any maritime transaction" or "a contract evidencing a transaction involving commerce," or written agreements to submit to arbitration any existing dispute under such contracts, are:

    . . . valid, irrevocable, and enforceable
    . . . except on "such grounds as exist at law or in equity for the revocation of any contract."

This section expressly counters the common law's hostility toward arbitration. It reverses court precedents making pre-dispute arbitration agreements unenforceable and puts arbitration agreements on equal footing with other types of contracts. It also makes clear that parties can raise standard state law contract defenses to challenge an arbitration clause. Courts must enforce an arbitration agreement unless a valid defense is raised to the arbitration agreement.

- **Section 1** defines two categories of contracts covered by the FAA:

  . . . "maritime transactions" and
  . . . contracts involving "commerce," meaning "commerce among the several States or with foreign nations," or involving U.S. Territories.

The Supreme Court has broadly construed "commerce"—or, to be more explicit, "interstate commerce"—to include most economic transactions in our modern national (and global) economy. For this reason, it is not at all difficult to find some interstate elements in a transaction, and therefore a predicate for the application of the FAA to enforcement of arbitration agreements. Decisions exploring the breadth of this provision are included in Section C.4 below. *See, e.g., Citizens Bank v. Alafabco, Inc.*, 539 U.S. 32 (2003); *Allied-Bruce Terminix Cos. v. Dobson*, 513 U.S. 265 (1995).

Section 1 excludes from the application of the FAA "contracts of employment of seamen, railroad employees, or any other class of workers engaged in foreign or interstate commerce." In *Circuit City Stores v. Adams*, 532 U.S. 105 (2001), the Court held that Section 1 exempts from the FAA only employment contracts of transportation workers. The FAA therefore applies to employees generally, even if their work involves interstate commerce. Thus, the FAA has been construed to provide a broad umbrella for enforcement of arbitration agreements. Importantly, as discussed in Section C.4, the U.S. Supreme Court in the mid-1980s identified FAA Section 2 as a source of substantive federal law providing for broad enforceability of arbitration agreements—a body of law that applies in state courts as well as federal courts.

- **Section 3** of the FAA provides that if one party to an arbitration contract sues "in any of the courts of the United States," the court *shall*, upon a finding that there is a valid, applicable arbitration agreement, stay the trial (i.e., court proceedings on the same controversy) until the arbitration is completed.

The language of Section 3 has been broadly construed so that courts are required to *stay*, or stop, all court proceedings, including pretrial phases, until arbitration proceedings are concluded. Courts also have been deemed to have discretion to stay other, non-arbitrable disputes in the same court proceeding. The FAA thus tries to avoid duplicative proceedings and the potentially conflicting outcomes that might occur if arbitrators and courts both conducted proceedings on the same matter simultaneously. As noted above and discussed below in C.4, if a transaction falls within the purview of the FAA, both federal and state courts must adhere to its broad policies supporting enforcement of arbitration agreements. Moreover, state courts have generally accepted that the procedures of Section 3 of the FAA, like Section 2, apply to them.[3]

- **Section 4** provides that if a party refuses to arbitrate, the opposing side can bring a motion in federal court for an order to compel the party to participate in arbitration. "If the making of the arbitration agreement or the failure, neglect or refusal to perform the same be in issue," the court is to "proceed summarily to the trial thereof."

This section attempts to ensure expeditious resolution of the question by mandating that courts issue orders to compel arbitration if an agreement to arbitrate is present. Its provisions make it relatively easy for a lawyer to go to federal court (and potentially state court), file a petition, and get a fairly speedy resolution of the issue, backed by the contempt power of the court. As Section 4 of the FAA makes reference to "any United States district court," its application at the state court level is much less clear than Section 3, and court decisions are in conflict regarding the applicability of Section 4 in state courts. Even if Section 4 does not apply in state courts, however, it is likely that parallel provisions of state arbitration law will authorize a court to compel arbitration.

To underscore the presumption in favor of courts not interfering with the progress of arbitration if any arbitration agreement is found, **Section 16** of the FAA provides that appellate courts can conduct interlocutory review of certain anti-arbitration rulings by a trial court (such as orders enjoining or stopping arbitration proceedings) but may not review orders *upholding* arbitration (e.g., orders directing parties to arbitrate or staying related litigation) on an interlocutory basis.

Sections 2, 3, and 4 of the FAA are prominently featured in the cases and materials in Section C below.

- **Section 5** of the FAA provides that if the parties fail to agree on an arbitrator, the court may appoint one.

The court's power to appoint an arbitrator is rarely exercised, as parties usually agree to other methods for selecting arbitrators and overcoming impasse or unforeseen difficulties. As explained in Chapters 2 and 3, many parties agree to employ arbitration procedures that include rules for selecting arbitrators, including default mechanisms if one or both parties fail to cooperate. Other parties incorporate their own ad hoc procedures for selection. Nevertheless, Section 5 of the FAA is an important fallback option for a party in those cases where a party attempts to evade or slow arbitration proceedings by refusing to cooperate in selecting arbitrators and there is no specified default mechanism, or where an agreed method for appointing arbitrators fails for some other reason. We touch briefly on this topic in Section E.1 below.

- **Section 7** of the FAA recognizes the power of arbitrators to issue "summonses" (subpoenas) for witnesses to appear before them and to bring material evidence. If a witness refuses, a court may compel attendance in accordance with the subpoena or hold the person in contempt of court.

Arbitrators, like courts, have the ability to summon (or subpoena) individuals (including nonparties) to provide critical evidence in arbitral proceedings. This power, like the subpoena power trial courts possess under the Federal Rules of Civil Procedure and state counterparts, makes arbitration a useful alternative to negotiation and mediation when a party is dependent on securing material evidence from the opposing party or nonparty witnesses to prove its claims. Curiously, the language of the FAA speaks of witnesses being compelled to appear "before the arbitrator(s)," and, moreover, makes no reference to subpoenas for pre-hearing discovery. Therefore, as discussed in Section E.2 below, some courts have interpreted the FAA to provide only for the enforcement of subpoenas to witnesses to attend hearings, and not to empower courts to enforce so-called discovery subpoenas.

- **Section 9** of the FAA provides that a party that has secured an award in arbitration may petition a court to enter the arbitration award as a court judgment if the parties have provided for this option in their agreement. If such a petition is filed within a year of the award's being issued, the court *must* grant judgment unless it vacates or modifies the award on the limited grounds described in Sections 10 and 11 of the FAA. Once a party secures a court judgment, it can execute on that judgment just as if it had won a victory in court.

While most students do not learn much about enforcing judgments during law school, this provision can make a great deal of practical difference. With a negotiated settlement or mediation agreement, enforcing compliance is sometimes difficult. On the other hand, a party who secures an arbitral award and has it entered as a judgment has access to the court's authority and processes for enforcement, including garnishing of wages, post-judgment discovery of assets, and so on. Thus, although most arbitration clauses are brief, it is common to include language providing for entry of judgment in court of any arbitral award rendered. (Indeed, as we discussed in Chapter 2, it is highly advisable to provide for court enforcement of arbitration awards in an agreement to arbitrate to avoid any question about the enforceability of an award.)

- Finally, **Section 10** of the FAA provides narrow grounds for judicial vacatur (or setting aside) of arbitral awards.

As you might imagine, the grounds for vacating or setting aside an arbitration award are of great interest to lawyers. In Chapter 6 we explore the statutory grounds for vacatur in some detail. For now, the main thing to keep in mind is that judicial review of arbitral rulings and awards is *extremely limited*, buttressing arbitration as a final, efficient, cost-effective dispute resolution option. However, the picture is complicated by the fact that some courts have appeared to enunciate additional grounds for judicial review of awards. Moreover, some parties have attempted to expand judicial scrutiny of awards by contract—with mixed, and sometimes unfortunate, results.

To sum up, the FAA is aimed at regulating the interface between the private forum of arbitration and the courts, with primary emphasis on the judicial enforcement of agreements to arbitrate and of resulting arbitration awards. It promotes the autonomy of parties by enforcing their agreements to arbitrate. It also serves channeling, evidentiary, and cautionary functions by judicially enforcing only those agreements evidenced by a writing or record, and against which no valid defense can be asserted. Finally, it establishes supplementary or default terms for different aspects of arbitration processes.

2. State Arbitration Laws—Another "Layer" of Arbitration Law

It is not enough for lawyers to be familiar with the FAA; they must also be aware of analogous arbitration statutes passed by the legislatures of U.S. states and territories. Although the FAA usually governs arbitration-related procedures in federal courts and also addresses some "arbitrability" issues in state court proceedings, it does not completely preempt the application of state law, as we will see in Section D. Of course, in most situations it will not matter which body of law is applicable, for the result will be the same. There are, however, important exceptions.

Two leading commercial states, New York and California, have unique arbitration statutes. N.Y. C.P.L.R. §§7501 et seq. (McKinney 2015); Cal. Civ. Proc. Code §§1280-1294.4 (West 2017). The overwhelming majority of states, however, have adopted some version of the Uniform Arbitration Act (UAA), which was originally approved by the National Conference of Commissioners on Uniform State Laws (NCCUSL) (now called the Uniform Law Commission) in 1955. Although the original UAA was a bare-bones statute like the FAA, recent revisions to that uniform law have produced a much lengthier, more detailed, and more prescriptive statutory framework for arbitration, the Revised Uniform Arbitration Act 2000 (RUAA).* These include a number of provisions setting forth default procedural elements—some of which are non-waivable by parties. The RUAA has been adopted, in whole or substantial part, by at least 21 states and by the District of Columbia, and is discussed briefly in Chapter 8.A. It is likely that some of the other states will eventually adopt the RUAA because 49 jurisdictions had adopted the UAA, the RUAA's predecessor, in whole or substantial part. Another very detailed statute is the California Arbitration Act, which among other things contains very specific disclosure requirements as "ethical standards" for arbitrators.

QUESTIONS

1. Can you list at least five functions performed by the FAA?
2. Take a look at the RUAA and compare it to the FAA in terms of the overall length, number of sections, and the subjects covered. What are some of the key differences? As you read the rest of this chapter, you may want to look back to see how the RUAA addresses many of the issues covered.

---

3. What Is "Arbitration" for the Purposes of Applying Federal or State Law?

What is "arbitration"? Curiously, neither the FAA nor state statutes define the term! Therefore, it is up to courts to reach their own conclusions about the applicability of arbitration law to different kinds of dispute resolution agreements.

---

* Available at http://www.uniformlaws.org/Act.aspx?title=Arbitration%20Act%20 (2000).

The fulfillment of parties' intent as expressed in their arbitration agreement is the dominant theme of U.S. arbitration.[4] Arbitration law gives parties a lot of flexibility to structure processes as they see fit. The principle of freedom to choose among procedural options has resulted in a very rich and diverse array of arbitration procedures. Arbitration law tends to promote broad legal enforcement of agreements regarding the nature and scope of arbitration, the precise breadth of the arbitrator's jurisdiction/authority, the selection of the tribunal, the character of the hearing, and pre- and post-hearing procedure. Additional flexibility inheres in the ability of parties to agree to modify or unilaterally waive elements of an agreed-upon process, even to the extent of forgoing participation in a hearing. "[T]he term 'arbitrate' need not appear in the contract in order to invoke the benefits of the FAA," and "it is not dispositive that an agreement fails to label the independent third party's conclusions 'final' or 'binding,' so long as the parties' intent in that regard is clear from the language of their contract." *Milligan v. CCC Info. Servs.*, 920 F.3d 146, 151-152 (2d Cir. 2019). This, however, begs the essential question: What, for the purposes of arbitration law, is "arbitration"? Put another way, when does arbitration law apply?

A determination that a particular dispute resolution procedure is not "arbitration" means that a number of questions, including the ability of courts to require participation in the process, to facilitate its implementation, or to enforce its results, must be decided on grounds other than arbitration law. These may be questions of first impression for courts, as may be questions about the confidentiality of related communications, the immunity of the third-party interveners or "neutrals" from legal process, and their obligation to make disclosures about potential conflicts of interest. "When one of these powers or duties is important," in the words of Judge Easterbrook, "the choice between 'arbitration' and other forms of private dispute resolution matters." *Omni Tech Corp. v. MPC Solutions Sales, LLC*, 432 F.3d 797, 799 (7th Cir. 2005). Some courts have concluded that if a procedure is not "arbitration," there is no basis for judicial enforcement.

So what kinds of dispute resolution agreements are covered by arbitration law? There are certainly strong clues in the overall form and content of the statutes. Viewed in full, both the FAA and the RUAA appear to contemplate *a process in which disputes are submitted to a hearing before a third party who renders a final and binding decision with respect to the disputes presented.* Moreover, standards for vacatur of arbitral decisions, or awards, envision some form of hearing before an impartial tribunal, as do provisions authorizing the issuance of summonses or subpoenas. In sum, some courts have identified at least four "signifying elements" of procedures that, when framed in an agreement, fall within the scope of arbitration law: (a) a process to settle disputes between parties; (b) a neutral third party; (c) an opportunity for the parties to be heard; and (d) a final, binding decision, or award, by the third party after the hearing. *See, e.g., Fit Tech, Inc. v. Bally Total Fitness Holding Corp.*, 374 F.3d 1, 7 (1st Cir. 2004). *See also Milligan v. CCC Info. Servs.*, 920 F.3d 146, 151-152 (2d Cir. 2019). These elements denote what we will refer to as *"classic" arbitration* for the purposes of comparison.

Given what has been characterized as the irresistible "gravitational force" of arbitration law—a body of well-established precedent according legitimacy, strong protection, and expedited enforcement to arrangements for resolving conflict—it is no wonder that many courts have swept aside "definitional niceties" and used arbitration law as a convenient hook for enforcement of other kinds of dispute resolution agreements, including mediation and nonbinding arbitration. Nonetheless, there are strong arguments supporting a more restrained application of arbitration law and the promotion of appropriate alternative grounds for the enforcement of nonbinding arbitration, mediation, and other alternatives to "classic" arbitration.[5]

QUESTIONS

3. Suppose your client enters into a contract that includes a provision requiring the parties to submit disputes to mediation before filing suit. If one party files suit without trying to mediate, should the other party be able to file for a judicial stay of litigation pending mediation under the FAA? *See, e.g., Advanced Bodycare Solutions, LLC v. Thione Int'l, Inc.*, 524 F.3d 1235 (11th Cir. 2008). What if the parties state that "[t]he Mediator shall render a [] decision" and "[a]ll decisions of the Mediator shall be binding"? *See Unite Here Loc. 30 v. Volume Services, Inc.*, 723 F. App'x 403, 404 (9th Cir. 2018) (unpublished).

4. Would your answer be different in Question 3 above if the contract called for the parties to enter into nonbinding arbitration — that is, arbitration culminating in a nonbinding, advisory award — before suit?[6]

C. ARBITRABILITY

The chief function of the FAA and other arbitration statutes is to require courts to enforce agreements to arbitrate. For example, the FAA calls upon U.S. courts to enforce written agreements to arbitrate unless they are presented with "grounds as exist at law or in equity for the revocation of any contract." If a particular dispute is within the scope of an enforceable arbitration agreement, courts have authority to stay pending litigation on the same issues and grant a motion to compel arbitration proceedings. Threshold jurisdictional or "arbitrability" questions exist — (a) whether there was an enforceable agreement to arbitrate, and (b) what kinds of disputes fall within the scope of the arbitration agreement.

Given the clarity and breadth of many standard contractual arbitration provisions in use today, "arbitrability" questions (e.g., Have the parties agreed to arbitrate? Are there defenses to enforceability of the agreement? Does the agreement cover the issues in dispute?) are less likely to arise. Moreover, prominent arbitration procedures now usually include language that purports to give *arbitrators* the authority to resolve these same kinds of questions. For example, the AAA Commercial Arbitration Rules state:

> The arbitrator shall have the power to rule on his or her own jurisdiction, including any objections with respect to the existence, scope or validity of the arbitration agreement.*

---

* AAA Commercial Arbitration Rules R-7(a) (amended and effective Oct. 1, 2013).

The Supreme Court decision below speaks to the division of functions between arbitrators and courts regarding certain arbitrability issues, and the impact of contract language that attempts to turn such questions over to arbitrators.

First Options of Chicago, Inc. v. Kaplan

514 U.S. 938 (1995)

[First Options of Chicago, Inc., a firm that clears stock trades on the Philadelphia Stock Exchange, entered into a "workout" agreement, embodied in four documents, that governed the "working out" of debts owed by Manuel Kaplan, Carol Kaplan, and their investment company ("MKI"). The Kaplans and MKI lost money in the October 1987 stock market crash and in 1989. First Options sought arbitration after its demands for payment were not satisfied. MKI, which had signed the only workout document containing an arbitration agreement, submitted to arbitration, but the Kaplans, who had not signed that document, objected on the basis that their dispute with First Options was not arbitrable. After concluding that the Kaplans' dispute was arbitrable, the arbitration tribunal ruled in First Options's favor on the merits of the dispute. The federal district court confirmed the award, but the Court of Appeals reversed, finding that the dispute with the Kaplans was not subject to the arbitration agreement. The U.S. Supreme Court granted a writ of certiorari. In the course of affirming the decision of the Court of Appeals, the Court had the opportunity to consider the question of whether courts or arbitrators should address questions relating to arbitrability.]

Justice BREYER delivered the opinion for a unanimous Court.
. . . The first question—the standard of review applied to an arbitrator's decision about arbitrability—is a narrow one. To understand just how narrow, consider three types of disagreements present in this case. First, the Kaplans and First Options disagree about whether the Kaplans are personally liable for MKI's debt to First Options. That disagreement makes up the *merits* of the dispute. Second, they disagree about whether they agreed to arbitrate the merits. That disagreement is about the *arbitrability* of the dispute. Third, they disagree about *who should have the primary power to decide the second matter.* Does that power belong primarily to the arbitrators (because the court reviews their arbitrability decision deferentially) or to the court (because the court makes up its mind about arbitrability independently)? We consider here only this third question.
Although the question is a narrow one, it has a certain practical importance. That is because a party who has not agreed to arbitrate will normally have a right to a court's decision about the merits of its dispute (say, as here, its obligation under a contract). But, where the party has agreed to arbitrate, he or she, in effect, has relinquished much of that right's practical value. The party still can ask a court to review the arbitrator's decision, but the court will set that decision aside only in very unusual circumstances. . . . Hence, who—court or arbitrator—has the primary authority to decide whether a party has agreed to arbitrate can make a critical difference to a party resisting arbitration.
We believe the answer to the "who" question (i.e., the standard-of-review question) is fairly simple. Just as the arbitrability of the merits of a dispute depends

upon whether the parties agreed to arbitrate that dispute . . . so the question "who has the primary power to decide arbitrability" turns upon what the parties agreed about *that* matter. Did the parties agree to submit the arbitrability question itself to arbitration? If so, then the court's standard for reviewing the arbitrator's decision about *that* matter should not differ from the standard courts apply when they review any other matter that parties have agreed to arbitrate. . . . That is to say, the court should give considerable leeway to the arbitrator, setting aside his or her decision only in certain narrow circumstances. . . . If, on the other hand, the parties did *not* agree to submit the arbitrability question itself to arbitration, then the court should decide that question just as it would decide any other question that the parties did not submit to arbitration, namely, independently. These two answers flow inexorably from the fact that arbitration is simply a matter of contract between the parties; it is a way to resolve those disputes — but only those disputes — that the parties have agreed to submit to arbitration. . . .

We agree with First Options, therefore, that a court must defer to an arbitrator's arbitrability decision when the parties submitted that matter to arbitration. Nevertheless, that conclusion does not help First Options win this case. That is because a fair and complete answer to the standard-of-review question requires a word about how a court should decide whether the parties have agreed to submit the arbitrability issue to arbitration. . . .

When deciding whether the parties agreed to arbitrate a certain matter (including arbitrability), courts generally (though with a qualification we discuss below) should apply ordinary state-law principles that govern the formation of contracts. . . . The relevant state law here, for example, would require the court to see whether the parties objectively revealed an intent to submit the arbitrability issue to arbitration. . . .

This Court, however, has . . . added an important qualification. . . . Courts should not assume that the parties agreed to arbitrate arbitrability unless there is "clear and unmistakable" evidence that they did so. . . . In this manner the law treats silence or ambiguity about the question "*who* (primarily) should decide arbitrability" differently from the way it treats silence or ambiguity about the question "*whether* a particular merits-related dispute is arbitrable because it is within the scope of a valid arbitration agreement" — for in respect to this latter question the law reverses the presumption. . . . [With respect to the pro-arbitration presumption that applies to a court's determination of whether a particular dispute is arbitrable, the Court cites *Mitsubishi Motors Corp. v. Soler Chrysler Plymouth, Inc.*, 473 U.S. 614, 626 (1985) (" '[A]ny doubts concerning the scope of arbitrable issues should be resolved in favor of arbitration' ") (quoting *Moses H. Cone Mem'l Hosp. v. Mercury Constr. Corp.*, 460 U.S. 1, 24-25 (1983)); *United Steelworkers of Am. v. Warrior & Gulf Navigation Co.*, 363 U.S. 574, 582-83 (1960).] . . .

The latter question [i.e., whether a particular dispute falls within the scope of the parties' arbitration agreement] arises when the parties have a contract that provides for arbitration of some issues. In such circumstances, the parties likely gave at least some thought to the scope of arbitration. And, given the law's permissive policies in respect to arbitration . . . one can understand why the law would insist upon clarity before concluding that the parties did *not* want to arbitrate a related matter. . . . On the other hand, the former question — the "who (primarily) should decide arbitrability" question — is rather arcane. A party often might not focus upon that question or upon the significance of having arbitrators decide the scope of their own powers. . . . And, given the principle that a party can be forced to arbitrate only those issues it specifically has agreed to submit to arbitration, one can understand why courts might hesitate to interpret silence or ambiguity on the "who should decide arbitrability" point as giving the arbitrators that power, for doing so might too often force unwilling parties to arbitrate a matter they reasonably would have thought a judge, not an arbitrator, would decide. . . .

On the record before us, First Options cannot show that the Kaplans clearly agreed to have the arbitrators decide (i.e., to arbitrate) the question of arbitrability. . . . We conclude that, because the Kaplans did not clearly agree to submit the question of arbitrability to arbitration, the Court of Appeals was correct in finding that the arbitrability of the Kaplan/First Options dispute was subject to independent review by the courts. The judgment of the Court of Appeals is *affirmed*.

QUESTION

5. As the Court indicates, the law's "permissive policies" respecting arbitration mean that courts are supposed to interpret arbitration provisions liberally when it comes to questions of the breadth or scope of coverage. In *Moses H. Cone Memorial Hospital v. Mercury Construction Corp.*, 460 U.S. 1, 24-25 (1983), in what proved to be the first in a long series of pro-arbitration pronouncements, the Court observed:

> Although our holding in *Prima Paint* extended only to the specific issue presented, the courts of appeals have since consistently concluded that questions of arbitrability must be addressed with a healthy regard for the federal policy favoring arbitration. We agree. The [Federal] Arbitration Act establishes that, as a matter of federal law, any doubts concerning the scope of arbitrable issues should be resolved in favor of arbitration, whether the problem at hand is the construction of the contract language itself or an allegation of waiver, delay, or like a defense to arbitration.

> Given its view that it is appropriate for courts to interpret arbitration provisions expansively when it comes to questions of arbitrability, why does the Court insist that a district court should itself make the decision whether a particular matter is arbitrable unless there is "clear and unmistakable" evidence that the parties intend such decisions to be made not by courts, but by arbitrators?

1. Separability (Severability)

In *Prima Paint Corp. v. Flood & Conklin Manufacturing Co.*, 388 U.S. 395 (1967), a party who had signed a contract containing a broad arbitration clause claimed that the entire contract was induced by fraud. The Supreme Court had to determine whether the arbitration clause should be considered separately from the underlying contract for the purpose of enforcement. The Court's decision—founded on the principle of separability (severability) of arbitration agreements—established an important limit on the authority of courts considering the enforceability of arbitration agreements. The separability doctrine is one of the cornerstones of modern arbitration law in the United States and throughout the world.

Prima Paint Corp. v. Flood & Conklin Manufacturing Co.

388 U.S. 395 (1967)

[In 1964, Prima Paint purchased Flood & Conklin's (F&C) paint business and entered into a consulting agreement with the chairman of F&C. Soon Prima Paint stopped making payments under the agreements, charging that F&C had breached both agreements by fraudulently representing that it was solvent when it intended to file for bankruptcy. F&C served a notice of intent to arbitrate. Three days before its answer to the notice was due, Prima Paint filed a lawsuit in federal district court in New York, seeking to rescind the consulting agreement on the basis that it was fraudulently induced. The federal court had subject matter jurisdiction because the parties were from New Jersey and Maryland and the dispute met the amount in controversy requirement of the diversity statute.]

Justice FORTAS delivered the opinion of the Court.

This case presents the question whether the federal court or an arbitrator is to resolve a claim of "fraud in the inducement," under a contract governed by the [FAA] where there is no evidence that the contracting parties intended to withhold that issue from arbitration.

. . . [T]he parties agreed to a broad arbitration clause, which read in part: "Any controversy or claim arising out of or relating to this Agreement, or the breach thereof, shall be settled by arbitration in the City of New York, in accordance with the rules then obtaining of the [AAA]. . . ."

Having determined that the contract in question is within the coverage of the Arbitration Act [because the underlying transaction involved interstate commerce], we turn to the central issue in this case: whether a claim of fraud in the inducement of the entire contract is to be resolved by the federal court, or whether the matter is to be referred to the arbitrators. The courts of appeals have differed in their approach to this question. The view of the Court of Appeals for the Second Circuit . . . is that—*except where the parties otherwise intend*—arbitration clauses as a matter of federal law are "separable" from the contracts in which they are embedded, and that where no claim is made that fraud was directed to the arbitration clause itself, a broad arbitration clause will be held to encompass arbitration of the claim that the contract itself was induced by fraud. . . . The Court of Appeals for the First Circuit, on the other hand, has taken the view that the question of "severability" is one of state law, and that where a State regards such a clause as inseparable a claim of fraud in the inducement must be decided by the court. . . . [Under the FAA], we think that Congress has provided an explicit answer. That answer is to be found in §4 of the Act, which provides a remedy to a party seeking to compel compliance with an arbitration agreement. Under §4 . . . , the federal court is instructed to order arbitration to proceed once it is satisfied that "the making of the agreement for arbitration or the failure to comply [with the arbitration agreement] is not in issue." Accordingly, if the claim is fraud in the inducement of the arbitration clause itself—an issue which goes to the "making" of the agreement to arbitrate—the federal court may proceed to adjudicate it. But the statutory language does not permit the federal court to consider claims of fraud in the inducement of the contract generally. . . . We hold, therefore . . . that a federal court may consider only issues relating to the making and performance of the agreement to arbitrate. In so concluding, we not only honor the plain meaning of the statute but also the unmistakably clear congressional purpose that the arbitration procedure, when selected by the parties to a contract, be speedy and not subject to delay and obstruction in the courts.

[The Court further concluded that such a rule was constitutionally permissible.]

. . . Accordingly, the decision below dismissing Prima Paint's appeal is *affirmed*.

Justice BLACK, with whom Justice DOUGLAS and STEWART join, dissenting:

The Court here holds that the [FAA] . . . compels a party to a contract containing a written arbitration provision to carry out his "arbitration agreement" even though a court might, after a fair trial, hold the entire contract—including the arbitration agreement—void because of fraud in the inducement. The Court holds, what is to me fantastic, that the legal issue of a contract's voidness because of fraud is to be decided by persons designated to arbitrate factual controversies arising out of a valid contract between the parties. And the arbitrators who the Court holds are to adjudicate the legal validity of the contract need not even be lawyers, and in all probability will be non-lawyers, wholly unqualified to decide legal issues, and even if qualified to apply the law, not bound to do so. I am by no means sure that thus forcing a person to forgo his opportunity to try his legal issues in the courts where, unlike the situation in arbitration, he may have a jury trial and right to appeal, is not a denial of due process of law. I am satisfied, however, that Congress did not impose any such procedures in the [FAA]. And I am fully satisfied that a reasonable and fair reading of that Act's language and history shows that both Congress and the framers of the Act were at great pains to emphasize that non-lawyers designated to adjust and arbitrate factual controversies arising out of valid contracts would not trespass upon the courts' prerogative to decide the legal question of whether any legal contract exists upon which to base an arbitration. . . .

QUESTIONS

6. What, practically speaking, is the effect of the holding and doctrine announced in *Prima Paint?* Consider the following case:

In *Rogers v. SWEPI LP*, 757 F. App'x 497 (6th Cir. 2018), *cert. denied*, 140 S. Ct. 484 (2019), Rogers entered into a lease agreement with

SWEPI LP (Shell), which contained an arbitration clause, which said that "any dispute that arises under this Lease . . . shall be resolved by binding arbitration" if the parties do not agree to nonbinding mediation. This lease governed extraction of petroleum from Rogers's property. Rogers claimed that Shell failed to pay a bonus, and Shell filed a motion to compel arbitration in federal district court to resolve the dispute. The district court found that the portion of the contract containing the arbitration clause never took effect and therefore denied Shell's motion. On appeal, the Sixth Circuit found that Rogers's challenge to the arbitration clause challenged the contract as a whole, rather than specifically the enforceability of only the arbitration clause. The Court held that such attacks on enforceability of an arbitration clause that broadly challenge the enforceability of the rest of the contract are matters for the arbitrator to decide, or arbitrations could be rendered meaningless in such cases. What practical or policy arguments support the separability doctrine? What, if any, concerns does it raise?

7. Should the doctrine of *Prima Paint* extend to circumstances where a party seeks to assert that the contract containing the arbitration clause was not just voidable, but illegal? The matter was addressed directly in *Buckeye Check Cashing, Inc. v. Cardegna,* 546 U.S. 440 (2006) (holding that issue of illegality of contract is arbitrable under broad form arbitration agreement), discussed below in Chapter 7.C.2.

8. Should *Prima Paint* apply with equal vigor in a situation involving a standardized consumer or employment contract? *See Buckeye, supra;* see also generally Chapters 23 and 24, discussing the use of arbitration provisions in standardized "adhesion" contracts and related fairness issues, and particularly, *Rent-A-Center, West v. Jackson,* 561 U.S. 63 (2010), discussed in Chapter 8.B.1.

2.   *Delegation Clauses*

Recall that most prominent arbitration procedures give arbitrators authority to resolve all jurisdictional issues. *See, e.g.,* AAA Commercial Arbitration Rules, R-7. Do such provisions reinforce the doctrine of *Prima Paint?*

The power of these "delegation clauses" that give the arbitrator power to decide their own jurisdiction was made clear in *Henry Schein, Inc. v. Archer and White Sales, Inc.,* 139 S. Ct. 524 (2019). In this case, the U.S. Supreme Court was asked whether it is consistent with the FAA for a court (rather than an arbitrator) to determine the arbitrability of a dispute when the argument for arbitration was allegedly "wholly groundless." The Supreme Court here held unanimously that when the parties' contract delegates the question of the arbitrability of a particular dispute to an arbitrator, a court may not override the contract, even if they think that the arbitration agreement applies to a dispute that is wholly groundless.

The Court noted that the "wholly groundless" exception used by some Courts of Appeals was inconsistent with the FAA. Writing for the Court, Justice Kavanaugh reiterated prior Court precedent holding that parties may delegate threshold arbitrability questions to the arbitrator, and in those cases a court may not decide on arbitrability. In so doing, Justice Kavanaugh eschewed arguments that Section 10 of the FAA, providing for judicial review of an arbitrator's decision if an arbitrator has exceeded his or her powers, supports the conclusion that the court should also be able to say that the underlying issue is not arbitrable in the first place. Kavanaugh also dismissed the argument that the "wholly groundless" exception is necessary to deter frivolous motions to compel arbitration. Kavanaugh says this exaggerates the potential problem, since arbitrators can efficiently take care of frivolous cases and there hasn't been a substantial problem with this before.

NOTE: ARBITRATION AGREEMENTS AND THE "BATTLE OF THE FORMS"

You may recall from your Contracts course that the process of determining the terms of an agreement is not always a simple one, especially when parties have exchanged standardized contract forms. In this regard you may remember (perhaps not fondly) U.C.C. §2-207, which was the drafters' effort to address the so-called battle of the forms that often occurs in sales of goods between merchants. One of the aims of §2-207 was to avoid the perceived unfairness and surprise that may result when the terms of the contract are determined by the provisions of the last form sent by either party—the usual result under the old common law "last shot" rule.

U.C.C. §2-207 provides, among other things, that if a response to an offer contains a term that materially alters the contract, then that term will not be included in the contract.

QUESTIONS

9. Why do you suppose the court in *Whoop, Inc. v. Ascent Int'l Holdings, Ltd.,* Civil No. 19-10210-LTS (D. Mass. May. 10, 2019) concluded that the inclusion of an arbitration agreement would "materially alter" the contract? Recall our comparison of arbitration and litigation in Chapter 1.
10. Might an arbitration agreement arise out of trade practices and usages in some contexts? If so, consider whether a party needs to have knowledge that arbitration forms part of a trade usage in order for it to become part of the relevant contract. *See In re Cotton Yarn Antitrust Litig.,* 505 F.3d 274 (4th Cir. 2007) (holding that an arbitration clause included in a written confirmation of an oral discussion of the price and quantity of certain goods became a part of the contract due to the trade usage of arbitration in the textile industry).

3.   *Procedural Questions*

The Supreme Court enunciated a "liberal federal policy favoring arbitration agreements" under the FAA. *Moses H. Cone Mem'l Hosp. v. Mercury Constr. Corp.,*

460 U.S. 1, 24-25 (1983). This policy is manifested in several ways. As discussed above, it is reflected in the liberality with which courts handle questions about whether issues in disputes are "arbitrable" under particular arbitration provisions, resolving doubts in favor of sending the disputes to arbitration. It is also illustrated by a long line of cases standing for the proposition that "procedural" questions that grow out of a dispute, even if they bear on its final disposition, are presumptively for the arbitrator, *not* for the judge, to decide. More than five decades ago the Supreme Court stated:

> Once it is determined, as we have, that the parties are obliged to submit the subject matter of a dispute to arbitration, "procedural" questions which grow out of the dispute and bear on its final disposition should be left to the arbitrator.

John Wiley & Sons, Inc. v. Livingston, 376 U.S. 543, 557 (1964). Since that time, the concept that arbitrators should have authority to resolve "procedural" issues associated with arbitration has been reaffirmed again and again. It has sometimes proven difficult, however, for courts to define the line between procedural issues growing out of a dispute and issues that should be reserved by the court in determining whether to enforce an arbitration clause.

In *Howsam v. Dean Witter Reynolds, Inc.*, 537 U.S. 79, 83 (2003), the Supreme Court noted that "one might call any potentially dispositive gateway question a 'question of arbitrability,' for its answer will determine whether the underlying controversy will proceed to arbitration on the merits." The Court's unanimous opinion concluded, however, that it has defined arbitrability much more narrowly, finding the "phrase applicable in the kind of narrow circumstance where contracting parties would likely have expected a court to have decided the gateway matter." This rather circular inquiry into parties' intent after a dispute has arisen can generate confusion, but the *Howsam* Court gave a few examples. A court should decide, for example, whether an arbitration contract binds parties who did not sign the agreement and whether an arbitration agreement survives a corporate merger to bind the resulting entity. (For another example, see *Marie v. Allied Home Mortg. Corp.*, 402 F.3d 1 (1st Cir. 2005) (issue of a party's alleged waiver of the right to arbitrate due to inconsistent activity in another litigation forum was an issue for court in the absence of "clear and unmistakable" delegation to the arbitrators).) On the other hand, matters such as whether required grievance procedures were completed prior to arbitration, or whether a party had thereby waived its right to arbitrate, were deemed by the Court to be the kinds of "procedural" questions relating to the dispute that were properly within the authority of arbitrators to address.

In *Howsam*, for example, Karen Howsam chose to arbitrate a dispute that arose with her brokerage firm under the National Association of Securities Dealers (NASD) Code of Arbitration Procedure. The Code provided that a dispute must be submitted to arbitration within six years of the occurrence or event giving rise to the dispute. The Supreme Court held that an NASD arbitrator, not a court, should apply the six-year limit to the underlying dispute to see if Ms. Howsam's arbitration submission was timely. Although the federal circuit courts were divided on the question of whether an arbitrator or court should determine this issue, the Court reasoned that what constitutes a question of arbitrability—presumed to be within the court's control absent party agreement to the contrary—should be narrowly construed. Characterizing the contractual time limit on submissions as involving a procedural question to be resolved by the arbitrators, the Court emphasized the comparative expertise of the NASD arbitrators in construing their own time limits, and expressed hope that this outcome would advance goals of both arbitration systems and judicial systems by "secur[ing] a fair and expeditious resolution of the underlying controversy."

A more recent illustration of these principles, and the difficulty judges sometimes have in assessing whether a question is substantive or procedural in nature, is *BG Grp. PLC v. Republic of Arg.*, 134 S. Ct. 1198 (2014), involving a dispute between a British company, BG Group, and the Argentine government under the UK-Argentina bilateral investment treaty (BIT). When BG Group filed a claim for arbitration under the BIT, Argentina argued that the BG Group's failure to first file suit in a local court in Argentina pursuant to the terms of the BIT precluded the arbitration tribunal from having jurisdiction. The arbitration panel disagreed and proceeded to make an award against Argentina, which filed a motion to vacate in federal district court. The district court denied the motion, but a court of appeals panel reversed the court's order and vacated the award. BG Group appealed to the Supreme Court, which reversed the appellate court decision in a majority decision. The Court majority concluded that the local litigation requirement in the BIT, which it labelled a "claims-processing rule," was a procedural matter that fell squarely within the authority of the arbitrators.

Similarly, in *Bamberger Rosenheim, Ltd., (Israel) v. OA Dev., Inc. (United States)*, 862 F.3d 1284 (11th Cir. 2017), the court held that questions related to a forum selection provision is just a question of where an arbitration will occur, not whether an arbitration will occur, and is therefore a question to be decided by the arbitrator. In this case, an Israeli real estate investment company (Bamberger) had a dispute with a U.S. real estate development company (OA), which was subject to an arbitration clause. The parties nonetheless disagreed regarding the proper venue for the arbitration. The district court confirmed the award based on arbitration in Atlanta, and the Eleventh Circuit affirmed the district court's judgment, deferring to arbitrators' determination on location.

As these cases demonstrate, parties can always agree expressly that arbitrators should handle certain types of threshold questions. But even if they do not vest such authority explicitly, courts that apply the FAA and state arbitration laws will often defer such decisions to arbitrators under a typical, broadly framed arbitration provision (e.g., covering "all disputes arising under or relating to the contract or the breach thereof").

QUESTION

11. Suppose you desire to include an arbitration agreement in your contract but you want a court, not arbitrators, to handle any determinations regarding the effect of a failure to file a claim within a certain period of time (e.g., a statute of limitations). Would you need to state that intent "clearly and unmistakably" because arbitrators are typically deemed to have authority over such determinations under the FAA?

Another set of issues related to what could be deemed "procedural questions" has to do with issues relating to a party's failure to comply with a contractual obligation to participate in negotiation or mediation prior to arbitration. Should such matters be handled by courts, or are they within the authority of arbitrators to handle procedural questions associated with an arbitrable dispute? Judicial responses vary.

PROBLEM 1: WHO SHOULD DETERMINE THE CONSEQUENCES OF A FAILURE TO NEGOTIATE OR MEDIATE UNDER A STEPPED DISPUTE RESOLUTION PROVISION?

Kalua Company entered into a long-term agreement to provide syrup to Rise 'n' Shine, a coffee shop chain. The parties' agreement included a stepped dispute resolution clause that stated in pertinent part:

> It is mutually agreed that the parties shall be free to bring any and all such matters to the attention of the other at any time without prejudicing their harmonious relationship and operations hereunder, and that the offices of either party shall be available at all times for the prompt and effective adjustment of any and all such differences, either by mail, telephone, or personal meeting under friendly and courteous circumstances.
>
> In the event that a dispute cannot be settled between the parties, the matter shall be mediated within fifteen (15) days after receipt of notice by either party that the other party requests the mediation of a dispute pursuant to this paragraph. If the parties are unable to select a mediator, the See You Out of Court! Mediation Group shall select a mediator. The parties agree to use their best efforts to mediate a dispute.
>
> In the event that the dispute cannot be settled through mediation, the parties shall submit the matter to arbitration within ten (10) days after receipt of notice by either party. The arbitration shall be conducted in accordance with the Commercial Arbitration Rules of the [AAA] then in effect. The parties shall each select an arbitrator and the two arbitrators thus selected shall select a third arbitrator. These three arbitrators shall constitute the arbitration panel. It is understood that a judgment or award rendered, which may include an award of damages, may be entered in any court having jurisdiction thereof.

Sadly, things did not go well under the contract. In May, Kalua made a demand on Rise 'n' Shine for payment of three months of unpaid invoices. On June 15, Rise 'n' Shine sent Kalua a notice acknowledging that it owed some of the money, but not all. A payment was not included with the notice. Kalua presented Rise 'n' Shine with another demand on June 28. Rise 'n' Shine did not respond. Kalua terminated the Agreement with Rise 'n' Shine on August 3.

On August 15, Kalua then brought this suit in federal district court (because the usual jurisdictional requirements were met). On September 20, Rise 'n' Shine filed a motion to stay the proceeding pending arbitration pursuant to FAA Section 3. Kalua seeks to defeat the motion and insists that the right to arbitrate has been waived because there was no effort by Rise 'n' Shine to negotiate or mediate.

A. If you are the federal district court judge charged with deciding how to address the motion to stay the proceeding pending arbitration, would you (1) grant the stay of the court proceeding and let the arbitrators address the impact of the failure to negotiate and mediate, or (2) deny the stay and have the parties stay in court? *See Kemiron Atl., Inc. v. Aguakem Int'l*, 290 F.3d 1287 (11th Cir. 2002); *HIM Portland LLC v. Devito Builders Inc.*, 317 F.3d 41, 44 (1st Cir. 2003). Note, however, the Fourth Circuit Court of Appeals in *Chorley Enterprises, Inc. v. Dickey's Barbecue Restaurants, Inc.*, 2015 WL 4637967 (4th Cir. 2015), calls into question the validity of *Kemiron* and *HIM Portland* (as well as *Perdue Farms Inc. v. Design Build Contracting Corp.*, 263 F. App'x 380, 383 (4th Cir. 2008)) in light of *Howsam* and *BG Group*. *Buffkin v. Dep't of Def.*, 957 F.3d 1327, 1328 (Fed. Cir. 2020) does not question the arbitrator's power to decide if one has properly filed for arbitration after first attempting mediation under the contract.

B. Might your answer be in any way affected by the provisions of the AAA Commercial Arbitration Rules?

4. Public Policy Limitations

Until relatively recently, courts routinely recognized significant public policy limitations on the enforcement of arbitration agreements. In particular, arbitration was not deemed amenable to the resolution of "public law" issues (i.e., rights created by the legislature, including federal antitrust or civil rights claims). "Less than twenty years ago, the concept of arbitrating federally created rights . . . was virtually unthinkable."[7] Traditionally, many arbitrators were not lawyers, and it was thought inappropriate to have them consider complex statutory claims, particularly when any legal decision they reached was not subject to a more public court process and appellate review. There were also concerns that arbitrators might prove insufficiently rigorous in upholding statutory protections and policing business peers.

An illustration of judicial unwillingness to allow arbitration of statutory claims is *Wilko v. Swan*, 346 U.S. 427 (1953). Although the FAA had been in existence since 1925, the *Wilko* Court held that an agreement to arbitrate disputes arising under the Securities Act of 1933 was unenforceable, because the Act prohibited waiver of "compliance with any provision of this title," which the Court interpreted as including the right to a judicial forum to resolve any disputes. The Court noted that arbitrators do not receive "judicial instruction on the law," "their award may be made without explanation of their reasons and without a complete record," and "the arbitrators' conception of the legal meaning of . . . statutory requirements" is not subject to judicial review. As Professor Judith Resnik summarizes:

> Three assumptions, central to *Wilko*, were key to its intellectual framework. First, arbitration was assumed to be something *different* from and less loyal to law than adjudication. Second, public judgments rendered by federal trial courts on factual questions, such as the claim of fraudulent inducement of a client by a firm to purchase stock, in individual cases, were viewed as desirable *mechanisms* of social regulation. Third, the judiciary viewed with skepticism the agreements of parties; parties' agreements were

insufficient, in and of themselves, to valorize all the decisions embodied in those agreements.[8]

For many years, "public policy" considerations served as a barrier to the arbitration of statutory claims. However, the attitude of the Supreme Court toward arbitration of statute-based claims shifted dramatically in the mid-1980s. Consider the following decision.

Mitsubishi Motors Corp. v. Soler Chrysler-Plymouth, Inc.

473 U.S. 614 (1985)

[Mitsubishi, an auto manufacturer, brought an action in federal district court against one of its dealers (Soler), to compel arbitration of a variety of claims for breach of contract. The contract contained a clause requiring arbitration by the Japan Commercial Arbitration Association of all disputes arising under the contract. Soler filed an answer and counterclaim alleging violation of the Sherman Antitrust Act as well as other causes of action. The district court ordered arbitration of most of the claims, including the federal antitrust issues. The Court of Appeals reversed the order compelling arbitration of the antitrust claim, relying on *American Safety Equipment Corp. v. J.P. Maguire & Co.*, 391 F.2d 821 (2d Cir. 1968), which held that rights conferred by the antitrust laws are inappropriate for arbitration.]

Justice BLACKMUN delivered the opinion of the Court.

. . . [W]e find no warrant in the [Federal] Arbitration Act for implying in every contract within its ken a presumption against arbitration of statutory claims. . . .

By agreeing to arbitrate a statutory claim, a party does not forgo the substantive rights afforded by the statute; it only submits to their resolution in an arbitral, rather than a judicial, forum. It trades the procedures and opportunity for review of the courtroom for the simplicity, informality, and expedition of arbitration (emphasis added). We must assume that if Congress intended the substantive protection afforded by a given statute to include protection against waiver of the right to a judicial forum, that intention will be deducible from text or legislative history. Having made the bargain to arbitrate, the party should be held to it unless Congress itself has evinced an intention to preclude a waiver of judicial remedies for the statutory rights at issue. Nothing, in the meantime, prevents a party from excluding statutory claims from the scope of an agreement to arbitrate. . . .

We now turn to consider whether Soler's antitrust claims are non-arbitrable even though it has agreed to arbitrate them. In holding that they are not [arbitrable], the Court of Appeals followed the decision of the Second Circuit in *American Safety Equipment Corp. v. J.P. Maguire & Co.*, 391 F.2d 821 (1968). Notwithstanding the absence of any explicit support for such an exception in either the Sherman Act or the [FAA], the Second Circuit there reasoned that "the pervasive public interest in enforcement of the antitrust laws, and the nature of the claims that arise in such cases, combine to make . . . antitrust claims . . . inappropriate for arbitration." . . .

At the outset, we confess to some skepticism of certain aspects of the *American Safety* doctrine. As distilled by the First Circuit, the doctrine comprises four ingredients. First, private parties play a pivotal role in aiding governmental enforcement of the antitrust laws by means of the private action for treble damages. Second, "the strong possibility that contracts which generate antitrust disputes may be contracts of adhesion militates against automatic forum determination by contract." Third, antitrust issues, prone to complication, require sophisticated legal and economic analysis, and thus are "ill-adapted to strengths of the arbitral process, i.e., expedition, minimal requirements of written rationale, simplicity, resort to basic concepts of common sense and simple equity." Finally, just as "issues of war and peace are too important to be vested in the generals, . . . decisions as to antitrust regulation of business are too important to be lodged in arbitrators chosen from the business community—particularly those from a foreign community that has had no experience with or exposure to our law and values."

Initially, we find the second concern unjustified. The mere appearance of an antitrust dispute does not alone warrant invalidation of the selected forum on the undemonstrated assumption that the arbitration clause is tainted. A party resisting arbitration of course may attack directly the validity of the agreement to arbitrate. . . . But absent such a showing—and none was attempted here—there is no basis for assuming the forum inadequate or its selection unfair.

Next, potential complexity should not suffice to ward off arbitration. We might well have some doubt that even the courts following *American Safety* subscribe fully to the view that antitrust matters are inherently insusceptible to resolution by arbitration, as these same courts have agreed that an undertaking to arbitrate antitrust claims entered into *after* the dispute arises is acceptable. And the vertical restraints which most frequently give birth to antitrust claims covered by an arbitration agreement will not often occasion the monstrous proceedings that have given antitrust litigation an image of intractability. In any event, adaptability and access to expertise are hallmarks of arbitration. The anticipated subject matter of the dispute may be taken into account when the arbitrators are appointed, and arbitral rules typically provide for the participation of experts either employed by the parties or appointed by the tribunal. Moreover, it is often a judgment that streamlined proceedings and expeditious results will best serve their needs that causes parties to agree to arbitrate their disputes; it is typically a desire to keep the effort and expense required to resolve a dispute within manageable bounds that prompts them mutually to forgo access to judicial remedies. In sum, the factor of potential complexity alone does not persuade us that an arbitral tribunal could not properly handle an antitrust matter. . . .

For similar reasons, we also reject the proposition that an arbitration panel will pose too great a danger of innate hostility to the constraints on business conduct that antitrust law imposes. International arbitrators frequently are drawn from the legal as well as the business community; where the dispute has an important legal component, the parties and the arbitral body with whose assistance they have agreed to settle their dispute can be expected to select arbitrators accordingly. We decline to indulge the presumption that the parties and arbitral body conducting a proceeding will be unable or unwilling to retain competent, conscientious, and impartial arbitrators. . . .

We are left, then, with the core of the *American Safety* doctrine—the fundamental importance to American democratic capitalism of the regime of the antitrust laws. As the Court of Appeals pointed out:

"A claim under the antitrust laws is not merely a private matter. The Sherman Act is designed to promote the national interest in a competitive economy; thus, the plaintiff asserting his rights under the Act has been likened to a private attorney-general who protects the public's interest." 723 F.2d at 168, quoting *American Safety*, 391 F.2d at 826.

The treble-damages provision wielded by the private litigant is a chief tool in the antitrust enforcement scheme, posing a crucial deterrent to potential violators.

The importance of the private damages remedy, however, does not compel the conclusion that it may not be sought outside an American court. . . . Having permitted the arbitration to go forward, the national courts of the United States will have the opportunity at the award-enforcement stage to ensure that the legitimate interest in the enforcement of the antitrust laws has been addressed. . . .

The judgment of the Court of Appeals is affirmed in part and reversed in part, and the cases are remanded for further proceedings consistent with this opinion.

Justice STEVENS filed a dissenting opinion.

. . . This Court agrees with the Court of Appeals' interpretation of the scope of the arbitration clause, but disagrees with its conclusion that the clause is unenforceable insofar as it purports to cover an antitrust claim against a Japanese company. This Court's holding rests almost exclusively on the federal policy favoring arbitration of commercial disputes and vague notions of international comity arising from the fact that the automobiles involved here were manufactured in Japan. . . . The plain language [of the FAA] encompasses Soler's claims that arise out of its contract with Mitsubishi, but does not encompass a claim arising under federal law, or indeed one that arises under its distributor agreement with Chrysler. Nothing in the text of the 1925 Act, nor its legislative history, suggests that Congress intended to authorize the arbitration of any statutory claims. . . .

Until today all of our cases enforcing agreements to arbitrate under the [FAA] have involved contract claims. . . . [T]his is the first time the Court has considered the question whether a standard arbitration clause referring to claims arising out of or relating to a contract should be construed to cover statutory claims that have only an indirect relationship to the contract. In my opinion, neither the Congress that enacted the Arbitration Act in 1925, nor the many parties who have agreed to such standard clauses, could have anticipated the Court's answer to that question. . . .

"Arbitral procedures, while well suited to the resolution of contractual disputes, make arbitration a comparatively inappropriate forum for the final resolution of rights created by [statute]. This conclusion rests first on the special role of the arbitrator, whose task is to effectuate the intent of the parties rather than the requirements of enacted legislation. . . . [T]he specialized competence of arbitrators pertains to the law of the shop, not the law of the land. . . ." (quoting *Alexander v. Gardner-Denver*, 415 U.S. 36, 56-57 (1974)).

[T]he informal procedures which make arbitration so desirable in the context of contractual disputes are inadequate to develop a record for appellate review of statutory questions. Such review is essential on matters of statutory interpretation in order to assure consistent application of important public rights*. . . . "Finally, not

---

* "Moreover, the fact-finding process in arbitration usually is not equivalent to judicial fact-finding. The record of the arbitration proceedings is not as complete; the usual rules of evidence do not apply; and rights and procedures common to civil trials, such as discovery, compulsory process, cross-examination, and testimony under oath, are often severely limited or unavailable."

only are arbitral procedures less protective of individual statutory rights than are judicial procedures, but arbitrators very often are powerless to grant the aggrieved employees as broad a range of relief.". . .

The Sherman and Clayton Acts reflect Congress' appraisal of the value of economic freedom; they guarantee the vitality of the entrepreneurial spirit. Questions arising under these Acts are among the most important in public law. . . . The provision for mandatory treble damages—unique in federal law when the statute was enacted—provides a special incentive to the private enforcement of the statute. . . .

There are . . . several unusual features of the antitrust enforcement scheme that unequivocally require rejection of any thought that Congress would tolerate private arbitration of antitrust claims in lieu of the statutory remedies that it fashioned. . . .

In view of the history of antitrust enforcement in the United States, it is not surprising that all of the federal courts that have considered the question have uniformly and unhesitatingly concluded that agreements to arbitrate federal antitrust issues are not enforceable. . . .

This Court would be well advised to endorse the collective wisdom of the distinguished judges of the Courts of Appeals who have unanimously concluded that the statutory remedies fashioned by Congress for the enforcement of the antitrust laws render an agreement to arbitrate antitrust disputes unenforceable. . . . Despotic decision making of this kind is fine for parties who are willing to agree in advance to settle for a best approximation of the correct result in order to resolve quickly and inexpensively any contractual dispute that may arise in an ongoing commercial relationship. Such informality, however, is simply unacceptable when every error may have devastating consequences for important businesses in our national economy and may undermine their ability to compete in world markets. Instead of "muffling a grievance in the cloakroom of arbitration," the public interest in free competitive markets would be better served by having the issues resolved "in the light of impartial public court adjudication."

NOTES AND QUESTIONS

12. This case involved an antitrust claim arising in the international context. Do you think the fact that the transaction was an international one influenced the assumptions of the Justices in *Mitsubishi*? Would the result be different if the case had involved a wholly domestic dispute where a party sought to compel arbitration of an antitrust claim? Is the *American Safety* doctrine, which holds that domestic antitrust claims are not subject to arbitration, still good law? You may consider the FAA's presumption in favor of arbitration, and cases such as *In re Evanston N.W. Corp. Antitrust Litig.*, 07-CV-04446, 2015 WL 13735423, at *1 (N.D. Ill. Sept. 4, 2015), directly analyzing the arbitrability of antitrust claims and citing *Seacoast Motors of Salisbury, Inc. v. DaimlerChrysler Motors Corp.*, 271 F.3d 6, 10 (1st Cir. 2001).

13. In this particular case, the arbitrators would likely be Japanese. They *might* be lawyers. How familiar would they be with, and how supportive would they be of, U.S. antitrust law? If the parties agreed in advance to use what Justice Stevens termed "despotic" decision makers (arbitrators), why should U.S. courts be concerned? If this dispute arose today, and it was understood that all civil claims, including antitrust issues, would be arbitrable, do you believe it would influence the choice of arbitrators? Explain.[9]

14. Writing for the majority, Justice Blackmun stated that "the national courts of the United States will have the opportunity at the award-enforcement stage to ensure that the legitimate interest in the enforcement of the antitrust laws has been addressed." Is this conclusion realistic? Keep this statement in mind as you read the decisions regarding judicial vacatur of arbitration awards in Chapter 6. *See Baxter Int'l v. Abbott Labs.*, 315 F.3d 829 (7th Cir. 2003) ("Legal errors are not among the grounds that the Convention gives for refusing to enforce international awards. Under domestic law, as well as under the Convention, arbitrators 'have completely free rein to decide the law as well as the facts and are not subject to appellate review' "), quoting *Commonwealth Coatings Corp. v. Continental Cas. Co.*, 393 U.S. 145, 149 (1968)).

15. Two years after *Mitsubishi*, the Court held that statutory claims arising under the Racketeer Influenced and Corrupt Organizations Act (RICO) are subject to mandatory arbitration. *See Shearson/American Express, Inc. v. McMahon*, 482 U.S. 220 (1987) (finding no basis for concluding that Congress intended to prevent enforcement of agreements to arbitrate RICO claims and concluding that a RICO claim can be effectively vindicated in an arbitral forum).

    The Court in *Shearson/American Express v. McMahon* also held that claims under the Securities Exchange Act of 1934 are subject to binding arbitration, rejecting the reasoning of *Wilko v. Swan*, 346 U.S. 427 (1953), which held that claims arising under the Securities Act of 1933 were not subject to binding arbitration. Not surprisingly, the Court overruled *Wilko* two years later in *Rodriguez de Quijas v. Shearson/American Express, Inc.*, 490 U.S. 477 (1989). *Gilmer v. Interstate/Johnson Lane Corp.*, 500 U.S. 20 (1991), supporting the arbitrability of statutory employment discrimination claims, narrowed the so-called public policy limitation even further. These developments are treated further in Chapter 7.

D. PREEMPTION OF STATE LAW BY THE FEDERAL ARBITRATION ACT

Another critical aspect of the evolution of modern arbitration law is the concept of preemption of state law by a "substantive law of arbitrability" — that is, a body of law supporting enforcement of arbitration agreements under the FAA. In the 1980s and 1990s, as evidenced by the decisions cited in the previous sections, the Supreme Court spent a significant portion of its time and effort determining controversies about the scope and force of the FAA. It construed the FAA broadly to cover arbitration of statutory claims. In doing so, it displaced the traditional role of state law in this arena.

These decisions conflict with what the Court has done during the same period in many other areas of law, as it delegated more power to states and reined in the role of federal law.[10] Two commentators offered a view on why the Court, in this series of "bold" decisions, rewrote the law governing arbitration:

> The Court's aggression has been the product of two worthy but overindulged impulses. One impulse has been to encourage international trade by enforcing dispute resolution provisions in international commercial contracts. The second has been to conserve scarce judicial resources by encouraging citizens to resolve disputes by private means.[11]

With some important exceptions, the Court came in the 1980s and 1990s to express unanimity in a number of these rulings, and frequently issued *per curiam* decisions. The agreement among the Justices in interpreting the FAA contrasted sharply with its 5-4 rulings in many areas of constitutional law, including other federalism decisions. This may have been a reflection of a prevailing view on the Court that in interpreting congressional intent, it could rely on Congress to revise the FAA if the Court misconstrued its scope and import. (As we will see, however, the most recent Court decisions have reflected a very clear split along political lines.)

As noted above, most states adopted versions of the UAA after Congress enacted the FAA. However, the operational scope of these statutes is now significantly qualified—at least in the fundamental area of enforcement of arbitration agreements—by the following Supreme Court decision and its progeny.

Southland Corp. v. Keating

465 U.S. 1 (1984)

[The Southland Corporation, which is the franchisor of the 7-Eleven convenience stores, had an arbitration clause in its standard franchise agreements requiring arbitration of "any controversy or claim arising out of or relating to this agreement." Keating, a franchisee, filed a class action in a California state court against Southland on behalf of approximately 800 California franchisees alleging fraud, oral misrepresentations, breach of contract, breach of fiduciary duty, and violation of the disclosure requirements of the California Franchise Investment Law. Southland petitioned the Superior Court to compel arbitration of all claims. The trial court granted the petition and compelled arbitration, except with respect to claims based on the California Franchise Investment Law, which provided as follows: "Any condition, stipulation or provision purporting to bind any person acquiring any franchise to waive compliance with any provision of this law or any rule or order hereunder is void." The California Supreme Court agreed with the trial court that the claims under the state statute were not arbitrable, and the decision was appealed to the U.S. Supreme Court. The U.S. Supreme Court did not question the California Court's interpretation of the statute, but instead granted cert on the basis that the law precluded enforcement of arbitration with respect to the California statutory claims.]

Chief Justice BURGER delivered the opinion of the Court.

[We noted probable jurisdiction to consider] (a) whether the California Franchise Investment Law, which invalidates certain arbitration agreements covered by the [FAA], violates the Supremacy Clause [of the United States Constitution]. . . .

In enacting §2 of the federal Act, Congress declared a national policy favoring arbitration and withdrew the power of the states to require a judicial forum for the resolution of claims which the contracting parties agreed to resolve by arbitration. The FAA provides:

> "A written provision in any maritime transaction or a contract evidencing a transaction involving commerce to settle by arbitration a controversy thereafter arising out of such contract or transaction, or the refusal to perform the whole or any part thereof, or an agreement in writing to submit to arbitration an existing controversy arising out of such a contract, transaction, or refusal, shall be valid, irrevocable, and enforceable, save upon such grounds as exist at law or in equity for the revocation of any contract." 9 U.S.C. §2 (1976).

Congress has thus mandated the enforcement of arbitration agreements.

We discern only two limitations on the enforceability of arbitration provisions governed by the [FAA]: they must be part of a written maritime contract or a contract "evidencing a transaction involving [interstate] commerce" and such clauses may be revoked upon "grounds as exist at law or in equity for the revocation of any contract." We see nothing in the Act indicating that the broad principle of enforceability is subject to any additional limitations under State law. . . .

At least since 1824 Congress' authority under the Commerce Clause has been held plenary. *Gibbons v. Ogden*, 22 U.S. 1 (1824). In the words of Chief Justice Marshall, the authority of Congress is "the power to regulate; that is, to prescribe the rule by which commerce is to be governed." Id. The statements of the Court in *Prima Paint* (388 U.S. 420) that the [Federal] Arbitration Act was an exercise of the Commerce Clause power clearly implied that the substantive rules of the Act were to apply in state as well as federal courts. . . .

Although the legislative history is not without ambiguities, there are strong indications that Congress had in mind something more than making arbitration agreements enforceable only in the federal courts. The House Report plainly suggests the more comprehensive objectives:

> "The purpose of this bill is to make valid and enforceable agreements for arbitration contained *in contracts involving interstate commerce* or within the jurisdiction or admiralty, *or* which may be the subject of litigation in the Federal courts." H.R. Rep. No. 96, 68th Cong., 1st Sess. 1 (1924) (Emphasis added.).

This broader purpose can also be inferred from the reality that Congress would be less likely to address a problem whose impact was confined to federal courts than a problem of large significance in the field of commerce. The [FAA] sought to "overcome the rule of equity, that equity will not specifically enforce any arbitration agreement." Hearing on S. 4214 Before a Subcomm. of the Senate Comm. on the Judiciary, 67th Cong., 4th Sess. 6 (1923) ("Senate Hearing") (remarks of Sen. Walsh). The House Report accompanying the bill stated:

> "[t]he need for the law arises from . . . the jealousy of the English courts for their own jurisdiction. . . . This jealousy survived for so [long] a period that the principle became firmly embedded in the English common law and was adopted with it by the American courts. The courts have felt that the precedent was too strongly fixed to be overturned without legislative enactment. . . ." H.R. Rep. No. 96, *supra*, 1-2 (1924).

Surely this makes clear that the House Report contemplated a broad reach of the Act, unencumbered by state law constraints. . . .

The problems Congress faced were therefore twofold: the old common law hostility toward arbitration, and the failure of state arbitration statutes to mandate enforcement of arbitration agreements. To confine the scope of the Act to arbitrations sought to be enforced in federal courts would frustrate what we believe Congress intended to be a broad enactment appropriate in scope to meet the large problems Congress was addressing. . . .

In creating a substantive rule applicable in state as well as federal courts, Congress intended to foreclose state legislative attempts to undercut the enforceability of arbitration agreements. We hold that §31512 of the California Franchise Investment Law violates the Supremacy Clause. . . . The judgment of the California Supreme Court denying enforcement of the arbitration agreement is reversed. . . .

Justice O'CONNOR with whom Justice REHNQUIST joins, dissenting.

Section 2 of the [FAA] provides that a written arbitration agreement "shall be valid, irrevocable, and enforceable, save upon such grounds as exist at law or in equity for the revocation of any contract." Section 2 does not, on its face, identify which judicial forums are bound by its requirements or what procedures govern its enforcement. The FAA deals with these matters in §§3 and 4. Section 3 provides:

> "If any suit or proceeding be brought *in any of the courts of the United States* upon any issue referable to arbitration . . . the court . . . shall on application of one of the parties stay the trial of the action until such arbitration has been had in accordance with the terms of the agreement. . . ."

Section 4 specifies that a party aggrieved by another's refusal to arbitrate "may petition *any United States district court* which, save for such agreement, would have jurisdiction under Title 28 . . . for an order directing that such arbitration proceed in the manner provided for in such agreement. . . ."

Today, the Court takes the facial silence of §2 as a license to declare that state as well as federal courts must apply §2. In addition, though this is not spelled out in the opinion, the Court holds that in enforcing this newly discovered federal right state courts must follow procedures specified in §3. The Court's decision is impelled by an understandable desire to encourage the use of arbitration, but it utterly fails to recognize the clear congressional intent underlying the FAA. Congress intended to require federal, not state, courts to respect arbitration agreements. . . . One rarely finds a legislative history as unambiguous as the FAA's. That history establishes conclusively that the 1925 Congress viewed the FAA as a procedural statute, applicable only in federal courts, derived, Congress believed, largely from the federal power to control the jurisdiction of the federal courts. . . .

If characterizing the FAA as procedural was not enough, the draftsmen of the Act, the House Report, and the early commentators all flatly stated that the Act was intended to affect only federal court proceedings. Mr. Cohen, the American Bar Association member who drafted the bill, assured two congressional subcommittees in joint hearings:

> "Nor can it be said that the Congress of the United States, *directing its own courts* . . . , would infringe upon the provinces or prerogatives of the States. . . . [T]he question of the enforcement relates to the law of remedies and not to substantive law. The rule must be changed for the jurisdiction in which the agreement is sought to be enforced. . . . There is no disposition therefore by means of the Federal bludgeon to force an individual State into an unwilling submission to arbitration enforcement." [Additional discussion of legislative history is omitted.]

Today's decision is unfaithful to congressional intent, unnecessary, and, in light of the FAA's antecedents and the intervening contraction of federal power, inexplicable. Although arbitration is a worthy alternative to litigation, today's exercise in judicial revisionism goes too far. I respectfully dissent.

NOTES AND QUESTIONS

16. The majority opinion concludes that the FAA is a source of substantive law governing the enforcement of arbitration agreements—a law based on the power of Congress under the Commerce Clause to regulate interstate commerce. It therefore applies in both federal and state courts. The dissent argues that it is a procedural statute based upon congressional power under Article III to establish and regulate federal courts and therefore applies only in federal proceedings. Who has the better of the argument?[12]

17. In another part of its opinion, the majority expressed concern that interpreting the FAA to apply only in federal courts and not state courts would "encourage and reward forum shopping." Justice O'Connor responded to this concern as follows:

    > Because the FAA makes the federal courts equally accessible to both parties to a dispute, no forum shopping would be possible even if we gave the FAA a construction faithful to the congressional intent. In controversies involving incomplete diversity of citizenship there is simply no access to federal court and therefore no possibility of forum shopping. In controversies *with* complete diversity of citizenship the FAA grants federal court access equally to both parties; no party can gain any advantage by forum shopping. Even when the party resisting arbitration initiates an action in state court, the opposing party can invoke FAA §4 and promptly secure a federal court order to compel arbitration.

18. *Southland* stands for the proposition that Section 2 of the FAA, which makes arbitration clauses "valid, irrevocable and enforceable," creates a substantive right that state courts must enforce under the Supremacy Clause of the Constitution. Because the FAA does not provide for federal court jurisdiction, arbitration disputes arising out of transactions involving interstate commerce end up being filed in state courts if there is no independent basis for federal court jurisdiction, such as diversity of citizenship of the parties or a federal question. In such circumstances, there are questions about what portions of the FAA would be applicable in state court. One important question is whether state courts are required to apply the enforcement mechanisms of the FAA, which include compelling arbitration and staying judicial proceedings. The majority apparently concluded the answer was "yes," but Justice O'Connor thought not:

> [A]bsent specific direction from Congress the state courts have always been permitted to apply their own reasonable procedures when enforcing federal rights. Before we undertake to read a set of complex and mandatory procedures into §2's brief and general language, we should at a minimum allow state courts and legislatures a chance to develop their own methods for enforcing the new federal rights. Some might choose to award compensatory or punitive damages for the violation of an arbitration agreement; some might award litigation costs to the party who remained willing to arbitrate; some might affirm the "validity and enforceability" of arbitration agreements in other ways. Any of these approaches could vindicate §2 rights in a manner fully consonant with the language and background of that provision.

> As discussed in Section B.1 above, however, state courts now often assume that FAA Section 3, authorizing judicial stays of litigation, applies in state court proceedings in which the FAA is determined to apply. However, the applicability of FAA Section 4, involving motions to compel arbitration in state courts is more controversial.

Southland concludes that the enactment of the FAA was an exercise of congressional power under the Commerce Clause. How broad an exercise of that power was intended? Consider the following case, in which the preemptive power of the FAA was tested against a state statute purporting to make pre-dispute arbitration agreements unenforceable.

Allied-Bruce Terminix Cos. v. Dobson

513 U.S. 265 (1995)

[The plaintiffs, Mr. and Mrs. G. William Dobson, purchased a house that had been subject to a lifetime "Termite Protection Plan" provided by Allied-Bruce Terminix. After the purchase they found the house to be severely infested with termites. They filed a lawsuit against defendant Allied-Bruce in Alabama state court. Defendant asked the court for a stay, citing the fact that the "Termite Protection Plan" contained an arbitration clause providing for arbitration of "any controversy or claim . . . arising out of or relating to the interpretation, performance or breach of any provision of this agreement." The Alabama court refused to grant the stay on the basis of a state statute making pre-dispute arbitration agreements invalid and unenforceable. The Alabama court found the FAA inapplicable because the connection between the termite contract and interstate commerce was too slight. Despite some interstate activities (e.g., Allied-Bruce was a multistate firm and shipped treatment and repair material from out of state), the court found that the parties "contemplated" a transaction that was primarily local and not "substantially" interstate. . . . The court took the view that the FAA applied only if at the time the parties entered a contract they "contemplated substantial interstate activity."]

Justice BREYER delivered the opinion of the Court.

This case concerns the reach of §2 of the [FAA]. That section makes enforceable a written arbitration provision in "a contract *evidencing* a transaction *involving* commerce." 9 U.S.C. §2 (emphasis added). Should we read this phrase broadly, extending the Act's reach to the limits of Congress' Commerce Clause power? Or, do the two italicized words—"involving" and "evidencing"—significantly restrict the Act's application? We conclude that the broader reading of the Act is the correct one, and we reverse a State Supreme Court judgment to the contrary. . . .

After examining the statute's language, background, and structure, we conclude that the word "involving" is broad and is indeed the functional equivalent of "affecting." For one thing, such an interpretation, linguistically speaking, is permissible. The dictionary finds instances in which "involve" and "affect" sometimes can mean about the same thing. For another, the Act's legislative history, to the extent that it is informative, indicates an expansive congressional intent. . . . Further, this Court has previously described the Act's reach expansively as coinciding with that of the Commerce Clause. . . .

Finally, a broad interpretation of this language is consistent with the Act's basic purpose, to put arbitration provisions on "the same footing" as a contract's other terms. Conversely, a narrower interpretation is not consistent with the Act's purpose, for (unless unreasonably narrowed to the flow of commerce) such an interpretation would create a new, unfamiliar test lying somewhere in a no man's land between "in commerce" and "affecting commerce," thereby unnecessarily complicating the law and breeding litigation from a statute that seeks to avoid it. We recognize arguments to the contrary: The pre-New Deal Congress that passed the Act in 1925 might well have thought the Commerce Clause did not stretch as far as has turned out to be the case. But, it is not unusual for this Court in similar circumstances to ask whether the scope of a statute should expand along with the expansion of the Commerce Clause power itself, and to answer the question affirmatively—as, for the reasons set forth above, we do here. . . .

Section 2 applies where there is "a contract *evidencing a transaction* involving commerce." The second interpretive question focuses on the italicized words. Does "evidencing a transaction" mean only that the transaction (that the contract "evidences") must turn out, *in fact*, to have involved interstate commerce? Or, does it mean more?

Many years ago, Second Circuit Chief Judge Lumbard said that the phrase meant considerably more. He wrote:

> "The significant question . . . is not whether, in carrying out the terms of the contract, the parties *did* cross state lines, but whether, *at the time they entered into it* and accepted the arbitration clause, they *contemplated* substantial interstate activity. Cogent evidence regarding their state of mind at the time would be the terms of the contract, and if it, on its face, evidences interstate traffic . . . , the contract should come within §2. In addition, evidence as to how the parties expected the contract to be performed and how it was performed is relevant to whether substantial interstate activity was contemplated." *Metro Industrial Painting Corp. v. Terminal Constr. Co.*, 287 F.2d 382, 387 (CA2 1961) (concurring opinion).

The Supreme Court of Alabama and several other courts have followed this view, known as the "contemplation of the parties" test.

We find the interpretive choice difficult, but for several reasons we conclude that the first interpretation ("commerce in fact") is more faithful to the statute than the second ("contemplation of the parties"). First, the "contemplation of the parties" interpretation, when viewed in terms of the statute's basic purpose, seems anomalous. That interpretation invites litigation about what was, or was not, "contemplated." Why would Congress intend a test that risks the very kind of costs and delay through litigation (about the circumstances of contract formation) that Congress wrote the Act to help the parties avoid?

Moreover, that interpretation too often would turn the validity of an arbitration clause on what, from the perspective of the statute's basic purpose, seems happenstance, namely, whether the parties happened to think to insert a reference to interstate commerce in the document or happened to mention it in an initial conversation. After all, parties to a sales contract with an arbitration clause might naturally think about the goods sold, or about arbitration, but why should they naturally think about an interstate commerce connection?

Further, that interpretation fits awkwardly with the rest of §2. That section, for example, permits parties to agree to submit to arbitration "an existing controversy arising out of" a contract made earlier. Why would Congress want to risk non-enforceability of this *later* arbitration agreement (even if fully connected with interstate commerce) simply because the parties did not properly "contemplate" (or write about) the interstate aspects of the earlier contract? The first interpretation, requiring only that the "transaction" *in fact* involve interstate commerce, avoids this anomaly, as it avoids the other anomalous effects growing out of the "contemplation of the parties" test.

Second, the statute's language permits the "commerce in fact" interpretation. . . .

Third, the basic practical argument underlying the "contemplation of the parties" test was, in Chief Judge Lumbard's words, the need to "be cautious in construing the act lest we excessively encroach on the powers which Congressional policy, if not the Constitution, would reserve to the states." The practical force of this argument has diminished in light of this Court's later holdings that the Act does displace state law to the contrary. See *Southland Corp. v. Keating.* . . .

The parties do not contest that the transaction in this case, in fact, involved interstate commerce. In addition to the multistate nature of Terminix and Allied-Bruce, the termite-treating and house-repairing material used by Allied-Bruce in its (allegedly inadequate) efforts to carry out the terms of the Plan, came from outside Alabama. Consequently, the judgment of the Supreme Court of Alabama is reversed, and the case is remanded for further proceedings not inconsistent with this opinion.

Justice O'CONNOR, concurring.

I agree with the Court's construction of §2 of the [FAA]. As applied in federal courts, the Court's interpretation comports fully with my understanding of congressional intent. A more restrictive definition of "evidencing" and "involving" would doubtless foster pre-arbitration litigation that would frustrate the very purpose of the statute. As applied in state courts, however, the effect of a broad formulation of §2 is more troublesome. The reading of §2 adopted today will displace many state statutes carefully calibrated to protect consumers, see, e.g., Mont. Code Ann. §27-5-114(2)(b) (1993) (refusing to enforce arbitration clauses in consumer contracts where the consideration is $5,000 or less), and state procedural requirements aimed at ensuring knowing and voluntary consent, see, e.g., S.C. Code Ann. §15-48-10(a) (Supp. 1993) (requiring that notice of arbitration provision be prominently placed on first page of contract). I have long adhered to the view, discussed below, that Congress designed the [FAA] to apply only in federal courts. But if we are to apply the Act in state courts, it makes little sense to read §2 differently in that context. In the end, my agreement with the Court's construction of §2 rests largely on the wisdom of maintaining a uniform standard.

I continue to believe that Congress never intended the [FAA] to apply in state courts, and that this Court has strayed far afield in giving the Act so broad a compass. . . . Yet, over the past decade, the Court has abandoned all pretense of ascertaining congressional intent with respect to the [FAA], building instead, case by case, an edifice of its own creation. I have no doubt that Congress could enact, in the first instance, a federal arbitration statute that displaces most state arbitration laws. But I also have no doubt that, in 1925, Congress enacted no such statute.

Were we writing on a clean slate, I would adhere to that view and affirm the Alabama court's decision. But, as the Court points out, more than 10 years have passed since *Southland*, several subsequent cases have built upon its reasoning, and parties have undoubtedly made contracts in reliance on the Court's interpretation of the Act in the interim. After reflection, I am persuaded by considerations of *stare decisis*, which we have said "have special force in the area of statutory interpretation," to acquiesce in today's judgment. Though wrong, *Southland* has not proved unworkable, and, as always, "Congress remains free to alter what we have done."

Today's decision caps this Court's effort to expand the [FAA]. Although each decision has built logically upon the decisions preceding it, the initial building block in *Southland* laid a faulty foundation. I acquiesce in today's judgment because there is no "special justification" to overrule *Southland*. It remains now for Congress to correct this interpretation if it wishes to preserve state autonomy in state courts.

NOTES AND QUESTIONS

19. Justice Breyer gives the FAA the broadest possible interpretation, holding that it can extend to any contracts involving matters "affecting" interstate commerce. How broad a scope is that? *See Wickard v. Filburn*, 317 U.S. 111 (1942) (giving an expansive interpretation to Commerce Clause); *but see United States v. Lopez*, 514 U.S. 549 (1995) (holding unconstitutional a federal statute prohibiting carrying of a gun within 1,000 feet of a school on grounds that it exceeded congressional authority under the Commerce Clause).

20. In *Citizen's Bank v. Alafabco, Inc.*, 539 U.S. 52 2037 (2003), the Court again construed the "commerce" requirement in the FAA broadly. There, residents of Alabama entered into debt-restructuring agreements providing for arbitration. Although all parties were Alabama residents, one of the parties had engaged in business throughout the southeastern United States using loans related to the agreements. The debt was secured by goods that contained out-of-state parts and raw materials. After *Allied-Bruce* and *Citizen's Bank*, what scope of operation is left for state arbitration statutes? What disputes can be viewed as involving matters that are purely intrastate?

In her concurring opinion, Justice O'Connor points out that the Court's broad interpretation of the FAA means that it will override statutory protections that have been enacted by state legislatures to protect their citizens from unknowing waiver of their rights by signing arbitration clauses. Consider the following case.

Doctor's Associates, Inc. v. Casarotto

517 U.S. 681 (1996)

Justice GINSBURG delivered the opinion of the Court.

This case concerns a standard form franchise agreement for the operation of a Subway sandwich shop in Montana. When a dispute arose between parties to the agreement, franchisee Paul Casarotto sued franchisor Doctor's Associates, Inc. (DAI), and DAI's Montana development agent, Nick Lombardi, in a Montana state court. DAI and Lombardi sought to stop the litigation pending arbitration pursuant to the arbitration clause set out on page nine of the franchise agreement.

The [FAA] declares written provisions for arbitration "valid, irrevocable, and enforceable, save upon such grounds as exist at law or in equity for the revocation of any contract." 9 U.S.C. §2. Montana law, however, declares an arbitration clause unenforceable unless "[n]otice that [the] contract is subject to arbitration" is "typed in underlined capital letters on the first page of the contract." Mont. Code Ann. §27-5-114(4) (1995). The question here presented is whether Montana's law is compatible with the federal Act. We hold that Montana's first-page notice requirement, which governs not "any contract," but specifically and solely contracts "subject to arbitration," conflicts with the FAA and is therefore displaced by the federal measure. . . .

Section 2 of the FAA provides that written arbitration agreements "shall be valid, irrevocable, and enforceable, save upon such grounds as exist at law or in equity for the revocation of *any* contract." 9 U.S.C. §2 (emphasis added). . . . [S]tate law may be applied "*if* that law arose to govern issues concerning the validity, revocability, and enforceability of contracts generally." Thus, generally applicable contract defenses, such as fraud, duress, or unconscionability, may be applied to invalidate arbitration agreements without contravening §2.

Courts may not, however, invalidate arbitration agreements under state laws applicable *only* to arbitration provisions. By enacting §2, we have several times said, Congress precluded States from singling out arbitration provisions for suspect status, requiring instead that such provisions be placed "upon the same footing as other contracts." Montana's §27-5-114(4) directly conflicts with §2 of the FAA because the State's law conditions the enforceability of arbitration agreements on compliance with a special notice requirement not applicable to contracts generally. The FAA thus displaces the Montana statute with respect to arbitration agreements covered by the Act. . . .

For the reasons stated, the judgment of the Supreme Court of Montana is *reversed*, and the case is remanded for further proceedings not inconsistent with this opinion.

NOTES AND QUESTIONS

21. Do you think decisions such as *Doctor's Associates* might create occasional tensions between state judges and federal judges, at least in states that have developed special protections for consumers with respect to arbitration clauses? Consider the specially concurring opinion of Justice Trieweiler in the decision of the Montana Supreme Court in *Casarotto v. Lombardi*, 268 Mont. 369, 382-385, 886 P.2d 931, 939-941 (1994):

   > To those federal judges who consider forced arbitration as the panacea for their "heavy case loads" and who consider the reluctance of state courts to buy into the arbitration program as a sign of intellectual inadequacy, I would like to explain a few things.
   >
   > In Montana, we are reasonably civilized and have a sophisticated system of justice which has evolved over time and which we continue to develop for the primary purpose of assuring fairness to those people who are subject to its authority. . . .
   >
   > What I would like the people in the federal judiciary, especially at the appellate level, to understand is that due to their misinterpretation of congressional intent when it enacted the [FAA], and due to their naive assumption that arbitration provisions and choice of law provisions are knowingly bargained for,

all of these procedural safeguards and substantive laws are easily avoided by any party with enough leverage to stick a choice of law and an arbitration provision in its pre-printed contract and require the party with inferior bargaining power to sign it. . . .

[I]f the [FAA] is to be interpreted as broadly as some of the decisions from our federal courts would suggest, then it presents a serious issue regarding separation of powers. What these interpretations do, in effect, is permit a few major corporations to draft contracts regarding their relationship with others that immunizes them from accountability under the laws of the states where they do business, and by the courts in those states.

These insidious erosions of state authority and the judicial process threaten to undermine the rule of law as we know it.

Nothing in our jurisprudence appears more intellectually detached from reality and arrogant than the lament of federal judges who see this system of imposed arbitration as "therapy for their crowded dockets." These decisions have perverted the purpose of the FAA from one to accomplish judicial neutrality, to one of open hostility to any legislative effort to assure that unsophisticated parties to contracts of adhesion at least understand the rights they are giving up.

22. Would the result in *Doctor's Associates* be different if the franchise agreement had provided that the agreement was to be governed by Montana law? *See Volt Info. Scis., Inc. v. Stanford*, 489 U.S. 468 (1989) (holding that where an arbitration agreement contained a choice-of-law clause providing that the contract was to be governed by the law of California, it was proper for a federal district judge to apply a California statute authorizing a stay of the arbitration proceeding pending resolution of related litigation between a party to the arbitration agreement and third parties not bound by it; even though such a state statute conflicts with the FAA, it is proper to apply state law where the parties have specified that state law controls). The majority in *Doctor's Associates* suggested that *Volt* is limited to state procedural rules regulating arbitration. The majority distinguished *Volt* as follows:

Volt involved an arbitration agreement that incorporated state procedural rules, one of which, on the facts of that case, called for arbitration to be stayed pending the resolution of a related judicial proceeding. The state rule examined in *Volt* determined only the efficient order of proceedings; it did not affect the enforceability of the arbitration agreement itself. . . . Applying [the Montana notice requirement], in contrast, would not enforce the arbitration clause in the contract between DAI and Casarotto; instead, Montana's first-page notice requirement would invalidate the clause. (517 U.S. at 688.)

23. What about the rights of state legislatures to alter application of the FAA by simply requiring that an agent cannot sign an arbitration agreement

for its principal unless that was expressly included in the power of attorney? For example, what if nursing home residents, through power of attorneys, sign home admission papers that include arbitration clauses without a sufficiently "clear statement" under such a state law? *See Kindred Nursing Centers Ltd. P'ship v. Clark*, 137 S. Ct. 1421 (2017) (holding that Kentucky's clear-statement rule regarding arbitration clauses in power of attorney documents disfavors arbitration agreements, and is therefore inconsistent with the FAA).

24. On January 1, 2020, a new law in California took effect to provide rights to consumers and employees facing arbitration. The law requires that the business must pay the initial fees or costs of arbitration where the employees or consumers are to arbitrate any claims related to their contracts or state/federal law. If the business doesn't pay fees and costs within 30 days of their due date, the business is in default and waives its right to compel arbitration. The consumer could then proceed in court or compel arbitration with the proviso that the business pay all reasonable attorneys' fees and costs related to the arbitration. The question is whether this will be preempted by the Federal Arbitration Act (FAA) where the arbitration emanates from a contract impacting interstate commerce.

In Chapters 7 and 8, we will return to the subject of enforcement of arbitration agreements with an emphasis on standardized contracts involving consumers and employees that raise special issues of fairness.

E. OTHER FORMS OF PRE-AWARD JUDICIAL SUPPORT OF ARBITRATION PROCEEDINGS

1. Judicial Appointment of Arbitrators

Where parties follow the common practice of incorporating standard arbitration procedures by reference in their agreement, such procedures normally include specific provisions setting forth an administrative procedure for the timely filling of vacancies on the arbitration tribunal and related procedural questions. *See, e.g.*, AAA Commercial Arbitration Rules R-20 "Vacancies" (amended and effective Oct. 1, 2013). Where, however, the parties neglect to incorporate such provisions by reference in their agreement, the death, incapacity, or resignation of an arbitrator during proceedings and prior to the rendition of an award may produce confusion and disagreement about the proper method of addressing the vacancy—and may even lead to a stalemate. In such circumstances, a party may seek judicial intervention under FAA Section 5, which states:

> If in the agreement provision be made for a method of naming or appointing an arbitrator or arbitrators or an umpire, such method shall be followed; but if no method be provided therein, or if a method be provided

and any party thereto shall fail to avail himself of such method, or if for any other reason there shall be a lapse in the naming of an arbitrator or arbitrators or umpire, or in filling a vacancy, then upon the application of either party to the controversy the court shall designate and appoint an arbitrator or arbitrators or umpire, as the case may require. . . .

Consider how this provision might be applied in the following scenario.

PROBLEM 2: COURT ASSISTANCE IN FILLING A VACANCY

A significant dispute arises under a contract for the chartering of a ship. The parties, Marine and Globe, have a contract that includes a provision calling for arbitration of disputes before a three-member panel consisting of one party-selected arbitrator nominated by each party and a third arbitrator selected jointly by the party arbitrators. During the course of arbitration hearings and prior to the making of an award, Globe's arbitrator dies. Neither the arbitration agreement in the Globe-Marine charterage contract nor the parties' submission to arbitration made any provision for the filling of vacancies on the panel. As the lawyer for Globe, you are concerned about what to do.

A. What options are open to you, and how specifically might a court, utilizing FAA Section 5, assist if you and Marine's counsel are unable to find a collaborative solution to this problem? Could a court, for example, direct the parties to essentially start the whole arbitration process over again? *See Nat'l Am. Ins. Co. v. Transamerica Occidental Life Ins. Co.*, 328 F.3d 462 (8th Cir. 2003) (holding a replacement arbitrator should be appointed instead of starting the proceedings over again after an arbitrator withdrew due to illness).

B. What is to prevent a party from having a party-appointed arbitrator resign late in the process to disrupt or delay an arbitration that does not seem to be going its way? *See Insurance Co. of N. Am v. Public Serv. Mut. Ins. Co.*, 609 F.3d 122 (2d Cir. 2010) (rule governing vacancies on arbitration tribunal caused by death of arbitrator did not apply in dealing with vacancy resulting from arbitrator's resignation).

---

2. *Judicial Enforcement of Arbitral Summonses and Subpoenas*

The FAA and most state arbitration statutes (aside from those based on the Revised Uniform Arbitration Act (RUAA), mentioned below) do not specifically address the subject of arbitration-related discovery. However, the FAA and corresponding state laws give arbitrators authority to issue summonses or subpoenas to parties or nonparties, and provide for their judicial enforcement. FAA Section 7, for example, states that arbitrators may "summon in writing any person to attend before them or any of them as a witness and in a proper case to bring with him or them any book, record, document, or paper which may be deemed material as evidence in the case." This language, with its reference to "attend[ing] before [one or more arbitrators]" fails to establish a clear predicate for ordering a party to appear at a deposition. Indeed, the section goes on to require subpoenas issued by arbitrators to be directed and served "in the same manner as subpoenas to appear and testify before the court." The RUAA, which is now law in a number of states, includes provisions that directly address these and other concerns through specific provisions for arbitrator-supervised discovery, including depositions.*

The FAA's silence respecting an arbitrator's power to compel testimony or production of documents *prior to an arbitration hearing* has produced conflicting judicial interpretations and rulings, although the issue is attenuated to some extent by the increasing attention given by arbitration procedural rules to the issue. For example, Rule L-3(f) (Management of Proceedings) of the Large Complex Commercial Disputes Procedures of the AAA Commercial Arbitration Rules (2013) provides that "in exceptional cases, at the discretion of the arbitrator, upon good cause shown and consistent with the expedited nature of arbitration, the arbitrator may order depositions to obtain the testimony of a person who may possess information determined by the arbitrator to be relevant and material to the outcome of the case."

The arbitration rules incorporated in parties' contracts are irrelevant, however, with respect to nonparty witnesses and documents. This is where the split of authority on Section 7 of the FAA has great import. Again, arbitrators need statutory authority to order discovery from nonparties to the arbitration.

This question is especially important in light of the growing use of virtual hearings. In *Managed Care Advisory Group, LLC v. CIGNA Healthcare, Inc.*, 939 F.3d 1145, 1160 (11th Cir. 2019), the Court of Appeals held that the district court did not have the authority to force nonparties to the arbitration to comply with the summons and provide testimony that would be transmitted via video conference. The court relied on a literal meaning of Section 7 of the FAA in finding that testimony via video does not comport with the statute. The court thus held that the arbitrator wasn't technically compelling their "attendance before" the arbitrator. Therefore, there was not authority for the district court to order attendance via video, cutting off access to discovery from third parties unless there is an in-person hearing.

This highlights a circuit split: The Second, Third, Fourth, and Ninth Circuits all have cases holding that Section 7 does not provide for pre-hearing discovery from nonparties to the arbitration agreement (they can only order them to produce documents if they are called as a witness at a hearing). *See Life Receivables Tr. v. Syndicate 102 at Lloyds of London*, 549 F.3d 210, 216 (2d Cir. 2008); *Hay Grp., Inc. v. E.B.S. Acquisitions Corp.*, 360 F.3d 404, 407 (3d Cir. 2004); *COMSAT Corp. v. Nat'l Sci. Found.*, 190 F.3d 269, 275-276 (4th Cir. 1999) (allowing an exception upon a showing of "special need or hardship"); and *CVS Health Corp. v. Vividus, LLC*, 878 F.3d 703, 708 (9th Cir. 2017). The Sixth and Eighth Circuits have held that there is implicit arbitral power to authorize subpoenas for pre-hearing discovery from third parties (looking at the documents without the witness needing to be present at a hearing). *See Am. Fed. of Television and Radio Artists, AFL-CIO v. WJBK-TV (New World Comm. of Detroit, Inc.)*, 164 F.3d 1004, 1109 (6th Cir. 1999); and *In re Sec. Life Ins. Co. of Am.*, 228 F.3d 865, 870-871 (8th Cir. 2000).

---

* Available at http://www.uniformlaws.org/Act.aspx?title=Arbitration%20Act%20 (2000), Section 17.

The above cases from the Second, Third, Fourth and Ninth Circuits read Section 7 of the FAA as saying that nonparty document disclosure is only allowed when the nonparty is at a hearing before the arbitrator. Although they don't address the issue of video or teleconferencing directly, they do seem to emphasize the importance of the witnesses being in the physical presence of the arbitrators. However, with the growth of online hearings in the wake of Covid-19, it is unclear whether the staunch view on Section 7 will remain. This creates a real issue for those facing arbitral hearings online in cases where they need discovery from third parties. Moreover, there is support for a "special need" exception, allowing a court to order pre-hearing discovery in cases such as where the evidence sought was on a ship that was scheduled to leave U.S. waters. *In re Deiulemar Compagnia Di Navigazione S.p.A.*, 198 F.3d 473 (4th Cir. 1999).

QUESTIONS

25. You are representing a client in arbitration and intend to conduct depositions of several witnesses. You are concerned that you may need judicial help to compel their attendance by enforcing arbitrator subpoenas. If you have a choice of going to federal court and applying for court assistance under FAA Section 5 or going to a state court and utilizing state arbitration law, which would you prefer? Why? (You may assume for the sake of this question that the state is one of those jurisdictions that adopted the RUAA.)

26. You are representing a client in a case in which you will need to subpoena witnesses who are not parties to the arbitration. You know that this evidence is crucial, and worry that the witness will not voluntarily appear. At the same time, you learn that it will be very costly for you and your client to travel to the hearing location, and your client is therefore urging that the arbitration take place online. The client also is a single parent and does not want to be away from home. What considerations come into play in deciding whether to proceed with a virtual hearing? Does discovery matter in this decision?

---

3.   Emergency Relief in Arbitration

Historically, although arbitral institutions provided relatively quick and efficient resolution of disputes, parties relied on the courts for emergency relief (including preliminary injunctions) rather than the arbitrators themselves. This was considered to be one of arbitration's shortcomings, particularly for intellectual property disputes.[13]

In response, some arbitral institutions created rules and procedures for emergency measures, including the appointment of an emergency arbitrator. For example, Rule 38 of the AAA Commercial Arbitration Rules (2013) (which provides emergency measures of protection) is applicable to any arbitration for which the underlying contract was entered into on or after October 1, 2013, without the necessity of a specific agreement to those measures (as was previously required). The AAA emergency measures of protection allow for the appointment of an emergency arbitrator within one business day of the AAA's receipt of a request for emergency relief.

In *Yahoo! Inc. v. Microsoft Corp.*, 983 F. Supp. 2d 310 (S.D.N.Y. 2013), a dispute between Microsoft and Yahoo arose from an agreement to merge their search capabilities internationally to better compete with Google, Inc. The merger was completed in all jurisdictions except for Taiwan and Hong Kong, where technical problems delayed the transfer of Yahoo's search capabilities and ad services to Bing. The last agreed deadline for completing the merger in those two markets was the end of October 2013. However, on September 20, 2013, Yahoo informed Microsoft that it would delay completion of its migration to Bing until "early 2014." This concerned Microsoft, as it had commitments to the Bing Ads platform. On the same day, Microsoft declared that Yahoo was in breach of the agreement; Microsoft initiated an emergency arbitration on September 26, 2013, under the AAA's emergency measures of protection.

The emergency arbitrator found that Yahoo had breached the agreement and that the breach justified emergency measures; it was critical that the transition proceed without delay "because advertiser orders and preferences change over time" — which could result in irreparable harm. The emergency arbitrator ordered injunctive relief, that Yahoo be "restrained and enjoined from continuing any pause in transitioning," and "commanded [Yahoo] to use all efforts" to complete the Taiwan transition by October 28, 2013 and the Hong Kong transition by November 11, 2013. The litigation over the arbitral award was equally expedient, with the award being confirmed only six days after Yahoo's motion to vacate was filed. The entire process of emergency arbitration and judicial confirmation was completed in just 25 days.

4. *Other Pre-Award Judicial Intervention*

Aside from the specific ways set forth in the FAA and state arbitration statutes, should parties be able to seek the intervention of courts to address issues that arise during the arbitration process? For example, should parties be able to go to court to challenge a procedural ruling by an arbitrator prior to the rendering of an award, or try to have an arbitrator replaced by a court in the middle of hearings because the arbitrator made prejudicial remarks? Why do you suppose courts nearly always resist such requests?

Consider the following case: In *Gold v. Maurer*, 251 F. Supp. 3d 127 (D.D.C. 2017), the plaintiffs sought a temporary restraining order against the defendant to stop him from repeating defamatory statements at a business meeting pending arbitration. The plaintiffs said this order was necessary because they could not appoint an arbitrator for at least a month. The court nonetheless denied the motion, noting that the plaintiffs had not attempted to seek an emergency arbitrator under AAA Rule 38, noted above, and this was not an otherwise extreme situation where relief was clearly necessary.

Endnotes

1. Stipanowich, Thomas J. (2001) *Contracts Symposium: Contract and Conflict Management,* 2001 Wis. L. Rev. 831.

2. Resnik, Judith. (1995) *Beyond* Mastrobuono: *Arbitrator's Guide to Arbitration, Employment Disputes, Punitive Damages, and the Implications of the Civil Rights Act of 1991.*

3. Kravitz, Mark & Dunham, Edward W. (1996) *Compelling Arbitration,* 23 Litig. 34.

4. Rau, Alan S. (2005) *Provisional Relief in Arbitration: How Things Stand in the United States,* 22 J. Int'l Arb. 1.

5. Stipanowich, Thomas J. (2007) *The Arbitration Penumbra: Arbitration Law and the Rapidly Changing Landscape of Dispute Resolution,* 8 Nev. L.J.; Schmitz, Amy J. (2006) *Confronting ADR Agreements' Contract/No-Contract Conundrum with Good Faith,* 56 DePaul L. Rev. 55.

6. *See, e.g., AMF, Inc. v. Brunswick Corp.,* 621 F. Supp. 456, 460 (E.D.N.Y. 1985), discussed in Stipanowich, Thomas J., *supra* note 5, at 427.

7. Offenkrantz, Ronald. (1997) *Arbitrating Rico: Ten Years After* Mcmahon, 1997 Colum. Bus. L. Rev. 1.

8. Resnik, Judith, *supra* note 2.

9. Korzun, Vera. (2015) *Arbitrating Antitrust Claims: From Suspicion to Trust,* 48 N.Y.U. J. Int'l L. & Pol. 867 (outlining the "remarkable but unnoticed transformation" of the national courts of most developed economies accepting (even mandating) adjudication of antitrust claims by private international arbitral tribunals).

10. Kloppenberg, Lisa. (2001) *Playing It Safe;* Noonan, John. (2002) *Narrowing the Nation's Power: The Supreme Court Sides with the States.*

11. Carrington, Paul D. & Haagen, Paul H. (1996) *Contract and Jurisdiction,* 1996 Sup. Ct. Rev. 331-402.

12. This is a complicated area of constitutional and statutory law; if these issues intrigue you, we recommend *Constitutional Law* by Erwin Chemerinsky (4th ed. 2011).

13. Landsman, Kim J. (2013) *Microsoft Case Is Great Example of Emergency Arbitration,* Law360.

CHAPTER 6

JUDICIAL ENFORCEMENT
OF ARBITRATION
AWARDS

A. *OVERVIEW OF STANDARDS FOR CONFIRMATION, VACATION, AND MODIFICATION UNDER THE FAA*

If a claim or controversy proceeds to arbitration and the arbitrators render an award, one likely result is that the parties will comply with the award and no judicial action will be necessary or appropriate. On the other hand, a party may seek to confirm the award, thereby converting it into a judgment of the court. The FAA provides:

§9. Award of arbitrators; confirmation; jurisdiction; procedure

If the parties in their agreement have agreed that a judgment of the court shall be entered upon the award made pursuant to the arbitration, and shall specify the court, then at any time within one year after the award is made any party to the arbitration may apply to the court so specified for an order confirming the award, and thereupon the court must grant such an order unless the award is vacated, modified, or corrected as prescribed in sections 10 and 11 of this title. If no court is specified in the agreement of the parties, then such application may be made to the United States court in and for the district within which such award was made. . . .

Confirmation of an award may be needed to harness the coercive authority of the court to locate and move against funds or property of a party against whom a monetary award was rendered.

It is also possible that one or both parties will seek a judicial order vacating (that is, overturning or setting aside) all or some part of the award. In addition or in the alternative, a motion might be made to the court to modify or correct the award. A careful study of Sections 10 and 11 of the FAA helps one to appreciate the very narrow scope of judicial scrutiny contemplated by arbitration statutes.

§10. Same; vacation; grounds; rehearing

(a) In any of the following cases the United States court in and for the district wherein the award was made may make an order vacating the award upon the application of any party to the arbitration—

(1) where the award was procured by corruption, fraud, or undue means;

(2) where there was evident partiality or corruption in the arbitrators, or either of them;

(3) where the arbitrators were guilty of misconduct in refusing to postpone the hearing, upon sufficient cause shown, or in refusing to hear evidence pertinent and material to the controversy; or of any other misbehavior by which the rights of any party have been prejudiced; or

(4) where the arbitrators exceeded their powers, or so imperfectly executed them that a mutual, final, and definite award upon the subject matter submitted was not made.

(b) If an award is vacated and the time within which the agreement required the award to be made has not expired, the court may, in its discretion, direct a rehearing by the arbitrators.

(c) The United States district court for the district wherein an award was made that was issued pursuant to section 580 of title 5 may make an order vacating the award upon the application of a person, other than a party to the arbitration, who is adversely affected or aggrieved by the award, if the use of arbitration or the award is clearly inconsistent with the factors set forth in section 572 of title 5.

§11. Same; modification or correction; grounds; order

In either of the following cases the United States court in and for the district wherein the award was made may make an order modifying or correcting the award upon the application of any party to the arbitration—

(a) Where there was an evident material miscalculation of figures or an evident material mistake in the description of any person, thing, or property referred to in the award.

(b) Where the arbitrators have awarded upon a matter not submitted to them, unless it is a matter not affecting the merits of the decision upon the matter submitted.

(c) Where the award is imperfect in matter of form not affecting the merits of the controversy.

The order may modify and correct the award, so as to effect the intent thereof and promote justice between the parties.

Both of the foregoing sections establish fairly clear boundaries for judicial action. Notable by its absence is any reference to judicial vacation or correction based upon arbitrator errors of law or fact, save clerical or mathematical mistakes evident on the face of the award.

In the following pages, we take a closer look at court decisions addressing various grounds for vacatur under FAA Section 10 or more-or-less parallel provisions of state arbitration law. Note that although the language of Section 10 clearly indicates it is a procedural rule applicable to federal courts, state courts may also end up applying the FAA's vacatur provisions if the parties' contract so requires. Courts applying the FAA have tended to construe these grounds for vacatur narrowly, reinforcing the finality of arbitral awards. They are generally much more deferential to arbitral awards and less likely to overturn them than the judgment of a lower court. Appellate courts typically review trial courts' findings on legal issues *de novo*, but they overturn trial courts' factual findings only if they are clearly erroneous and revise procedural choices only if the lower court abused its discretion. When it comes to arbitration awards, the deference is even greater, and extends to legal as well as factual determinations. As one prominent jurist summarized:

> [T]he question for decision by a federal court asked to set aside an arbitration award . . . is not whether the arbitrator or arbitrators erred in interpreting the contract; it is not whether they clearly erred in interpreting the contract; it is not whether they grossly erred in interpreting the contract; it is whether they interpreted the contract.

Hill v. Norfolk & W. Ry. Co., 814 F.2d 1192, 1194 (7th Cir. 1987) (Hon. Richard Posner). Thus, even if a judge would have reached a different conclusion on the merits, she is not supposed to substitute her judgment for that of the arbitrator(s).

Moreover, as a practical matter, a court is hampered in reviewing the merits of an arbitrator's ruling because written reasoning to support the decision is sometimes withheld, making it quite difficult to review an arbitrator's rulings pertaining to the making of the agreement to arbitrate or the merits of the underlying dispute. In international commercial arbitration and labor relations arbitration, however, arbitrators typically do provide reasoning to support their decisions, and the practice has probably become the norm in large commercial cases. While these rulings are not used as precedent in the same fashion as judicial precedent, they nevertheless provide a basis for parties to familiarize themselves with an arbitrator's work and give a court more assurance that the award was supported by actual contractual interpretation.

For these reasons, motions to vacate awards under the FAA are seldom successful, although grounds for vacatur vary considerably by degree of use and relative likelihood of success. On the other hand, vacatur motions before state courts applying state arbitration law (which may be less deferential to arbitrators and their awards) may have a higher likelihood of success than comparable motions in federal courts. A survey by John Burritt McArthur of court decisions addressing motions to vacate U.S. arbitration awards using the West keynote system for the years 2010-2017 indicates that motions based on allegations that arbitrators "exceeded their powers" were by far the most common (387 cases). Two other grounds not expressly mentioned in the FAA or most state arbitration statutes, "manifest disregard of the law" (211 cases) and "public policy" bases (158 cases), were the second and third most common grounds. Less frequent were motions based on arbitrators' "evident partiality" (127 cases), arbitrator misconduct (58 cases), or misconduct by a party (19 cases). Overall, motions based on arbitrators exceeding powers also tend to be the most likely to succeed (17.6% of motions granted), while motions based on manifest disregard are rarely successful (2.4%).

Regardless of the nature of the motion to vacate, the likelihood of vacatur in state courts is much higher; for motions based on allegations that arbitrators exceeded their powers, for example, the vacatur rate was 7.3 percent in federal courts and 23.2 percent in state courts.[1] Of course, there is also great variation among states in rate of vacatur. The following sections explore in more detail various grounds for vacatur of awards and include exemplary court decisions under the FAA or state law. Most of these grounds are expressly enumerated in arbitration statutes, but some, such as manifest disregard of the law or public policy, have been developed in case law or through other statutes.

B.   WAS THE AWARD PROCURED BY CORRUPTION, FRAUD, OR UNDUE MEANS?

Awards are seldom vacated on the basis of "corruption, fraud, or undue means," but there are notable exceptions. In one Eleventh Circuit case, an arbitral award was vacated under the FAA on the basis that an expert witness whose testimony influenced the arbitral award had committed perjury. The circumstances were unusual in that there was very clear evidence of perjury with respect to a central issue in the case, and the aggrieved party was not in a position to discover the evidence until after the arbitration proceedings ended. *Bonar v. Dean Witter Reynolds, Inc.*, 835 F.2d 1378 (11th Cir. 1988). Interestingly, the court in *Bonar* did not require "the movant to establish that the result of the proceedings would have been different had the fraud not occurred." However, in a decision four years later, the U.S. Court of Appeals for the Ninth Circuit held that plaintiffs are required to show that the fraud was material to the outcome of the arbitration. *See A.G. Edwards & Sons*, 967 F.2d 1401, 1403 (9th Cir. 1992). *See also Odeon Capital Group LLC v. Ackerman*, 864 F.3d 191 (2d Cir. 2017) (refusing to vacate an arbitration award based on Ackerman's perjury during the arbitration because it was not material to the award).

In most cases where claims of perjury or improper evidence are raised after arbitrators have rendered an award, courts are very reluctant to allow parties to reopen the case. For example, the court in *Hoolahan v. IBC Adv. Alloys Corp.*, 947 F.3d 101 (1st Cir. 2020), refused to vacate an award under "undue means" based on "ethically improper" statements of Hoolahan's lawyer. IBC alleged that Hoolahan's lawyer improperly called IBC seeking evidence without disclosing his representation of Hoolahan. The court nonetheless denied the vacatur motion, emphasizing that there is a high bar for overturning an arbitration award based on undue means. Similarly, the court in *MCI Constructors, LLC v. City of Greensboro*, 610 F.3d 849 (4th Cir. 2010), refused to vacate an arbitral award based on the City's alleged misrepresentation of facts and other misconduct. The Fourth Circuit held that to vacate an award for undue means, the party must show that the facts constituting fraud or undue means were (1) not discoverable upon the exercise of due diligence prior to the arbitration, (2) materially related to an issue in the arbitration, and (3) established by clear and convincing evidence. The court also noted that the scope of review for an arbitral award is extremely narrow because making it otherwise would frustrate the purposes of arbitration (avoiding expense and delay).

C.   WAS THERE EVIDENT PARTIALITY OR CORRUPTION IN THE ARBITRATORS?

In Chapter 3, we examined requirements for arbitrator disclosure of potential conflicts of interest and other facts that might raise questions regarding the independence and impartiality of arbitrators, as well as related procedures for challenge to and removal of arbitrators, under arbitration rules and ethical standards. Concerns regarding arbitrator partiality and bias may also be addressed by courts reviewing motions to vacate awards under the FAA and state arbitration statutes. As the Second

Circuit stated, "Evident partiality within the meaning of 9 U.S.C. §10 will be found where a reasonable person would have to conclude that an arbitrator was partial to one party to the arbitration." *Morelite Const. Corp. v. New York City Dist. Council Carpenters Ben. Funds*, 748 F.2d 79, 82 (2d Cir. 1984). In light of strong policies supporting the finality of arbitration awards, however, courts tend to be hesitant to allow parties who are disappointed by an award to use a claim of bias or partiality as a way to undermine the finality of arbitration. It is unusual to find decisions in which the statements or acts of arbitrators during arbitration demonstrate actual partiality or bias.

On the other hand, motions to vacate an arbitration award are often based on an arbitrator's failure to disclose actual or perceived conflicts of interest. In the seminal decision in *Commonwealth Coatings Corp. v. Continental Casualty Co.*, 393 U.S. 145 (1968), the Supreme Court established that an arbitrator's failure to disclose a business relationship with one of the parties was sufficient to support judicial vacation of an arbitration award on the ground of "evident partiality" under Section 10 of the FAA. The case involved an arbitration tribunal made up of two arbitrators chosen by each of the parties and a third "neutral" arbitrator who had previously had a business relationship with one of the parties to the arbitration. The neutral arbitrator voted with the panel for an award in favor of the party with whom he had done business. Thereafter, the party that lost the arbitration challenged the award, claiming that the failure of the arbitrator to disclose his significant business relationship with the winning party amounted to "evident partiality" under 9 U.S.C. §10, warranting vacatur of the award. A majority of the Court reached the conclusion that vacatur was warranted even though there was no proof of actual bias or partiality on the part of the arbitrator and no proof that the undisclosed connection had any direct impact on the deliberations leading to the award. The mere fact that the relationship had not been disclosed on a timely basis was sufficient to warrant the finding of "evident partiality" and to strike down the award.

Justice Black, writing for a four-member plurality, offered the following rationale for the holding:

> It is true that arbitrators cannot sever all their ties with the business world, since they are not expected to get all their income from their work deciding cases, but we should, if anything, be even more scrupulous to safeguard the impartiality of arbitrators than judges, since the former have completely free rein to decide the law as well as the facts and are not subject to appellate review. We can perceive no way in which the effectiveness of the arbitration process will be hampered by the simple requirement that arbitrators disclose to the parties any dealings that might create an impression of possible bias.

Justice White and Justice Marshall joined in the holding, but Justice White's concurring opinion arguably reflects a more restrained view of what kinds of undisclosed relationships may justify vacatur of a subsequent award:

> [A]rbitrators are not automatically disqualified by a business relationship with the parties before them if both parties are informed of the relationship in advance, or if they are unaware of the facts but the relationship is trivial. I see no reason automatically to disqualify the best informed and most capable potential arbitrators.

The arbitration process functions best when an amicable and trusting atmosphere is preserved and there is voluntary compliance with the decree, without need for judicial enforcement. This end is best served by establishing an atmosphere of frankness at the outset, through disclosure by the arbitrator of any financial transactions which he has had or is negotiating with either of the parties. In many cases the arbitrator might believe the business relationship to be so insubstantial that to make a point of revealing it would suggest he is indeed easily swayed, and perhaps a partisan of that party. But if the law requires the disclosure, no such imputation can arise. And it is far better that the relationship be disclosed at the outset, when the parties are free to reject the arbitrator or accept him with knowledge of the relationship and continuing faith in his objectivity, than to have the relationship come to light after the arbitration, when a suspicious or disgruntled party can seize on it as a pretext for invalidating the award. The judiciary should minimize its role in arbitration as judge of the arbitrator's impartiality. That role is best consigned to the parties, who are the architects of their own arbitration process, and are far better informed of the prevailing ethical standards and reputations within their business.

Since the Court's decision in *Commonwealth Coatings*, alleged "evident partiality" based on arbitrator nondisclosure has become one of the most common grounds for a motion to vacate an arbitration award. Yet, despite the outcome in *Commonwealth Coatings*, relatively few court decisions have overturned awards on the basis of undisclosed relationships or facts. The McArthur survey of West keynoted cases from 2010-2017 indicated that only 11.0 percent of motions to vacate for evident partiality were granted (although there was a significant disparity between federal courts (3.0% of motions granted) and state courts (20.0% granted)).[2] As explained in the following decision, the difference of perspective reflected in the Black and White opinions in *Commonwealth Coatings* led to variations in the rigor with which courts police undisclosed relationships. However, the Fifth Circuit majority's stance in *Positive Software* exemplifies the strong trend of decisions under the FAA.

Positive Software Solutions, Inc. v. New Century Mortgage Corp.

476 F.3d 278 (5th Cir. 2007)

Appeal from the United States District Court for the Northern District Texas.
. . .

JONES, Chief Judge, joined by JOLLY, HIGGINBOTHAM, DAVIS, SMITH, BARKSDALE, DEMOSS, CLEMENT, PRADO and OWEN, Circuit Judges:

The court reconsidered this case en banc in order to determine whether an arbitration award must be vacated for "evident partiality," 9 U.S.C. §10(a)(2), where an arbitrator failed to disclose a prior professional association with a member of one of the law firms that engaged him. We conclude that the [FAA] does not mandate the extreme remedy of vacatur for nondisclosure of a trivial past association, and we reverse the district court's contrary judgment, but it is necessary to remand for consideration of appellee's other objections to the arbitral award. . . .

[New Century Mortgage Corporation ("New Century") licensed a software program from Positive Software Solutions, Inc. ("Positive Software") in 2001. Later, Positive Software alleged that New Century copied the program in violation of the parties' contract and applicable copyright law. Positive Software sued New Century in the Northern District of Texas alleging numerous causes of action. The district court later submitted the matter to arbitration under AAA rules as provided for in the parties' contract.]

[T]he AAA provided the parties with a list of potential arbitrators and asked the parties to rank the candidates. After reviewing biographical information, the parties selected Peter Shurn to arbitrate the case. . . . The AAA contacted Shurn about serving as an arbitrator, and he agreed, after stating that he had nothing to disclose regarding past relationships with either party or their counsel.

After a seven-day hearing, Shurn issued an eighty-six page written ruling, concluding that New Century did not infringe Positive Software's copyrights, did not misappropriate trade secrets, did not breach the contract, and did not defraud or conspire against Positive Software. He ordered that Positive Software take nothing on its claims and granted New Century $11,500 on its counterclaims and $1.5 million in attorney's fees.

Upon losing the arbitration, Positive Software conducted a detailed investigation of Shurn's background. It discovered that several years earlier, Shurn and his former law firm, Arnold, White, & Durkee ("Arnold White"), had represented the same party as New Century's counsel, Susman Godfrey, L.L.P., in a patent litigation between Intel Corporation and Cyrix Corporation ("the Intel litigation"). One of Susman Godfrey's attorneys in the New Century arbitration, Ophelia Camiña, had been involved in the Intel litigation.

The Intel litigation involved six different lawsuits in the early 1990s. Intel was represented by seven law firms and at least thirty-four lawyers, including Shurn and Camiña. The dispute involved none of the parties to the arbitration. Camiña participated in representing Intel in three of the lawsuits from August 1991 until July 1992, although her name remained on the pleadings in one of the cases until June 1993. In September 1992, Shurn, along with twelve other Arnold White attorneys, entered an appearance in two of the three cases on which Camiña worked. Although their names appeared together on pleadings, Shurn and Camiña never attended or participated in any meetings, telephone calls, hearings, depositions, or trials together.

Positive Software filed a motion to vacate the arbitration award, alleging [among other things that] . . . despite the lack of contact between Shurn and Camiña, Shurn had been biased, as evidenced by his failure to disclose his past connection to Camiña. In September 2004, the district court granted Positive Software's motion and vacated the award, finding that Shurn failed to disclose "a significant prior relationship with New Century's counsel," thus creating an appearance of partiality requiring vacatur. . . . New Century appealed, and a panel of this court affirmed the district court's vacatur on the ground that the prior relationship "might have conveyed an impression of possible partiality to a reasonable person." . . . Neither the district court nor the appellate panel found that Shurn was actually biased toward New Century. This court granted New Century's petition for rehearing en banc.

DISCUSSION

To assure that arbitration serves as an efficient and cost-effective alternative to litigation, and to hold parties to their agreements to arbitrate, the FAA narrowly restricts judicial review of arbitrators' awards. The ground of vacatur alleged here is that "there was evident partiality" in the arbitrator. . . . The meaning of evident partiality is discernible definitionally and as construed by the Supreme Court and a number of our sister circuits.

On its face, "evident partiality" conveys a stern standard. Partiality means bias, while "evident" is defined as "clear to the vision or understanding" and is synonymous with manifest, obvious, and apparent. *Webster's Ninth New Collegiate Dictionary* 430 (1985). The statutory language, with which we always begin, seems to require upholding arbitral awards unless bias was clearly evident in the decision makers.

The panel decision here disagreed with the straightforward interpretation, however, and concluded that, in "a nondisclosure case in which the parties chose the arbitrator," the "arbitrator selected by the parties displays evident partiality by the very failure to disclose facts that might create a reasonable impression of the arbitrator's partiality." . . . The panel acknowledged a lack of any actual bias in this award even as it substituted a reasonable impression of partiality standard for "evident" partiality in cases of an arbitrator's nondisclosure to the parties. The panel believed this different standard to be required by the Supreme Court's decision in *Commonwealth Coatings Corp. v. Continental Cas. Co.* . . .

How *Commonwealth Coatings* guides this court is a critical issue. Reasonable minds can agree that *Commonwealth Coatings*, like many plurality-plus Supreme Court decisions, is not pellucid. Justice Black delivered the opinion of the Court and imposed "the simple requirement that arbitrators disclose to the parties any dealings that might create an impression of possible bias." . . . He noted that, while arbitrators are not expected to sever all ties with the business world, courts must be scrupulous in safeguarding the impartiality of arbitrators, who are given the ability to decide both the facts and the law and whose decisions are not subject to appellate review. . . . Thus, arbitrators "not only must be unbiased but also must avoid even the appearance of bias," . . . in order to maintain confidence in the arbitration system.

Justice White, the fifth vote in the case, together with Justice Marshall, purported to be "glad to join" Justice Black's opinion, but he wrote to make "additional remarks." . . . Justice White emphasized that "[t]he Court does not decide today that arbitrators are to be held to the standards of judicial decorum of Article III judges, or indeed of any judges." . . . Indeed, Justice White wrote that arbitrators are not "automatically disqualified by a business relationship with the parties before them if . . . [the parties] are unaware of the facts but the relationship is trivial." . . . While supporting a policy of disclosure by arbitrators to enhance the selection process, Justice White also concluded, in a practical vein, that an arbitrator "cannot be expected to provide the parties with his complete and unexpurgated business biography." . . . His opinion fully envisions upholding awards when arbitrators fail to disclose insubstantial relationships. . . .

A majority of circuit courts have concluded that Justice White's opinion did not lend majority status to the plurality opinion. . . . While these courts' interpretations of *Commonwealth Coatings* may differ in particulars, they all agree that nondisclosure alone does not require vacatur of an arbitral award for evident partiality. An arbitrator's failure to disclose must involve a significant compromising connection to the parties.

This court's prior case law is also consistent with a narrow reading of *Commonwealth Coatings*. In *Bernstein Seawell & Kove v. Bosarge*, 813 F.2d 726 (5th Cir. 1987), the losing party in the arbitration challenged the award because of the alleged evident partiality of one of the arbitrators. The arbitrator owned a fractional share of the disputed property and had received commissions on the sale of certain interests. The court held the party had waived his objection to the composition of the panel. Nevertheless, "[e]ven assuming no waiver," he had not produced evidence of evident partiality, . . . because "[t]he appearance of impropriety, standing alone, is insufficient." . . . The court also noted that "[e]vident partiality means more than a mere appearance of bias." . . .

Only the Ninth Circuit has interpreted *Commonwealth Coatings*, as the panel majority did, to de-emphasize Justice White's narrowing language. See *Schmitz v. Zilveti*, 20 F.3d 1043 (9th Cir. 1994). In *Schmitz*, the court criticized case law suggesting "that an impression of bias is sufficient while an appearance [of bias] is not." . . . *Commonwealth Coatings*, it held, does not merit such a "hairline distinction." . . .

As we have concluded, the better interpretation of *Commonwealth Coatings* is that which reads Justice White's opinion holistically. The resulting standard is that in nondisclosure cases, an award may not be vacated because of a trivial or insubstantial prior relationship between the arbitrator and the parties to the proceeding. The "reasonable impression of bias" standard is thus interpreted practically rather than with utmost rigor.

According to this interpretation of *Commonwealth Coatings*, the outcome of this case is clear: Shurn's failure to disclose a trivial former business relationship does not require vacatur of the award. The essential charge of bias is that the arbitrator, Peter Shurn, worked on the same litigation as did Ophelia Camiña, counsel for one of the parties. They represented Intel in protracted patent litigation that lasted from 1990 to 1996. Camiña and Shurn each signed the same ten pleadings, but they never met or spoke to each other before the arbitration. They were two of thirty-four lawyers, and from two of seven firms, that represented Intel during the lawsuit, which ended at least seven years before the instant arbitration.

No case we have discovered in research or briefs has come close to vacating an arbitration award for nondisclosure of such a slender connection between the arbitrator and a party's counsel. In fact, courts have refused vacatur where the undisclosed connections are much stronger. . . .

The relationship in this case pales in comparison to those in which courts have granted vacatur. See, e.g., *Commonwealth Coatings*, 393 U.S. at 146, 89 S. Ct. at 338 (business relationship between arbitrator and party was "repeated and significant"; the party to the arbitration was one of the arbitrator's "regular customers"; "the relationship even went so far as to include the rendering of services on the very projects involved in this lawsuit"); *Olson v. Merrill Lynch, Pierce, Fenner & Smith, Inc.*, 51 F.3d 157, 159 (8th Cir. 1995) (arbitrator was a high-ranking officer in a company that had a substantial ongoing business relationship with one of the parties); *Schmitz*, 20 F.3d at 1044 (arbitrator's law firm represented parent company of a party for decades, including within two years of the arbitration); *Morelite Constr. Corp. v. New York City Dist. Council Carpenters Benefit Funds*, 748 F.2d 79, 83 n. 3 (2d Cir. 1984) (arbitrator's father was General President of the union involved in the arbitrated dispute).

Finally, even if Justice White's "joinder" is not read as a limitation on Justice Black's opinion in *Commonwealth Coatings*, and the controlling opinion emphatically requires arbitrators to "disclose to the parties any dealings that might create an impression of possible bias," . . . we cannot find the standard breached in this case. The facts of *Commonwealth Coatings* are easily distinguishable. In *Commonwealth Coatings*, the arbitrator and a party had a "repeated and significant" business relationship. . . . The relationship involved fees of about $12,000 paid to the arbitrator by the party, extended over a period of four or five years, ended only one year before the arbitration, and even included the rendering of services on the very projects involved in the arbitration before him. . . . Such a relationship bears little resemblance to the tangential, limited, and stale contacts between Shurn and Camiña. Nothing in *Commonwealth Coatings* requires vacatur for the undisclosed relationship in this case.

CONCLUSION

Awarding vacatur in situations such as this would seriously jeopardize the finality of arbitration. Just as happened here, losing parties would have an incentive to conduct intensive, after-the-fact investigations to discover the most trivial of relationships, most of which they likely would not have objected to if disclosure had been made. Expensive satellite litigation over nondisclosure of an arbitrator's "complete and unexpurgated business biography" will proliferate. Ironically, the "mere appearance" standard would make it easier for a losing party to challenge an arbitration award for nondisclosure than for actual bias.

Moreover, requiring vacatur based on a mere appearance of bias for nondisclosure would hold arbitrators to a higher ethical standard than federal Article III judges. In his concurrence, Justice White noted that the Court did not decide whether "arbitrators are to be held to the standards of judicial decorum of Article III judges, or indeed of any judges." . . . This cannot mean that arbitrators are held to a higher standard than Article III judges. Had this same relationship occurred between an Article III judge and the same lawyer, neither disclosure nor disqualification would have been forced or even suggested. . . . While it is true that disclosure of prior significant contacts and business dealings between a prospective arbitrator and the parties furthers informed selection,* it is not true, as Justice White's opinion perceptively explains, that "the best informed and most capable potential arbitrators" should be automatically disqualified (and their awards nullified) by failure to inform the parties of trivial relationships. . . .

* The American Arbitration Association ("AAA"), whose rules governed this proceeding, requires broad prophylactic disclosure of "any circumstance likely to affect impartiality or create an appearance of partiality," so that parties may rely on the integrity of the selection process for arbitrators. Whether Shurn's nondisclosure ran afoul of the AAA rules, however, is not before us and plays no role in applying the federal standard embodied in the FAA.

Finally, requiring vacatur on these attenuated facts would rob arbitration of one of its most attractive features apart from speed and finality—expertise. Arbitration would lose the benefit of specialized knowledge, because the best lawyers and professionals, who normally have the longest lists of potential connections to disclose, have no need to risk blemishes on their reputations from post-arbitration lawsuits attacking them as biased.

Neither the FAA nor the Supreme Court, nor predominant case law, nor sound policy countenances vacatur of FAA arbitral awards for nondisclosure by an arbitrator unless it creates a concrete, not speculative impression of bias. Arbitration may have flaws, but this is not one of them. The draconian remedy of vacatur is only warranted upon nondisclosure that involves a significant compromising relationship. This case does not come close to meeting this standard.

The judgment of the district court is Reversed, and the case is Remanded for Further Proceedings.

REAVLEY, Circuit Judge, dissenting, joined by WIENER, GARZA, BENAVIDES and STEWART, Circuit Judges:

In 1968 the Supreme Court held that an arbitral award could not stand where the arbitrator had failed to disclose a past relationship that might give the impression of possible partiality. . . . The Court has never changed that holding; it is the law that rules us today. . . .

The majority opinion manages to substitute actual bias, or the reasonable impression of bias, or concrete impression of bias for the Supreme Court's ruling that dealings that might create only an impression of possible bias must be disclosed. And it purports to join other circuits to hold that non-disclosure alone does not require vacatur of an arbitral award. If the circuit courts could overrule the Supreme Court, the majority might be on a bit firmer ground, because the *Commonwealth Coatings* ruling has not been well received by some of the circuit courts. . . .

While I can understand the desire to protect the finality of arbitration awards and avoid a return to extended court expense and delay, this does not justify evading the law of the Supreme Court by misstating it or by avoiding it by bleaching the evidence of possible partiality. Nor should we miss the need to promote the impartiality of arbitrators in this time when that is the favored method of dispute resolution. Influence can so easily corrupt the decision-making process even when it is not recognized by the magistrate or arbitrator himself. And to prove bias or improper influence is rarely possible. It is imperative that we not allow even the good faith or memory of the potential arbitrator to control the disclosure decision for, as the Justices made clear in *Commonwealth Coatings*, it is the protection and reassurance of the party that matters most. . . .

[The dissent discusses the instant action and the efforts of the federal district court to assist Positive Software in getting its software back from New Century, and the court's issuance of an injunction and protective order "based on a finding that New Century had copied Positive Software's material and enjoining New Century from use of Loan Force software, its database, or the software New Century was claiming to be its own products." Later, the district court "found that its orders had been violated in an order telling the disturbing story."]

Meanwhile the dispute had gone to arbitration where the award favored New Century completely. The award found that there had been no infringement or breach of the licensing contract and charged Positive Software with several million dollars of damages, fees, and costs.

At the outset of his ruling the arbitrator ridiculed Positive Software's claim and wrote: "It involves a saga of how failure to renew an $86,100 software license has led to a claim for $500,000,000 in damages in this arbitration, and for $38,000,000,000 in Federal Court." The district court expressed curiosity about the explanation for this statement of the arbitrator's disdain. . . .

Positive Software searched for an answer to this award and found a prior relationship between counsel for New Century, the Susman Godfrey law firm, and the arbitrator, Peter J. Shurn, a member of the Arnold White & Durkee firm. These two prominent law firms in Houston both represented Intel in its protracted patent litigation with Cyrix. . . . [The dissent discusses the fact that Shurn and Susman Godfrey lawyers' names appeared together on multiple pleadings and motions, and that various questions remained about the extent of the relationship.] The district court said that the fact that Camiña's name remained on pleadings and court records, for years after she claimed to have ended her participation, itself gives the appearance of impropriety. . . .

When Shurn was being considered to arbitrate this dispute, he was told the names of counsel and told of the importance of disclosing any relationship with them. He signed a disclosure for the [AAA] saying that he had nothing to disclose of past relationship with the parties or their counsel, "direct or indirect, whether financial, professional, social or of any other kind." He was further instructed: "If any relationship arises during the course of the arbitration, or if there is any change . . . it must also be disclosed." When Shurn was appointed he was asked: "Have you had any professional or social relationship with counsel for any party in this proceeding or the firms for which they work?" He checked: "I have nothing to disclose." And he signed an oath that he would act in accord with the rules of the [AAA].

The majority opinion portrays this relationship as trivial by reducing the record to Camiña's statement that she did no work with Shurn. The district court had a different picture of the relationship, one that would have been remembered if Shurn or the other lawyers had given any thought to it, and certainly would have prevented Positive Software from resting its case with Peter Shurn.

Positive Software asked the district court for more discovery of the relationship between the arbitrator and the Susman Godfrey firm, but this request was not granted because the record had already established a failure to disclose a relationship requiring vacatur under the rule of *Commonwealth Coatings*. . . .

[The dissent concludes that the district court judgment vacating the arbitration award should be affirmed.]

WIENER, Circuit Judge, Specially Concurring in Circuit Judge REAVLEY's dissent, joined by REAVLEY, Circuit Judge:

As I wholeheartedly concur in Judge Reavley's dissent, I write separately only to add a perspective that I find helpful in analyzing this case and demonstrating that Judge Reavley has gotten it right. I refer in general to the key differences between arbitration under the FAA and litigation in federal court. . . .

The tradeoffs attendant on the dispute-resolution choice between litigation and arbitration are well and widely known: The principal benefits usually ascribed to arbitration are speed, informality, cost-savings, confidentiality, and services of a decision-maker with expertise and familiarity with the subject matter of the dispute. These "pluses," however, are not without offsetting "minuses." The informalities attendant on proceedings in arbitration come at the cost of the protections automatically afforded to parties in court, which reside in such venerable institutions as the rules of evidence and civil procedure. Likewise sacrificed at the altar of quick and economical finality is virtually the entire system of appellate review. . . . By dispensing with such basic standards of review as clearly erroneous, de novo, and abuse of discretion, there remain to parties in arbitration only the narrowest of appellate recourse. . . .

A less frequently encountered and less frequently discussed distinction and its tradeoffs is the one implicated here: the vital difference between the method by which a federal judge is selected to hear a case in litigation vis-à-vis the method by which arbitrators are selected—a distinction hinted at by Justice White but frequently overlooked or misinterpreted. All know that trial judges in the federal system are nominated and confirmed only after a rigorous testing of their capabilities, experience, and integrity. In contrast, arbitrators are quickly selected by the parties alone, who frequently have unequal knowledge of or familiarity with the full history of potential arbitrators. Federal trial judges are full-time dispute resolvers; the experience of arbitrators falls all along the experience spectrum, from those who might serve but once or twice in a lifetime to those who conduct arbitration with increasing regularity. The trial judge who is to hear a case is almost never "selected" by or agreed on by the parties; rather, such judge is "selected" or designated by objectively random or blind assignment through long established court procedures (except in the rare case of a party's successful forum shopping in a single-judge district, or consenting to try a case to a known magistrate judge). In stark contrast, it is the parties to arbitration themselves who have sole responsibility for the selection of their arbitrator or arbitrators.

It follows then that because they alone do the selecting, the parties to arbitration must be able to depend almost entirely on the potential arbitrator's good faith, sensitivity, understanding, and compliance with the rules of disclosure by candidates for the post. And, even then, appellate relief is an *avis rara* when it comes to questions of bias, prejudice, or non-disclosure in arbitration. Consequently, except for such background checks that the parties might be able to conduct, the only shield available to the parties against favoritism, prejudice, and bias is full and frank disclosure, "up front," by each potential arbitrator. And even that is far less efficacious than the safeguards that are afforded to parties in litigation through the elaborate rules of professional conduct, disqualification, and recusal, and the body of law and procedure thereon developed in the crucible of the very formal and extensive judicial system.

The point that I belabor here is that, because parties to arbitration have virtually none of the protections against prejudice and bias (or the appearances thereof) that are automatically and routinely afforded to litigants in federal court, the single arrow remaining in the otherwise-empty quiver of protection afforded to parties in arbitration—full, unredacted disclosure of every prior relationship—must be rigorously adhered to and strenuously enforced. Indeed, it is these very differences in the disclosure standards—not disqualification standards—to which judges are held vis-à-vis those to which arbitrators are held that demand unyielding fealty to both the letter and spirit of the disclosure requirement: With such a slim safeguard against bias or the appearance of bias in arbitration, the reason is obvious why such mandated disclosure of every relationship, without self-abridgment by the potential arbitrator, must be assiduously enforced. . . .

NOTES AND QUESTIONS

1. *Positive Software* reflects the key policy and practical concerns that underlie judicial interpretation of the "evident partiality" standard of the FAA. The majority correctly notes that courts tend to be loath to overturn awards on the basis of undisclosed relationships. Why do you suppose this is the case? In *Merit Insurance Co. v. Leatherby Insurance Co.*, 714 F.2d 673 (7th Cir. 1983), the court refused to find grounds for vacatur on the basis of an undisclosed prior business relationship with a party that had ended 14 years before the dispute. The court stated that it "d[id] not want to encourage the losing party to every arbitration to conduct a background investigation of each of the arbitrators in an effort to uncover evidence of a former relationship with the adversary. This would only increase the cost and undermine the finality of arbitration."

2. Consider the opinions of the dissenting judges in *Positive Software*. What is their apparent perception of what was going on in the arbitration? What other arguments did they advance?

3. What was the standard of disclosure required of Arbitrator Shurn under the AAA Commercial Arbitration Rules? Should the particular disclosure standard applicable under the parties' arbitration agreement have an impact on a judicial finding of "evident partiality." Why or why not?

4. In *Monster Energy Co. v. City Beverages, LLC*, 940 F.3d 1130 (9th Cir. 2019), the Court of Appeals vacated an award by a JAMS arbitrator for evident partiality because he did not disclose that he was one of the neutrals on JAMS's list who had an ownership interest in JAMS. Although he disclosed that he had a general economic interest in the arbitral institution, Olympic Eagle (the party seeking vacatur) did not know that he had an ownership interest until after he issued an award in favor of Monster. The court found that Olympic Eagle did not have the necessary constructive notice of the arbitrator's interest. Do you think that the fact that a prospective arbitrator has an ownership interest in an organization administering arbitration, as opposed to simply having an arrangement to market and/or deliver her services through a particular organization, is an important piece of information for a party to have in making

decisions on arbitral appointment? What additional information might be relevant to your answer?

5. *A Glaring Example. Thomas Kinkade Co. v. White*, 711 F.3d 719 (6th Cir. 2013), dealt with an exceptionally troubling scenario in which an arbitrator's apparent conflicts of interest coincided with highly irregular procedural rulings. This resulted in vacatur of the resulting award. In that decision, the Court of Appeals affirmed a district court judgment vacating award for evident partiality and corruption where, after nearly five years (and 50 hearing days of arbitration), the chair of the arbitration panel, Kowalsky, announced to Kinkade that the other party, White, and the Whites' party-arbitrator had each hired Kowalsky's firm for matters likely to be substantial. Over Kinkade's objections, Kowalsky continued forward with the arbitration. Thereafter, in the words of the appellate court,

> [Kowalsky] gave the Whites a second and then a third chance to bolster the proofs for their claims. He allowed the Whites to rely upon 8,800 documents they had deliberately and wrongfully withheld for more than four years. He denied Kinkade any relief on a straightforward breach-of-contract claim that was virtually uncontested during the hearings. . . . Kowalsky failed to offer any response to serious objections that Kinkade had raised to his decisions as an arbitrator. And Kowalsky awarded the Whites nearly $500,000 in attorneys' fees after the plain terms of the Interim Award indicated that the Whites' request for fees had been denied. These actions, when combined with the late-arbitration dealings between the Whites and Kowalsky's firm, are more than sufficient to show his evident partiality.

The Eighth Circuit affirmed the district court's vacatur.

6. *Deference to Arbitral Authority.* Courts may decline to vacate an arbitration award in deference to arbitrators' plenary authority over procedural matters. For example, in *Bain Cotton Co. v. Chesnutt Cotton Co.*, 531 F. App'x 500 (mem.) (5th Cir. 2013), Bain Cotton sought to vacate an adverse award on the ground that the arbitrators' failure to grant Bain's discovery requests "evidenced partiality or corruption on their part." In upholding the district court's denial of Bain's motion to vacate, the court of appeals panel noted:

> Had this discovery dispute arisen in and been ruled on by the district court, it is not unlikely that Bain's pleas [for discovery] would have led to reversal; however, under the "strong federal policy favoring arbitration, judicial review of an arbitration award is exceedingly narrow."

PROBLEM 1A: ARBITRATOR NONDISCLOSURE AND VACATUR OF AWARD

(Before doing this exercise, you may wish to refer back to Problem 2A on Arbitrator Disclosure in Chapter 3 for purposes of comparison. The earlier exercise deals with disclosure and challenge procedures under standard arbitration rules.)

You are attorney for Carmin Co., a manufacturer of high-tech GPS units used in automobiles, in a dispute with SamCo, Inc., a national "buying club" with stores all over the country. The parties have a contract containing an arbitration provision that incorporates the AAA Commercial Arbitration Rules. A dispute arises between the parties, and Carmin demands arbitration. Arbitration proceedings are conducted before a single arbitrator under the AAA Rules; the arbitrator renders an award in favor of SamCo.

A. Shortly after the award is rendered, you discover that the arbitrator failed to disclose that she had approached SamCo about serving as an attorney for them in a series of cases unrelated to the present action. The contact had occurred about two months before the arbitration. What are your options? Will a court vacate the award on grounds of "evident partiality" under the FAA? *See, e.g., University Commons-Urbana, Ltd. v. Universal Constructors Inc.*, 304 F.3d 1331 (11th Cir. 2002).

B. In Chapter 5.B.2, you were introduced to the UAA and its revised version, the RUAA. Among other things, the RUAA sets forth affirmative guidelines for arbitrator disclosure and more specific guidance on the impact of nondisclosure on judicial action. Suppose you were seeking to vacate the award in a state court proceeding in which the RUAA was applicable. How, if at all, does §12 of the RUAA affect your analysis in this problem? Under the RUAA, could Carmin Co. sue the arbitrator for failing to disclose the relationship?

C. Suppose instead that you are seeking to vacate the award in a California state court, and California arbitration law applies. Consider the effect of the California Ethics Standards for Neutral Arbitrators in Contractual Arbitration of the California Rules of Court, Cal. Civ. Proc. Code §1281.85 (West 2015).

PROBLEM 1B: NONDISCLOSURE BY A "PARTY ARBITRATOR" AND VACATUR

You will recall from Chapter 3 that tripartite arbitration panels are a common feature of the landscape. The concept—each party picking an arbitrator, and the two "party arbitrators" agreeing on a third arbitrator—is seemingly straightforward and fair. Such arrangements, however, often bring unanticipated results and, sometimes, litigation. The issue inevitably comes down to the precise role of party arbitrators and their obligation of disclosure.

We saw that under current leading arbitration rules and the revised *Code of Ethics for Arbitrators in Commercial Disputes*, arbitrators appointed by a single party are subject to disclosure requirements similar to other arbitrators, and rules make them subject to similar administrative challenge procedures. Now we consider the impact of a "party arbitrator's" failure to disclose, and the possibility of judicial vacation of award on grounds of "evident impartiality."

(Before doing this exercise, you may wish to refer back to Problem 2B on Disclosure by Party Arbitrators in Chapter 3 for purposes of comparison. The earlier exercise deals with disclosure and challenge procedures under standard arbitration rules.)

Again, assume you represent Carmin Co. in arbitration proceedings with SamCo, Inc. In this scenario, however, the arbitration procedures in the parties' agreement provide that the wing arbitrators appointed unilaterally by the respective parties "should not be subject to requirements of independence and impartiality." Each party selects an arbitrator, and the party arbitrators jointly select a third individual to serve as chair of the panel. After the arbitration tribunal renders a binding award in favor of SamCo, you find out for the first time that the arbitrator appointed by SamCo worked directly with SamCo before and during the proceedings on virtually every aspect of SamCo's case. You and your client are horrified by the situation.

A. Are these circumstances grounds for judicial vacatur of award under the FAA on grounds of "evident partiality"? In *Certain Underwriting Members of Lloyds of London v. Fla. Dep't of Financial Servs.*, 892 F.3d 501 (2d Cir. 2018), a party (ICA) appealed a district court order vacating an arbitration award on the basis that ICA's party arbitrator had failed to disclose close relationships with present and former directors and employees of ICA. The Second Circuit reversed on the basis that "a party seeking to vacate an award under [FAA] Section 10(a)(2) must sustain a higher burden to prove evident partiality on the part of an arbitrator who is appointed by a party and who is expected to espouse the view or perspective of the appointing party." *Id.* at 503-504. The court went on to state:

> An undisclosed relationship between a party and its party-appointed arbitrator constitutes evident partiality, such that vacatur of the award is appropriate if: (1) the relationship violates the contractual requirement of disinterestedness (see *Sphere Drake Ins. v. All American Life Ins.*, 307 F.3d 617, 620 (7th Cir. 2002)); or (2) it prejudicially affects the award (see *Delta Mine Holding Co. v. AFC Coal Properties, Inc.*, 280 F.3d 815, 821-22 (8th Cir. 2001)).

Compare this approach to the standards for neutral arbitrators under *Commonwealth Coatings*. The court's decision contains considerable dicta to the effect that party-appointed wing arbitrators may be expected to be less than neutral — something that raises troublesome issues for parties and counsel. Suppose, for example, parties enter into an ad hoc arbitration agreement without incorporated arbitration procedures, and provide for a "tripartite" arbitration panel with each party appointing a wing arbitrator and the chair being jointly appointed. If the parties have no specific agreement as to the arbitrators' independence and impartiality, what standards would govern motions to vacate an award for "evident partiality" by a party-appointed arbitrator?

B. In *Delta Mine Holding Co. v. AFC Coal Props., Inc.*, 280 F.3d 815 (8th Cir. 2001), *cert. denied*, 537 U.S. 817 (2002), a party-appointed arbitrator and his entire consulting firm surreptitiously assisted his appointing party's law firm in preparing elements of the case in arbitration under rules that provided party-appointees were not required to be independent and impartial. The Eighth Circuit overturned a district court order that had vacated the subsequent award on grounds of evident partiality of the arbitrator. Among other reasons, the appellate court concluded that because the parties had specifically agreed that the party-appointed wing arbitrators did not have to be independent and impartial (under the provisions of the *old* AAA commercial rules), a party seeking to vacate the award on the basis of an arbitrator's evident partiality faced a higher burden than that established in *Commonwealth Coatings*. To what extent does *Delta Mine Holding* reinforce — or undermine — the following policies associated with arbitration: party autonomy, finality of award, and respect for the integrity of arbitration as an adjudication process?

NOTE: CAN A PARTY, OR AN EMPLOYEE OF A PARTY, BE A SOLE ARBITRATOR?

Where parties agree, as part of a pre-dispute dispute resolution agreement, that one of the parties, or an individual very closely associated with one of the parties (such as counsel) is empowered to arbitrate disputes between the parties and render an award that is enforceable under applicable arbitration statutes, is the agreement enforceable? Is an award by the arbitrator subject to vacatur for evident partiality, or on public policy grounds? These issues, touched on briefly at the end of Chapter 3, will now be explored in detail.

Arbitration is broadly understood to be a process involving independent and impartial adjudication — a corollary of the principle that no man should be a judge in his own case. The legal principle that "no man should be judge in his own cause" can be traced back to its Latin articulation — *nemo judex in causa sua* — and the Justinian Codex (circa 529-565 A.D.). That principle underpins a number of modern decisions. As observed in *Cross & Brown Co. v. Nelson*, 167 N.Y.S.2d 573 (1957):

> A well-recognized principle of "natural justice" is that a man may not be a judge in his own cause. Irrespective of any proof of actual bias or prejudice, the law presumes that a party to a dispute cannot have that disinterestedness and impartiality necessary to act in a judicial or quasi-judicial capacity regarding that controversy. This absolute

disqualification to act rests upon sound public policy. Any other rule would be repugnant to a proper sense of justice.

. . .

"What we do hold is that no party to a contract, or someone so identified with the party as to be in fact, even though not in name, the party, can be designated as an arbitrator to decide disputes under it. Apart from outraging public policy, such an agreement is illusory; for while in form it provides for arbitration, in substance it yields the power to an adverse party to decide disputes under the contract."

See also Astoria Med. Group v. Health Ins. Plan of Greater N.Y., 11 N.Y.2d 128, n.1 (1962) (noting that when an agreement authorizes a party to "appoint" an arbitrator, it is implicit in that very provision that he may not appoint himself); *Manes v. Dallas Baptist College*, 638 S.W.2d 143 (Tex. App. 1982) (allowing a party to act as arbitrator in its own cases "is totally inconsistent with the theory of arbitration"); *In re Phelps Dodge Magnet Wire Co.*, 225 S.W.3d 599 (Tex. App. 2005) (procedure was not true arbitration because the entire pool of potential arbitrators were employees of a party).

In *McConnell v. Howard University*, 818 F.2d 58 n.2 (D.C. Cir. 1987), the court declared:

Although courts will often take a deferential posture in reviewing decisions made by arbitral bodies, this deference is premised on the fact that the arbitral remedy is one agreed upon by the parties and is fair. Even if it could be said that the parties "agreed" to make the Board of Trustees [of one of the parties the]. . . arbitral body, we cannot say that this remedy would be a fair one.

The international arbitration community overwhelmingly rejects the notion that a party to a dispute can serve as arbitrator in its own case, as reflected in the *International Bar Association Rules on Conflicts of Interests* (2014). This document includes a "Non-waivable Red List" identifying arbitrator conflicts of interest that are so offensive to a sense of justice that even a party's informed consent will not cure the foundational defect. The very first item on the Non-Waivable Red List is: "There is an identity between a party and the arbitrator, or the arbitrator is a legal representative or employee of an entity that is a party in the arbitration."

Given this fundamental concern about permitting parties to act as arbitrators in their own cases, you may be surprised to learn that there are a number of U.S. decisions enforcing agreements or awards in cases in which a party, or counsel for a party, or a party's employee, or another individual with close ties to a party, is appointed as arbitrator. You may recall the "Deflategate" controversy, in which NFL Commissioner Roger Goodell delegated himself arbitrator to review his own decision to suspend New England Patriots quarterback Tom Brady (discussed in Chapter 3). Goodell's award upholding his earlier decision was vacated upon the motion of the Football Players Association, but the Second Circuit overturned the decision, stating in part:

The Association's final contention is that the Commissioner was evidently partial with regard to the delegation issue and should have recused himself from hearing at least that portion of the arbitration because it was improper for him to adjudicate the propriety of his own conduct. This argument has no merit.

The party seeking vacatur must prove evident partiality by "clear and convincing evidence.". . . However, arbitration is a matter of contract, and consequently, the parties to an arbitration can ask for no more impartiality than inheres in the method they have chosen. *Williams v. Nat'l Football League*, 582 F.3d 863, 885 (8th Cir. 2009).

Here, the parties contracted in the CBA to specifically allow the Commissioner to sit as the arbitrator in all disputes brought pursuant to Article 46, Section 1(a). They did so knowing full well that the Commissioner had the sole power of determining what constitutes "conduct detrimental," and thus knowing that the Commissioner would have a stake both in the underlying discipline and in every arbitration brought pursuant to Section 1(a). Had the parties wished to restrict the Commissioner's authority, they could have fashioned a different agreement.

Nat'l Football League Mgmt. Council v. Nat'l Football Players Ass'n, 820 F.3d 527, 548 (2d Cir. 2016).

How is this kind of scenario, where the agreement identifies a sole arbitrator who is employed by a party, different from tripartite arbitration panels involving party-appointed wing arbitrators? Should parties be able to agree to have anyone, including a party, serve as their arbitrator, or should there be some legal limits that can be imposed on motion of a party? Should "arbitration" by a party's employee even be treated as a kind of arbitration, or should it be handled like some other kind of contractual arrangement for decision making by a party?

D. WAS THERE ARBITRAL MISCONDUCT (A FAILURE TO POSTPONE THE HEARING OR REFUSAL TO HEAR PERTINENT AND MATERIAL EVIDENCE, ETC.)?

Arbitrator misconduct such as a failure to postpone a hearing for cause or refusing to hear pertinent and material evidence is not often a basis for vacation. Arbitrators generally understand that such mistakes should be avoided and they tend to err on the side of allowing evidence to be heard. Moreover, arbitrators enjoy broad discretion regarding the management of hearings and the receipt of evidence under the law of arbitration, and such discretion is reinforced by standard arbitration rules. Most courts are therefore very deferential to arbitrators' evidentiary determinations and other rulings.

For a recent case, see *Balch v. Oracle Corp.*, CV DKC 19-133, 2019 WL 6052670 (D. Md. Nov. 15, 2019). In that case, Balch moved to vacate an arbitration award, in part arguing that the arbitrator deprived him of a fair hearing when the arbitrator issued a summary judgment. Balch argued that the testimony and the language of the contract created material questions of fact that required an evidentiary hearing. The court nonetheless noted that federal courts have read the FAA to provide arbitrators with broad discretion to decide cases on summary judgment. The court also emphasized that "not every failure of an arbitrator to receive relevant evidence constitutes misconduct requiring vacatur of an arbitrator's award." Based on this logic, the court upheld the arbitration award in favor of Oracle Corp.

E.   DID THE ARBITRATORS "EXCEED THEIR POWERS"?

It appears that, generally speaking, the most "frequently asserted and sustained" of the grounds for judicial vacatur of arbitration awards is a finding that arbitrators "exceeded their powers."[3] Such a finding usually employs as its touchstone the agreement of the parties; vacation is warranted when an arbitrator's action is clearly beyond the scope of her authority as set forth in the agreement, or in contravention of that agreement. Of course, as illustrated by the following decision, the breadth of most arbitration provisions and the liberality with which courts tend to interpret arbitration agreements often cut against vacatur on such grounds.

David Co. v. Jim Miller Construction, Inc.

444 N.W.2d 836 (Minn. 1989)

[Miller Construction, Inc., contracted with David Co. to construct townhouses in two phases on property owned by David Co. After phase one was complete, a dispute between the parties regarding defective workmanship arose. Following arbitration of the dispute, the arbitrators, as part of their award, ordered the general contractor (Miller) to purchase the real property on which the subject buildings had been erected. The issue presented to the court is whether in so doing the arbitrators exceeded their powers. A divided court of appeals panel affirmed a district court order that had affirmed the award. The Minnesota Supreme Court heard Miller's appeal and issued the following decision.]

KELLEY, Justice.

The construction contract at issue was entitled "General Conditions of the Contract for Construction." It included an arbitration clause by which the parties agreed that "[a]ll claims, disputes and other matters in question . . . arising out of, or relating to, the contract documents or the breach thereof . . ." would be subject to arbitration with the exception of claims waived by the making of final payment. . . .

Shortly after the commencement of construction on Phase I of the project, construction problems began to surface and thereafter continued throughout construction. David Company attributed the recurrence of these problems to Miller's inadequate supervision of subcontractors and its tolerance of poor workmanship by them. Primarily because of those problems, completion of construction on Phase I was delayed beyond the contract completion date of May 1984 to October of that year. David Company claimed this delay not only caused it to lose sales of the units and to incur additional interest and other expense, but, in addition, left it with shoddily constructed units which were unmarketable as the luxury-type units originally contemplated by the project.

David Company was aware of numerous construction deficiencies, knew they had not been rectified, and that Phase I completion had been delayed for months, when it made final payment to Miller on Phase I in November 1984. Miller argues that the final payment constituted waiver under subparagraphs 9.9.4 and 9.9.5 of the contract. In response, David Company claims it made the payment reluctantly and only after it had been induced to do so by Miller's reaffirmation of its contractual and other legal obligations to remedy all construction deficiencies in its work.

Shortly after making final payment, David Company learned of additional previously unknown extensive and serious construction defects. Moreover, further nonconformities with contract requirements and building code violations emerged. After Miller refused to correct the newly discovered deficiencies, David Company filed its Demand for Arbitration with the [AAA]. In its Demand it alleged breach of contract, negligence and misrepresentation. For relief it requested "compensation for damages in excess of $250,000, including damages which continue to accrue, plus costs, disbursements, attorney fees and interest." It likewise expressly reserved the right to later amend the demand.

A building contractor and two professional engineers were selected by the parties to arbitrate the dispute. The arbitrators heard evidence presented by the parties over a span of three days, heard submissions of counsel for each party, and physically visited the project site to inspect and evaluate the quality of construction. Evidence presented to the arbitrators revealed numerous and serious construction defects and deficiencies . . . resulting in rescission demands from owners to whom David had sold units prior to completion, and [rendering] the unsold units, in a practical sense, unmarketable absent extensive and costly repairs.

During the course of his closing argument before the arbitration panel, one of David Company's attorneys, while highlighting the numerous and substantial items of shabby workmanship, observed that his client, and, perhaps as well, vendees who had purchased the units, might be saddled with contingent future liabilities under statutory warranties. He noted that Miller was not only a building contractor, but, as well a developer and owner of real estate thereby implying that, as such, Miller might well better bear that risk than could the respondents. Thereupon, the arbitrators suggested to the parties that they might consider an award resulting in Miller ending up with the project and the property on which it was located in exchange for a cash payment to David Company. Miller's counsel promptly objected on the ground that to so structure an award, the arbitrators would exceed the power granted to them. Nonetheless, David Company's lawyers prepared an itemized "sell back" option claiming $884,476 in damages. . . . The arbitrators' award incorporated the "sell back" option. Alternatively, in the event David Company was unable to convey the property free of liens within 45 days, the award provided for a monetary damages award of $497,925 to be paid to David Company. David Company chose to exercise the "sell back" option, and pursuant thereto, made timely tender of performance. When Miller refused to perform by making the payment as required by the arbitrators' award, David Company commenced an action in district court to confirm the award. . . .

Before this court Miller contends that the arbitrators exceeded their powers within the meaning of Minn. Stat. §572.19.1(3) (1988) when they ordered it to purchase real property from David Company when an alternative damage award was likewise made because: (a) the compelled purchase violated strong public policy as codified by the statute of frauds, and, (b) the order for compelled purchase of real estate was not authorized by either the contract between the parties nor the submittal. Miller further asserts that the arbitrators exceeded their powers by inclusion in the purchase figure that was part of the ultimate award, certain claims which, pursuant to the contract documents, Miller claims had been waived by David Company when it made final payment of Phase I of the project in October 1984.

We first address the claim that the arbitrators did exceed their powers. Because David Company's Demand for Arbitration claimed relief for negligence, breach of contract and misrepresentation, all of which arose out of, or were relevant to, the contract documents, the issue raised here relates not to the question of arbitrability, but rather to the question of whether the arbitrators exceeded their powers in structuring a remedy. If they did, of course, their award may be vacated (Minn. Stat. §572.19, subd. 1(3)). While the parties, either by contract or by written submission circumscribing the arbitrator's authority, may limit the arbitrator's authority, absent such consensual limitations, the arbitrators are the final judges of both the facts and the law concerning the merits. *State v. Berthiaume*, 259 N.W.2d 904, 910 (Minn. 1977). Moreover, an award will not be vacated merely because the court may believe the arbitrators erred.

The innovative and unique remedy structured by the arbitrators in the instant case, unlike the customary award ordering payment of monetary damages, may be considered equitable in nature. However, merely because the relief granted is equitable in nature does not, by itself, preclude arbitrators from employing it when otherwise appropriate. Indeed, it appears that our statute contemplates "equitable" as well as "legal" remedies in that it provides that upon confirmation of an award, a "judgment or *decree*" shall be entered. Minn. Stat. §572.21 (1988). No prior holdings of this court which involved comparable types of awards in construction disputes have been brought to our attention. However, in the area of labor relations although an agreement itself contained no provision relative to the scope of the authority of the arbitrators to structure a remedy, we observed that "we defer to the arbitrator's discretion, preserving the flexibility which commends arbitration as an effective means of resolving labor disputes." *Children's Hosp. v. Minnesota Nurses Ass'n*, 265 N.W.2d 649 (Minn. 1978) (a case where arbitrators "mandated" collective bargaining—arguably an equitable remedy—as an alternative in their award). . . .

Our cases as well as those from other jurisdictions . . . reveal the emergence of a general trend of courts, in the absence of limiting language in the contract itself, to accord judicial deference and afford flexibility to arbitrators to fashion awards comporting with the circumstances out of which the disputes arose. Recognition by us in this case that arbitration awards of an equitable nature may be appropriately fashioned would be entirely consistent with this court's long tradition of favoring the use of arbitration in dispute resolution and rejecting challenges to its employment, which, if granted, would limit, rather than expand, its utility. Thus, we hold that merely because the novel relief structured by the arbitrators in this case may have been equitable in nature does not support appellant's claim that they thereby exceeded their authority. Nonetheless, the power exercised in fashioning the award must have its genesis either from the underlying contract, the arbitration clause itself, or the submission. . . .

In the instant case the basis for the award cannot be found in the submission. The original demand sought "compensation for damages in excess of $250,000" (later increased to $598,622.45). Prior to the close of the final arguments before the arbitrators, never did David amend its submission demand to seek relief of the nature provided in the award. Rather, it was one of the arbitrators who, after argument, suggested the "sell back" option. When he did so, appellant promptly voiced its objection. Neither expressly nor tacitly did Miller agree that the submission be expanded to authorize a remedy of this type. Nor, with the exception of the arbitration clause itself in the "General Conditions of the Contract for Construction," does the underlying contract provide any basis for the remedy formulated by the arbitrators. Accordingly, the basis, if any, for the award which was fashioned must depend upon construction of the contract's arbitration clause. . . .

The scope of the arbitration clause is extremely broad. It authorizes arbitrators to decide "[a]ll claims, disputes and other matters in question . . . relating to, the Contract . . . or the breach thereof. . . ." No provision in the arbitration clause expressly or implicitly limits the arbitrators to structuring only a remedy calling for the payment of a monetary award nor does any provision expressly authorize, or prohibit, arbitrators from formulating remedies that are equitable in nature. However, in conformity with our long established policy favoring expansion of the arbitration remedy, we conclude that implicit in the exceedingly broad powers which were granted by the parties to the arbitrators to decide "[a]ll claims, disputes, and other matters in question" is a grant of authority to structure an award which is commensurate with the extent, the pervasiveness, and nature of the poor workmanship resulting in construction deficiencies of such patent magnitude which existed. The appellant, and the dissenter in the court of appeals' opinion, argue that the arbitration clause should be more restrictively construed to limit the type of relief to the more traditional monetary award. While it may be correct to surmise that initially neither party specifically contemplated that in case of dispute between them this type of an equitable award might ensue from arbitration, yet both, neither of whom were inexperienced in construction projects of this nature, knew that the project involved the construction of luxury style residential townhomes for immediate resale to third parties, and each were undoubtedly aware of the potential future warranty liability to vendees and subvendees. Nonetheless, the parties executed a contract containing an arbitration clause affording to arbitrators wide and virtually unlimited latitude to fashion a remedy. By their agreement, either initially or in the submission, the parties could have limited the arbitrators' authority. . . . They failed to do so. We decline to judicially restrict the powers of the arbitrators which the parties themselves have so broadly granted to them. Nor, in our opinion, does the fact that the arbitrators were able to make an alternative monetary award have relevance to the determination of the scope of the powers delegated to them. By fashioning the award, the arbitrators not only acted within the scope of the broad grant of authority in fashioning the "sell back" option, but also placed the obligation on Miller, the party responsible for the gross construction deficiencies, to remedy them and bear the risk of potential future warranty liabilities. . . .

[The court then went on to address Miller's claims that the arbitration award violated the Statute of Frauds, and that David Co. had waived its right to collect damages by rendering final payment to Miller.]

Accordingly, because we hold that the award structured by the arbitrators was within the powers granted to them by the arbitration clause of the general contract; that the award did not do violence to the underlying policy of the Statute of Frauds; and that the award did not include items which were "waived" by final payment, we *affirm*.

NOTES AND QUESTIONS

7. How does the remedy-making power of arbitrators as described by the Minnesota Supreme Court in *David Co.* differ from that of a civil court? Would a court have been able to render similar relief had the case been brought in court?

8. Do you believe the makeup of the panel of arbitrators had anything to do with the nature of the final arbitration award?

9. What specific elements of the arbitration agreement reinforced the court's conclusion regarding the breadth of the arbitrators' authority? Could the parties have limited the scope of their remedial power by a specific statement in the agreement?

10. *Categorizing Damages.* The arbitration award in the *David Co.* case was highly unusual; arbitrators usually render straightforward awards of damages similar to courts. Arbitrators may be called upon to interpret contracts that include provisions limiting recovery of certain categories of damages, such as consequential damages. In *Kemper Corp. Servs., Inc. v. Computer Scis. Corp.*, 946 F.3d 817 (5th Cir. 2020), Computer Sciences Corporation sought vacatur of an arbitration award in favor of Kemper Corporation Services on the grounds that the arbitrator exceeded his powers by categorizing damages as either consequential or direct in the course of enforcing a contractual limitation on consequential damages. The Fifth Circuit held that because courts are required to resolve all doubts in favor of arbitration, the final award was subject to very deferential review as long as the arbitrator did not exceed his powers since such categorization was required in order to comply with the terms of the contract. The lower court's ruling upholding the arbitration award was affirmed.

11. *"Late" Award of Attorneys' Fees.* In recent years, many arbitrators have become accustomed to bifurcating hearings in order to address claims for attorneys' fees after other substantive claims have been adjudicated. This makes sense since the predicate for obtaining attorneys' fees is often being

the "prevailing party." In *Floridians for Solar Choice, Inc. v. Paparella*, 802 F. App'x 519 (11th Cir. 2020), the losing party sought to vacate an award of attorneys' fees on the basis that the arbitrator exceeded their authority by issuing the award past the post-hearing deadline for final awards prescribed by the AAA Rules. The court denied the motion on the basis that the parties had stipulated that all motions for attorneys' fees would be addressed after the completion of hearings on substantive claims, and had conducted themselves consistent with that understanding.

12. *Vacatur on Multiple Grounds.* Often, motions to vacate are supported by multiple grounds; however, actual vacatur on several different grounds is relatively rare. In early 2022, considerable attention was garnered by a Georgia superior court decision vacating an arbitration award in favor of defendant Wells Fargo by a FINRA securities arbitration tribunal on five different grounds. First, the court ruled, Wells Fargo's refusal to utilize the FINRA neutral computer-generated arbitrator list and striking an arbitrator initially selected by Wells Fargo violated 9 U.S.C. §10(a)(4). Second, the arbitrators violated 9 U.S.C. §10(a)(3) in denying the plaintiff investors' request to postpone the hearing. Third, the arbitrators violated 9 U.S.C. §10(a)(3) by refusing to hear relevant, non-cumulative testimony from a third-party witness and unfairly limiting the cross examination of one of Wells Fargo's expert witnesses. Fourth, the award was procured by fraud in violation of 9 U.S.C. §10(a)(1). Finally, the court held, the arbitrators exceed their powers (9 U.S.C. § 10(a)(3)) in their grant of an award of costs and session fees against the plaintiff. *Leggett v. Wells Fargo Clearing Services, LLC*, No. 2019CV328949 (Ga. Super. Jan. 25, 2022), https://www.finra.org/sites/default/files/aao_documents/17-01077%283%29.pdf.

COMMENT ON PUNITIVE DAMAGES IN ARBITRATION

Should arbitrators have the authority to consider and render awards for punitive or exemplary damages? U.S. courts make such awards in some civil actions under the authority of common law or statutes; their fundamental purpose is to punish those who engage in certain proscribed behavior and to deter others from engaging in similar behavior. A generation ago, in a decision by Chief Judge Charles Breitel, the New York Court of Appeals vacated an arbitration award of punitive damages on the basis that arbitrators had no business considering or awarding "socially exemplary remedies." *Garrity v. Lyle Stuart, Inc.*, 40 N.Y.2d 354 (1976). Among other things, Breitel's opinion reflected a highly skeptical view of arbitrators' abilities and motivations, and a concern that punitive damages might become an instrument of oppression in private hands.

Given the subsequent evolution of arbitration into a highly favored alternative under judicial interpretations of the FAA, you may not be surprised to learn that the New York court's strong stance against arbitration of punitive damages under New York law did not hold sway in decisions governed by the FAA. *See* Thomas J. Stipanowich, *Punitive Damages in Arbitration: Garrity v. Lyle*

Stuart, Inc. Reconsidered, 66 B.U. L. Rev. 953 (1986). In *Mastrobuono v. Shearson Lehman Hutton, Inc.*, 514 U.S. 52 (1995), the Supreme Court concluded that where a broad-form arbitration agreement was governed by the FAA, the agreement should be read to permit arbitral awards of punitive damages in the absence of specific terms to the contrary. Although punitive or exemplary damages are rarely awarded in commercial arbitration cases, they are frequently sought in employment and securities brokerage disputes.

NOTES AND QUESTIONS

13. Judge Breitel's specter of unbridled, oppressive awards does not appear to have been borne out by experience with punitive damages. On the other hand, what happens if a seemingly extreme punitive award is rendered? What, if any, oversight should courts have of arbitral awards of punitive damages? *See Sawtelle v. Waddell & Reed*, No. 2330 (N.Y. App. Div. 1st Dep't 2003) (overturning judgment affirming $25 million punitive damages award against brokerage firm on the ground that it was grossly disproportionate to the harm suffered by the plaintiff, a mutual funds broker, and thus "arbitrary and irrational" under New York law).

14. Arbitral awards of punitive damages may be granted in commercial as well as non-commercial settings, but the arena in which we are most aware of punitive awards is investor-broker disputes. An empirical analysis of punitive damages in securities arbitrations based on a data set of more than 6,800 securities arbitration awards found that claimants prevailed in 48.9 percent of arbitrations and that 9.1 percent of those claimant victories included an award of punitive damages. The authors found that punitive damages tended to be awarded for "claims that suggested egregious misbehavior" and with higher awards of compensatory damages. The relationship between punitive and compensatory awards in securities arbitration did not differ substantially from data on juries from Civil Justice Surveys by the Bureau of Justice Statistics.[4]

15. Should parties be able to avoid punitive or exemplary damages by contract? Since it is generally within the power of the parties to arbitration agreements to include or exclude particular claims or controversies as they see fit, would it be possible to structure an arbitration provision that functions as a partial or complete pre-dispute waiver of claims for punitive damages? What, if any, policy concerns might weigh against such provisions? In *Galloway v. Priority Imports Richmond, LLC*, 426 F. Supp. 3d 236 (E.D. Va. 2019), the plaintiff argued that an arbitration provision violated public policy and was unenforceable because it did not allow the arbitrator to award punitive damages. The district court disagreed, and held that the limitation of the statutory right to recover punitive damages did not make the arbitration unenforceable. In contrast, in *Life Care Centers of Am., Inc. v. Est. of Deal*, 18-CV-187-MV, 2019 WL 1283006 (D.N.M. Mar. 20, 2019), the district court found that an arbitration agreement that prohibited the arbitrator from

awarding punitive damages was unconscionable because it contravened New Mexico statutory tort law. However, instead of voiding the arbitration clause, the court merely severed the provisions prohibiting punitive damages. As we will see in Chapter 7, these "remedy-stripping" provisions are most problematic in the context of a standardized contract of adhesion, such as an individual employment contract or a consumer contract.

F.   CONTRACTUAL PROVISIONS ATTEMPTING TO EXPAND OR NARROW GROUNDS FOR VACATUR OF AWARD

In the late 1990s, some parties were attempting to expand the grounds of judicial review of arbitral awards by contract. For example, in *Lapine Technology Corp. v. Kyocera Corp.*, 130 F.3d 884, 887 (9th Cir. 1997), the parties expressly provided grounds for judicial review beyond those available under the FAA, including court modification or vacatur if arbitrators made findings not supported by substantial evidence or made erroneous legal conclusions. The federal circuits were divided on whether to permit this expansion of judicial review by contract, with some honoring contractual autonomy and others finding that expansion of review would undercut the efficiency of arbitration.[5]

Hall Street Associates, L.L.C. v. Mattel, Inc.

552 U.S. 576 (2008)

Justice SOUTER delivered the opinion of the Court. . . .

The Federal Arbitration Act (FAA or Act), 9 U.S.C. §1 *et seq.*, provides for expedited judicial review to confirm, vacate, or modify arbitration awards. §§9-11. The question here is whether statutory grounds for prompt vacatur and modification may be supplemented by contract. We hold that the statutory grounds are exclusive.

I

This case began as a lease dispute between landlord, petitioner Hall Street Associates, L.L.C., and tenant, respondent Mattel, Inc. The property was used for many years as a manufacturing site, and the leases provided that the tenant would indemnify the landlord for any costs resulting from the failure of the tenant or its predecessor lessees to follow environmental laws while using the premises.

Tests of the property's well water in 1998 showed high levels of trichloroethylene (TCE), the apparent residue of manufacturing discharges by Mattel's predecessors between 1951 and 1980. After the Oregon Department of Environmental Quality (DEQ) discovered even more pollutants, Mattel stopped drawing from the well and, along with one of its predecessors, signed a consent order with the DEQ providing for cleanup of the site.

After Mattel gave notice of intent to terminate the lease in 2001, Hall Street filed this suit, contesting Mattel's right to vacate on the date it gave, and claiming that the lease obliged Mattel to indemnify Hall Street for costs of cleaning up the TCE, among other things. Following a bench trial before the United States District Court for the District of Oregon, Mattel won on the termination issue, and after an unsuccessful try at mediating the indemnification claim, the parties proposed to submit to arbitration. The District Court was amenable, and the parties drew up an arbitration agreement, which the court approved and entered as an order. One paragraph of the agreement provided that

> "[t]he United States District Court for the District of Oregon may enter judgment upon any award, either by confirming the award or by vacating, modifying or correcting the award. The Court shall vacate, modify or correct any award: (i) where the arbitrator's findings of facts are not supported by substantial evidence, or (ii) where the arbitrator's conclusions of law are erroneous."

Arbitration took place, and the arbitrator decided for Mattel. In particular, he held that no indemnification was due, because the lease obligation to follow all applicable federal, state, and local environmental laws did not require compliance with the testing requirements of the Oregon Drinking Water Quality Act (Oregon Act); that Act the arbitrator characterized as dealing with human health as distinct from environmental contamination.

Hall Street then filed a District Court Motion for Order Vacating, Modifying And/Or Correcting the arbitration decision on the ground that failing to treat the Oregon Act as an applicable environmental law under the terms of the lease was legal error. The District Court agreed, vacated the award, and remanded for further consideration by the arbitrator. The court expressly invoked the standard of review chosen by the parties in the arbitration agreement, which included review for legal error, and cited *LaPine Technology Corp. v. Kyocera Corp.* for the proposition that the FAA leaves the parties "free . . . to draft a contract that sets rules for arbitration and dictates an alternative standard of review."

On remand, the arbitrator followed the District Court's ruling that the Oregon Act was an applicable environmental law and amended the decision to favor Hall Street. This time, each party sought modification, and again the District Court applied the parties' stipulated standard of review for legal error, correcting the arbitrator's calculation of interest but otherwise upholding the award. Each party then appealed to the Court of Appeals for the Ninth Circuit, where Mattel switched horses and contended that the Ninth Circuit's recent en banc action overruling *LaPine* in *Kyocera Corp. v. Prudential-Bache Trade Servs., Inc.* left the arbitration agreement's provision for judicial review of legal error unenforceable. Hall Street countered that *Kyocera* (the later one) was distinguishable, and that the agreement's judicial review provision was not severable from the submission to arbitration.

The Ninth Circuit reversed in favor of Mattel in holding that, "[u]nder *Kyocera* the terms of the arbitration agreement controlling the mode of judicial review are unenforceable and severable." The Circuit instructed the District Court on remand to

> "return to the application to confirm the original arbitration award (not the subsequent award revised after reversal), and . . . confirm that award,

unless . . . the award should be vacated on the grounds allowable under 9 U.S.C. §10, or modified or corrected under the grounds allowable under 9 U.S.C. §11."

After the District Court again held for Hall Street and the Ninth Circuit again reversed, we granted certiorari to decide whether the grounds for vacatur and modification provided by §§10 and 11 of the FAA are exclusive. We agree with the Ninth Circuit that they are, but vacate and remand for consideration of independent issues.

II

Congress enacted the FAA to replace judicial indisposition to arbitration with a "national policy favoring [it] and plac[ing] arbitration agreements on equal footing with all other contracts." As for jurisdiction over controversies touching arbitration, the Act does nothing, being "something of an anomaly in the field of federal-court jurisdiction" in bestowing no federal jurisdiction but rather requiring an independent jurisdictional basis. But in cases falling within a court's jurisdiction, the Act makes contracts to arbitrate "valid, irrevocable, and enforceable," so long as their subject involves "commerce." §2. And this is so whether an agreement has a broad reach or goes just to one dispute, and whether enforcement be sought in state court or federal.

The Act also supplies mechanisms for enforcing arbitration awards: a judicial decree confirming an award, an order vacating it, or an order modifying or correcting it. §§9-11. An application for any of these orders will get streamlined treatment as a motion, obviating the separate contract action that would usually be necessary to enforce or tinker with an arbitral award in court §6. Under the terms of §9, a court "must" confirm an arbitration award "unless" it is vacated, modified, or corrected "as prescribed" in §§10 and 11. Section 10 lists grounds for vacating an award, while §11 names those for modifying or correcting one. . . .

The Courts of Appeals have split over the exclusiveness of these statutory grounds when parties take the FAA shortcut to confirm, vacate, or modify an award, with some saying the recitations are exclusive, and others regarding them as mere threshold provisions open to expansion by agreement. As mentioned already, when this litigation started, the Ninth Circuit was on the threshold side of the split, see *LaPine*, 130 F.3d, at 889, from which it later departed en banc in favor of the exclusivity view, see *Kyocera*, 341 F.3d, at 1000, which it followed in this case. We now hold that §§10 and 11 respectively provide the FAA's exclusive grounds for expedited vacatur and modification.

III

Hall Street makes two main efforts to show that the grounds set out for vacating or modifying an award are not exclusive, taking the position, first, that expandable judicial review authority has been accepted as the law since *Wilko v. Swan*, 346 U.S. 427, 74 S. Ct. 182, 98 L. Ed. 168 (1953). This, however, was not what *Wilko* decided, which was that §14 of the Securities Act of 1933 voided any agreement to arbitrate claims of violations of that Act, see *id.*, at 437-438, 74 S. Ct. 182, a holding since overruled *by Rodriguez de Quijas v. Shearson/American Express, Inc.*, 490 U.S. 477,

484, 109 S. Ct. 1917, 104 L. Ed. 2d 526 (1989). Although it is true that the Court's discussion includes some language arguably favoring Hall Street's position, arguable is as far as it goes.

The *Wilko* Court was explaining that arbitration would undercut the Securities Act's buyer protections when it remarked (citing FAA §10) that "[p]ower to vacate an [arbitration] award is limited," 346 U.S., at 436, 74 S. Ct. 182, and went on to say that "the interpretations of the law by the arbitrators in contrast to manifest disregard [of the law] are not subject, in the federal courts, to judicial review for error in interpretation," *id.*, at 436-437, 74 S. Ct. 182. Hall Street reads this statement as recognizing "manifest disregard of the law" as a further ground for vacatur on top of those listed in §10, and some Circuits have read it the same way. . . . Hall Street sees this supposed addition to §10 as the camel's nose: if judges can add grounds to vacate (or modify), so can contracting parties.

But this is too much for *Wilko* to bear. Quite apart from its leap from a supposed judicial expansion by interpretation to a private expansion by contract, Hall Street overlooks the fact that the statement it relies on expressly rejects just what Hall Street asks for here, general review for an arbitrator's legal errors. Then there is the vagueness of *Wilko*'s phrasing. Maybe the term "manifest disregard" was meant to name a new ground for review, but maybe it merely referred to the §10 grounds collectively, rather than adding to them. . . . Or, as some courts have thought, "manifest disregard" may have been shorthand for §10(a)(3) or §10(a)(4), the subsections authorizing vacatur when the arbitrators were "guilty of misconduct" or "exceeded their powers." . . . We, when speaking as a Court, have merely taken the *Wilko* language as we found it, without embellishment, . . . and now that its meaning is implicated, we see no reason to accord it the significance that Hall Street urges.

Second, Hall Street says that the agreement to review for legal error ought to prevail simply because arbitration is a creature of contract, and the FAA is "motivated, first and foremost, by a congressional desire to enforce agreements into which parties ha[ve] entered." *Dean Witter Reynolds Inc. v. Byrd*, 470 U.S. 213, 220, 105 S. Ct. 1238, 84 L. Ed. 2d 158 (1985). But, again, we think the argument comes up short. Hall Street is certainly right that the FAA lets parties tailor some, even many features of arbitration by contract, including the way arbitrators are chosen, what their qualifications should be, which issues are arbitrable, along with procedure and choice of substantive law. But to rest this case on the general policy of treating arbitration agreements as enforceable as such would be to beg the question, which is whether the FAA has textual features at odds with enforcing a contract to expand judicial review following the arbitration.

To that particular question we think the answer is yes, that the text compels a reading of the §§10 and 11 categories as exclusive. To begin with, even if we assumed §§10 and 11 could be supplemented to some extent, it would stretch basic interpretive principles to expand the stated grounds to the point of evidentiary and legal review generally. Sections 10 and 11, after all, address egregious departures from the parties' agreed-upon arbitration: "corruption," "fraud," "evident partiality," "misconduct," "misbehavior," "exceed[ing] . . . powers," "evident material miscalculation," "evident material mistake," "award[s] upon a matter not submitted"; the only ground with any softer focus is "imperfect[ions]," and a court may correct those only if they go to "[a] matter of form not affecting the merits." Given this emphasis on extreme arbitral conduct, the old rule of *ejusdem generis* has an implicit lesson to teach here. Under that rule, when a statute sets out a series of specific items ending with a general term, that general term is confined to covering subjects comparable to the specifics it follows. Since a general term included in the text is normally so limited, then surely a statute with no textual hook for expansion cannot authorize contracting parties to supplement review for specific instances of outrageous conduct with review for just any legal error. "Fraud" and a mistake of law are not cut from the same cloth.

That aside, expanding the detailed categories would rub too much against the grain of the §9 language, where provision for judicial confirmation carries no hint of flexibility. On application for an order confirming the arbitration award, the court "must grant" the order "unless the award is vacated, modified, or corrected as prescribed in sections 10 and 11 of this title." There is nothing malleable about "must grant," which unequivocally tells courts to grant confirmation in all cases, except when one of the "prescribed" exceptions applies. This does not sound remotely like a provision meant to tell a court what to do just in case the parties say nothing else. . . .

Instead of fighting the text, it makes more sense to see the three provisions, §§9-11, as substantiating a national policy favoring arbitration with just the limited review needed to maintain arbitration's essential virtue of resolving disputes straightaway. Any other reading opens the door to the full-bore legal and evidentiary appeals that can "rende[r] informal arbitration merely a prelude to a more cumbersome and time-consuming judicial review process," and bring arbitration theory to grief in post-arbitration process.

When all these arguments based on prior legal authority are done with, Hall Street and Mattel remain at odds over what happens next. Hall Street and its *amici* say parties will flee from arbitration if expanded review is not open to them. One of Mattel's *amici* foresees flight from the courts if it is. We do not know who, if anyone, is right, and so cannot say whether the exclusivity reading of the statute is more of a threat to the popularity of arbitrators or to that of courts. But whatever the consequences of our holding, the statutory text gives us no business to expand the statutory grounds.

IV

In holding that [FAA] §§10 and 11 provide exclusive regimes for the review provided by the statute, we do not purport to say that they exclude more searching review based on authority outside the statute as well. The FAA is not the only way into court for parties wanting review of arbitration awards: they may contemplate enforcement under state statutory or common law, for example, where judicial review of different scope is arguable. But here we speak only to the scope of the expeditious judicial review under §§9, 10, and 11, deciding nothing about other possible avenues for judicial enforcement of arbitration awards. . . .

We express no opinion on these matters beyond leaving them open for Hall Street to press on remand. . . .

Although we agree with the Ninth Circuit that the FAA confines its expedited judicial review to the grounds listed in 9 U.S.C. §§10 and 11, we vacate the judgment and remand the case for proceedings consistent with this opinion.

It is so ordered.

NOTES AND QUESTIONS

The Supreme Court's pronouncement in *Hall Street* failed to fully resolve questions surrounding the enforcement of contractual provisions for expanded judicial scrutiny of arbitration awards. The majority concluded that agreements for expanded review were inconsistent with the specific language of FAA Sections 10 and 11, which "substantiat[e] a national policy favoring arbitration with just the limited review needed to maintain arbitration's essential virtue of resolving disputes straightaway." But the Court proceeded to invite consideration of other avenues to the same ends, as where parties "contemplate enforcement under state statutory or common law . . . where judicial review of different scope is arguable." Although it may be some time before the full import of this invitation is clarified, it is likely that some state statutes or controlling judicial decisions promoting contractually expanded review will become "safe harbors" for such activity. New Jersey is perhaps the sole example of a statutory template for parties that wish to "opt in" to the legislative framework for elevated scrutiny of awards. *See* N.J. Stat. Ann. §2A:23A-12 (West 2015). In *Cable Connection, Inc. v. DIRECTV, Inc.*, 190 P.3d 586 (Cal. 2008), California's highest court recognized a more general "safe harbor" for contractually expanded judicial review under that state's law. The court indicated, however, that any provision for an expanded scope of review of arbitral awards must be unequivocal and explicit: "[T]o take themselves out of the general rule that the merits of the award are not subject to judicial review, the parties must clearly agree that legal errors are an excess of arbitral authority that is reviewable by the courts." 190 P.3d at 603. Similarly, the Texas Supreme Court in *Nafta Traders, Inc. v. Quinn*, 339 S.W.3d 84 (Tex. 2011), held that the Texas Arbitration Act (TAA) permits parties to contract for expanded judicial review of arbitration awards. The parties in *Nafta Traders* agreed that "[t]he arbitrator does not have authority (i) to render a decision which contains a reversible error of state or federal law, or (ii) to apply a cause of action or remedy not expressly provided for under existing state or federal law." The Texas Supreme Court held that the TAA permits parties to agree to expanded judicial review of arbitration awards, and the FAA does not preempt state law permitting such expanded review.

16. In *Katz, Nannis & Solomon, P.C. v. Levine*, 46 N.E.3d 541, 547 (Mass. 2016), the Massachusetts Supreme Judicial Court reached a different conclusion on the issue, holding that parties to a commercial arbitration agreement cannot alter the scope of judicial review of an arbitration award under the Massachusetts Uniform Arbitration Act for Commercial Disputes (MAA). In this case, the parties' agreement provided for judicial review of an award to see if there was a material, gross, and flagrant error made by the arbitrator. The court here held that even though arbitration is a creature of contract, the parties cannot modify the scope of judicial review set out in the MAA, which this court read to mimic the FAA. They relied on the Supreme Court's decision in *Hall Street Associates*, holding that the grounds for vacating or modifying an arbitration award in the FAA are the exclusive grounds, and parties cannot expand the scope of

judicial review by their agreement. *Cable Connection* appears to be a rational interpretation of the vacatur provisions of the California Arbitration Act (which is virtually identical in pertinent part to the FAA). However, even if your client had a legal right to contract for expanded judicial review of arbitration awards (e.g., provide that a reviewing court could vacate awards for errors of fact or law), is it something that you would want to include in your contract? What would be the likely impact on the cost and length of the dispute resolution process? Recall, moreover, that effective judicial review requires a variety of implementing steps, including the creation of a record, the preparation of a rationale to accompany the award, clear standards of review, and other elements.

17. *Manifest Disregard of the Law.* In addition to the statutory grounds for vacation of award included in the FAA and state analogues, courts have infrequently recognized non-statutory grounds for vacating arbitral awards. In unusual circumstances, courts might vacate awards as being "arbitrary and capricious" or irrational. *See, e.g., Ainsworth v. Skurnick*, 960 F.2d 939 (11th Cir. 1992) (district court upheld the decision of an arbitration panel finding Skurnick negligent, but vacated the arbitration judgment as being in manifest disregard of the law for failing to provide for mandatory damages under Florida law, rendering the panel's denial of damages arbitrary or capricious). The most prominent of these judicially declared grounds for vacatur, however, is "manifest disregard of the law." As explained in *Hall Street*, the notion that courts might vacate an award on such grounds sprang from dicta by Justice Black in a 1953 decision, *Wilko v. Swan*. Yet while parties often move to vacate an award on the basis that the arbitrators acted in "manifest disregard of the law," such motions seldom succeed. The Second Circuit described the basic contours of the doctrine as follows:

> The party seeking to vacate an award on the basis of the arbitrator's alleged "manifest disregard" of the law bears a "heavy burden." Our review under the [judicially constructed] doctrine of manifest disregard is "severely limited." . . . "It is highly deferential to the arbitral award and obtaining judicial relief for arbitrators' manifest disregard of the law is rare." . . .
>
> In this light, "manifest disregard" has been interpreted "clearly [to] mean more than error or misunderstanding with respect to the law." . . . A federal court cannot vacate an arbitral award merely because it is convinced that the arbitration panel made the wrong call on the law. On the contrary, the award should be enforced, despite a court's disagreement with it on the merits, if there is a barely colorable justification for the outcome reached.
>
> In the context of contract interpretation, we are required to confirm arbitration awards despite "serious reservations about the soundness of the arbitrator's reading of th[e] contract." . . .
>
> The concept of "manifest disregard" is well illustrated by *New York Telephone* Co. *v. Communication Workers*. There the

arbitrator recognized binding Second Circuit case law but deliberately refused to apply it, saying—no doubt to the astonishment of the parties—"Perhaps it is time for a new court decision." Because the arbitrator explicitly rejected controlling precedent, we concluded that the arbitral decision was rendered in manifest disregard of the law. . . .

[We doubt it is] necessary for arbitrators to state that they are deliberately ignoring the law. If the arbitrator's decision "strains credulity" or "does not rise to the standard of barely colorable," a court may conclude that the arbitrator "willfully flouted the governing law by refusing to apply it. . . ."

There are three components to our application of the "manifest disregard" standard. First, we must consider whether the law that was allegedly ignored was clear, and in fact explicitly applicable to the matter before the arbitrators. An arbitrator obviously cannot be said to disregard a law that is unclear or not clearly applicable. Thus, misapplication of an ambiguous law does not constitute manifest disregard.

Second, once it is determined that the law is clear and plainly applicable, we must find that the law was in fact improperly applied, leading to an erroneous outcome. We will, of course, not vacate an arbitral award for an erroneous application of the law if a proper application of law would have yielded the same result. In the same vein, where an arbitral award contains more than one plausible reading, manifest disregard cannot be found if at least one of the readings yields a legally correct justification for the outcome. Even where explanation for an award is deficient or non-existent, we will confirm it if a justifiable ground for decision can be inferred from the facts of the case.

Third, once the first two inquiries are satisfied, we look to a subjective element, that is, the knowledge actually possessed by the arbitrators. In order to intentionally disregard the law, the arbitrator must have known of its existence, and its applicability to the problem before him. In determining an arbitrator's awareness of the law, we impute only knowledge of governing law identified by the parties to the arbitration. Absent this we will infer knowledge and intentionality on the part of the arbitrator only if we find an error that is so obvious that it would be instantly perceived as such by the average person qualified to serve as an arbitrator.

Stolt-Nielsen S.A. v. AnimalFeeds Int'l Corp., 548 F.3d 85 (2d Cir. 2008), *rev'd and remanded*, 559 U.S 662 (2010). Based on your reading of *Hall Street*, do you believe the Supreme Court in that decision affected the "scope or vitality" of the doctrine of "manifest disregard"?

Since that time, the Second Circuit in *Weiss v. Sallie Mae, Inc.*, 939 F.3d 105 (2d Cir. 2019), remanded a case to the arbitrator after the lower court vacated an arbitration award based on manifest disregard of the law. The award had granted Weiss damages against the lender under the Telephone Consumer Protection Act, even though the arbitrator determined that Weiss was a class member in a class action against Sallie Mae that had been resolved by a settlement agreement containing a release that barred members from bringing TCPA claims against Sallie Mae. The court here held that because the arbitrator did not explain the reasoning behind his determinations, they could not decide whether he disregarded the law, as the district court ruled. They remanded to ask the arbitrator to clarify the basis of the award. They also noted that following the Supreme Court decision in *Hall Street*, the "manifest disregard" standard remains a basis for overturning an award, regardless of whether it is an independent reason for review or a "judicial gloss" on the enumerated grounds under the FAA.

According to the McArthur survey of reported cases from 2010-2017, manifest disregard is the second most frequent ground for a motion to vacate (after "exceeded powers"), but it is the least successful of all grounds for vacatur. After exhaustive study of the subject, McArthur concludes:

> Extreme facts and outcomes do attract efforts to vacate, and increase the odds of success. Vacatur, though rare, not uncommonly does rectify very unusual, unexpected outcomes when it is granted. Manifest disregard certainly requires an extreme fact—an arbitrator or panel that intentionally disregards the law. Reasons are the perfect antidote to this attack. Almost any good-faith reason should remove the predicate for manifest-disregard vacatur.[6]

18. *Appellate Arbitration Procedures.* Leading U.S. arbitration institutions (including JAMS, CPR, and the AAA) have established processes that are private counterparts of appellate courts. *Compare, e.g.,* JAMS Optional Arbitration Appeal Procedure and the AAA Optional Appellate Arbitration Rules.[7] How do these appellate arbitration procedures compare? Would you consider such an alternative in place of a contractual provision for expanded judicial review?

19. *Stolt-Nielsen S.A. v. AnimalFeeds Int'l Corp.*, 559 U.S. 662 (2010), a decision mentioned above, laid the groundwork for later rulings by a 5-4 majority of Supreme Court Justices enforcing class action waivers accompanying agreements to arbitrate. Those decisions are discussed in Chapter 8.B.2.

G.   TREATMENT OF FOREIGN ARBITRAL AWARDS UNDER THE NEW YORK CONVENTION

As discussed in Chapter 1, the Convention on the Recognition and Enforcement of Foreign Arbitral Awards (New York Convention) is a primary reason why arbitration is so extensively used as a substitute for litigation in international commerce and trade. Because of the New York Convention, adopted by more than 150 sovereign States worldwide, it is much easier to enforce arbitration awards rendered in other countries than it is to enforce foreign court judgments. In the United States, the New York Convention was adopted as Chapter 2 of the FAA (§§201-208).

Put most simply, the New York Convention establishes a mechanism for the recognition and/or enforcement of an award made in one sovereign nation (State A) in another nation (State B). "Recognition" means formal judicial acknowledgment of the legally binding status of an award vis-à-vis involved parties and issues. It is used most commonly in situations where parties are engaged in court litigation in State B over the same issues that were addressed in arbitration in State A. Judicial recognition of a prior arbitration would serve as a basis for ending the court proceedings as res judicata based on the earlier award. Thus, recognition is usually employed defensively against a court action brought by a party that lost in arbitration. Recognition of a prior award may also serve as the foundation of a right of setoff of damages against a current claim.

Judicial enforcement of a prior award goes a step further. It involves not only recognition by the court in State B but also steps to carry out the award through seizure of property and other assets and forfeiture of bank accounts in State B. In extreme cases a court might go so far as to imprison corporate officers. As the foregoing suggests, a party that succeeded in obtaining a favorable arbitration award in State A typically seeks enforcement in State B because that is where the party against whom the arbitration award was rendered has assets.

Under Article IV of the Convention, all that is needed to commence a procedure for recognition or enforcement is a "duly authenticated original award" or certified copy, and an original or certified copy of the arbitration agreement. Also, a party need not have obtained a judicial confirmation of the award in State A in order to get recognition or enforcement in State B.

Of course, the widespread adoption of the New York Convention does not guarantee uniformity in its application. First of all, it should be noted that Article I(3) permits countries to sign onto the Convention subject to different kinds of limitations or reservations. States enacting the Convention subject to a "reciprocity reservation" contract to recognize and enforce only awards rendered in countries that are also signatories to the Convention. States may also limit recognition and enforcement to awards rendered in arbitrations arising under or in connection with commercial relationships.

Beyond this, the Convention provides a relatively uniform framework but leaves its application in the hands of courts that are applying the procedural rules of their respective states. Although Article III of the Convention says that in applying such rules courts cannot discriminate against foreign arbitral awards by imposing requirements that are more stringent than usual, it is possible that lack of familiarity with the Convention or forms of protectionism will affect court decisions. In some cases, moreover, state public policies may prevent recognition and enforcement.

Article I(1) of the Convention provides that it applies "to the recognition and enforcement of arbitral awards made in the territory of a State other than the State where the recognition and enforcement of such awards are sought" and "to arbitral awards not considered as domestic awards in the State where their recognition and enforcement are sought." In order to enforce an arbitral award under the Convention, the arbitral award has to be of a "foreign" nature, which is generally determined by the domestic law. This was the issue in *Yusuf Ahmed Alghanim & Sons v. Toys "R" Us, Inc.*, 126 F.3d 15 (1997), and the Second Circuit further clarified the FAA shall be applied to the non-domestic award made in the United States to decide whether setting aside the award is appropriate.

Yusuf Ahmed Alghanim & Sons v. Toys "R" Us, Inc.

126 F.3d 15 (2d Cir. 1997)

MINER, Circuit Judge:

. . .

In November of 1982, respondent-appellant Toys "R" Us, Inc. (collectively with respondent-appellant TRU (HK) Limited, "Toys 'R' Us") and petitioner-appellee Yusuf Ahmed Alghanim & Sons, W.L.L. ("Alghanim"), a privately owned Kuwaiti business, entered into a License and Technical Assistance Agreement (the "agreement") and a Supply Agreement. Through the agreement, Toys "R" Us granted Alghanim a limited right to open Toys "R" Us stores and use its trademarks in Kuwait and 13 other countries located in and around the Middle East (the "territory."). Toys "R" Us further agreed to supply Alghanim with its technology, expertise and assistance in the toy business.

From 1982 to the December 1993 commencement of the arbitration giving rise to this appeal, Alghanim opened four toy stores, all in Kuwait. According to Toys "R" Us, the first such store, opened in 1983, resembled a Toys "R" Us store in the United States, but the other three, two of which were opened in 1985 and one in 1988, were small storefronts with only limited merchandise. It is uncontested that Alghanim's stores lost some $6.65 million over the 11–year period from 1982 to 1993, and turned a profit only in one year of this period.

On July 20, 1992, Toys "R" Us purported to exercise its right to terminate the agreement, sending Alghanim a notice of non-renewal stating that the agreement would terminate on January 31, 1993. Alghanim responded on July 30, 1992, stating that because its most recently opened toy store had opened on January 16, 1988, the initial term of the agreement ended on January 16, 1993. Alghanim asserted that Toys "R" Us's notice of non-renewal was four days late in providing notice six months before the end of the initial period. According to Alghanim, under the termination provision of the agreement, Toys "R" Us's failure to provide notice more than six months before the fifth year after the opening of the most recent store automatically extended the term of the agreement for an additional two years, until January 16, 1995.

Through the balance of 1992 and 1993, the parties unsuccessfully attempted to renegotiate the agreement or devise a new arrangement. In September of 1993, the parties discussed Alghanim's willingness to relinquish its rights under the agreement. In one discussion, Amin Kadrie, Alghanim's chief operating officer and the head of its toy business, offered to "release the business right now" if Toys "R" Us would "give us $2 million for the losses we've incurred [in] trying to develop this business." (J.A. 457.) Toys "R" Us declined, offering instead to buy Alghanim's inventory at Alghanim's cost. The parties could not agree upon a reconciliation.

At the end of 1993, Toys "R" Us contracted with Al-Futtaim Sons Co., LLC ("Al-Futtaim") for the post-Alghanim rights to open Toys "R" Us stores in five of the countries under the agreement, including Kuwait, and with ATA Development Co. ("ATA") for the post-Alghanim rights to open Toys "R" Us stores in Saudi Arabia. These two companies initially offered $30 million for the rights, and eventually paid a total of $22.5 million. On December 20, 1993, Toys "R" Us invoked the dispute-resolution mechanism in the agreement, initiating an arbitration before the American Arbitration Association. Toys "R" Us sought a declaration that the agreement was terminated on December 31, 1993. Alghanim responded by counterclaiming for breach of contract.

On July 11, 1996, the arbitrator awarded Alghanim $46.44 million for lost profits under the agreement, plus 9 percent interest to accrue from December 31, 1994. The arbitrator's findings and legal conclusions were set forth in a 47-page opinion. Alghanim petitioned the district court to confirm the award under the Convention on the Recognition and Enforcement of Foreign Arbitral Awards of June 10, 1958 ("Convention"), 21 U.S.T. 2517, 330 U.N.T.S. 38, reprinted at 9 U.S.C. §201. 1 Toys "R" Us cross-moved to vacate or modify the award under the Federal Arbitration Act ("FAA"), 9 U.S.C. §1 *et seq.*, arguing that the award was clearly irrational, in manifest disregard of the law, and in manifest disregard of the terms of the agreement.

DISCUSSION

I. Availability of the FAA's Grounds for Relief in Confirmation Under the Convention

A. Applicability of the Convention

Neither party seriously disputes the applicability of the Convention to this case and it is clear to us that the Convention does apply. The Convention provides that it will "apply to the recognition and enforcement of arbitral awards made in the territory of a State other than the State where the recognition and enforcement of such awards are sought, and arising out of differences between persons, whether physical or legal." It shall also apply to arbitral awards not considered as domestic awards in the State where their recognition and enforcement are sought. Convention art. I(1).

The Convention does not define nondomestic awards. See *Bergesen v. Joseph Muller Corp.*, 710 F.2d 928, 932 (2d Cir. 1983). However, 9 U.S.C. §202, one of the provisions implementing the Convention, provides that "[a]n agreement or award arising out of such a relationship which is entirely between citizens of the United States shall be deemed not to fall under the Convention unless that relationship involves property located abroad, envisages performance or enforcement abroad, or has some other reasonable relation with one or more foreign states."

In *Bergesen*, we held "that awards 'not considered as domestic' denotes awards which are subject to the Convention not because made abroad, but because made within the legal framework of another country, e.g., pronounced in accordance with foreign law or involving parties domiciled or having their principal place of business outside the enforcing jurisdiction." 710 F.2d at 932 (quoting 9 U.S.C. §201). The Seventh Circuit similarly has interpreted §202 to mean that "any commercial arbitral agreement, unless it is between two United States citizens, involves property located in the United States, and has no reasonable relationship with one or more foreign states, falls under the Convention." *Jain v. de Méré*, 51 F.3d 686, 689 (7th Cir.), *cert. denied*, 516 U.S. 914, 116 S. Ct. 300, 133 L. Ed. 2d 206 (1995).

The Convention's applicability in this case is clear. The dispute giving rise to this appeal involved two nondomestic parties and one United States corporation, and principally involved conduct and contract performance in the Middle East. Thus, we consider the arbitral award leading to this action a non-domestic.

B. Authority Under the Convention to Set Aside an Award Under Domestic Arbitral Law

Toys "R" Us argues that the district court properly found that it had the authority under the Convention to apply the FAA's implied grounds for setting aside the award. We agree.

Under the Convention, the district court's role in reviewing a foreign arbitral award is strictly limited: "The court shall confirm the award unless it finds one of the grounds for refusal or deferral of recognition or enforcement of the award specified in the said Convention." 9 U.S.C. §207; see *Andros Compania Maritima, S.A. v. Marc Rich & Co., A.G.*, 579 F.2d 691, 699 n. 11 (2d Cir. 1978). Under Article V of the Convention, the grounds for refusing to recognize or enforce an arbitral award are: [the court quoted the seven grounds from Article V of the New York Convention].

Enforcement may also be refused if "[t]he subject matter of the difference is not capable of settlement by arbitration," or if "recognition or enforcement of the award would be contrary to the public policy" of the country in which enforcement or recognition is sought. Id. art. V(2). These seven grounds are the only grounds explicitly provided under the Convention.

In determining the availability of the FAA's implied grounds for setting aside, the text of the Convention leaves us with two questions: (1) whether, in addition to the Convention's express grounds for refusal, other grounds can be read into the Convention by implication, much as American courts have read implied grounds for relief into the FAA, and (2) whether, under Article V(1)(e), the courts of the United States are authorized to apply United States procedural arbitral law, i.e., the FAA, to nondomestic awards rendered in the United States. We answer the first question in the negative and the second in the affirmative.

1. Authority Under the Convention to Set Aside an Award Under Domestic Arbitral Law

We have held that the FAA and the Convention have "overlapping coverage" to the extent that they do not conflict. *Bergesen*, 710 F.2d at 934; see 9 U.S.C. §208 (FAA may apply to actions brought under the Convention "to the extent that [the FAA] is not in conflict with [9 U.S.C. §§201-208] or the Convention as ratified by the United States"); *Lander Co. v. MMP Invs., Inc.*, 107 F.3d 476, 481 (7th Cir. 1997), *cert. denied*, 522 U.S. 811, 118 S. Ct. 55, 139 L. Ed. 2d 19, (1997). However, by that same token, to the extent that the Convention prescribes the exclusive grounds for relief from an award under the Convention, that application of the FAA's implied grounds would be in conflict, and is thus precluded. See, e.g., *M & C Corp. v. Erwin Behr GmbH & Co., KG*, 87 F.3d 844, 851 (6th Cir. 1996).

In *Parsons & Whittemore Overseas Co. v. Societe Generale de L'Industrie du Papier (Rakta)*, 508 F.2d 969 (2d Cir. 1974), we declined to decide whether the implied defense of "manifest disregard" applies under the Convention, having decided that even if it did, appellant's claim would fail. See id. at 977. Nonetheless, we noted that "[b]oth the legislative history of Article V and the statute enacted to implement the United States' accession to the Convention are strong authority for treating as exclusive the bases set forth in the Convention for vacating an award." Id. (citation and footnote omitted).

There is now considerable case law holding that, in an action to confirm an award rendered in, or under the law of, a foreign jurisdiction, the grounds for relief enumerated in Article V of the Convention are the only grounds available for setting aside an arbitral award. See, e.g., *M & C*, 87 F.3d at 851 (concluding that the Convention's exclusive grounds for relief "do not include miscalculations of fact or manifest disregard of the law"); *International Standard Elec. Corp. v. Bridas Sociedad Anonima Petrolera, Industrial Y Comercial*, 745 F. Supp. 172, 181-82 (S.D.N.Y.1990) (refusing to apply a "manifest disregard of law" standard on a motion to vacate a foreign arbitral award); *Brandeis Intsel Ltd. v. Calabrian Chems. Corp.*, 656 F.Supp. 160, 167 (S.D.N.Y.1987) ("In my view, the 'manifest disregard' defense is not available under Article V of the Convention or otherwise to a party . . . seeking to vacate an award of foreign arbitrators based upon foreign law."); see also *Albert Jan van den Berg, The New York Arbitration Convention of 1958: Towards a Uniform Judicial Interpretation* 265 (1981) ("the grounds mentioned in Article V are exhaustive"). . . . We join these courts in declining to read into the Convention the FAA's implied defenses to confirmation of an arbitral award.

2. *Nondomestic Award Rendered in the United States*

Although Article V provides the exclusive grounds for refusing confirmation under the Convention, one of those exclusive grounds is where "[t]he award . . . has been set aside or suspended by a competent authority of the country in which, or under the law of which, that award was made." Convention art. V(1)(e). Those courts holding that implied defenses were inapplicable under the Convention did so in the context of petitions to confirm awards rendered abroad. These courts were not presented with the question whether Article V(1)(e) authorizes an action to set aside an arbitral award under the domestic law of the state in which, or under which, the award was rendered. We, however, are faced head-on with that question in the case before us, because the arbitral award in this case was rendered in the United States, and both confirmation and vacatur were then sought in the United States.

Our conclusion also is consistent with the reasoning of courts that have refused to apply non-Convention grounds for relief where awards were rendered outside the United States. For example, the Sixth Circuit in *M & C* concluded that it should not apply the FAA's implied grounds for vacatur, because the United States did not provide the law of the arbitration for the purposes of Article V(1)(e) of the Convention. 87 F.3d at 849. Similarly, in International Standard, the district court decided that only the state under whose procedural law the arbitration was conducted has jurisdiction under Article V(1)(e) to vacate the award, whereas on a petition for confirmation made in any other state, only the defenses to confirmation listed in Article V of the Convention are available. 745 F. Supp. at 178.

This interpretation of Article V(1)(e) also finds support in the scholarly work of commentators on the Convention and in the judicial decisions of our sister signatories to the Convention. There appears to be no dispute among these authorities that an action to set aside an international arbitral award, as contemplated by Article V(1)(e), is controlled by the domestic law of the rendering state. As one commentator has explained:

> The possible effect of this ground for refusal [Article V(1)(e)] is that, as the award can be set aside in the country of origin on all grounds contained in the arbitration law of that country, including the public policy of that country, the grounds for refusal of enforcement under the Convention may indirectly be extended to include all kinds of particularities of the arbitration law of the country of origin. This might undermine the limitative character of the grounds for refusal listed in Article V . . . and thus decrease the degree of uniformity existing under the Convention . . . The defense in Article V(1)(e) incorporates the entire body of review rights in the issuing jurisdiction. . . . If the scope of judicial review in the rendering state extends beyond the other six defenses allowed under the New York Convention, the losing party's opportunity to avoid enforcement is automatically enhanced: The losing party can first attempt to derail the award on appeal on grounds that would not be permitted elsewhere during enforcement proceedings.

There is no indication in the Convention of any intention to deprive the rendering state of its supervisory authority over an arbitral award, including its authority to set aside that award under domestic law. The Convention succeeded and replaced the *Convention on the Execution of Foreign Arbitral Awards* ("Geneva Convention"), Sept. 26, 1927, 92 L.N.T.S. 301. The primary defect of the Geneva Convention was that it required an award first to be recognized in the rendering state before it could be enforced abroad, see Geneva Convention arts. 1(d), 4(2), 92 L.N.T.S. at 305, 306, the so-called requirement of "double exequatur." See Jane L. Volz & Roger S. Haydock, *Foreign Arbitral Awards: Enforcing the Award Against the Recalcitrant Loser*, 21 Wm. Mitchell L.Rev. 867, 876-77 (1996); W. Laurence Craig, *Some Trends and Developments in the Laws and Practice of International Commercial Arbitration*, 30 Tex. Int'l L.J. 1, 9 (1995). This requirement "was an unnecessary time-consuming hurdle," van den Berg, *supra*, at 267, and "greatly limited [the Geneva Convention's] utility," Craig, *supra*, at 9.

The Convention eliminated this problem by eradicating the requirement that a court in the rendering state recognize an award before it could be taken and enforced abroad. In so doing, the Convention intentionally "liberalized procedures for enforcing foreign arbitral awards," Volz & Haydock, *supra*, at 878; see *Scherk*, 417 U.S. at 519-20 & n. 15, 94 S. Ct. at 2457 & n. 15; *Parsons*, 508 F.2d at 973 (noting "[t]he general pro-enforcement bias informing the Convention and explaining its supersession of the Geneva Convention").

Nonetheless, under the Convention, the power and authority of the local courts of the rendering state remain of paramount importance. "What the Convention did not do. . . was provide any international mechanism to insure the validity of the award where rendered. This was left to the provisions of local law. The Convention provides no restraint whatsoever on the control functions of local courts at the seat of arbitration." Craig, *supra*, at 11. Another commentator explained:

> Significantly, [Article V(1)(e)] fails to specify the grounds upon which the rendering State may set aside or suspend the award. While it would have provided greater reliability to the enforcement of awards under the Convention had the available grounds been defined in some way, such action

would have constituted meddling with national procedure for handling domestic awards, a subject beyond the competence of the Conference.

Leonard V. Quigley, *Accession by the United States to the United Nations Convention on the Recognition and Enforcement of Foreign Arbitral Awards*, 70 Yale L.J. 1049, 1070 (1961). From the plain language and history of the Convention, it is thus apparent that a party may seek to vacate or set aside an award in the state in which, or under the law of which, the award is rendered. Moreover, the language and history of the Convention make it clear that such a motion is to be governed by domestic law of the rendering state, despite the fact that the award is nondomestic within the meaning of the Convention as we have interpreted it in *Bergesen*, 710 F.2d at 932.

In sum, we conclude that the Convention mandates very different regimes for the review of arbitral awards (1) in the state in which, or under the law of which, the award was made, and (2) in other states where recognition and enforcement are sought. The Convention specifically contemplates that the state in which, or under the law of which, the award is made, will be free to set aside or modify an award in accordance with its domestic arbitral law and its full panoply of express and implied grounds for relief. See Convention art. V(1)(e). However, the Convention is equally clear that when an action for enforcement is brought in a foreign state, the state may refuse to enforce the award only on the grounds explicitly set forth in Article V of the Convention.

. . .

II. Application of FAA Grounds for Relief

. . .

A. Manifest Disregard of the Law

. . .

B. Manifest Disregard of the Agreement

. . .

CONCLUSION

For the foregoing reasons, the judgment of the district court is affirmed.

The central "battleground" of the Convention is Article V, which sets forth the grounds for refusal of recognition and enforcement of a foreign arbitral award:

1. Recognition and enforcement of the award may be refused, at the request of the party against whom it is invoked, only if that party furnishes to the competent authority where the recognition and enforcement is sought, proof that:

(a) The parties to the agreement referred to in article II were, under the law applicable to them, under some incapacity, or the said agreement is not valid under the law to which the parties have subjected it or, failing any indication thereon, under the law of the country where the award was made; or

(b) The party against whom the award is invoked was not given proper notice of the appointment of the arbitrator or of the arbitration proceedings or was otherwise unable to present his case; or

(c) The award deals with a difference not contemplated by or not falling within the terms of the submission to arbitration, or it contains decisions on matters beyond the scope of the submission to arbitration, provided that, if the decisions on matters submitted to arbitration can be separated from those not so submitted, that part of the award which contains decisions on matters submitted to arbitration may be recognized and enforced; or

(d) The composition of the arbitral authority or the arbitral procedure was not in accordance with the agreement of the parties, or, failing such agreement, was not in accordance with the law of the country where the arbitration took place; or

(e) The award has not yet become binding on the parties, or has been set aside or suspended by a competent authority of the country in which, or under the law of which, that award was made.

2. Recognition and enforcement of an arbitral award may also be refused if the competent authority in the country where recognition and enforcement is sought finds that:

(a) The subject matter of the difference is not capable of settlement by arbitration under the law of that country; or

(b) The recognition or enforcement of the award would be contrary to the public policy of that country.

With respect to the foregoing, a few general observations are in order. First of all, the grounds listed in Article V are the sole and exclusive grounds for refusal to recognize or enforce an award, and they should be construed/applied narrowly. In this regard, note that Article V (like Section 10 of the FAA) makes no provision for review or refusal to recognize or enforce arbitration awards for errors of fact or law. Second, the burden of proof under Article V is on the party seeking to avoid recognition or enforcement. Finally, and significantly, the decision to refuse recognition or enforcement is not mandatory, but instead a matter of discretion for a court.

As you review the grounds for refusing recognition and enforcement in Article V, it should be evident that they are in many respects similar to the grounds for vacatur of award set out in FAA Section 10 — an invalid arbitration agreement, procedural deficiencies preventing a fair hearing, and arbitrators acting outside their jurisdiction/authority. However, judicial action under Article V is sometimes complicated by the fact that a court in State B may be called upon not only to interpret and apply the arbitration law and related public policies of State B, but also to interpret and apply the law of the "seat" of arbitration — State A. The latter law may come into play, for example, under subsection (e) where there are issues regarding compliance with special procedures for issuance of a valid award in State A.

When all is said and done, however, remember that Article V is permissive and not mandatory, and courts have a degree of discretion in making the decision to refuse to recognize or enforce a foreign arbitration award. Therefore, there are situations in which a court in State B has enforced an arbitration award even though the award was set aside or vacated by the courts of State A. In addition, the

New York Convention contains what might be described as a "loophole" provision in Article VII that allows a party seeking recognition and enforcement to use more favorable local law.

> *The provisions of the present Convention shall not affect the validity of multilateral or bilateral agreements concerning the recognition and enforcement of arbitral awards entered into by the Contracting States nor deprive any interested party of any right he may have to avail himself of an arbitral award in the manner and to the extent allowed by the law or the treaties of the country where such award is sought to be relied upon.*

In the controversial decision in *Chromalloy Aeroservices v. Arab Republic of Egypt,* 939 F. Supp. 907 (D.D.C. 1996), a federal court cited this provision in the course of enforcing an award that had been set aside by a court in Egypt. The court contrasted the language of Article VII with the permissive language of Article V, and held that "[a] decision by this Court to recognize the decision of the Egyptian court would violate [the] clear U.S. public policy" in favor of enforcement of binding arbitration clauses. 939 F. Supp. 907, 913.

Chromalloy Aeroservices v. Arab Republic of Egypt

939 F. Supp. 907 (D.D.C. 1996)

Appeal from the United States District Court for the Northern District Texas.

. . .

JUNE L. GREEN, District Judge:

This matter is before the Court on the Petition of Chromalloy Aeroservices, Inc., ("CAS") to Confirm an Arbitral Award, and a Motion to Dismiss that Petition filed by the Arab Republic of Egypt ("Egypt"), the defendant in the arbitration. This is a case of first impression. The Court GRANTS Chromalloy Aeroservices' Petition to Recognize and Enforce the Arbitral Award, and DENIES Egypt's Motion to Dismiss, because the arbitral award in question is valid, and because Egypt's arguments against enforcement are insufficient to allow this Court to disturb the award.

[On June 16, 1988, Egypt and CAS entered into a contract under which CAS agreed to provide parts, maintenance, and repair for helicopters belonging to the Egyptian Air Force. On December 2, 1991, Egypt terminated the contract by notifying CAS representatives in Egypt. On December 4, 1991, Egypt notified CAS headquarters in Texas of the termination. On December 15, 1991, CAS notified Egypt that it rejected the cancellation of the contract "and commenced arbitration proceedings on the basis of the arbitration clause contained in Article XII and Appendix E of the Contract." Egypt then drew down CAS's letters of guarantee in an amount totaling some $11,475,968.

On February 23, 1992, the parties began appointing arbitrators, and shortly thereafter, commenced a lengthy arbitration. On August 24, 1994, the arbitral panel ordered Egypt to pay to CAS the sums of $272,900 plus 5 percent interest from July 15, 1991 (interest accruing until the date of payment) and $16,940,958 plus 5 percent interest from December 15, 1991 (interest accruing until the date of payment). The panel also ordered CAS to pay to Egypt the sum of 606,920 pounds sterling, plus 5 percent interest from December 15, 1991 (interest accruing until the date of payment).

On October 28, 1994, CAS applied to this Court for enforcement of the award. On November 13, 1994, Egypt filed an appeal with the Egyptian Court of Appeal, seeking nullification of the award. On March 1, 1995, Egypt filed a motion with this Court to adjourn CAS's Petition to enforce the award. On April 4, 1995, the Egyptian Court of Appeal suspended the award, and on May 5, 1995, Egypt filed a Motion in this Court to Dismiss CAS's petition to enforce the award. On December 5, 1995, Egypt's Court of Appeal at Cairo issued an order nullifying the award. (Decision of Egyptian Court of Appeal ("Egypt Ct.") at 11.) This Court held a hearing in the matter on December 12, 1995.

Egypt argues that this Court should deny CAS's Petition to Recognize and Enforce the Arbitral Award out of deference to its court. CAS argues that this Court should confirm the award because Egypt "does not present any serious argument that its court's nullification decision is consistent with the New York Convention or United States arbitration law."]

DISCUSSION

While Article V provides a discretionary standard, Article VII of the Convention requires that, "The provisions of the present Convention shall not . . . deprive any interested party of any right he may have to avail himself of an arbitral award in the manner and to the extent allowed by the law . . . of the count[r]y where such award is sought to be relied upon." 9 U.S.C. §201 note (emphasis added). In other words, under the Convention, CAS maintains all rights to the enforcement of this Arbitral Award that it would have in the absence of the Convention. Accordingly, the Court finds that, if the Convention did not exist, the Federal Arbitration Act ("FAA") would provide CAS with a legitimate claim to enforcement of this arbitral award. See 9 U.S.C. §§1-14. Jurisdiction over Egypt in such a suit would be available under 28 U.S.C. §§1330 (granting jurisdiction over foreign states "as to any claim for relief in personam with respect to which the foreign state is not entitled to immunity . . . under sections 1605-1607 of this title") and 1605(a)(2) (withholding immunity of foreign states for "an act outside . . . the United States in connection with a commercial activity of the foreign state elsewhere and that act causes a direct effect in the United States"). . . .

Under the laws of the United States, 9 U.S.C. §10. 3., arbitration awards are presumed to be binding, and may only be vacated by a court under very limited circumstances:

> (a) In any of the following cases the United States court in and for the district wherein the award was made may make an order vacating the award upon the application of any party to the arbitration—
> (1) Where the award was procured by corruption, fraud, or undue means.
> (2) Where there was evident partiality or corruption in the arbitrators, or either of them.
> (3) Where the arbitrators were guilty of misconduct in refusing to postpone the hearing, upon sufficient cause shown, or in refusing to hear

evidence pertinent and material to the controversy; or of any other misbehavior by which the rights of any party have been prejudiced.

(4) Where the arbitrators exceeded their powers, or so imperfectly executed them that a mutual, final, and definite award upon the subject matter submitted was not made.

An arbitral award will also be set aside if the award was made in " 'manifest disregard' of the law." *First Options of Chicago v. Kaplan*, 514 U.S. 938, ___, 115 S. Ct. 1920, 1923, 131 L. Ed. 2d 985 (1995). "Manifest disregard of the law may be found if [the] arbitrator[s] understood and correctly stated the law but proceeded to ignore it." *Kanuth v. Prescott, Ball, & Turben, Inc.*, 949 F.2d 1175, 1179 (D.C. Cir. 1991).

In the United States, "[W]e are well past the time when judicial suspicion of the desirability of arbitration and of the competence of arbitral tribunals inhibited the development of arbitration as an alternative means of dispute resolution." *Mitsubishi Motors Corp. v. Soler Chrysler-Plymouth, Inc.*, 473 U.S. 614, 626-27, 105 S. Ct. 3346, 3354, 87 L. Ed. 2d 444 (1985). In Egypt, however, "[I]t is established that arbitration is an exceptional means for resolving disputes, requiring departure from the normal means of litigation before the courts, and the guarantees they afford." (Nullification Decision at 8.) Egypt's complaint that, "[T]he Arbitral Award is null under Arbitration Law, . . . because it is not properly 'grounded' under Egyptian law," reflects this suspicious view of arbitration, and is precisely the type of technical argument that U.S. courts are not to entertain when reviewing an arbitral award. . . .

The Court has already found that the arbitral award is proper as a matter of U.S. law, and that the arbitration agreement between Egypt and CAS precluded an appeal in Egyptian courts. The Egyptian court has acted, however, and Egypt asks this Court to grant res judicata effect to that action. The "requirements for enforcement of a foreign judgment . . . are that there be 'due citation' [i.e., proper service of process] and that the original claim not violate U.S. public policy." *Tahan v. Hodgson*, 662 F.2d 862, 864 (D.C. Cir. 1981) (citing *Hilton v. Guyot*, 159 U.S. 113, 202, 16 S. Ct. 139, 158, 40 L. Ed. 95 (1895)). The Court uses the term 'public policy' advisedly, with a full understanding that, "[J]udges have no license to impose their own brand of justice in determining applicable public policy." *Northwest Airlines Inc. v. Air Line Pilots Association, Int'l*, 808 F.2d 76, 78 (D.C. Cir. 1987). Correctly understood, "[P]ublic policy emanates [only] from clear statutory or case law, 'not from general considerations of supposed public interest.' " Id. (quoting *American Postal Workers Union v. United States Postal Service*, 789 F.2d 1 (D.C. Cir. 1986)).

The U.S. public policy in favor of final and binding arbitration of commercial disputes is unmistakable, and supported by treaty, by statute, and by case law. The Federal Arbitration Act "and the implementation of the Convention in the same year by amendment of the Federal Arbitration Act," demonstrate that there is an "emphatic federal policy in favor of arbitral dispute resolution," particularly "in the field of international commerce." *Mitsubishi v. Soler Chrysler-Plymouth*, 473 U.S. 614, 631, 105 S. Ct. 3346, 3356, 87 L. Ed. 2d 444 (1985) (internal citation omitted); cf. *Revere Copper & Brass Inc., v. Overseas Private Investment Corporation*, 628 F.2d 81, 82 (D.C. Cir. 1980) (holding that, "There is a strong public policy behind judicial enforcement of binding arbitration clauses"). A decision by this Court to recognize the decision of the Egyptian court would violate this clear U.S. public policy.

"No nation is under an unremitting obligation to enforce foreign interests which are fundamentally prejudicial to those of the domestic forum." *Laker Airways Ltd. v. Sabena, Belgian World Airlines*, 731 F.2d 909, 937 (D.C. Cir. 1984). "[C]omity never obligates a national forum to ignore 'the rights of its own citizens or of other persons who are under the protection of its laws.'" Id. at 942 (emphasis added) (quoting *Hilton v. Guyot*, 159 U.S. 113, 164, 16 S. Ct. 139, 143-44, 40 L. Ed. 95 (1895). Egypt alleges that, "Comity is the chief doctrine of international law requiring U.S. courts to respect the decisions of competent foreign tribunals." However, comity does not and may not have the preclusive effect upon U.S. law that Egypt wishes this Court to create for it.

As a final matter, Egypt argues that "Chromalloy's use of [A]rticle VII [to invoke the Federal Arbitration Act] contradicts the clear language of the Convention and would create an impermissible conflict under 9 U.S.C. §208," by eliminating all consideration of Article V of the Convention. See *Vimar Seguros y Reaseguros, S.A. v. M/V Sky Reefer*, 515 U.S. 528, ___, 115 S. Ct. 2322, 2325, 132 L. Ed. 2d 462 (1995) (holding that, "[W]hen two statutes are capable of coexistence . . . it is the duty of the courts, absent a clearly expressed congressional intention to the contrary, to regard each as effective"). As the Court has explained, however, Article V provides a permissive standard, under which this Court may refuse to enforce an award. Article VII, on the other hand, mandates that this Court must consider CAS' claims under applicable U.S. law.

Article VII of the Convention provides that "The provisions of the present Convention shall not . . . deprive any interested party of any right he may have to avail himself of an arbitral award in the manner and to the extent allowed by the law . . . of the count[r]y where such award is sought to be relied upon." 9 U.S.C. §201 note. Article VII does not eliminate all consideration of Article V; it merely requires that this Court protect any rights that CAS has under the domestic laws of the United States. There is no conflict between CAS' use of Article VII to invoke the FAA and the language of the Convention.

CONCLUSION

The Court concludes that the award of the arbitral panel is valid as a matter of U.S. law. The Court further concludes that it need not grant res judicata effect to the decision of the Egyptian Court of Appeal at Cairo. Accordingly, the Court GRANTS Chromalloy Aeroservices' Petition to Recognize and Enforce the Arbitral Award, and DENIES Egypt's Motion to Dismiss that Petition. . . .

In *Baker Marine*, the Second Circuit rejected Baker Marine's reliance on *Chromalloy* to enforce annulled foreign arbitral awards. This was because the factual relationship and the fact that appellees did not violate any promise in appealing the arbitration award within Nigeria are distinguishable from *Chromalloy*. The court then held that the "[r]ecognition of the Nigerian judgment in this case does not conflict with United States public policy." 191 F.3d at 197 n.3. It also noted that "[i]f a party whose arbitration award has been vacated at the site of the award can automatically obtain enforcement of the awards under the domestic laws of other nations, a losing party will have every reason to pursue its adversary 'with enforcement actions from country to country until a court is found, if any, which grants the enforcement.'" (quoting Albert Jan van den Berg, *The New York Arbitration Convention of 1958: Towards a Uniform Judicial Interpretation* 355 (1981)). Similarly, in *TermoRio*, the D.C Court of Appeals distinguished its case at hand from *Chromalloy*; however, it set a more clear role of enforcing annulled foreign arbitral awards under the New York Convention by accepting that "there is a narrow public policy gloss on Article V(1)(e) of the Convention and that a foreign judgment is unenforceable as against public policy to the extent it is 'repugnant to fundamental notions of what is decent and just in the United States.'" 487 F.3d 928, 939. Neither *Baker Marine* nor *TermoRio* disaffirmed the judgment in *Chromalloy*; therefore, *Chromalloy* still survives as binding authority that makes a district court hesitate to defer to a foreign judgment of nullification of an arbitral award that conflicts with fundamental notions of fairness prescribed by U.S. public policy. *See Pemex*, 962 F.Supp.2d 642, 656.

In *Pemex*, the U.S District Court of New York held that an arbitration award that had been set aside by the Mexican courts could be enforced in the United States under the terms of the Panama Convention even though the latter does not contain an equivalent to Article VII of the New York Convention. The district court in *Pemex* considered previous cases by stressing that *Chromalloy*, *Baker Marine*, and *TermoRio* all stand solid as precedents, and held that the nullification judgment from a foreign court that is in conflict with the fundamental notions of fairness in the United States should not be recognized. Given the legitimate expectation of the parties and due to the "retroactive application of laws and the unfairness associated with such application", the district court refused to recognize the Mexican court's nullification of an arbitral award that violated basic notions of justice and enforced the annulled ICC award.

Corporación Mexicana de Mantenimiento Integral, S. de R.L. de C.V. v. Pemex-Exploración y Producción

962 F. Supp. 2d 642 (S.D.N.Y. 2013)

Remanded from The United States Court of Appeals for the Second Circuit.

. . .

Alvin K. HELLERSTEIN, District Judge:

Generally, arbitration awards issued in one nation can be enforced by judgments and executions granted by the courts of another nation. However, arbitration awards also can be nullified, and if nullified by the courts of the nation in which, or according to the law of which, the arbitration was conducted, a conflict is created for the courts of other nations. Which is to be given primacy, the award or the nullifying judgment?

This is the issue of the case. After a vigorously contested arbitration, a panel of arbitrators in Mexico City issued an award (the "Award") in favor of petitioner, Corporación Mexicana de Mantenimiento Integral, S. de R.L. de C.V. ("COMMISA"). The Award, with interest, is now worth almost four hundred million U.S. dollars. COMMISA obtained judgment in this court confirming the Award. Respondent, PEMEX–Exploración y Producción (PEP), an instrumentality of Mexico, continued to resist, appealing from the judgment to the Second Circuit of Appeals, and filing litigation proceedings in the Mexican courts to nullify the Award.

PEP was successful in the Mexican courts. On September 21, 2011, the Eleventh Collegiate Court on Civil Matters of the Federal District (the "Eleventh Collegiate Court," generally equivalent in hierarchy and authority to the U.S. Court of Appeals for the D.C. Circuit) issued a 486–page decision that held that the Award was invalid. It reversed the Mexican district court, and remanded the case to it to issue a judgment in favor of PEP. On October 25, 2011, the district court issued such a judgment with its own 46–page opinion.

The Eleventh Collegiate Court held that arbitrators are not competent to hear and decide cases brought against the sovereign, or an instrumentality of the sovereign, and that proper recourse of an aggrieved commercial party is in the Mexican district court for administrative matters. Hence, it nullified the Award. The court based its decision in part on a statute that was not in existence at the time the parties' entered their contract, and the decision left COMMISA without the apparent ability to obtain a hearing on the merits of its case.

THE PANAMA CONVENTION AND ENFORCEMENT OF ARBITRATION AWARDS

COMMISA's petition to confirm the Award in its favor invokes the Inter–American Convention on International Commercial Arbitration (the "Panama Convention"). See 9 U.S.C. §305; John Bowman, *The Panama Convention and its Implementation Under the Federal Arbitration Act*, 11 Am. Rev, Int'l. Arb. 1, 91-94 (2000). *The Panama Convention and the Convention on the Recognition and Enforcement of Foreign Arbitral Awards* (the "New York Convention") are largely similar, and so precedents under one are generally applicable to the other. See *Productos Mercantiles E Industriales, S.A. v. Faberge USA, Inc.*, 23 F.3d 41, 45 (2d Cir. 1994) ("The legislative history of the [Panama] Convention's implementing statute. . . clearly demonstrates that Congress intended the [Panama] Convention to reach the same results as those reached under the New York Convention" such that "courts in the United States would achieve a general uniformity of results under the two conventions."). Article 4 of the Panama Convention provides that an arbitration decision reached in a foreign country can be recognized in U.S. courts "in the same manner as that of decisions handed down by national or foreign ordinary courts, in accordance with the procedural laws of the country where it is to be executed and the provision of international treaties."

The Panama Convention is enforceable pursuant to the Federal Arbitration Act ("FAA"). 9 U.S.C. §301. . . . The FAA allows a party to an arbitral award falling under the Panama Convention to apply to a court for an order confirming the award. 9 U.S.C. §§302, 207. If the court determines it has jurisdiction, that court "shall confirm the award unless it finds one of the grounds for refusal or deferral of recognition or enforcement of the award specified in the said Convention." Id. "Under Article [5] of the [Panama Convention], '[t]he recognition and execution of the decision may be refused, at the request of the party against which it is made, only if such party is able to prove the existence of certain carefully specified defenses.'" *Figueiredo Ferraz E Engenharía de Projeto Ltda. v. Republic of Peru*, 665 F.3d 384, 397 (2d Cir. 2011) (quoting Panama Convention Art. 5). While courts have some freedom to set aside arbitration awards if the award followed an arbitration in the court's own nation, "when an action for enforcement is brought in a foreign state, the state may refuse to enforce the award only on the grounds explicitly set forth in Article [5] of the Convention." *Yusuf Ahmed Alghanim & Sons v. Toys "R" Us, Inc.*, 126 F.3d 15, 23 (2d Cir. 1997).

The broad holding of *Chromalloy* has been criticized. See *TermoRio*, 487 F.3d at 937 (declining to determine whether Chromalloy was correctly decided while noting that courts should defer to nullifications despite "the Convention policy in favor of enforcement of arbitration awards"); see also *Int'l Trading & Indus. Inv. Co. v. DynCorp Aerospace Tech.*, 763 F. Supp. 2d 12, 30 (D.D.C. 2011). However, *Chromalloy* remains alive, for both *Baker Marine* and *TermoRio* recognized that a district court should hesitate to defer to a judgment of nullification that conflicts with fundamental notions of fairness. See *TermoRio*, 487 F.3d at 939 (concluding that deferral is not warranted if doing so would violate "basic notions of justice"); *Baker Marine*, 191 F.3d at 197 n. 3 (distinguishing Chromalloy on the ground that "recognition of the Nigerian judgment in this case does not conflict with United States public policy").

DISCUSSION

Under Article 5 of the Panama Convention as applied by the Federal Arbitration Act, "recognition and execution of [the arbitral award] may be refused" if the award has been nullified by a "competent authority" of the state in which, or according to the law of which, the arbitration was conducted. The statutory phrase, "may," gives me discretion but, it appears from the two important court of appeals cases on the subject, a narrow discretion. The Second Circuit in *Baker Marine* did not define the scope of discretion, ruling only that the party that had won the arbitration did not give an "adequate reason" why comity should not be given to the foreign court's judgment 191 F.3d at 197. In *TermoRio*, the D.C. Circuit gave a more substantive definition of the enforcing court's discretion; if the judgment of nullification "is repugnant to fundamental notions of what is decent and just in the United States" or, stated another way, if the judgment "violated any basic notions of justice in which we subscribe," then it need not be followed. 487 F.3d at 939.

I find that under the standard announced in *TermoRio*, the decision vacating the Award violated "basic notions of justice," and that deference is therefore not required.

When COMMISA initiated arbitration at the end of 2004, it had every reason to believe that its dispute with PEP could be arbitrated. Twice PEP had signed an agreement stating that disputes related to the gas platforms contracts would be arbitrated. The arbitration clause was broadly worded and mandatory, providing that "[a]ny controversy, claim, difference, or dispute that may arise from or that is related to, or associated with, the present Contract or any instance of breach with the present Contract, shall be definitely settled through arbitration. . . ." Ex. 2 §23.3. PEP had the authority to enter into such an arbitration provision, as the organic law that gave PEP its existence specifically authorized it to resolve commercial disputes by arbitration. See Ex. MMM at 443, Section 14 of the PEMEX and Affiliates Organic Law ("In the event of international legal acts, Petróleos Mexicanos or its Affiliates may agree upon the application of foreign law, the jurisdiction of foreign courts in trade matters, and execute arbitration agreements whenever deemed appropriate in furtherance of their purpose.").

[R]etroactive application of laws and the unfairness associated with such application is at the center of the dispute before me.

Elementary considerations of fairness dictate that individuals should have an opportunity to know what the law is and to conform their conduct accordingly; settled expectations should not be lightly disrupted. For that reason, the "principle that the legal effect of conduct should ordinarily be assessed under the law that existed when the conduct took place has timeless and universal appeal." In a free, dynamic society, creativity in both commercial and artistic endeavors is fostered by a rule of law that gives people confidence about the legal consequences of their actions. *Landgraf v. USI Film Products*, 511 U.S. 244, 265-66, 114 S. Ct. 1483, 128 L. Ed. 2d 229 (1994) (citation omitted). Here, the law at the time of the parties' contracting gave COMMISA the "settled expectation" that its dispute could be arbitrated. The 1994 Mexican Supreme Court decision was not sufficient to put COMMISA on notice that the statute that specifically empowered PEP to arbitrate and the arbitration clauses PEP had agreed to should have been ignored.

Further, this retroactive application of Section 98 was undertaken to favor a state enterprise over a private party. The Eleventh Collegiate Court explained that administrative rescissions helped "safeguard [the state's] financial resources" and that "the State should be granted . . . suitable mechanisms to fulfill [this] objective[]," *Ex. MMM* at 422, 431. This rationale flouts a basic principle of justice; where a sovereign has waived its immunity and has agreed to contract with a private party, a court hearing a dispute regarding that contract should treat the private party and the sovereign as equals. See *United States v. Winstar Corp.*, 518 U.S. 839, 895, 116 S. Ct. 2432, 135 L. Ed. 2d 964 (1996) ("When the United States enters into contract relations, its rights and duties therein are governed generally by the law applicable to contracts between private individuals.") (citation omitted); *United States v. Bostwick*, 94 U.S. 53, 66, 24 L. Ed. 65 (1877) ("The United States, when they contract with their citizens, are controlled by the same laws that govern the citizen in that behalf."); *Cooke v. United States*, 91 U.S. 389, 398, 23 L. Ed. 237 (1875) (finding that when the United States "comes down from its position of sovereignty, and enters the domain of commerce, it submits itself to the same laws that govern individuals there").

Applying a law that came into effect well after the parties entered into their contract was troubling. But this unfairness was exacerbated by the fact that the Eleventh Collegiate Court's decision left COMMISA without a remedy to litigate the merits of the dispute that the arbitrators had resolved in COMMISA's favor.

In 2006, the Mexican Supreme Court observed that "there is no obstacle or restriction whatever against a private party . . . [filing] within the relevant time periods . . . an administrative dispute proceeding, thereby triggering intervention by the relevant court, if [the aggrieved party] . . . has been adversely affected by the cancellation of the administrative contract for public works to which it was a party." *Ex. LLL* at 71. This right to judicial recourse was essential to the Mexican Supreme Court's conclusion that administrative rescissions were constitutional, and not arbitrary cancellations of the contract rights of private counter-parties. Thus, the Eleventh Collegiate Court justified its judgment of nullification by observing that the case "may have been contested by filing a federal ordinary administrative action before a District Judge in Administrative Matters to analyze the substantive matter," *Ex, MMM* at 434.

But by the time the Eleventh Collegiate Court issued its opinion, this option was no longer available to COMMISA. Article 14(VII) of the Organic Law of the Federal Court in Tax and Administrative Matters, a 2007 statute, gave the Tax and Administrative Court jurisdiction over public works cases involving Mexican state entities. That court has a short, 45-day statute of limitations. Based on that statute, the Mexican Supreme Court held in 2010 that the Tax and Administrative Court was the exclusive forum for such cases. The necessary implication is that the District Courts for Administrative Matters, in which a 10-year statute of limitations applies, are not available to hear disputes like this one. COMMISA tested this issue, filing suit in the Tax and Administrative Court on November 6, 2012, arguing that the 10-year statute of limitations should apply, but COMMISA's argument was rejected and the case was dismissed barely a month after its filing. The Tax and Administrative Court held that COMMISA's suit was barred by both the statute of limitations and by res judicata. This lack of remedy is particularly unjust because COMMISA has been deemed to owe damages to PEP, even though there has been no full hearing on the merits outside arbitration, simply because PEP issued an administrative rescission.

For these reasons, this is a very different case from *Baker Marine* and from *TermoRio*. In neither of those cases did the annulling court rely on a law that did not exist at the time of the parties' contract. In both *Baker Marine* and *TermoRio*, the nullification was based on the failure of arbitrators to follow proper procedure. The courts of Nigeria and Colombia did not hold that the cases could not be subject to arbitration, and therefore there was no contradiction between the government entities' agreements to arbitrate and the courts' rulings. Here, in contrast, the Eleventh Collegiate Court ruled that the entire case was not subject to arbitration based on public policy grounds, a ruling that was at odds with PEP's own agreement, the PEMEX enabling statute, and the law of Mexico at the time of contracting and the commencement of arbitration.

In declining to defer to the Eleventh Collegiate Court, I am neither deciding, nor reviewing, Mexican law. I base my decision not on the substantive merit of a particular Mexican law, but on its application to events that occurred before that law's adoption. At the time COMMISA brought its claims against PEP, there was no statute, case law, or any other source of authority that put COMMISA on notice that it had to pursue its claims in court, instead of in arbitration. COMMISA reasonably believed that it was entitled to arbitrate the case, and the Eleventh Collegiate Court's decision disrupted this reasonable expectation by applying a law and policy that were not in existence at the time of the parties' contract, thereby denying COMMISA an opportunity to obtain a hearing on the merits of its claims. The decision therefore violated basic notions of justice, and I hold that the Award in favor of COMMISA should be confirmed. . . .

This chapter and Chapter 5 have charted the dramatic evolution of U.S. arbitration as a strongly favored alternative to litigation under the broad aegis of the FAA. They have shown how the U.S. Supreme Court has promoted broad enforcement of agreements to arbitrate through a body of substantive federal law applicable in both federal and state courts. They have examined the gradual expansion of arbitration into a full-blown court surrogate, given responsibility to address statute-based claims as well as common law actions, and even "socially exemplary remedies" such as punitive damages. We have also seen the expansion of arbitration provisions into the realm of employment and consumer contracts—standardized documents that are often presented to individuals seeking a job, or consumer goods or services, on a "take it or leave it" basis. Chapters 7 and 8 focus on these latter scenarios, which have given rise to a host of fairness concerns and stimulated a variety of responses from courts, legislatures, agencies, and other bodies.

Endnotes

1. McArthur, John B. (forthcoming) *The Reasoned Arbitration Award in the United States: Its Promise, Problems, Preparation and Preservation.*
2. *Id.*
3. Brewer, Thomas J. & Mills, Lawrence R. (2009) *When Arbitrators "Exceed Their Powers": A New Study of Vacated Arbitration Awards,* 64 Disp. Resol. J. 46.
4. Choi, Stephen J. & Eisenberg, Theodore. (2010) *Punitive Damages in Securities Arbitration: An Empirical Study,* 39 J. Legal Stud. 497.
5. Schmitz, Amy J. (2002) *Ending a Mud Bowl: Defining Arbitration's Finality Through Functional Analysis,* 37 Ga. L. Rev. 123 (predicting the resolution of the split).
6. McArthur, John B., *supra* note 1.
7. http://www.jamsadr.com/rules/optional; https://www.adr.org/sites/default/files/AAA-ICDR_Optional_Appellate_Arbitration_Rules.pdf.

CHAPTER 7

FAIRNESS IN ARBITRATION PART I: EMPLOYMENT, CONSUMER, AND ADHESION CONTRACTS

A. INTRODUCTION

A generation ago, U.S. consumers usually encountered arbitration in the form of short procedures for determining whether a motor vehicle was a "lemon" under state statutes. A decision in the buyer's favor would require the manufacturer to pay damages, give a refund, or provide a replacement vehicle. If the buyer lost, however, she could still sue in court. Such systems are skewed toward the consumer, and, overseen by state attorneys general, appear to work fairly well.

Beginning in the mid-1980s, however, the Supreme Court began dramatically expanding the reach of arbitration agreements under the Federal Arbitration Act (FAA)—a series of developments charted in Chapter 5. These developments encouraged companies to incorporate pre-dispute binding arbitration clauses in all kinds of consumer contracts and individual employment contracts. As private arbitration awards suddenly bound individuals, questions were raised about the fairness of different aspects of these procedures.

In the last two decades, binding arbitration became a part of everyday life. Binding arbitration clauses are commonplace in transactions such as banking, credit card agreements, contracts for wireless services, insurance policies, sales of consumer goods, smartphone "apps," and more! Very often, people enter into contracts that contain boilerplate arbitration clauses without focusing on those clauses and are sometimes not even aware of the presence or meaning of the arbitration provision.[1]

A recent empirical study explores the extent to which consumers are aware of and understand the effect of arbitration clauses in consumer contracts, and the "results suggest a profound lack of understanding about the existence and effect of arbitration agreements among consumers."[2] While 43 percent of the respondents to the survey recognized that the sample contract provided to them included an arbitration clause, 61 percent of those believed that they would still have the right to have a court decide a dispute too large for a small claims court. Less than 9 percent realized both that the contract had an arbitration clause and that it would prevent consumers from proceeding in court.

Another recent study adds to the picture, noting the prevalence of arbitration clauses. Professor Imre Szalai found that at least 447,437,000 visitors to the Web sites of Amazon, Walmart, and eBay were subject to arbitration clauses.[3] The arbitration agreements for these companies are so broad that these agreements purport to cover anyone who visits their Web sites. In July 2018, JPMorgan Chase and Wells Fargo combined reportedly had about 53.6 million users of their mobile banking apps, which are also covered by broad arbitration clauses. Furthermore, during the second quarter of 2018, it was estimated that AT&T had about 147.3 million and Verizon had about 152.7 million wireless subscribers subject to arbitration clauses. Internet subscribers in the United States are similarly subject to arbitration provisions. Szalai concluded that at least a majority of U.S. citizens are subject to arbitration provisions. The ubiquity of arbitration clauses causes one to question the notion of consumer "consent" to arbitration.[4]

Of course, that does not mean all arbitration is "bad" or unfair. A private arbitration process may well provide individuals with a fundamentally fair, inexpensive, and relatively speedy alternative to going to court. This is especially true if it can be completed online with little to no cost.[5] However, process fairness depends on the details—and the suitability of defined procedures to the circumstances. Some arbitration procedures fall short of parties' reasonable expectations of fairness and have a dramatic impact on consumers' or employees' substantive rights and remedies.

Concerns are magnified where such provisions are presented as part of a "take it or leave it" deal—requiring an individual to accept the terms or seek other alternatives for goods or employment. The presence of arbitration provisions in these so-called contracts of "adhesion" has generated considerable debate and provoked a variety of responses. In fact, the United States is an outlier when it comes to laws respecting arbitration of consumer and individual employment disputes. No other developed nation so liberally enforces arbitration agreements, and most have established significant limits on the use of arbitration in these settings.[6]

This chapter focuses on the wide range of fairness concerns raised by binding pre-dispute arbitration agreements in consumer or employment transactions. It explores concerns surrounding the making of the agreement, including lack of awareness of the arbitration provision and of waiver of the right to trial, as well as lack of access to information about the arbitration program and related rules and procedures. It also examines key process-related concerns, including the independence and impartiality of decision makers, and of the administering institution, if any; the secrecy of the process; the cost, location, and time frame of arbitration; the ability to present a claim as part of a class action; the right to representation; the ability to secure needed information (discovery); and the fundamental fairness of hearings. Also relevant are outcome-related concerns: the nature of arbitral remedies, including the availability of punitive damages in cases where they would be available in court; the scope of judicial review of arbitration awards; and the availability of binding precedents for the future guidance of actors in various arenas.

Such concerns have triggered litigation over the enforcement of arbitration agreements in adhesion contracts, or resulting arbitration awards. Although federal and state courts have tended to reinforce the ability of companies to require their employees or customers to arbitrate, they have, to varying degrees, established limits on the contracting process and the kinds of procedures companies can impose. To some extent, these judicial efforts have been supplemented or reinforced by state or federal legislation governing arbitration, and by the collective efforts of organizations to create minimum due process standards — or protocols — for arbitration in these settings.

Over the years, there have been various bills proposed for a national statute designed to amend the FAA to outlaw pre-dispute arbitration agreements in consumer, employment, civil rights, and other adhesive contracts. These have included the "Arbitration Fairness Act" (AFA) and most recently, the "Ending Forced Arbitration of Sexual Assault and Sexual Harassment Act of 2021," which became law in 2022. The law, discussed in Chapter 8, adds a new chapter to Title 9 of the U.S. Code. H.R. 4445, 117th Cong. (2022); Actions Overview H.R. 4445 — 117th Congress (2021-2022), CONGRESS.GOV, https://www.congress .gov/bill/117th-congress/house-bill/4445/actions (last visited Feb. 11, 2022).

At the same time, the Dodd-Frank Wall Street Reform and Consumer Protection Act gave agencies authority to place limits on the enforceability of arbitration agreements in certain settings. Accordingly, after much study, the Consumer Financial Protection Bureau (CFPB) issued an arbitration rule barring the use of arbitration clauses to preclude class actions with respect to financial services and contracts disputes. The rule would have prohibited banks and other consumer financial companies from including mandatory arbitration clauses that block group lawsuits in any new contracts after the compliance date. Although the rule would not have barred arbitration clauses outright, it would have restored the ability of consumers to file or join group lawsuits. This may have provided companies with more incentive to comply with the law, and the new rule also would have required more transparency regarding arbitrations. Nonetheless, in 2019, then–Vice President Pence broke the tie in the Senate to overturn CFPB's proposed rule on arbitration.[8] Furthermore, a series of Supreme Court decisions (usually decided by a 5-4 margin) have strongly reinforced the Court's pro-arbitration positions and gave a green light to terms in arbitration agreements that waive parties' right to press claims through class actions.

This chapter will briefly explore the trend of strengthened enforcement of arbitration agreements in standardized contracts for employment or consumer goods or services. It will also consider the impact of private efforts to establish minimum standards for arbitration of employment and consumer disputes and court decisions reflecting different approaches to judicial policing of such agreements. Chapter 8 will examine key legislative developments, as well as key Supreme Court decisions and other precedents affecting employees and consumers.

B.   PRO-CONSUMER DISPUTE RESOLUTION: STATE LEMON LAWS AND THE MAGNUSON-MOSS WARRANTY ACT

1.   State Lemon Laws

If you buy a car and it appears to have fundamental defects, you probably have rights and remedies under a state lemon law. Lemon laws typically permit disgruntled car buyers with the opportunity to have a streamlined hearing before an arbitration tribunal empowered to award a speedy, out-of-court remedy, and give buyers the option of proceeding to court if they are unhappy with the result.[9] Maine's lemon law, for example, provides that all manufacturers submit to state-certified new car arbitration if arbitration is requested by the consumer within three years from the date of original delivery of a new car to the consumer or within the term of the express warranties, whichever comes first. This state-certified arbitration panel consists of one or more neutral arbitrators selected by the Department of the Attorney General. The Attorney General's office is responsible for administering the proceedings under such rules as will "promote fairness and efficiency."[10]

QUESTION

1. Does state regulation of arbitration promote confidence in the process? How do you view the pro-consumer orientation of these processes?

---

2. *Magnuson-Moss Warranty Act*

An analogous attempt by the federal government to encourage the use of ADR in the consumer setting can be seen in the Magnuson-Moss Warranty Act (MMWA), enacted in 1975 in response to increasing consumer protection concerns.[11] The MMWA allows warrantors to require that consumers enter into ADR if a dispute arises, but it specifies that the ADR be nonbinding and that the consumer be able to assert claims in court if ADR is unsuccessful. The Act attempts to provide common ground and a fair process for resolving certain types of consumer disputes.

For some time after the enactment of the MMWA, every federal court that had a Magnuson-Moss case come before it concluded that the Act vested a non-waivable right of court access and thus that the Act precluded binding arbitration. One of the first and most prominent cases dealing with the MMWA was *Wilson v. Waverlee Homes Inc.*, in which a federal district court held that the Act makes clear that the "informal dispute resolution procedures" allowed by the Act "are a prerequisite, not a bar, to relief in court." 954 F. Supp. 1530, 1537 (M.D. Ala. 1997), *aff'd*, 127 F.3d 40 (11th Cir. 1997). In subsequent years, other courts followed this approach. As late as 2000, in *Pitchford v. Oakwood Mobile Homes, Inc.*, a federal district court in Virginia held that the clear intent behind the implementation of the MMWA was to encourage ADR without stripping parties of their access to the judicial system, 124 F. Supp. 2d 958 (W.D. Va. 2000).

However, Supreme Court decisions expanding the FAA's scope led to questions regarding the validity of this interpretation of the MMWA. In *Krol v. FCA US, LLC*, 273 So. 3d 198 (Fla. 5th Dist. Ct. App. 2019), the buyer of a used truck filed an action against a dealership because of defects in the truck it sold under the MMWA. The dealer moved to compel arbitration under their agreement, and the buyer opposed the arbitration, arguing that MMWA claims are exempt from binding arbitration. The court agreed with the dealer, holding that the MMWA permits enforcement of pre-dispute binding arbitration clauses in written warranty agreements. While the court acknowledged that the Supreme Court has not addressed whether MMWA claims are arbitrable, and state and lower federal courts are divided on the issue, it concluded that it would join with the federal circuit courts that have decided that the MMWA does not stop enforcement of arbitration clauses (the Eleventh Circuit in *Davis v. S. Energy Homes*, and the Fifth Circuit in *Walton v. Rose Mobile Homes*). *See also Sheinfeld v. BMW Fin. Services NA, LLC*, 218CV02083JADEJY, 2019 WL 4667323, at *1 (D. Nev. Sept. 24, 2019) (holding that Sheinfeld was required to arbitrate his claims since the MMWA does not preclude binding arbitration of MMWA claims).

QUESTIONS

2. In *Davis v. Southern Energy Homes, Inc.*, 305 F.3d 1268 (11th Cir. 2002), a federal circuit that previously ruled that the Act prevented binding arbitration in warranty agreements held that homeowners who signed a pre-dispute arbitration agreement must arbitrate their claims against the builder, including their MMWA claim. The Eleventh Circuit reasoned that the MMWA does not expressly preclude arbitration and that the Act's "legislative history only addresses 'internal dispute settlement procedures'; it never directly addresses the role of binding arbitration or the FAA." The court added that the purposes of the MMWA—" 'to improve the adequacy of information available to consumers, prevent deception, and improve competition in the marketing of consumer products' "—do not conflict with the FAA. The Fifth Circuit Court of Appeals in *Walton v. Rose Mobile Homes*, 298 F.3d 470 (5th Cir. 2002), agreed with this conclusion. From a public policy standpoint, why do you think courts switched from refusing enforcement of arbitration clauses in these contexts to allowing it?

3. The MMWA fails to mention binding arbitration or the FAA directly—probably because it was passed at a time before the pro-arbitration judicial activism of the 1980s and 1990s. However, Congress did not amend the MMWA during the 1980s or 1990s to address the Supreme Court's precedents favoring arbitration. Recall that in *Shearson/American Express, Inc. v. McMahon*, 482 U.S. 220 (1987), the Supreme Court stated that in reviewing the text, legislative history, and the existence of any "inherent conflict between arbitration" and a federal statute's purpose, courts must be mindful of the federal policy favoring arbitration, and that the party opposing arbitration bears the burden of showing that Congress intended to preclude arbitration. *Id.* at 226-227.

C. EXPANSION OF PRE-DISPUTE ARBITRATION AGREEMENTS INTO CONSUMER AND EMPLOYMENT REALMS

1. Impact of Changed Judicial Attitudes Toward Arbitrators and Role of Arbitration

As discussed in Chapter 5 and referred to above, the U.S. Supreme Court's broad, pro-arbitration interpretations of the FAA in the 1980s and 1990s ushered in a sea change in judicial attitudes toward binding arbitration and the role of arbitrators in administering civil justice. *Southland Corp. v. Keating*, 465 U.S. 1 (1984), and its progeny reinforced strong pro-arbitration policies under the FAA and recognized a body of substantive law governing the enforcement of arbitration agreements applicable to federal courts (and potentially state courts) in cases regarding transactions involving interstate commerce—a truly broad rubric. *See, e.g., Allied-Bruce Terminix Cos. v. Dobson*, 513 U.S. 265 (1995). State laws designed to single out arbitration clauses from other contractual clauses, even if meant to protect consumers from arbitral abuses, are preempted by the FAA's national pro-arbitration policies. *See, e.g., Doctor's Assocs., Inc. v. Casarotto*, 517 U.S. 681 (1996). Decisions such as *Mitsubishi* and *Shearson/American Express* were among the early precedents expanding the authority of arbitrators to resolve various kinds of statutory claims. None was more significant than the decision below, which opened the door to widespread use of pre-dispute arbitration agreements in employment contracts.

Gilmer v. Interstate/Johnson Lane Corp.

500 U.S. 20 (1991)

[Robert Gilmer was employed by Interstate as a Manager of Financial Services, which required him to register as a securities representative with the New York Stock Exchange (NYSE). His registration application provided that he agreed to arbitrate "any dispute, claim or controversy" arising between him and his employer. After Interstate terminated Gilmer's employment in 1987, at which time Gilmer was 62 years of age, he filed an action in federal court under the Age Discrimination in Employment Act (ADEA). Interstate filed a motion to compel arbitration pursuant to the NYSE rules. The Fourth Circuit ruled in favor of Interstate that the dispute should be resolved by arbitration.]

Justice WHITE delivered the opinion of the Court.

. . . Congress enacted the ADEA in 1967 "to promote employment of older persons based on their ability rather than age; to prohibit arbitrary age discrimination in employment; [and] to help employers and workers find ways of meeting problems arising from the impact of age on employment." To achieve those goals, the ADEA, among other things, makes it unlawful for an employer "to fail or refuse to hire or to discharge any individual or otherwise discriminate against any individual with respect to his compensation, terms, conditions, or privileges of employment, because of such individual's age." . . .

As Gilmer contends, the ADEA is designed not only to address individual grievances, but also to further important social policies. We do not perceive any inherent inconsistency between those policies, however, and enforcing agreements to arbitrate age discrimination claims. It is true that arbitration focuses on specific disputes between the parties involved. The same can be said, however, of judicial resolution of claims. Both of these dispute resolution mechanisms nevertheless also can further broader social purposes. . . .

We also are unpersuaded by the argument that arbitration will undermine the role of the EEOC in enforcing the ADEA. An individual ADEA claimant subject to an arbitration agreement will still be free to file a charge with the EEOC, even though the claimant is not able to institute a private judicial action. . . .

Gilmer also argues that compulsory arbitration is improper because it deprives claimants of the judicial forum provided for by the ADEA. Congress, however, did not explicitly preclude arbitration or other nonjudicial resolution of claims, even in its recent amendments to the ADEA. . . . Moreover, Gilmer's argument ignores the ADEA's flexible approach to resolution of claims. The EEOC, for example, is directed to pursue "informal methods of conciliation, conference, and persuasion," which suggests that out-of-court dispute resolution, such as arbitration, is consistent with the statutory scheme established by Congress. . . .

In arguing that arbitration is inconsistent with the ADEA, Gilmer also raises a host of challenges to the adequacy of arbitration procedures. Initially, we note that in our recent arbitration cases we have already rejected most of these arguments as insufficient to preclude arbitration of statutory claims. . . .

Gilmer first speculates that arbitration panels will be biased. However, "[w]e decline to indulge the presumption that the parties and arbitral body conducting a proceeding will be unable or unwilling to retain competent, conscientious and impartial arbitrators." . . .

Gilmer also complains that the discovery allowed in arbitration is more limited than in the federal courts, which he contends will make it difficult to prove discrimination. It is unlikely, however, that age discrimination claims require more extensive discovery than other claims that we have found to be arbitrable, such as RICO and antitrust claims.

A further alleged deficiency of arbitration is that arbitrators often will not issue written opinions, resulting, Gilmer contends, in a lack of public knowledge of employers' discriminatory policies, an inability to obtain effective appellate review, and a stifling of the development of the law. The NYSE rules, however, do require that all arbitration awards be in writing, and that the awards contain the names of the parties, a summary of the issues in controversy, and a description of the award issued. In addition, the award decisions are made available to the public. Furthermore, judicial decisions addressing ADEA claims will continue to be issued because it is unlikely that all or even most ADEA claimants will be subject to arbitration agreements. Finally, Gilmer's concerns apply equally to settlements of ADEA claims, which, as noted above, are clearly allowed. . . .

It is also argued that arbitration procedures cannot adequately further the purposes of the ADEA because they do not provide for broad equitable relief and class actions. As the court below noted, however, arbitrators do have the power to fashion equitable relief. Indeed, the NYSE rules applicable here do not restrict the types of relief an arbitrator may award, but merely refer to "damages and/or other relief." But "even if the arbitration could not go forward as a class action or class relief could not be granted by the arbitrator, the fact that the [ADEA] provides for the possibility of bringing a collective action does not mean that individual attempts at conciliation were intended to be barred." *Nicholson v. CPC Int'l Inc.*, 877 F.2d 221, 241 (CA3 1989) (Becker, J., dissenting). Finally, it should be remembered that arbitration agreements will not preclude the EEOC from bringing actions seeking class-wide and equitable relief.

An additional reason advanced by Gilmer for refusing to enforce arbitration agreements relating to ADEA claims is his contention that there often will be unequal bargaining power between employers and employees. Mere inequality in bargaining power, however, is not a sufficient reason to hold that arbitration agreements are never enforceable in the employment context. Relationships between securities dealers and investors, for example, may involve unequal bargaining power, but we nevertheless held in *Rodriguez de Quijas* and *McMahon* that agreements to arbitrate in that context are enforceable. As discussed above, the FAA's purpose was to place arbitration agreements on the same footing as other contracts. Thus, arbitration agreements are enforceable "save upon such grounds as exist at law or in equity for the revocation of any contract." 9 U.S.C. §2. "Of course, courts should remain attuned to well-supported claims that the agreement to arbitrate resulted from the sort of fraud or overwhelming economic power that would provide grounds 'for the revocation of any contract.' " *Mitsubishi*, 473 U.S. at 627, 105 S. Ct. at 3354. There is no indication in this case, however, that Gilmer, an experienced businessman, was coerced or defrauded into agreeing to the arbitration clause in his registration application. As with the claimed procedural inadequacies discussed above, this claim of unequal bargaining power is best left for resolution in specific cases. . . .

We conclude that Gilmer has not met his burden of showing that Congress, in enacting the ADEA, intended to preclude arbitration of claims under that Act. Accordingly, the judgment of the Court of Appeals is Affirmed.

Justice STEVENS filed a dissenting opinion.

. . . There is little dispute that the primary concern animating the FAA was the perceived need by the business community to overturn the common-law rule that denied specific enforcement of agreements to arbitrate in contracts between business entities. . . . At the [legislative hearing regarding the FAA], Senator Walsh stated:

> "The trouble about the matter is that a great many of these contracts that are entered into are really not [voluntary] things at all. Take an insurance policy; there is a blank in it. You can take that or you can leave it. . . . It is the same with a good many contracts of employment. A man says, 'These are our terms. All right, take it or leave it.' Well, there is nothing for the man to do except to sign it; and then he surrenders his right to have his case tried by the court, and has to have it tried before a tribunal in which he has no confidence at all." . . .

Not only would I find that the FAA does not apply to employment-related disputes between employers and employees in general [based on construction of Section 1 of the Act], but also I would hold that compulsory arbitration conflicts with the congressional purpose animating the ADEA. . . . [A]uthorizing the courts to issue broad injunctive relief is the cornerstone to eliminating discrimination in society. . . . Because commercial arbitration is typically limited to a specific dispute between the particular parties and because the available remedies in arbitral forums do not provide for class-wide injunctive relief, . . . an essential purpose of the ADEA is frustrated by compulsory arbitration of employment discrimination claims. Moreover, as Chief Justice Burger explained:

> "Plainly, it would not comport with the congressional objectives behind a statute seeking to enforce civil rights protected by Title VII to allow the

very forces that had practiced discrimination to contract away the right to enforce civil rights in the courts. For federal courts to defer to arbitral decisions reached by the same combination of forces that had long perpetuated discrimination would have made the foxes guardians of the chickens."

NOTES AND QUESTIONS

4. Did Congress intend the FAA to apply to employment disputes such as Gilmer's ADEA claim? The FAA provides in Section 1 that "nothing herein contained shall apply to contracts of seamen, railroad employees, or any other class of workers engaged in foreign or interstate commerce." Doesn't this mean that arbitration clauses cannot bind employees whose work involves interstate commerce, as Gilmer's surely did? The Court refused to address the question in *Gilmer* but resolved it ten years later in *Circuit City Stores, Inc. v. Adams*, 532 U.S. 105 (2001). There, the Court held that Section 1 exempts from the FAA only employment contracts of transportation workers, not contracts of employees generally even though their work may involve interstate commerce.

5. In *Alexander v. Gardner-Denver Co.*, 415 U.S. 36 (1974), the Court held that even though an employment dispute has been arbitrated pursuant to a collective bargaining agreement, the employee was not precluded from filing a subsequent lawsuit for employment discrimination under Title VII. The Court in *Gilmer* distinguished the *Alexander* case on three grounds: (1) the arbitration clause in *Alexander* authorized arbitration only of claims under the collective bargaining agreement, not statutory claims; (2) the claimant in *Alexander* was represented by his union in the arbitration proceeding rather than proceeding individually; and (3) *Alexander* was not decided under the FAA. In *14 Penn Plaza LLC v. Pyett*, 556 U.S. 247 (2009), the Court held that *Alexander* and its progeny controlled only where the arbitration agreement did not specifically grant the arbitrator the authority to arbitrate statutory claims. *Pyett*, 556 U.S. at 263-264. Does *Alexander* survive at all? The Court in *Pyett* further held that the dicta in *Alexander*, which claimed that an agreement to arbitrate statutory claims amounted to a waiver of the employee's statutory rights, was erroneous. The Court reasoned that agreeing to arbitrate does not waive a person's rights; it only elects a different forum for their vindication. *Id.* at 266.

6. What role does the Equal Employment Opportunity Commission (EEOC) have in pursuing employment discrimination claims? *See EEOC v. Waffle House, Inc.*, 534 U.S. 279 (2002) (agreement between employer and employee to arbitrate specific employment-related disputes does not bar the EEOC from pursuing judicial relief (including back pay, reinstatement, and damages, in an Americans with Disabilities Act of 1990 (ADA) enforcement action) on behalf of the victim).

7. Which do you find more persuasive—the arguments of the majority or those of the dissent in *Gilmer*? Would it make any difference to know that Mr. Gilmer eventually was awarded $200,000 in arbitration—essentially a victory on the merits?

2. *Extension of the Separability Doctrine*

Recall that in Chapter 5, we encountered the doctrine of separability of arbitration agreements as annunciated in the Supreme Court's decision in *Prima Paint*, a case involving commercial interests. Nearly 40 years after that case came *Buckeye Check Cashing, Inc. v. Cardegna*, 546 U.S. 440 (2006), in which the Court addressed "whether a court or an arbitrator should consider the claim that a contract containing an arbitration provision is void for illegality." In *Buckeye*, the plaintiffs filed a putative class action alleging that the interest rates in various deferred-payment transactions with Buckeye Check Cashing "in which they received cash in exchange for a personal check in the amount of the cash plus a finance charge" were usurious. The plaintiffs also alleged that the Deferred Deposit and Disclosure Agreement (which contained an arbitration clause) violated Florida lending and consumer protection statutes. The trial court denied Buckeye's motion to compel arbitration, "holding that a court rather than an arbitrator should resolve a claim that a contract is illegal and void ab initio." The Florida appellate court reversed on the ground that the plaintiffs challenged the Agreement in its entirety, not the arbitration clause alone, so "the agreement to arbitrate was enforceable, and the question of the contract's legality should go to the arbitrator." The Florida Supreme Court in turn reversed the appellate court, and the United States Supreme Court granted certiorari. In a decision by Justice Scalia, the Court reaffirmed the principle that "regardless of whether the challenge is brought in federal or state court, a challenge to the validity of the contract as a whole, and not specifically to the arbitration clause, must go to the arbitrator."

NOTES AND QUESTIONS

8. Do you see any potential concerns associated with giving arbitrators authority to address questions such as those at the heart of *Buckeye Check Cashing*, which involved a standardized "pay-day" contract aimed at consumers, and allegations that a contract was illegal and therefore void? Consider, also, that many arbitration rules now give arbitrators plenary authority over all questions relating to and challenging their jurisdiction.[12] For a discussion of potential limitations on arbitral authority and a role for courts in the context of adhesion contracts, see Section E below.

9. A contract between Ferrer, who appears on television as "Judge Alex," and Preston, an entertainment lawyer, required arbitration of "any dispute . . . relating to the [contract] terms . . . or the breach, validity, or legality thereof . . . in accordance with the [AAA] Rules." When Preston demanded arbitration, seeking fees allegedly due under the contract, Ferrer petitioned the California Labor Commissioner for a determination that the contract was invalid and unenforceable under the California Talent Agencies Act because Preston had failed to acquire a license as a talent agent. Should a court enforce the arbitration agreement or direct the parties to proceed before the Labor Commissioner? *See Preston v. Ferrer*, 552 U.S. 346 (2008).

10. Should a court or arbitrator decide whether an arbitration agreement allows for class proceedings? In *Spirit Airlines, Inc. v. Maizes*, 899 F.3d 1230 (11th Cir. 2018), *cert. denied*, 139 S. Ct. 1322 (2019), the Court of Appeals held that the issue of whether or not the agreement allowed for class arbitration was for the arbitrator, not the court, looking to the AAA rules that give the arbitrator power to decide their own jurisdiction. Why do you think that the Supreme Court denied cert in this case? See Chapter 8 for more discussion of delegation clauses.

D. FAIRNESS ISSUES IN ARBITRATION UNDER STANDARDIZED CONSUMER AND EMPLOYMENT CONTRACTS

1. Fairness in the Contracting Process

A decision by the U.S. Fifth Circuit Court of Appeals is exemplary of judicial approaches to the enforcement of arbitration provisions in standardized consumer and employment contracts. The court found that life insurance purchasers had agreed to submit to arbitration because they signed a document that contained the following clause, located just above the signature lines:

THE PARTIES UNDERSTAND THAT BY SIGNING THIS ARBITRATION AGREEMENT, THEY ARE LIMITING ANY RIGHT TO PUNITIVE DAMAGES AND GIVING UP THE RIGHT TO A TRIAL IN COURT, BOTH WITH AND WITHOUT A JURY.

The court found that the consumers had thereby waived their right to a judicial forum and "their corresponding right to a jury trial." *American Heritage Life Ins. Co. v. Orr*, 294 F.3d 702 (5th Cir. 2002). Other court decisions have enforced "agreements" to arbitrate based on a consumer's indication of assent. *Hill v. Gateway 2000, Inc.*, 105 F.3d 1147 (7th Cir. 1997) (enforcing arbitration provision in terms and conditions that came in the box containing computer goods); *Davis v. Dell, Inc.*, 2007 U.S. Dist. LEXIS 94767 (D.N.J. 2007) (assent to terms and conditions that included an arbitration clause shown by clicking a box in an online Web site); *Hauenstein v. Softwrap Ltd.*, 2007 WL 2404624, 2007 U.S. Dist. LEXIS 60618 (W.D. Wash. Aug. 17, 2007) (same).

Nonetheless, some courts have looked at whether consent to arbitration is lacking. In *Shockley v. PrimeLending*, 929 F.3d 1012 (8th Cir. 2019), the Court of Appeals held that even if a delegation provision in an employee handbook qualified as an offer, the employee's online review and acknowledgment that they reviewed the handbook was not an unequivocal acceptance of the arbitration clause buried in the handbook. The court applied Missouri contract law to find that there was no real acceptance of an agreement to arbitrate claims under the Fair Labor Standards Act.

Accordingly, some courts acknowledge the reality that consumers and employees generally do not see, read, or understand arbitration clauses. They usually do not realize that they are agreeing to forgo rights to trial, including jury trial, with its procedural protections, including judicial review.[13] Fairness concerns in arbitration also arise due to a lack of transparency in the arbitration process and a lack of understanding about how the process works. As you have come to understand by reading Chapters 1-4, even a relatively sophisticated attorney may not have more than a general idea of how arbitration will proceed without knowing what particular arbitration rules are governing the process. Modern dispute resolution procedures contain numerous provisions covering many pages, similar to court procedure rules. These governing provisions are usually only incorporated by reference in the contract, usually requiring that one find them on the Internet.

Concerns about how consumers and employees become bound to arbitrate and how arbitration procedures are set up have stimulated considerable academic commentary, state legislative measures, and court decisions addressing the enforceability, formation, and contents of arbitration agreements. Courts and legislatures occasionally take steps to make arbitration a more "user-friendly" process—an effort supplemented by initiatives of the American Arbitration Association (AAA) and other dispute resolution organizations. The 2008 financial crisis spurred some legislators to pay closer attention to the role of arbitration in consumer disputes.

NOTES AND QUESTIONS

11. *Contract Law and Arbitration.* You may remember from your Contracts course that one of the requisites in contract formation is mutual assent; this principle is often an important issue for courts examining the validity of arbitration clauses. Under classic contract theory, mutual assent is often found through the "objective manifestations" of parties, including acts that somehow signify that one is entering into a bargain. The cases above should help you see how contract formation principles matter in these cases. In Section E below, we further examine various doctrines that have come into play in judicial efforts to police arbitration agreements, including unconscionability, fraud, and breach of contract.

12. *Critical Commentary.* Commentators have explored a wide variety of concerns about the growth of pre-dispute arbitration clauses, including the foreclosure of access to juries and judges, restriction of remedies (e.g., classwide relief), and process failures (arbitral bias, cost, etc.). Most scholarly commentary has been quite critical of consumer and employment arbitration.[14] Despite the concerns fostered by pre-dispute arbitration

clauses, many courts uphold such arbitration agreements. What value might enforcement of such agreements yield for the contracting parties and court systems?[15]

13. *Punitive Damages.* As noted in Chapter 6, some have challenged arbitration agreements that purport to "waive" punitive damages. Should such a limitation in adhesion contracts be enforced?[16] There are a number of court decisions striking down such "waiver" provisions on grounds of unconscionability, *see, e.g., Armendariz v. Foundation Health Psychcare Serv., Inc.*, 24 Cal. 4th 83 (2000); *Trinity Mission of Clinton, LLC v. Barber*, 988 So. 2d 910 (Miss. Ct. App. 2007). However, as noted in Chapter 6, there are also courts upholding such damages waivers. What view do you think is correct? Should the context of the agreement matter? If a court finds a waiver provision unconscionable, should the court sever the waiver and still order arbitration? Why or why not?

2. *Fairness of Arbitration Procedures and Outcomes*

The most pointed criticisms of pre-dispute arbitration provisions in consumer, employment, and other potentially "adhesive" contracts usually stem from perceived unfairness in arbitration procedures and remedies. It is worth reviewing some of the advantages of arbitration you have learned about in these chapters and comparing and contrasting the consumer and employment contexts from the business-to-business and international agreements in which arbitration has long been popular. Rational consumers and employees, like business counterparts, may conclude that in some cases arbitration procedures provide a speedier and less expensive alternative to going to court, as well as a greater likelihood of getting to a hearing.

However, where one party is a company that "sets the stage" for binding arbitration by putting arbitration provisions in its contracts with consumers or employees, some of the arbitration terms may appear to produce one-sided advantages. The party drafting the provision may have more power in choosing an arbitration provider, the scope of information exchange and discovery, location of proceedings, confidentiality of the process, nature of hearings, availability of remedies (including punitive damages and attorneys' fees), scope and format of awards, and the ability to challenge awards.

An individual forced to arbitrate may be unfamiliar with the process, while the party who drafted the arbitration clause may be a repeat player who is familiar with the process and with particular arbitrators. Although in one sense an arbitrator is like a judge without a robe, that lack of a robe can sometimes be a cause for concern. In the judicial system, a party is unable to choose the adjudicator, unlike parties in arbitration. Thus, while businesses may look for commercial or technical expertise in an arbitrator, consumers may be wary of the perceived bias borne of experience as an "insider." This becomes particularly concerning when certain companies continue to give repeat business to the same arbitrators, and those same companies provide all or a large part of the arbitrators' fees. While the FAA provides that a court may overturn an arbitration award if an arbitrator engages in "evident partiality," this is not easy to prove and is rarely found, 9 U.S.C. §10(a)(2); see Chapter 6. Clearly, these concerns call into question the viability of arbitration when significant gaps in bargaining power exist between parties entering arbitral agreements.

Finally, arbitration may be a mechanism to shield the company from consolidated consumer efforts (e.g., class action lawsuits). Many companies include clear class waivers in their arbitration clauses, and these clauses have been essentially "blessed" by the Supreme Court in cases such as *AT&T Mobility v. Concepcion*, 563 U.S. 333 (2011), discussed in Chapter 8.B.2, holding (in a 5-4 decision) that a class action waiver in a standardized consumer contract was enforceable. *See also Epic Sys. Corp. v. Lewis*, 138 S. Ct. 1612 (2018) (the Supreme Court holding that arbitration agreements calling for individualized proceedings are enforceable per not only the FAA, but also the Fair Labor Standards Act (FLSA) and National Labor Relations Act (NLRA)).

PROBLEM 1

You are very probably a party to a contract that contains arbitration provisions. Arbitration provisions appear in contracts for wireless services, for medical services, for employment, in apartment leases, and even in "apps" for your phone.

Your assignment is to examine a contract to which you are a party that includes an arbitration provision and answer the following questions:

A. Did you take the time to read these contents before signifying your acceptance of the agreement? (Remember that, generally speaking, a failure to read terms and conditions will not operate as a defense against their enforcement under U.S. contract law.)

B. *Clarity and Transparency.* Where is the agreement to arbitration contained in your contract? How easy is it to locate? Under what heading or section title does it appear? Is the language clear and understandable? Does the provision reference or incorporate separate rules or procedures, and, if so, how easy is it to locate and review them?

C. *Administration.* Can you tell how the program is administered, and by whom? Is it an independent organization? Can you tell who pays the fees of administration?

D. *Arbitrators.* How are the arbitrators selected, and by whom? Are they selected from a panel, or subject to experiential or other requirements? Who pays the arbitrators' fees and expenses?

E. *Procedures.* How are filings of claims made, and what kind of notice is required for the filing of a demand? May you be represented by an attorney, if desired? If need be, can you obtain critical documents or testimony from the company? What kind of a hearing are you entitled to, and when and where will it be held? Might you get an online hearing, eliminating travel and time off work? How long will it take to obtain relief? Can you bring a claim as part of a class action or collective action by other consumers/employees? To what extent is the proceeding confidential, and how does this affect your ability to share information with third parties? Are you permitted the option of pursuing relief in small claims court?

F. *Outcomes (Awards and Remedies).* Are there any limitations on your ability to obtain relief that might be available in court, including punitive damages or statutory remedies? Will the award contain any form of rationale? Is the loser required to pay for attorneys' fees and arbitration costs?

G. Are you comfortable with these procedures? What relative advantages or disadvantages do they present in comparison to going to court? In reaching your answer, what difference does it make whether any claims you might have are likely to be relatively small—say, no more than $100 or $200?

3.   Fairness Concerns and Administering Institutions

Some years ago, a Minnesota-based organization called the National Arbitration Forum (NAF) was at the center of a very colorful and troubling episode in consumer arbitration. NAF administered arbitrations of consumer debt actions. In the summer of 2009, NAF ceased its consumer arbitration program as part of a settlement with the Minnesota Attorney General. The latter had sued over its management of debt actions involving consumers and credit card companies. NAF was accused of violating state consumer fraud, deceptive trade practices, and false advertising laws by hiding financial connections to collection agencies and credit card companies.[17] The Minnesota Attorney General alleged that NAF had handled more than 214,000 collection claims in 2006, 60 percent of which were filed by law firms with ties to the collection industry. NAF denied the allegations. Under the settlement, NAF was permitted to continue to arbitrate certain types of claims performed under supervision of government entities or non-government organizations. The NAF story—that of a provider with an apparent deep-seated conflict of interest—resonates with concerns long expressed by some scholars that consumers and employees cannot find equitable treatment in justice systems set up by companies who are "repeat players" in the system.

NOTES AND QUESTIONS

14. How might a company that wanted to continue to use arbitration prevent such bias or mitigate perceptions of bias?

15. Do the data support the repeat player concept? The early quantitative underpinning of the concept was primarily the work of Professor Lisa Bingham. Extensive research conducted by Professor Bingham on issues in employment arbitration did not produce clear evidence to reinforce such concerns, although the author concludes that "superior bargaining power is affecting the outcomes of arbitration."[18] One researcher suggested that the data do not clearly support the concept that repeated

experiences with a single arbitrator are a critical factor in outcomes.[19] However, it is easy to imagine scenarios in which repeat players reap advantages over their opponents through superior information about procedures and neutrals, personal familiarity, perceived economic leverage, or other factors.

16. Do arbitrators in employment and labor cases ignore the law? In a recent study, researchers reviewed hundreds of labor arbitration awards over the last decade to determine that the majority of awards do not cite to external authority like case law.[20] However, only a small number decline to address a statutory issue or fail to address external authority that the parties bring up in their arguments. The researchers also note that there is more likely to be a citation to external authority if the parties are represented by attorneys, and that arbitrators selected through the AAA or the Federal Mediation and Conciliation Service are more likely to cite to external authority. Specifically, they studied 602 labor awards and found that only 17 cite to or rely on a statute, 11 mention a statute but don't analyze it, and 5 explicitly decline to address a statutory issue. Additionally, 78 (12.96%) of the awards cite or rely on at least one judicial opinion, while 23 awards (3.82%) cite to administrative authority like the EEOC or NLRB. Of all 602, 99 awards (16.4%) cite to at least some external authority, while 83 percent cite no external authority. Should it matter whether arbitrators cite to authority? Note, too, that these studies address arbitration under collective bargaining agreements, but not arbitration under individual contracts of employment.

17. What does arbitration *mean* in the aftermath of the #MeToo movement? Stephanie Greene and Christine Neylon O'Brien argue that the Supreme Court's decision in *Epic Systems* strikes a blow to employees' rights by limiting class arbitration.[21] They argue that these arbitration clauses generally fall disproportionately on low-wage employees who may fear retaliation, and have difficulty finding attorneys to represent individual employees when the recovery is small. Furthermore, they worry that the secrecy of arbitration in the workplace allows problems like wage theft and sexual harassment to continue. Do you think that these concerns are warranted? What remedies should policymakers seek?

18. Notably, some companies (Microsoft, Uber, Lyft) have decided independently not to arbitrate sexual harassment cases. Do you think that this is due to the #MeToo movement? See Greene and O'Brien's discussion, referenced above.

NOTE: NONDISCLOSURE AGREEMENTS (NDAs)

Arbitration is private but not confidential. Arbitration is private in that only the parties to the arbitration agreement, the arbitrators, witnesses, and others that the parties invite, may attend the proceedings. However, arbitration proceedings are not necessarily secret, or confidential. Information revealed during the process may become public, and parties may talk to others about the arbitration proceedings unless they agree to keep the information confidential. This is where nondisclosure agreements (NDAs) come in. Often arbitration agreements include confidentiality clauses that are essentially NDAs. Some parties do include confidentiality clauses in their agreements, especially when they are concerned with guarding sensitive information or preventing unwanted publicity. This is often true in sophisticated business contexts involving parties who are cognizant of distinctions between privacy and confidentiality in arbitration. Indeed, parties are wise to include confidentiality clauses in their arbitration contracts when they expect possible disputes to involve business secrets or copyright-protected information.

However, confidentiality clauses may be sources of concern where they hinder the public's access to information impacting health and safety. These clauses also are problematic when they impede individuals' abilities to obtain information regarding prior claims that they may need to prove patterns of discrimination or other legal violations they may need to succeed on statutory claims. It is in these cases that courts have held such agreements unconscionable or otherwise unenforceable under contract law defenses. This is especially true when there is disparate bargaining power, such as is often the case in consumer and employment contexts.

What are the benefits to secrecy in arbitration? Why might a party want to include an NDA or confidentiality clause in their arbitration agreement? What are some drawbacks? Should there be legal limits on NDAs in arbitration? California recently enacted a law barring settlement agreements from containing NDAs preventing the disclosure of facts related to claims of sexual harassment and sex discrimination. Further, the U.S. Congress recently passed legislation to end mandatory arbitration in lawsuits involving sexual assault and harassment claims. As discussed in Chapter 8, the Ending Forced Arbitration of Sexual Assault and Sexual Harassment Act of 2021 is likely to dramatically change the landscape of sexual harassment disputes in the workplace.

NOTE: THE DUE PROCESS PROTOCOLS

Some leading dispute resolution organizations undertook initiatives to address fairness concerns regarding consumer and employment arbitration. The AAA co-sponsored several national efforts to establish due process standards—all of which have underpinned changes to its own rules and procedures while encouraging the development of analogous rules by some other provider organizations. A Due Process Protocol for Mediation and Arbitration of Statutory Disputes Arising Out of the Employment Relationship (Employment Due Process Protocol) was one of the first attempts to resolve the problems arising from mandated arbitration of statutory claims, 91 Daily Lab. Rep. (BNA) A-8, E-11 (May 11, 1995). The Employment Due Process Protocol, which was adopted by AAA and JAMS, was geared specifically to deal with due process issues for one-shot disputants in employment arbitration. It attempted to address these problems by recommending that certain procedural and substantive aspects of litigation be employed in arbitration. For example, the Protocol recommends allowing employees to be represented by an attorney, having the employer reimburse the employee for attorneys' fees, encouraging the use of pretrial discovery, and allowing the arbitrator to provide any type of relief that would be similar to that available in a court proceeding. These recommendations would, in many situations, give an employee a greater sense of fairness, preserving some protections available in litigation and further reducing the cost of arbitration.

The Employment Due Process Protocol was the primary model for the 1998 Due Process Protocol for Mediation and Arbitration of Consumer Disputes (Consumer Due Process Protocol), a statement of 15 principles to "establish clear benchmarks for conflict resolution processes involving consumers," embodying consumers' "fundamental reasonable expectation" of a fair process.[22] The Consumer Due Process Protocol is a major step beyond the Employment Due Process Protocol in several respects. In addition to requiring an independent administration of ADR if participation is mandated by a pre-dispute agreement, the Consumer Due Process Protocol sets forth many elements of a "fundamentally fair process," a few of which are (1) provision of "full and accurate information regarding Consumer ADR programs," (2) independent and impartial neutrals, and (3) the right of parties "to seek relief in a small claims court for disputes or claims within the scope of its jurisdiction." The principles' call for full disclosure of information about consumer arbitration programs means that consumers are aware of what rights they are surrendering by agreeing to submit to the process. The ability to resolve some issues in small claims courts may assuage consumers by allowing them to feel that a public airing of the dispute before an independent judiciary remains an option.

In 1998, a leading group of organizations involved in ADR, law, and medicine issued a special variant of the Consumer Due Process Protocol, the Due Process Protocol for Mediation and Arbitration of Health Care Disputes. The latter encourages the use of ADR to resolve disputes over health care coverage and access arising out of the relationship between patients and private health plans and managed care organizations. The sponsoring organizations agreed, however, that the use of pre-dispute arbitration agreements should be limited in the health care arena for disputes involving patients. The drafters sought to promote efficiency as well as fairness and did find mandatory, pre-dispute arbitration appropriate in disputes not involving patients.

Notably, the AAA has made efforts to require companies that incorporate AAA procedures in consumer or employment contracts to comply with its procedures; JAMS has similar policies. The AAA's Protocol-influenced procedures appear to have produced tangible positive results when effectively put into practice. The AAA will decline to administer cases it feels deviate from minimum due process standards.[23] Similarly, JAMS takes some measures aimed to ensure fairness, although it will abide by contract terms.[24] If the arbitration is based on an agreement that is required as a condition of employment, the only fee an employee is required to pay is the JAMS Case Management Fee, although there may be other fees and expenses involved.

One study compared randomly selected arbitrated cases under the AAA National Rules for Resolution of Employment Disputes in 1999-2000 with state court trial outcomes reported by the Civil Trial Court Network.[25] Researchers concluded that higher-paid employees pursuing non-civil-rights employment claims, the group most likely to be able to afford representation to go to court and therefore most represented in state court trials, won more frequently in arbitration than at trial. The authors found no statistically significant difference in median or mean awards in trial and arbitration. Moreover, the evidence indicated that the mean and median times to resolution were much shorter in arbitration than in litigation. They also observed that some pro-employee arbitration awards would probably have ended up as pro-employer summary judgments in litigation, as courts are significantly more likely than arbitrators to dismiss claims prior to trial on the merits. The authors considered it important that the AAA adhered to the Employment Due Process Protocol.

Research by Professor Bingham supports the conclusion that the imposition of community due process standards in private arbitration has positive implications for employees.[26] Moreover, an independent investigation of AAA-administered consumer credit cases by a task force of Northwestern University's Searle Civil Justice Institute indicates that consumer-debtors prevailed more often in debt collection actions in AAA-administered debt collection arbitration than in court, and creditor recovery rates tended to be lower than, or comparable to, recovery rates in court.[27]

Critics remain concerned, however, that providers' adherence to the Protocols is voluntary and that the Protocols may be insufficient to guarantee fairness in some circumstances. Although the Protocols have had an impact on arbitration, they do not have the force of law. The effectiveness of the Protocols thus lies in the voluntary agreement by arbitrators and arbitration service providers to require adherence to the procedures called for in the Protocols. By committing themselves to ensuring that due process protections are provided, the decision by some institutional providers to regulate themselves may have helped to legitimize the prevalent and growing use of pre-dispute arbitration clauses in contracts of adhesion. Such efforts may also have been instrumental in fending off more direct government regulation of the arbitration industry and in maintaining the favored status the Supreme Court has bestowed upon arbitration.[28]

NOTE AND QUESTION

19. While the AAA and some other organizations have been particularly attentive to due process issues and have actively sought to administer arbitration accordingly, there is no requirement that all providers of arbitration services adopt or adhere to the Protocols. Recall, for example, the reported conflicts of interest that undermined the NAF consumer arbitration program (discussed above) that demonstrated the potential for abuse of private arbitration. In 2009, in the wake of NAF's withdrawal from the arena of consumer arbitration, the AAA suspended that part of its own consumer arbitration program relating to consumer credit card contracts. Following this, several major credit card issuers also agreed to temporarily stop enforcing the mandatory arbitration clauses in their contracts.

20. Do any of the Protocols (all but one of which were developed in the 1990s) take a position on provisions purporting to prevent class actions or classwide arbitration of claims—provisions that are at the heart of the current debate over pre-dispute arbitration provisions in consumer and employment contracts?

E.   *JUDICIAL POLICING OF ARBITRATION AGREEMENTS IN CONSUMER AND EMPLOYMENT CONTRACTS*

Courts have been moved to intervene to protect consumers and employees from egregious unfairness in arbitration by striking down specific terms in the arbitration agreement or by denying enforcement to the whole arbitration provision. They have used a variety of defenses to contract, including fraud and misrepresentation, breach of contract, and unconscionability. As we will see, however, these efforts must be seen against the backdrop of the broader pro-arbitration policy that has led most courts to enforce arbitration agreements in all kinds of contracts, even standardized agreements. *See, e.g., Gilmer v. Interstate/Johnson Lane Corp.*, 500 U.S. 20 (1991), discussed above in Section C.1. Judges find themselves trying to strike the right balance between upholding the federal and state laws promoting arbitration and reining in some of the more egregious examples of unfairness—with varied and conflicting results.

As you read each of the decisions below, note the different approaches the courts used to establish limits on arbitration agreements in the interest of promoting fairness. Consider, also, the array of procedural concerns that gave rise to and were addressed by these decisions.

Engalla v. Permanente Medical Group, Inc.

15 Cal. 4th 951 (1997)

[Plaintiffs in this case were the surviving family of Wilfredo Engalla, who through his employer was enrolled in Kaiser Permanente Medical Group's health maintenance organization (Kaiser). Part of the standard insurance agreement contained an arbitration clause providing for binding arbitration of disputes related to Kaiser's services. Alleging that Kaiser had lost X-rays, failed to follow its physician's recommendations, and otherwise negligently failed to diagnose his cancer until it was inoperable, Mr. Engalla initiated arbitration. Although Kaiser represented that an arbitration within its self-administered program would reach a hearing within several months' time, the final arbitrator was not even selected until more than five months after the service of Mr. Engalla's claim. Mr. Engalla died before an arbitral hearing could be held. After his death, his family initiated a medical malpractice action in superior court.]

Mosk, J.:
. . . The arbitration clause contained in the Service Agreement . . . provides that each side "shall" designate a party arbitrator within 30 days of service of the claim and that the 2 party arbitrators "shall" designate a third, neutral arbitrator within 30 days thereafter. . . . The arbitration program is designed, written, mandated, and administered by Kaiser. It does not . . . employ or contract with any independent person or entity to provide such administrative services, or any oversight or evaluation of the arbitration program or its performance. Rather, administrative functions are performed by outside counsel retained to defend Kaiser in an adversarial capacity. . . . The fact that Kaiser has designed and administers its arbitration

program from an adversarial perspective is not disclosed to Kaiser members or subscribers. . . . [In materials distributed to Kaiser members,] Kaiser represented that an arbitration in its program would reach a hearing within several months' time, and that its members would find the arbitration process to be a fair approach to protecting their rights. [The opinion recounts in detail multiple requests from Mr. Engalla's counsel for expeditious processing of the claim due to his terminal condition. It details delays on the part of the lawyers for Kaiser in the selection of arbitrators so that the final, neutral arbitrator was not appointed until more than five months after the service of Mr. Engalla's claim, well beyond the representations made by Kaiser, and shortly before his death.] . . .

In order to defeat a petition to compel arbitration, the parties opposing a petition to compel must show that the asserted fraud claim goes specifically " 'to the "making" of the agreement to arbitrate,' " rather than to the making of the contract in general. . . .

The Engallas claim that Engalla was fraudulently induced to enter the arbitration agreement—in essence a claim of promissory fraud. " 'Promissory fraud' is a subspecies of fraud and deceit. A promise to do something necessarily implies the intention to perform; hence, where a promise is made without such intention, there is an implied misrepresentation of fact that may be actionable fraud. . . ."

Here the Engallas claim (1) that Kaiser misrepresented its arbitration agreement in that it entered into the agreement knowing that, at the very least, there was a likelihood its agents would breach the part of the agreement providing for the timely appointment of arbitrators and the expeditious progress towards an arbitration hearing; (2) that Kaiser employed the above misrepresentation in order to induce reliance on the part of Engalla and his employer; (3) that Engalla relied on these misrepresentations to his detriment. The trial court found evidence supporting those claims. . . .

First, evidence of misrepresentation is plain. "[F]alse representations made recklessly and without regard for their truth in order to induce action by another are the equivalent of misrepresentations knowingly and intentionally uttered." As recounted above, section 8.B. of the arbitration agreement provides that party arbitrators "shall" be chosen within 30 days and neutral arbitrators within 60 days, and that the arbitration hearing "shall" be held "within a reasonable time thereafter." Although Kaiser correctly argues that these contractual representations did not bind it to appoint a neutral arbitrator within 60 days, since the appointment of that arbitrator is a bilateral decision that depends on agreements of the parties, Kaiser's contractual representations were at the very least commitments to exercise good faith and reasonable diligence to have the arbitrators appointed within the specified time. This good faith duty is underscored by Kaiser's contractual assumption of the duty to administer the health service plan as a fiduciary.

Here there are facts to support the Engallas' allegation that Kaiser entered into the arbitration agreement with knowledge that it would not comply with its own contractual timelines, or with at least a reckless indifference as to whether its agents would use reasonable diligence and good faith to comply with them. As discussed, a survey of Kaiser arbitrations between 1984 and 1986 submitted into evidence showed that a neutral arbitrator was appointed within 60 days in only 1 percent of the cases, with only 3 percent appointed within 180 days, and that on average the neutral arbitrator was appointed 674 days—almost 2 years—after the demand for arbitration. Regardless of when Kaiser became aware of these precise statistics, which were part of a 1989 study, the depositions of two of Kaiser's in-house attorneys demonstrate that Kaiser was aware soon after it began its arbitration program that its contractual deadlines were not being met, and that severe delay was endemic to the program. Kaiser nonetheless persisted in its contractual promises of expeditiousness.

Kaiser now argues that most of these delays were caused by the claimants themselves and their attorneys, who procrastinated in the selection of a neutral arbitrator. But Kaiser's counterexplanation is without any statistical support, and is based solely on anecdotal evidence related by Kaiser officials. Moreover, the explanation appears implausible in view of the sheer pervasiveness of the delays. While it is theoretically possible that 99 percent of plaintiffs' attorneys did not seek a rapid arbitration, a more reasonable inference, in light of common experience, is that in at least some cases Kaiser's defense attorneys were partly or wholly responsible for the delays, and Kaiser's former general counsel conceded as much in deposition testimony. It is, after all, the defense which often benefits from delay, thereby preserving the status quo to its advantage until the time when memories fade and claims are abandoned. Indeed, the present case illustrates why Kaiser's counsel may sometimes find it advantageous to delay the selection of a neutral arbitrator. There is also evidence that Kaiser kept extensive records on the arbitrators it had used, and may have delayed the selection process in order to ensure that it would obtain the arbitrators it thought would best serve its interests. Thus, it is a reasonable inference from the documentary record before us that Kaiser's contractual representations of expeditiousness were made with knowledge of their likely falsity, and in fact concealed an unofficial policy or practice of delay.

The systemwide nature of Kaiser's delay comes into clearer focus when it is contrasted with other arbitration systems. As the Engallas point out, many large institutional users of arbitration, including most health maintenance organizations (HMOs), avoid the potential problems of delay in the selection of arbitrators by contracting with neutral third party organizations, such as the American Arbitration Association (AAA). These organizations will then assume responsibility for administering the claim from the time the arbitration demand is filed, and will ensure the arbitrator or arbitrators are chosen in a timely manner. Though Kaiser is not obliged by law to adopt any particular form of arbitration, the record shows that it did not attempt to create within its own organization any office that would neutrally administer the arbitration program, but instead entrusted such administration to outside counsel retained to act as advocates on its behalf. In other words, there is evidence that Kaiser established a self-administered arbitration system in which delay for its own benefit and convenience was an inherent part, despite express and implied contractual representations to the contrary. . . .

We turn then to the Engallas' unconscionability argument. We have required that "contractual arrangement[s] for the nonjudicial resolution of disputes" must possess "'minimum levels of integrity.'" Thus, in *Graham v. Scissor-Tail, Inc.*, we held that an arbitration agreement that called for the selection of an arbitrator affiliated with one of the parties to the contract was unconscionable. . . . In addition to the general doctrine of unconscionability derived from contract law, HMO's such as Kaiser are regulated by the Knox-Keene Health Care Service Plan Act, which provides among other things that all contracts made in connection with a health service plan be "fair, reasonable, and consistent with the objectives" of that statute. HMO's are therefore especially obligated not to impose contracts on their subscribers that are one-sided and lacking in fundamental fairness.

In determining whether a contract term is unconscionable, we first consider whether the contract between Kaiser and Engalla was one of adhesion. In [*Madden*], we held that an agreement between Kaiser and a state employee was not a true contract of adhesion, although Kaiser's health plan was offered to state employees "on a 'take it or leave it' basis without opportunity for individual bargaining." We reasoned that the Kaiser contract was not adhesive because (1) it "represents the product of negotiation between two parties, Kaiser and the [State Employees Retirement System], possessing parity of bargaining strength" and (2) the state employee could choose from among a number of different health plans, and thus was not confronted with the choice typical of a contract of adhesion of "either adher[ing] to the standardized agreement or forego[ing] the needed service." We also found that the arbitration clause in question was not, unlike the unconscionable clauses in adhesion contracts, a term that limits the liability or obligations of a stronger party, but rather "could prove helpful to all parties."

The present agreement, which was also offered to Engalla on a "take it or leave it" basis, has more of the characteristics of an adhesion contract than the one considered in *Madden*. First, although Oliver Tire [Engalla's employer] is a corporation of considerable size, it has had only a small number of employees enrolled in Kaiser, and did not have the strength to bargain with Kaiser to alter the terms of the contract. Second, Engalla did have one other health plan from which to choose, but not several plans as was the case in *Madden*. Finally, unlike in *Madden*, the Engallas do not claim that the arbitration clause itself is unconscionable, but that the arbitration program Kaiser established was biased against them.

Nonetheless, although the present contract has some of the attributes of adhesion, it did not, on its face, lack "'minimum levels of integrity.'" The unfairness that is the substance of the Engallas' unconscionability argument comes essentially to this: The Engallas contend that Kaiser has established a system of arbitration inherently unfair to claimants, because the method of selecting neutral arbitrators is biased. They claim that Kaiser has an unfair advantage as a "repeat player" in arbitration, possessing information on arbitrators that the Engallas themselves lacked. They also argue that Kaiser, under its arbitration system, has sought to maximize this advantage by reserving for itself an unlimited right to veto arbitrators proposed by the other party. This method is in contrast to arbitration programs run by neutral, third party arbitration organizations such as the AAA, which give parties a very limited ability to veto arbitrators from its preselected panels.

Yet none of these features of Kaiser's arbitration program renders the arbitration agreement per se unconscionable. . . . The alleged problem with Kaiser's arbitration in this case was not any defect or one-sidedness in its contractual provisions, but rather in the gap between its contractual representations and the actual workings of its arbitration program. It is the doctrines of fraud and waiver, rather than of unconscionability, that most appropriately address this discrepancy between the contractual representation and the reality. Thus, viewing the arbitration agreement on its face, we cannot say it is unconscionable.

[Reversed and remanded to the trial court for a determination of the Engallas' waiver claim. The Engallas argued that arbitration should not be compelled because of Kaiser's conduct.]

BROWN, J., dissenting:

. . . Almost lost in the majority's exhaustive procedural summary is one key fact—namely, the arbitration process was already underway by the time the plaintiffs unilaterally withdrew. . . . The reason the Engallas withdrew from the arbitration was that Kaiser declined to stipulate that Mrs. Engalla's separate loss of consortium claim survived her husband's death. It is this unilateral withdrawal from a pending arbitration that the majority's decision validates. . . .

In evaluating both the Engallas' fraudulent inducement claim and their waiver claim, the majority focuses on Kaiser's performance during the course of the aborted private arbitration. According to the majority, the sine qua non of successful fraudulent inducement and waiver claims is unreasonable or bad faith delay by Kaiser. . . .

Although the majority's desire to penalize Kaiser's obduracy is understandable, the consequences of validating a party's unilateral withdrawal from a pending arbitration based on the conduct of its arbitration adversary will reverberate far beyond the bad facts of the instant case. In stark contrast to the legislative response, which enhances the procedures for keeping a case in private arbitration, . . . the majority expands the procedures for removing a case from arbitration. . . .

In this case, having previously submitted their dispute to private arbitration and having already completed the arbitrator selection process, the Engallas should have sought relief for Kaiser's dilatory conduct in the pending arbitration. For example, the Engallas could have presented their fraud and waiver claims directly to the arbitrators and requested that they not enforce the arbitration provision. Likewise, the Engallas could have requested that the arbitrators sanction Kaiser's dilatory conduct by deeming Mrs. Engalla's separate loss of consortium claim to have survived her husband's death [describing broad remedial powers of arbitrators]. In fact, at oral argument, the Engallas' counsel conceded that this case could likely have remained in private arbitration if Mrs. Engalla's economic loss had been ameliorated.

The one thing the Engallas should not be permitted to do, however, is to circumvent the arbitrators altogether. The consequences of validating a party's unilateral withdrawal from a pending arbitration will be dramatic. Jurisdictional disputes will inevitably arise. Suppose, for example, that following the Engallas' unilateral withdrawal, Kaiser had elected to continue to pursue the pending arbitration and that the arbitrators had ultimately entered a default judgment in favor of Kaiser. Would that default judgment have been valid? Would the same have been true if the trial court had simultaneously entered a default judgment in favor of the Engallas in the pending litigation?

In addition, . . . other parties to pending arbitrations will doubtlessly engage in the same conduct. Counsel's answer to this dilemma was that this court should "trust the trial courts." The majority's answer is to "emphasize . . . that the delay must be substantial, unreasonable, and in spite of the claimant's own reasonable diligence" and not "the result of reasonable and good faith disagreements between the parties."

Neither answer is satisfactory. Under the majority's holding, which has all the precision of a "SCUD" missile, the resolution of fraudulent inducement and waiver claims will necessarily entail fact-intensive, case-by-case determinations. The disruptive, time-consuming nature of these determinations is well illustrated by the facts of the present case, in which "[t]he Engallas ultimately had five months to complete discovery [on the petition to compel arbitration], during which time thirteen motions were filed and more than a dozen depositions were taken." Even assuming that the trial courts ultimately resolve all future claims correctly, the interim disruption to pending arbitrations will be simply intolerable.

Great cases like hard cases make bad law. For great cases are called great, not by reason of their real importance in shaping the law of the future, but because of some accident of immediate overwhelming interest which appeals to the feelings and distorts the judgment. These immediate interests exercise a kind of hydraulic pressure which makes what previously was clear seem doubtful, and before which even well settled principles of law will bend. Although legislators, practitioners, and courts have all expressed concern that disparities in bargaining power may affect the procedural fairness of consumer arbitration agreements, this case amply demonstrates why any solutions should come from the Legislature, whose ability to craft precise exceptions is far superior to that of this court.

However well-intentioned the majority and however deserving its intended target, today's holding pokes a hole in the barrier separating private arbitrations and the courts. Unfortunately, like any such breach, this hole will eventually cause the dam to burst. Ironically, the tool the majority uses to puncture its hole is the observation that "those who enter into arbitration agreements expect that their dispute will be resolved without necessity for any contact with the courts." Because I suspect that parties to private arbitrations will be having quite a bit more contact with the courts than they ever bargained for, I dissent.

NOTE AND QUESTION

21. *Role of the Arbitrator.* The dissent states that although Kaiser's process did have unreasonable delays, the issues regarding delay should have been first brought up with the arbitrator because the arbitration had already begun. Judge Brown, in dissent, believes the majority essentially created more problems than it solved because now parties will find it easier to circumvent arbitrators in favor of the courts during the arbitral proceeding. Can you think of better solutions to address the delay problem? (Note: After this ruling, Kaiser formed a "Blue Ribbon Panel" of outside experts to suggest reforms to its arbitration process designed to speed up the process and ensure greater fairness.)

22. As discussed in Section D.3 above, the Health Care Due Process Protocol (proposing some limits on pre-dispute arbitration provisions) was developed in the 1990s. Would the Kaiser approach pass muster under the Health Care Due Process Protocol?

NOTE: THE USE OF UNCONSCIONABILITY DOCTRINE IN POLICING ARBITRATION AGREEMENTS

The *Engalla* majority declined to find the Kaiser arbitration provision unconscionable. Although the agreement had certain "adhesive" characteristics (that is, the consumer's relevant options were limited and Kaiser's control was great), the procedures spelled out in the agreement did not fail to meet "minimum levels of integrity" because, on their face, they did not appear to be unfair. Rather, the court reasoned, Kaiser misled the public as to its ability to meet the promised schedule.

Although unconscionability is the legal doctrine that is most often used to police fairness in arbitration agreements, what constitutes an unconscionable arbitration clause varies widely from state to state and court to court. The California courts have been especially active in using unconscionability as a basis for striking down arbitration agreements in whole or in part. In *Armendariz v. Foundation Health Psychcare Service, Inc.*, 24 Cal. 4th 83 (2000), for example, the California Supreme Court used the unconscionability doctrine as the basis for considering what procedural protections would be requisites for the arbitration of statutory discrimination claims under an employment agreement. Such elements included an independent and impartial arbitrator, the opportunity for the employee to have adequate discovery, limits on the cost of arbitration, remedies akin to those available in court, a written decision allowing limited judicial review, and procedural "bilaterality." Because not all of these requirements were met, the court struck down the entire agreement as unconscionable. Of course, the strong presumption in favor of enforcing arbitration agreements might lead other courts to take a more tailored approach and reform the agreement to address fairness concerns, thus allowing arbitration to proceed in a "fairer" way.

In any event, an arbitration clause will not be deemed unconscionable solely because it is contained in a preprinted sales agreement that was prepared by the seller and that the buyer may not have fully read. In *Harper v. J.D. Byrider of Canton*, 772 N.E.2d 190 (Ohio Ct. App. 9th Dist. 2002), for example, the court explained that a used car buyer who believed that the car he purchased had a false odometer reading was bound to arbitrate his dispute with the car dealer: "Preprinted forms are a fact of commercial life and do not serve to demonstrate prima facie unconscionability with regard to arbitration clauses." Normally, unconscionability comes into play when significant disparities in bargaining power are coupled with terms unreasonably favorable to the stronger, drafting party.

Courts have a good deal of flexibility in how to address perceived unconscionability, and this is another point of potential variation among courts. They might strike down individual provisions, modify those provisions, or deny enforcement to the entire arbitration agreement, as the California court did in *Armendariz*. As a general rule, the more suspect terms an arbitration agreement contains, the more likely it is that the whole arbitration agreement will be struck down. *See, e.g., Geiger v. Ryan's Family Steakhouses, Inc.*, 134 F. Supp. 2d 985 (S.D. Ind. 2001) (refusing to enforce an arbitration agreement that allowed the employer to select the arbitration panel, forced the employees to pay half or more of the cost of arbitration, and limited discovery to one deposition).

Interestingly, concerns about arbitration provisions in consumer and employment contracts may be said to have "reinvigorated" the doctrine of unconscionability. Most first-year Contracts casebooks now introduce the doctrine of unconscionability with a case about arbitration. Did your casebook do so? How did the casebook authors, and your teacher, characterize arbitration?

Hooters of America, Inc. v. Phillips

173 F.3d 933 (4th Cir. 1999)

[Annette R. Phillips alleges that she was sexually harassed while working as a bartender at a Hooters restaurant in Myrtle Beach, South Carolina. After quitting her job, Phillips threatened to bring a suit against Hooters under Title VII. Arguing that Phillips had agreed to arbitrate employment-related disputes, Hooters preemptively filed suit to compel arbitration under Section 9 of the FAA. She responded, asserting individual and class counterclaims against Hooters. The federal district court refused to compel arbitration, finding the agreement unconscionable and void for reasons of public policy.]

WILKINSON, Chief Judge:

. . . This agreement arose in 1994 during the implementation of Hooters' alternative dispute resolution program. As part of that program, the company conditioned eligibility for raises, transfers, and promotions upon an employee signing an "Agreement to arbitrate employment-related disputes." The agreement provides that Hooters and the employee each agree to arbitrate all disputes arising out of employment, including "any claim of discrimination, sexual harassment, retaliation, or wrongful discharge, whether arising under federal or state law." The agreement further states that:

> The employee and the company agree to resolve any claims pursuant to the company's rules and procedures for alternative resolution of employment-related disputes, as promulgated by the company from time to time ("the rules"). Company will make available or provide a copy of the rules upon written request of the employee.

The employees of Hooters were initially given a copy of this agreement at an all-staff meeting held on November 20, 1994. Hooters' general manager, Gene Fulcher, told the employees to review the agreement for five days and that they would then be asked to accept or reject the agreement. No employee, however, was given a copy of Hooters' arbitration rules and procedures. Phillips signed the agreement on November 25, 1994. When her personnel file was updated in April 1995, Phillips again signed the agreement. . . .

Pre-dispute agreements to arbitrate Title VII claims are thus valid and enforceable. The question remains whether a binding arbitration agreement between Phillips and Hooters exists and compels Phillips to submit her Title VII claims to arbitration. . . . "It [i]s for the court, not the arbitrator, to decide in the first instance

whether the dispute [i]s to be resolved through arbitration." . . . In so deciding, we
" 'engage in a limited review to ensure that the dispute is arbitral—i.e., that a valid
agreement to arbitrate exists between the parties and that the specific dispute falls
within the substantive scope of that agreement.' ". . .

. . . The judicial inquiry, while highly circumscribed, is not focused solely on
an examination for contractual formation defects such as lack of mutual assent
and want of consideration. . . . Courts also can investigate the existence of "such
grounds as exist at law or in equity for the revocation of any contract." 9 U.S.C.
§2. . . . In this case, the challenge goes to the validity of the arbitration agreement
itself. Hooters materially breached the arbitration agreement by promulgating
rules so egregiously unfair as to constitute a complete default of its contractual obligation to draft arbitration rules and to do so in good faith. . . .

The Hooters rules when taken as a whole . . . are so one-sided that their only
possible purpose is to undermine the neutrality of the proceeding. The rules
require the employee to provide the company notice of her claim at the outset,
including "the nature of the Claim" and "the specific act(s) or omissions(s) which
are the basis of the Claim." Rule 6-2(1), (2). Hooters, on the other hand, is not
required to file any responsive pleadings or to notice its defenses. Additionally, at
the time of filing this notice, the employee must provide the company with a list of
all fact witnesses with a brief summary of the facts known to each. Rule 6-2(5). The
company, however, is not required to reciprocate.

The Hooters rules also provide a mechanism for selecting a panel of three
arbitrators that is crafted to ensure a biased decision maker. Rule 8. The employee
and Hooters each select an arbitrator, and the two arbitrators in turn select a third.
Good enough, except that the employee's arbitrator and the third arbitrator must
be selected from a list of arbitrators created exclusively by Hooters. This gives Hooters control over the entire panel and places no limits whatsoever on whom Hooters
can put on the list. Under the rules, Hooters is free to devise lists of partial arbitrators who have existing relationships, financial or familial, with Hooters and its management. In fact, the rules do not even prohibit Hooters from placing its managers
themselves on the list. Further, nothing in the rules restricts Hooters from punishing
arbitrators who rule against the company by removing them from the list. Given the
unrestricted control that one party (Hooters) has over the panel, the selection of an
impartial decision maker would be a surprising result.

Nor is fairness to be found once the proceedings are begun. Although Hooters
may expand the scope of arbitration to any matter, "whether related or not to the
Employee's Claim," the employee cannot raise "any matter not included in the Notice
of Claim." Rules 4-2, 8-9. Similarly, Hooters is permitted to move for summary dismissal of employee claims before a hearing is held whereas the employee is not permitted to seek summary judgment. Rule 14-4. Hooters, but not the employee, may
record the arbitration hearing "by audio or videotaping or by verbatim transcription."
Rule 18-1. The rules also grant Hooters the right to bring suit in court to vacate or
modify an arbitral award when it can show, by a preponderance of the evidence, that
the panel exceeded its authority. Rule 21-4. No such right is granted to the employee.

In addition, the rules provide that upon 30 days notice Hooters, but not the
employee, may cancel the agreement to arbitrate. Rule 23-1. Moreover, Hooters
reserves the right to modify the rules, "in whole or in part," whenever it wishes and
"without notice" to the employee. Rule 24-1. Nothing in the rules even prohibits
Hooters from changing the rules in the middle of an arbitration proceeding.

If by odd chance the unfairness of these rules were not apparent on their face, leading arbitration experts have decried their one-sidedness. George Friedman, senior vice president of the American Arbitration Association (AAA), testified that the system established by the Hooters rules so deviated from minimum due process standards that the Association would refuse to arbitrate under those rules. [Other expert testimony omitted.] . . . In a similar vein, two major arbitration associations have filed amicus briefs with this court. The National Academy of Arbitrators stated that the Hooters rules "violate fundamental concepts of fairness . . . and the integrity of the arbitration process." Likewise, the Society of Professionals in Dispute Resolution noted that "[i]t would be hard to imagine a more unfair method of selecting a panel of arbitrators." It characterized the Hooters arbitration system as "deficient to the point of illegitimacy" and "so one-sided, it is hard to believe that it was even intended to be fair."

We hold that the promulgation of so many biased rules — especially the scheme whereby one party to the proceeding so controls the arbitral panel — breaches the contract entered into by the parties. The parties agreed to submit their claims to arbitration — a system whereby disputes are fairly resolved by an impartial third party. Hooters by contract took on the obligation of establishing such a system. By creating a sham system unworthy even of the name of arbitration, Hooters completely failed in performing its contractual duty.

Moreover, Hooters had a duty to perform its obligations in good faith. . . . Good faith "emphasizes faithfulness to an agreed common purpose and consistency with the justified expectations of the other party." Restatement (Second) of Contracts §205 cmt. a. Bad faith includes the "evasion of the spirit of the bargain" and an "abuse of a power to specify terms." Id. §205 cmt. d. By agreeing to settle disputes in arbitration, Phillips agreed to the prompt and economical resolution of her claims. She could legitimately expect that arbitration would not entail procedures so wholly one-sided as to present a stacked deck. Thus we conclude that the Hooters rules also violate the contractual obligation of good faith.

Given Hooters' breaches of the arbitration agreement and Phillips' desire not to be bound by it, we hold that rescission is the proper remedy. Generally, "rescission will not be granted for a minor or casual breach of a contract, but only for those breaches which defeat the object of the contracting parties." . . . As we have explained, Hooters' breach is by no means insubstantial; its performance under the contract was so egregious that the result was hardly recognizable as arbitration at all. We therefore permit Phillips to cancel the agreement and thus Hooters' suit to compel arbitration must fail. . . .

We respect fully the Supreme Court's pronouncement that "questions of arbitrability must be addressed with a healthy regard for the federal policy favoring arbitration." *Moses H. Cone*, 460 U.S. at 24. Our decision should not be misread: We are not holding that the agreement before us is unenforceable because the arbitral proceedings are too abbreviated. An arbitral forum need not replicate the judicial forum. "[W]e are well past the time when judicial suspicion of the desirability of arbitration and of the competence of arbitral tribunals inhibited the development of arbitration as an alternative means of dispute resolution." . . . Nor should our decision be misunderstood as permitting a full-scale assault on the fairness of proceedings before the matter is submitted to arbitration. Generally, objections to the nature of arbitral proceedings are for the arbitrator to decide in the first instance. Only after arbitration may a party then raise such challenges if they meet the narrow grounds set out in 9 U.S.C. §10 for vacating an arbitral award. In the case before us, we only reach the content of the arbitration rules because their promulgation was the duty of one party under the contract. The material breach of this duty warranting rescission is an issue of substantive arbitrability and thus is reviewable before arbitration. . . . This case, however, is the exception that proves the rule: fairness objections should generally be made to the arbitrator, subject only to limited post-arbitration judicial review as set forth in section 10 of the FAA.

By promulgating this system of warped rules, Hooters so skewed the process in its favor that Phillips has been denied arbitration in any meaningful sense of the word. To uphold the promulgation of this aberrational scheme under the heading of arbitration would undermine, not advance, the federal policy favoring alternative dispute resolution. This we refuse to do. . . .

Affirmed and Remanded.

QUESTIONS

23. Are there other possible grounds on which the court could have held that Ms. Phillips should not be required to arbitrate? Might another court have used unconscionability doctrine?
24. If you were advising a restaurant chain, what advice would you give if it sought to establish a process for settling disputes between the chain and its employees? Do the Due Process Protocols, discussed above in Section D.3, offer any guideposts?

The following excerpt from *Cole v. Burns International Security Services*, written by Judge Harry Edwards, should help you reflect on these controversies. The case involved the enforcement of an arbitration claim of employment discrimination pursuant to Title VII of the Civil Rights Act of 1964 under the AAA Employment Rules. Accepting the Supreme Court's decision in *Gilmer v. Interstate/Johnson Lane Corp.*, 500 U.S. 20 (1991), as a qualified mandate for arbitration as a condition of employment, Judge Edwards set forth a number of "minimal standards of procedural fairness" for employees entering into binding arbitration of statutory discrimination claims. In the conclusion of the ruling, excerpted below, he offers a thoughtful discourse on binding employment arbitration.

Cole v. Burns International Security Services

105 F.3d 1465 (D.C. Cir. 1997)

HARRY T. EDWARDS, Chief Judge:

. . . We acknowledge the concerns that have been raised regarding arbitration's ability to vindicate employees' statutory rights. However, for all of arbitration's shortcomings, the process, if fairly conducted, is not necessarily inferior to litigation as a mechanism for the resolution of employment disputes. As the Dunlop Commission recognized:

[L]itigation has become a less-than-ideal method of resolving employees' public law claims. . . . [E]mployees bringing public law claims in court must endure long waiting periods as governing agencies and the over-burdened court system struggle to find time to properly investigate and hear the complaint. Moreover, the average profile of employee litigants . . . indicates that lower-wage workers may not fare as well as higher-wage professionals in the litigation system; lower-wage workers are less able to afford the time required to pursue a court complaint, and are less likely to receive large monetary relief from juries. Finally, the litigation model of dispute resolution seems to be dominated by "ex-employee" complain-ants, indicating that the litigation system is less useful to employees who need redress for legitimate complaints, but also wish to remain in their current jobs. . . .

Arbitration also offers employees a guarantee that there will be a hearing on the merits of their claims; no such guarantee exists in litigation where relatively few employees survive the procedural hurdles necessary to take a case to trial in the federal courts.

As a result, it is perhaps misguided to mourn the Supreme Court's endorse-ment of the arbitration of complex and important public law claims. Arbitrators, however, must be mindful that the Court's endorsement has been based on the assumption that "competent, conscientious, and impartial arbitrators" will be avail-able to decide these cases. . . . Therefore, arbitrators must step up to the challenges presented by the resolution of statutory issues and must be vigilant to protect the important rights embodied in the laws entrusted to their care.

Greater reliance on private process to protect public rights imposes a profes-sional obligation on arbitrators to handle statutory issues only if they are prepared to fully protect the rights of statutory grievants. . . . To meet that obligation, arbi-trators must educate themselves about the law. . . . They must follow precedent and must adopt an attitude of judicial restraint when entering undefined areas of the law. . . . Arbitrators must actively ensure that the record is adequately developed and that procedural fairness is provided. . . . And appointing agencies like AAA must be certain that only persons who are able to satisfy these criteria are added to arbitrator-panel lists. For if arbitrators and agencies do not meet these obligations, the courts will have no choice but to intercede.

NOTE ON *COLE v. BURNS INTERNATIONAL*

Judge Edwards's opinion in Cole was notable in that it drew upon the 1994 recommendations of the Presidential Commission on the Future of Worker-Management Relations, chaired by Harvard economist and former Labor Secretary John T. Dunlop. His intent was to set forth minimum due process standards for arbitration processes — including (1) a neutral arbi-trator schooled in the relevant law; (2) a fair method for securing informa-tion necessary to present a claim; (3) affordable access to arbitration; (4) the right to independent representation; (5) a range of remedies equal to those available in court; (6) a written opinion explaining the reasons for the award; and (7) sufficient judicial review to ensure compliance with governing laws. While *Cole* has undoubtedly had some influence, no other court has gone quite so far as the *Cole* decision.

Endnotes

1. Schmitz, Amy J. (2016) *Remedy Realities in Business to Consumer Contracting,* 58 Ariz. L. Rev. 213.
2. Sovern, Jeff, Greenberg, Elayne E., Kirgis, Paul F. & Liu, Yuxiang. (2015) *"Whimsy Little Contracts" with Unexpected Consequences: An Empirical Analysis of Consumer Understanding of Arbitration Agreements,* 75 Md. L. Rev. 1.
3. Szalai, Imre S. (2019) *The Prevalence of Consumer Arbitration Agreements by America's Top Companies,* 52 U.C. Davis L. Rev. Online 233.
4. Schmitz, Amy J. (2008) *Curing Consumer Warranty Woes Through Regulated Arbitration,* 23 Ohio St. J. on Disp. Resol. 627 (proposing legislative reforms that address the realities of consumer arbitration that threaten and deny consumers' access to remedies for companies' violations of public, or statutory, warranty remedies under the MMWA).
5. Schmitz, Amy J. (2020) *Addressing the Class Claim Conundrum with Online Dispute Resolution (ODR),* 2020 J. Disp. Resol. 361. *See also* Schmitz, Amy J. (2021) *Considering Uber Technologies, Inc. v. Heller Under U.S. Law,* 1(2) Can. J. Com. Arb. 163; Schmitz, Amy J. (2021) *Reviving the "New Handshake" in the Wake of a Pandemic,* Mediation Theory and Practice, 32-54, Vol. 5, issue 1; Schmitz, Amy J (2016) *Remedy Realities in Business to Consumer Contracting,* 58 Arizona L. Rev. 213-261.
6. Schmitz, Amy J. (2013) *American Exceptionalism in Consumer Arbitration,* 10 Loy. U. Chi. Int'l L. Rev. 81.
7. https://www.congress.gov/bill/116th-congress/house-bill/1423/all-actions-without-amendments. For the committee report, see https://www.congress.gov/congressional-report/116th-congress/house-report/204/1?s=1&r=4.
8. https://www.wsj.com/articles/congress-votes-to-overturn-cfpb-arbitration-rule-1508897968.
9. Mass. Gen. Laws ch. 90, §7N1/2 (West 2015).
10. Me. Rev. Stat. Ann. tit. 10, §1169 (2015).
11. 15 U.S.C. §§2301-2312 (2004).
12. Ware, Stephen J., *Arbitration Law's Separability Doctrine After Buckeye Check Cashing, Inc. v. Cardegna.* Nevada Law Journal, Vol. 8, No. 107, 2007.
13. Schwartz, David S. (1997) *Enforcing Small Print to Protect Big Business: Employee and Consumer Rights Claims in an Age of Compelled Arbitration,* 1 Wis. L. Rev. 33; Schmitz, Amy J. (2012) *Access to Consumer Remedies in the Squeaky Wheel System,* 39 Pepp. L. Rev. 279.
14. Bingham, Lisa B. (2004) *Control over Dispute-System Design and Mandatory Commercial Arbitration,* 67 Law & Contemp. Prob. 221; Sternlight, Jean R. (2005) *Creeping Mandatory Arbitration: Is It Just?,* 57 U. Nev. Las Vegas L. Rev. 1631.

15. Ware, Stephen J. (2003) *Teaching Arbitration Law*, 14 Am. Rev. Int'l Arb. 231.

16. Stipanowich, Thomas J. (1997) *Punitive Damages and the Consumerization of Arbitration*, 92 Nw. U. L. Rev. 1.

17. *Firm Agrees to End Role in Arbitrating Card Debt*, N.Y. Times, July 20, 2009, at B8.

18. Amsler, Lisa B. (1998) *On Repeat Players, Adhesive Contracts, and the Use of Statistics in Judicial Review of Employment Arbitration Awards*, 29 McGeorge L. Rev. 223. *See also* Schmitz, Amy J. (2010) *Legislating in the Light: Considering Empirical Data in Crafting Arbitration Reforms*, 15 Harvard Negotiation L. Rev. 115-194.

19. Hill, Elizabeth. (2003) *Due Process at Low Cost: An Empirical Study of Employment Arbitration Under the Auspices of the American Arbitration Association*, 18 Ohio St. J. on Disp. Resol. 3.

20. Levinson, Ariana R., O'Hara O'Connor, Erin A. & Skiba, Paige M. (2020) *Predictability of Arbitrators' Reliance on External Authority?* 69 Am. U. L. Rev. 1827.

21. Green, Stephanie & O'Brien, Christine N. (2019) *Epic Backslide: The Supreme Court Endorses Mandatory Individual Arbitration Agreements — #TimesUp on Workers' Rights*, 15 Stan. J. C.R. & C.L. 43.

22. https://www.adr.org/sites/default/files/document_repository/Consumer %20Due%20Process%20Protocol%20(1).pdf.

23. *Employment Arbitration Rules and Mediation Procedures*, AAA (July 1, 2016), at https://www.adr.org/sites/default/files/Employment%20Rules.pdf.

24. *JAMS Employment Arbitration Rules & Procedures*, JAMS (July 1, 2014), at https://www.jamsadr.com/rules-employment-arbitration/english.

25. Eisenberg, Theodore & Hill, Elizabeth. (2004) *Arbitration and Litigation of Employment Claims: An Empirical Comparison*, 58 Disp. Resol. J. 44 (2003-2004).

26. Bingham, Lisa B. & Sharaf, Shimon. (2004) *Employment Arbitration Before and After the Due Process Protocol for Mediation and Arbitration of Statutory Disputes Arising Out of Employment: Preliminary Evidence That Self-Regulation Makes a Difference*, in *Alternative Dispute Resolution in the Employment Arena, Proceedings of New York University 53rd Annual Conference on Labor* (Estreicher & Sherwyn, eds.).

27. Drahozal, Christopher R. & Zyontz, Samantha. (2011) *Creditor Claims in Arbitration and In Court*, 7 Hastings Bus. L.J. 77.

28. Harding, Margaret M. (2004) *The Limits of the Due Process Protocols*, 38 Ohio St. J. on Disp. Resol. 369.

CHAPTER 8

FAIRNESS IN ARBITRATION PART II: RECENT LEGISLATIVE AND JUDICIAL DEVELOPMENTS

A. LEGISLATIVE RESPONSES TO FAIRNESS CONCERNS

Concerns about the fairness of arbitration under pre-dispute arbitration agreements binding consumers and employees also prompted repeated efforts to pass laws outlawing or limiting such agreements. However, state statutory initiatives were repeatedly blunted by the preemptive effect of the FAA, discussed in Chapter 5. Nevertheless, revisions to the Uniform Arbitration Act and a California law purporting to promote "ethics" among arbitrators and arbitration institutions made inroads in this area. More recently, efforts in Congress to outlaw pre-dispute arbitration agreements in consumer and employment contracts led to repeated efforts to pass an Arbitration Fairness Act. Although these failed, other congressional enactments have limited, or have the potential to place limits on, enforcement of such agreements.

1. The Revised Uniform Arbitration Act

The Revised Uniform Arbitration Act (RUAA) was published by the National Conference of Commissioners on Uniform State Laws (NCCUSL) (now called the Uniform Law Commission) in 2000, and by 2020, it had been enacted into law in 21 states and the District of Columbia.[1] The 21 states are Alaska, Arizona, Arkansas, Colorado, Connecticut, Florida, Hawaii, Kansas, Michigan, Minnesota, Nevada, New Jersey, New Mexico, North Carolina, North Dakota, Oklahoma, Oregon, Pennsylvania, Utah, Washington, and West Virginia. In the 2019-2020 session, both Massachusetts and Vermont proposed adoption, but the bills are still pending.[2]

The NCCUSL drafting committee was warned against any categorical treatment of consumer and employee contracts that might run afoul of the preemptive effect of the FAA; they therefore made do with a commentary regarding the role of unconscionability and other means of policing overreaching in adhesive arbitration agreements. Concerns about mass arbitration involving consumer and employee "outsiders," however, formed a subtext for other, substantive elements of the RUAA. Like its close federal counterpart, the FAA, the original UAA was carefully tailored to provide a "bare-bones" legal framework to facilitate very limited judicial intervention to specifically enforce arbitration agreements and awards, including a limited statute of frauds, key default provisions (including authority for judicial appointment of arbitrators where the stipulated method failed), and severely restrained judicial review challenges to awards. But the RUAA is a much more expansive document. It incorporates many more procedural default rules and, more importantly, a number of mandatory (required and non-waivable) procedural elements. These elements represent an effort to restrict the party autonomy that is a traditional hallmark of arbitration in favor of certain perceived requirements of due process. Arguably superfluous in a statute aimed at traditional business-to-business arbitration agreements incorporating detailed and varied arbitration procedures, these provisions appear to be intended primarily for the protection of consumers, employees, and other "adhering parties" from overreaching.

These include RUAA §16, which states: "A party to an arbitration proceeding may be represented by a lawyer." The right to legal representation is not waivable by a pre-dispute agreement under RUAA §4(b). Legal representation is taken for granted in most commercial arbitration processes, while in some traditional industry or trade settings lawyers are actually excluded from hearings by the rules. Section 16 works little, if any, benefit in the former scenarios and may entail undesirable transaction costs if raised in the latter context. Section 16 therefore centers on the special concerns of individual employees or consumers who find themselves in arbitration.

Also non-waivable by executory agreement are §17(a) and (b) regarding the authority of arbitrators to issue subpoenas and to "permit the deposition of a witness to be taken for use as evidence at the hearing." To say that parties cannot, by pre-dispute agreement, limit the ability of arbitrators to order pre-hearing depositions is a significant turnabout on traditional "no discovery" arbitration, and justifiable primarily on the basis of concerns about employees', consumers', and other adhering parties' not having access to information and witnesses. One commentator described the RUAA's approach as a "complicated arrangement" aiming to balance competing interests. On the one hand, it provides certain non-waivable protections to consumers, employees, and others who may be 'forced' into arbitration through pre-dispute agreements. On the other hand, the RUAA provides enough room for sophisticated corporations and other repeat players to incorporate features that favor their own needs. It is probable that neither group is entirely happy with the compromise.

Finally, §21 provides that arbitrators "may award punitive damages or other exemplary relief if such an award is authorized by law in a civil action involving the same claim. . . ." Although the provision is waivable under the RUAA, the commentary clarifies that limits or waivers of certain remedies may run afoul of judicial decisions requiring that employees and other parties "[have] the right to obtain the same relief in arbitration as is available in court." While punitive damages are known in the commercial arena, it is not uncommon for business parties to limit their arbitration agreement to exclude punitive damages from the arbitral arsenal of remedies, especially in international agreements. Again, this provision is motivated primarily by the concerns of parties to adhesion contracts, a reality reflected in the cases and standards cited in the commentary.

Although each of these statutory elements is likely to be brought to bear most directly in adhesion settings involving consumers or employees, they will undoubtedly have an impact on the law and practice of commercial arbitration. As noted previously, the expansive discovery provisions of the RUAA are already being cited to arbitrators as a standard for practice.[3]

QUESTIONS

1. The RUAA differs from the various versions of the Arbitration Fairness Act, which were intended to outlaw pre-dispute arbitration agreements in certain categories of contracts. Which approach is likely to yield more satisfactory results?
2. What impact, if any, are the noted provisions of the RUAA likely to have on the practice of business-to-business arbitration?

---

2. Ending Forced Arbitration of Sexual Assault and Sexual Harassment Act of 2021

This Act passed both the House of Representatives and the Senate in early 2022, and was signed into law by President Biden. This was the biggest arbitration news in a long time and indicates a significant change in the law. The law adds a new chapter to Title 9 of the U.S. Code. H.R. 4445, 117th Cong. (2022); Actions Overview H.R. 4445 — 117th Congress (2021-2022), CONGRESS.GOV, https://www.congress.gov/bill/117th-congress/house-bill/4445/actions (last visited Feb. 11, 2022). Specifically, the Act invalidates any pre-dispute arbitration agreement or pre-dispute joint action waiver when an individual or collective group alleges conduct constituting a sexual harassment or sexual assault dispute in a case filed under federal, tribal, or state law. H.R. 4445, 117th Cong. §402(a) (2022). Any issues about applying this chapter to a dispute must be determined by federal law and must be determined by a court. *Id.* §402(b). This reverses common delegation clauses giving the arbitrator power to rule over his or her jurisdiction in these matters. Instead, the court must determine the applicability of this chapter, even where the contract includes a delegation clause. The Act applies to any dispute or claim that arises or accrues on or after the Act's enactment date. *Id.*

As soon as the bill passed the House and Senate, practitioners and scholars began debating the issues. One question that arises is whether the employee-claimants actually prefer arbitration for various reasons (e.g., confidentiality and privacy). Reasonable minds differ on this issue, but the debate continues. Also, it is unclear whether parties can ignore the law and agree to arbitrate sexual harassment claims via consensual post-dispute agreement. The law says, in part: "no predispute arbitration agreement or predispute joint-action waiver shall be valid or enforce-able with respect to a case [that] . . . relates to the sexual assault dispute or the sex-ual harassment dispute." Does that mean that even if employee and employer both affirmatively agree to arbitrate, a court could refuse to confirm the award based on this new law?

3.   The California "Ethics Standards"

Due to concern about the proliferation of pre-dispute arbitration clauses in consumer, health care, and employment contracts, the California legislature in 2001 directed the California Judicial Council to implement ethics strictures governing pri-vate arbitrators in "mandatory" arbitration. The 2002 Standards established a general duty of impartiality and included, among other matters, rules governing arbitrator disclosures, confidentiality, and written fee explanations. "One of the more controver-sial new disclosure requirements is the arbitrator's policy regarding acceptance of new employment as a neutral from any current party, lawyer or lawyer's firm," designed to address the appearance of favoritism.[4] The California standards are broad because they render disclosure grounds for disqualification upon the motion of any party, even if the disclosures might not be considered material to a finding of evident par-tiality under traditional arbitration law. Some critics expressed concerns that the Eth-ics Standards might give rise to cynical manipulation of the arbitration process and increase the risk that arbitration might be detailed midstream. By way of illustration, consider the situation in which, months or years into the arbitration of a complex commercial case, a party who fears it may lose hires new counsel or identifies a witness having some relationship to the arbitrator for the purpose of creating a requirement for the arbitrator to make a supplemental disclosure under the statute. An arbitrator who elects to disclose the relationship gives the parties an automatic right to have that arbitrator disqualified, no matter how insignificant the relationship. Should the arbi-trator fail to make the disclosure and the "aggrieved" party learns of the nondisclosed relationship, the arbitration award may be vacated if the nondisclosure is found to be "a ground for disqualification of which the arbitrator was then aware."[5] In practice, however, it appears that such scenarios have rarely if ever occurred.

Conflicts between the applicability of the California Ethics Standards and other standards (e.g., the National Association of Securities Dealers (NASD) and the New York Stock Exchange Standards, overseen by the Securities & Exchange Com-mission) soon ensued.[6] While federal and state courts have found that federal secu-rities arbitration rules preempt the California Ethics Standards in investor-broker disputes (*see, e.g., Credit Suisse First Bos. Corp. v. Grunwald*, 400 F.3d 1119 (9th Cir. 2005) (holding that the Securities Exchange Act preempted application of the Cal-ifornia Ethics Standards to NASD-appointed arbitrators), under the SEC-supervised arbitration system, the exact extent of the preemption remains uncertain.

4.   The Arbitration Fairness Act

In recent years, Congress has considered numerous bills intended to out-law or limit the use of arbitration agreements in standardized contracts, but many failed to gather sufficient traction to become law. One early exception was the Motor Vehicle Franchise Contract Arbitration Fairness Act of 2002, 15 U.S.C. §1226(a)(2), which requires that, before car manufacturers and their dealerships settle a dispute through arbitration, all parties must consent in writing after the controversy arises. The bill found bipartisan support. *See, e.g., Volkswagen of Am., Inc. v. Sud's of Peoria, Inc.*, 474 F.3d 966 (7th Cir. 2007) (affirming district court holding that arbitration of claim by car manufacturer against car dealership was not authorized under Motor Vehicle Franchise Contract Arbitration Fairness Act). Section 1226(a)(2) has not been repealed, and even the U.S. Supreme Court has given the law apparent credence. *See Epic Systems Corp. v. Lewis*, 138 S. Ct. 1612, 1617, 1626 (2018) (comparing the language of §1226 with the language of the National Labor Relations Act, concluding that "Congress . . . knows how to override the Arbitration Act" given its language in §1226(a)(2)).

As noted in Chapter 7, the Arbitration Fairness Act (AFA), which was originally proposed in 2007 and again in 2009, 2011, 2013, 2015, and 2017, stimulated considerable debate among lawyers and scholars. All versions of the AFA sought to limit the enforceability of pre-dispute arbitration agreements in generally adhesive settings, like consumer, employment, and civil rights, among others.

The 2009 version was aimed at preventing the enforcement of pre-dispute arbitration agreements in all consumer, employment, and franchise contracts, and with respect to statutory claims protecting civil rights, and was an improvement over the vague language of the 2007 version, which provided for the non-enforceability of disputes under "any statute intended to protect civil rights or to regulate contracts or transactions between parties of unequal bargaining power." The failure to provide more specific definitions (e.g., affecting "civil rights") created a grey area of non-enforceability that could have been exploited by parties seeking to avoid or delay the commencement of arbitration. Some also opposed language providing that "the validity or enforceability of an agreement to arbitrate shall be determined by the court, rather than the arbitrator. . . ." The impact of this provision was rendered far greater by a materially ambiguous provision that gave courts initial authority to address not only "challenges [of] the arbitration agreement specifically," but also challenges to the arbitration provision "in conjunction with other terms of the contract containing such agreement." This provision undermined the separability principle first enunciated in *Prima Paint*. While such a limitation may be appropriate in the context of certain categories of contracts, which are normally adhesive, such as employment or consumer contracts, some have argued that it would be wholly inconsistent with expectations in the typical business-to-business setting. Professor Emmanuel Gaillard warned that the Act "pos[ed] a serious threat to the promotion of efficient international dispute resolution and of the United States as a friendly place to arbitrate."[7]

Although the 2009 version was markedly different, it prohibited pre-dispute arbitration agreements in franchise agreements. While many countries outlaw or restrict the use of pre-dispute arbitration agreements in consumer or employment contracts, research has revealed no statutory prohibitions or regulations regarding arbitration provisions in franchise agreements anywhere else in the world with the exception of Puerto Rico. Thus, where arbitration is readily available to private parties as a mean of resolving disputes, no distinction is made with respect to arbitration agreements contained in franchise contracts.

The AFA was re-introduced in 2011. The revised bills reflected a tightening of the legislation to address various concerns associated with earlier drafts, including the following:

A. more moderate findings focused on concerns about pre-dispute arbitration agreements affecting consumer and employment disputes, and Supreme Court decisions that "have changed the meaning of the [FAA] so that it now extends to consumer disputes and employment disputes";

B. the creation of a new part of the FAA denying the validity or enforceability of pre-dispute arbitration agreements requiring arbitration of employment, consumer, or civil rights disputes; and

C. specific definitions of relevant terms such as "employment dispute," "consumer dispute," "civil rights dispute," and "pre-dispute arbitration agreement."

The 2011 bills contained no reference to franchise agreements, a major bone of contention under prior versions. They continued to omit controversial language from the 2007 drafts outlawing provisions authorizing arbitrators to address "gateway" issues relating to the validity or enforceability of arbitration agreements that would have had a significant "spillover" effect on commercial arbitration.

The AFA re-introduced in 2017[8] is similar in language to its 2011 counterpart in that it made pre-dispute arbitration agreements invalid or unenforceable in employment, consumer, and civil rights disputes. However, the 2017 AFA included antitrust disputes as well. Similar to the previous iterations of the AFA, the issues of enforceability and validity and applicability of the AFA were to be decided by a court under federal law rather than by an arbitrator. The AFA of 2017 was referred to the Subcommittee on Regulatory Reform, Commercial and Antirust Law in the same month that it was introduced. This version of the AFA was introduced in the Senate in 2018, where it was read twice and referred to the Committee on the Judiciary.

5.   The Arbitration Fairness for Consumers Act

The Arbitration Fairness for Consumers Act[9] (hereinafter AFCA) of 2019 was a narrow offshoot from the more broad AFA. The AFCA had two stated purposes: first, to prohibit pre-dispute arbitration agreements that force arbitration of future consumer financial product or service disputes; and second, to prohibit agreements and practices that interfere with the right of individuals and small businesses to participate in a joint, class, or collective action related to the aforementioned types of disputes. The AFCA contained the same language as the AFA in the form of its non-enforceability and provides that where it states "notwithstanding any other provision of law, no predispute arbitration agreement or predispute joint-action waiver shall be valid or enforceable with respect to a consumer dispute between a covered person and a consumer that relates to a consumer financial product or service."[10] The AFCA included the same review parameters as the AFA, requiring applicability and enforceability to be decided under federal law by a court rather than an arbitrator.[11] The AFCA was read twice in the Senate in 2019, and referred to the Committee on Banking, Housing, and Urban Affairs.

6.   *The Forced Arbitration Injustice Repeal Act*

The Forced Arbitration Injustice Repeal (FAIR) Act was a return to the ideas in the AFA, and in many ways the FAIR Act might be seen as a resurrection of the AFA. As noted in Chapter 7, the FAIR Act aimed to prevent the enforcement of pre-dispute arbitration agreements in employment, consumer, antitrust, and civil rights disputes. The Act sought to prohibit practices and agreements that interfere with the right of individuals, workers, and small businesses to participate in joint, class, or collective action related to any of the aforementioned types of disputes.[12] The FAIR Act included the familiar provision that applicability, enforceability, and validity are to be decided under federal law by a court rather than an arbitrator.[13] The FAIR Act was intended not to apply to an arbitration provision in a contract between an employer and a labor organization, except to the extent that an arbitration provision may not require workers to waive their right to seek judicial enforcement of a right arising under the Constitution of the United States, a state constitution, or a federal or state statute, or public policy.[14] The FAIR Act passed through the House with a 225-186 vote. It was received in the Senate and read twice in September of 2019. The Act resurfaced in 2021 and passed the House but did not pass the Senate.

7.   *The Franken Amendment and the Consumer Protection Act (Dodd-Frank)*

Section 8116 of the 2010 Department of Defense Appropriations Act, signed by President Obama in late 2009, also known as the Franken Amendment, prohibited federal contractors who receive funds under the Act for contracts in excess of $1 million from requiring their employees or independent contractors to arbitrate "claims involving Title VII of the civil rights act or any tort arising out of alleged sexual assault or harassment." The same prohibition applies to federal defense subcontractors on subcontracts valued at more than $1 million; prime contractors must obtain contractual commitments from subcontractors that they will not enter into nor enforce any arbitration agreement as to the specified legal claims. Senator Franken's amendment was a reaction to the public furor over the facts underlying *Jones v. Halliburton Co.*, 583 F.3d 228 (5th Cir. 2009), and the general debate over pre-dispute arbitration agreements in employment and consumer contracts. Its solution to the problem of pre-dispute arbitration agreements is categorical and complete—within its scope, a draconian counterpart to the Supreme Court's jurisprudence.

The Dodd-Frank Wall Street Reform and Consumer Protection Act (Consumer Protection Act) had the potential to effect sweeping reforms of mandatory binding pre-dispute arbitration agreements in the broad arenas of consumer finance and investment. Signed into law by President Obama on July 21, 2010, the Consumer Protection Act included several different provisions that aim to restrict or to consider possible restrictions in the use of pre-dispute arbitration agreements. Under the provisions of §748(n)(1-2) and §922, the Act provides special protections and incentives to whistleblowers. An employee cannot waive his right to a judicial forum regarding a dispute that arises under the whistleblower protection section of the Act. This prevents an employer from forcing arbitration of the issue of whether a particular employee qualifies for the extensive enumerated protections listed under the section. Section 1414 amends the Truth in Lending Act to provide that no mortgage lender may include a pre-dispute arbitration clause in its loan agreements.

The Consumer Protection Act is largely concerned with regulation of the newly established Consumer Financial Protections Bureau (CFPB). Section 1028 of the Consumer Protection Act gave the CFPB broad power to regulate all pre-dispute arbitration contracts in the area of consumer financial products and services. The CFPB was directed to study and prepare a report to Congress on the use of pre-dispute arbitration agreements "in connection with the offering or providing of consumer financial products or services." If deemed to be in the public interest, it "may prohibit or impose conditions or limitations on the use" of such agreements. Section 928 gave the Securities and Exchange Commission (SEC) the same authority with regard to securities products and services.

In March 2015, the CFPB released its study on the use of pre-dispute arbitration clauses in consumer financial markets. The study concluded that arbitration agreements restrict consumers' relief for disputes with financial service providers by limiting class actions. It found that, in the consumer finance markets studied, very few consumers individually seek relief through arbitration or the federal courts, while millions of consumers are eligible for relief each year through class action settlements. The CFPB's findings echo the concept discussed in Chapter 7.D, that many consumers are unaware that they are a party to arbitration agreements. The CFPB reported that 75 percent of consumers surveyed did not know whether they were subject to an arbitration clause in their agreements with their financial service providers, and fewer than 7 percent of those covered by arbitration clauses realized that the clauses restricted their ability to sue in court.

In October 2015, the CFPB announced its plan to propose rules that would prevent consumer financial services companies from using arbitration clauses to block class actions. The proposed rule never came to fruition, as it was reversed with the administration change in 2016.

In prior years, the CFPB had implored the SEC to use its authority (granted in the Consumer Protection Act) to investigate the impact of similar clauses used by securities broker-dealers and investment advisors, and prohibit or restrict their use in the public interest and for the protection of investors. Some consider an SEC review to be less important as securities arbitration is highly regulated by the Financial Industry Regulatory Authority (FINRA). Furthermore, complaints about the FINRA system are balanced and perhaps outweighed by the track record of programs that have been overseen by the SEC and related entities such as the Securities Industry Conference on Arbitration. Moreover, the passage of the bill may have prodded FINRA to announce a new regulatory proposal to make permanent its pilot "all-public" arbitrator program. Now, investors have the opportunity to appoint a panel of three arbitrators, none of whom have affiliations with the securities industry; the requirement of a single "industry" arbitrator—long a focus of complaints by investor advocates—has been eliminated.

In 2012, another regulatory agency, the Federal Deposit Insurance Corporation (FDIC), published a rule banning pre-dispute arbitration agreements in retail foreign exchange transactions between smaller investors (both individuals and small business) and "state non-member banks"—for which the FDIC is the primary U.S. regulator. About two months before, the FDIC had issued a proposed Notice of Rulemaking prohibiting such agreements and placing certain restrictions on post-dispute arbitration agreements. The accompanying FDIC commentary suggested that the FDIC's posture was motivated by the congressional concerns toward arbitration reflected in the Dodd-Frank financial reform, even though the latter did not apply to retail foreign exchange transactions. Having received no feedback on its proposed limitations during the comment period, the FDIC approved the proposed rule.[15]

B. CONTINUING ACTIVISM ON THE HIGH COURT: DELEGATION CLAUSES AND CLASS ACTION WAIVERS

To the extent congressional action has left leeway for the further development of the body of substantive law promoting strong enforcement of arbitration agreements under the FAA, the Supreme Court has continued to take full advantage of the opportunity in a series of split decisions with important implications for individuals entering into standardized agreements as customers or employees.

1. Enforcing Delegation Clauses in Consumer or Employment Arbitration Agreements

As explained in Chapter 5, the Supreme Court in *First Options of Chicago, Inc. v. Kaplan*, 514 U.S. 938 (1995), indicated that although issues regarding the enforceability and scope of arbitration agreements are normally for the courts, the parties may agree that such arbitrability issues are to be submitted to the determination of arbitrators if the parties' agreement to that effect is "clear and unmistakable." Moreover, if such issues are to be handled by the arbitrator, courts should give great leeway to the arbitrators' determinations on issues of arbitrability if later asked to review such determinations. What if you have an arbitration agreement in a standardized employment or consumer contract that contains terms that the consumer or employee alleges to be grossly unfair? Suppose the arbitration agreement "clearly and unmistakably" states that all arbitrability issues, including allegations relating to the enforceability of the arbitration agreement, should be handled by the arbitrator. Should courts, following the guidance of *First Options*, enforce the provision? The Supreme Court addressed the issue in the following decision.

Rent-A-Center, West, Inc. v. Jackson

561 U.S. 63 (2010)

[Jackson filed an employment discrimination suit (alleging race discrimination and retaliation) against Rent-A-Center, his former employer. As a condition of his employment, Jackson had signed an agreement providing for the arbitration of all claims and controversies arising in relation to his employment. The agreement also included a "delegation clause" providing that the arbitrator (and not the courts) should have authority to resolve any dispute relating to the interpretation of the applicability, enforceability, or formation of the arbitration agreement (including, but not limited to, any claim that all or any part of the agreement is void or voidable). Rent-A-Center brought a motion to dismiss Jackson's suit and compel arbitration under the FAA before the United States District Court for the District of Nevada. That court granted the motion and Jackson appealed the decision to the Court of Appeals for the Ninth Circuit, which reversed. The Supreme Court granted Rent-A-Center's motion for certiorari. A key issue before the Court was whether the provision delegating issues relating to the enforceability or formation of the arbitration agreement required that the arbitrator and not a court should address the issue of the alleged unconscionability of the arbitration agreement.]

Justice SCALIA delivered the opinion of the Court, in which ROBERTS, C.J., and KENNEDY, THOMAS and ALITO, JJ., joined.

. . . The FAA . . . places arbitration agreements on an equal footing with other contracts, [*Buckeye Check Cashing, Inc. v. Cardegna*, 540 U.S. 440, 443 (2006)], and requires courts to enforce them according to their terms, *Volt Information Sciences, Inc. v. Board of Trustees of Leland Stanford Junior Univ.*, 489 U.S. 468, 478 (1989). Like other contracts, however, they may be invalidated by "generally applicable contract defenses, such as fraud, duress, or unconscionability." *Doctor's Associates, Inc. v. Casarotto*, 517 U.S. 681, 687 (1996). . . .

The Agreement here contains multiple "written provision[s]" to "settle by arbitration a controversy," §2. . . . First, the section titled "Claims Covered By The Agreement" provides for arbitration of all "past, present or future" disputes arising out of Jackson's employment with Rent-A-Center. . . . Second, the section titled "Arbitration Procedures" provides that "[t]he Arbitrator . . . shall have exclusive authority to resolve any dispute relating to the . . . enforceability . . . of this Agreement including, but not limited to any claim that all or any part of this Agreement is void or voidable." The current "controversy" between the parties is whether the Agreement is unconscionable. It is the second provision, which delegates resolution of that controversy to the arbitrator, that Rent-A-Center seeks to enforce. Adopting the terminology used by the parties, we will refer to it as the delegation provision.

The delegation provision is an agreement to arbitrate threshold issues concerning the arbitration agreement. We have recognized that parties can agree to arbitrate "gateway" questions of "arbitrability," such as whether the parties have agreed to arbitrate or whether their agreement covers a particular controversy. See, e.g., [*Howsam v. Dean Witter Reynolds, Inc.*, 537 U.S., at 83-85 (2002)]; *Green Tree Financial Corp. v. Bazzle*, 539 U.S. 444, 452 (2003) (plurality opinion). This line of cases merely reflects the principle that arbitration is a matter of contract. *First Options of Chicago, Inc. v. Kaplan*, 514 U.S. 938, 943 (1995). An agreement to arbitrate a gateway issue is simply an additional, antecedent agreement the party seeking arbitration asks the federal court to enforce, and the FAA operates on this additional arbitration agreement just as it does on any other. . . . The question before us, then, is whether the delegation provision is valid under §2 [of the FAA].

There are two types of validity challenges under §2: "One type challenges specifically the validity of the agreement to arbitrate," and "[t]he other challenges the contract as a whole, either on a ground that directly affects the entire agreement (e.g., the agreement was fraudulently induced), or on the ground that the illegality of one of the contract's provisions renders the whole contract invalid." *Buckeye*, 546 U.S., at 444. In a line of cases neither party has asked us to overrule, we held that only the first type of challenge is relevant to a court's determination whether the arbitration agreement at issue is enforceable. See *Prima Paint Corp. v. Flood & Conklin Mfg. Co.*, 388 U.S. 395, 403-404 (1967); *Buckeye*, supra, at 444-446; *Preston v. Ferrer*, 552 U.S. 346, 353-354 (2008). That is because §2 states that a "written provision" "to settle by arbitration a controversy" is "valid, irrevocable, and enforceable" without mention of the validity of the contract in which it is contained. Thus, a party's challenge to another provision of the contract, or to the contract as a whole, does not prevent a court from enforcing a specific agreement to arbitrate. "[A]s a matter of substantive federal arbitration law, an arbitration provision is severable from the remainder of the contract." *Buckeye*, 546 U.S., at 445; see also id., at 447 (the severability rule is based on §2). . . .

Here, the "written provision . . . to settle by arbitration a controversy," 9 U.S.C. §2, that Rent-A-Center asks us to enforce is the delegation provision—the provision that gave the arbitrator "exclusive authority to resolve any dispute relating to the . . . enforceability . . . of this Agreement,". . . The "remainder of the contract," *Buckeye*, supra, at 445, is the rest of the agreement to arbitrate claims arising out of Jackson's employment with Rent-A-Center. To be sure this case differs from *Prima Paint, Buckeye*, and *Preston*, in that the arbitration provisions sought to be enforced in those cases were contained in contracts unrelated to arbitration—contracts for consulting services, see *Prima Paint*, supra, at 397, check-cashing services, see *Buckeye*, supra, at 442, 126 S. Ct. 1204, and "personal management" or "talent agent" services, see *Preston*, supra, at 352. In this case, the underlying contract is itself an arbitration agreement. But that makes no difference. Application of the severability rule does not depend on the substance of the remainder of the contract. Section 2 operates on the specific "written provision" to "settle by arbitration a controversy" that the party seeks to enforce. Accordingly, unless Jackson challenged the delegation provision specifically, we must treat it as valid under §2, and must enforce it under §§3 and 4, leaving any challenge to the validity of the Agreement as a whole for the arbitrator.

The District Court correctly concluded that Jackson challenged only the validity of the contract [that is, the arbitration agreement] as a whole. Nowhere in his opposition to Rent-A-Center's motion to compel arbitration did he even mention the delegation provision. . . .

As required to make out a claim of unconscionability under Nevada law, see 581 F.3d, at 919, [Jackson] contended that the [arbitration] Agreement was both procedurally and substantively unconscionable. . . . But we need not consider that claim because none of Jackson's substantive unconscionability challenges was specific to the delegation provision. . . .

[The Court concluded that Jackson's substantive unconscionability arguments regarding procedures in the arbitration agreement that called for a splitting of arbitration fees and limitations on discovery applied to the arbitration agreement as a whole, but not the delegation provision specifically.]

Jackson's appeal to the Ninth Circuit confirms that he did not contest the validity of the delegation provision in particular. . . .

[However] [i]n his brief to this Court, Jackson made the contention . . . that the delegation provision itself is substantively unconscionable because the quid pro quo he was supposed to receive for it—that "in exchange for initially allowing an arbitrator to decide certain gateway questions," he would receive "plenary post-arbitration judicial review"—was eliminated by the Court's subsequent holding in *Hall Street Associates, L.L.C. v. Mattel, Inc.*, 552 U.S. 576 (2008), that the nonplenary grounds for judicial review in §10 of the FAA are exclusive. . . . He brought this challenge to the delegation provision too late, and we will not consider it. [We reverse the judgment of the Court of Appeals for the Ninth Circuit. *It is so ordered.*]

Justice STEVENS, with whom Justice GINSBURG, Justice BREYER, and Justice SOTOMAYOR join, dissenting.

. . . The Court asserts that its holding flows logically from *Prima Paint Corp. v. Flood & Conklin Mfg. Co.*, 388 U.S. 395 (1967), in which the Court held that consideration of a contract revocation defense is generally a matter for the arbitrator, unless the defense is specifically directed at the arbitration clause, id., at 404, 87 S. Ct. 1801. We have treated this holding as a severability rule: When a party challenges a contract, "but not specifically its arbitration provisions, those provisions are enforceable apart from the remainder of the contract." *Buckeye Check Cashing, Inc. v. Cardegna*, 546 U.S. 440, 446 (2006). The Court's decision today goes beyond *Prima Paint.* Its breezy assertion that the subject matter of the contract at issue—in this case, an arbitration agreement and nothing more—"makes no difference," . . . is simply wrong. This written arbitration agreement is but one part of a broader employment agreement between the parties, just as the arbitration clause in *Prima Paint* was but one part of a broader contract for services between those parties. Thus, that the subject matter of the agreement is exclusively arbitration makes all the difference in the *Prima Paint* analysis. . . .

Two different lines of cases bear on the issue of who decides a question of arbitrability respecting validity, such as whether an arbitration agreement is unconscionable. Although this issue, as a gateway matter, is typically for the court, we have explained that such an issue can be delegated to the arbitrator in some circumstances. When the parties have purportedly done so, courts must examine two distinct rules to decide whether the delegation is valid.

The first line of cases looks to the parties' intent. . . . The second line of cases bearing on who decides the validity of an arbitration agreement, as the Court explains, involves the *Prima Paint* rule. . . . That rule recognizes two types of validity challenges. One type challenges the validity of the arbitration agreement itself, on a ground arising from an infirmity in that agreement. The other challenges the validity of the arbitration agreement tangentially—via a claim that the entire contract (of which the arbitration agreement is but a part) is invalid for some reason. See *Buckeye*, 546 U.S., at 444. Under *Prima Paint*, a challenge of the first type goes to the court; a challenge of the second type goes to the arbitrator. See 388 U.S., at 403-404; see also *Buckeye*, 546 U.S., at 444-445. The *Prima Paint* rule is akin to a pleading standard, whereby a party seeking to challenge the validity of an arbitration agreement must expressly say so in order to get his dispute into court.

In sum, questions related to the validity of an arbitration agreement are usually matters for a court to resolve before it refers a dispute to arbitration. But questions of arbitrability may go to the arbitrator in two instances: (1) when the parties have demonstrated, clearly and unmistakably, that it is their intent to do so; or (2) when the validity of an arbitration agreement depends exclusively on the validity of the substantive contract of which it is a part.

We might have resolved this case by simply applying the *First Options* rule: Does the arbitration agreement at issue "clearly and unmistakably" evince petitioner's and respondent's intent to submit questions of arbitrability to the arbitrator? The answer to that question is no. . . .

In other words, when a party raises a good-faith validity challenge to the arbitration agreement itself, that issue must be resolved before a court can say that he clearly and unmistakably intended to arbitrate that very validity question. This case well illustrates the point: If respondent's unconscionability claim is correct—i.e., if the terms of the agreement are so one-sided and the process of its making so unfair—it would contravene the existence of clear and unmistakable assent to arbitrate the very question petitioner now seeks to arbitrate. Accordingly, it is necessary for the court to resolve the merits of respondent's unconscionability claim in order to decide whether the parties have a valid arbitration agreement under §2. Otherwise, that section's preservation of revocation issues for the Court would be meaningless.

This is, in essence, how I understand the Court of Appeals to have decided the issue below. See 581 F.3d 912, 917 (9th Cir. 2009) ("[W]e hold that where, as here, a party challenges an arbitration agreement as unconscionable, and thus asserts that he could not meaningfully assent to the agreement, the threshold question of unconscionability is for the court"). I would therefore affirm its judgment, leaving, as it did, the merits of respondent's unconscionability claim for the District Court to resolve on remand.

Rather than apply *First Options*, the Court takes us down a different path, one neither briefed by the parties nor relied upon by the Court of Appeals. In applying *Prima Paint*, the Court has unwisely extended a "fantastic" and likely erroneous decision. 388 U.S., at 407 (Black, J., dissenting).

. . . [T]his case lies at a seeming crossroads in our arbitration jurisprudence. It implicates cases such as *First Options*, which address whether the parties intended to delegate questions of arbitrability, and also those cases, such as *Prima Paint*, which address the severability of a presumptively valid arbitration agreement from a potentially invalid contract. . . .

Prima Paint and its progeny allow a court to pluck from a potentially invalid contract a potentially valid arbitration agreement. Today the Court adds a new layer of severability—something akin to Russian nesting dolls—into the mix: Courts may now pluck from a potentially invalid arbitration agreement even narrower provisions that refer particular arbitrability disputes to an arbitrator. . . . I do not think an agreement to arbitrate can ever manifest a clear and unmistakable intent to arbitrate its own validity. But even assuming otherwise, I certainly would not hold that the *Prima Paint* rule extends this far. . . .

The Court, however, reads the delegation clause as a distinct mini-arbitration agreement divisible from the contract in which it resides—which just so happens also to be an arbitration agreement. . . . Although the Court simply declares that it "makes no difference" that the underlying subject matter of the agreement is itself an arbitration agreement . . . that proposition does not follow from—rather it is at odds with—*Prima Paint*'s severability rule. . . .

It would seem the Court reads *Prima Paint* to require, as a matter of course, infinite layers of severability: We must always pluck from an arbitration agreement the specific delegation mechanism that would—but for present judicial review—commend the matter to arbitration, even if this delegation clause is but one sentence within one paragraph within a standalone agreement. And, most importantly, the party must identify this one sentence and lodge a specific challenge to its validity. Otherwise, he will be bound to pursue his validity claim in arbitration. . . .

. . . While I may have to accept the "fantastic" holding in *Prima Paint* . . . (Black, J., dissenting), I most certainly do not accept the Court's even more fantastic reasoning today. I would affirm the judgment of the Court of Appeals, and therefore respectfully dissent.

QUESTIONS

3. What is the practical significance of the Court's ruling in *Rent-A-Center*? Is it likely to affect the drafting of arbitration provisions in consumer and employment contracts?[16]

4. Under *Rent-A-Center*, what kinds of defenses may still be brought before a court if there is a broad clause in the arbitration agreement delegating enforcement issues and arbitrability issues to arbitrators? Can you think of specific examples of the kinds of allegations that might trigger court involvement?

5. Is there any reason why arbitrators who rule on the unconscionability of terms in the arbitration agreement would reach a different conclusion than that of a court? Is there reason for concern about having arbitrators make these determinations?

6. Should a court still punt the case to arbitration per a delegation clause if it appears that the underlying claim is "wholly groundless" under this arbitrability jurisprudence? In *Henry Schein, Inc. v. Archer and White Sales, Inc.*, 139 S. Ct. 524 (2019), the Court held that when the parties' contract delegates the question of arbitrability to an arbitrator, a court may not decide arbitrability—even if the court thinks that the arbitration agreement applies to a wholly groundless dispute. The Court reinforced its endorsement of delegation clauses. Furthermore, the Court eschewed the "wholly groundless" exception used by some Courts of Appeals to promote efficiency by denying motions to compel arbitration where the case appears to lack any merit. Instead, the Court opined that the "wholly groundless" exception is not necessary to deter frivolous motions to compel arbitration. Do you agree?

7. In the same year, the Supreme Court decided *New Prime Inc. v. Oliveira*, 139 S. Ct. 532 (2019). One of the issues in that case was whether a court or the arbitrator should decide disputes over the application of Section 1 of the FAA's exception for transportation workers in interstate commerce. In this case, a former truck driver brought a class action against

an interstate trucking company, alleging that it violated the FLSA and Missouri and Maine labor laws by failing to pay its drivers minimum wage. The plaintiff worked under an agreement that had a mandatory arbitration provision, which also included a clause delegating arbitrability questions to the arbitrator. When the defendant moved to compel arbitration, the plaintiff argued that the court lacked authority to compel arbitration because Section 1 of the FAA excepts from coverage disputes involving "contracts of employment" of certain transportation workers. Writing for the Court, Justice Gorsuch opined that a court must decide application of Section 1, even where a delegation clause is present, because a court simply lacks power until it gets past Section 1. The FAA says that "nothing" in the Act "shall apply" to "contracts and employment of . . . any other class of workers engaged in foreign or interstate commerce." Accordingly, a court should first decide whether the Section 1 exclusion applies before it can order arbitration and use Sections 2-4. Furthermore, the Court found that the delegation clause was only enforceable if it's in a contract without a Section 1 exception, and the severability principle would not matter in this instance. Does this opinion seem in line with prior opinions regarding delegation clauses?

8. The Supreme Court is poised to weigh in again on the "transportation worker" exception in 2022. SCOTUS granted cert. on the question of whether workers who load or unload goods from vehicles that travel in interstate commerce, but do not physically transport such goods themselves, are interstate "transportation workers" exempt from the Federal Arbitration Act. The focus is going to be on what level of involvement an employee needs to have in order to be considered a transportation worker who engages in interstate or foreign commerce. *Saxon v. Southwest Airlines Co.*, 993 F.3d 492, *cert. granted*, 142 S. Ct. 638 (2021). The plaintiff in this case is a ramp supervisor employed by Southwest Airlines Co. *Saxon v. Southwest Airlines Co.*, 993 F.3d 492, 494, *cert. granted*, 142 S. Ct. 638 (2021). As part of her job, she often filled in for other workers, including loading and unloading cargo from the planes. *Id.* As part of her employment contract, plaintiff agreed to arbitrate wage disputes. *Id.* The Court of Appeals was asked whether Saxon, as a ramp supervisor, is engaged in commerce and therefore falls into the residual category of employees exempt from the Federal Arbitration Act under §1. The court held that she was within the class of workers engaged in the actual transportation of goods and therefore within the exception under FAA §1. *Id.* at 498. Using the *ejusdem generis* canon of statutory interpretation and examining the two enumerated categories of workers in the statute, the Court of Appeals determined that an employee cannot simply be employed by a transportation employer to be considered a transportation worker. *Id.* at 497. The worker must also be engaged in either interstate or foreign commerce. *Id.* For purposes of §1, engaged in commerce is "to perform work analogous to that of seamen and railroad employees, whose occupations are centered on the transportation of goods in interstate and foreign commerce." *Id.* at 496. Here, for ramp supervisors to

be engaged in interstate or foreign commerce, the interstate movement of goods must be a central part of the job description. *Id.* In this case, the record indicates ramp supervisors cover three full ramp agent shifts per week. Thus, ramp supervisors spend a great deal of time loading and unloading cargo from planes traveling to and coming from interstate and foreign locations. *Id.* Therefore, a central part of their job is engaging in interstate and foreign commerce. SCOTUS will now weigh in on this interpretive question. As of the publication of this book, the decision had not been rendered.

2. Class Action Waivers and Arbitration Agreements

A major stimulus to efforts to outlaw pre-dispute arbitration agreements in consumer and employment contracts was and is the use of class action waivers—terms in arbitration agreements purporting to prevent individuals from presenting their claims as part of a class action. This idea is a running theme throughout many of the recent arbitration cases, including *Green Tree Financial Corp. v. Bazzle*, 539 U.S. 444, 453 (2003), reaching the U.S. Supreme Court in recent years. The *Bazzle* opinion left the decision of whether a particular arbitration agreement provides for or prohibits classwide arbitration to the arbitrators rather than the courts. That, in turn, caused financial services companies and other corporations to include provisions in consumer or employment contracts purporting to reflect the intent of the parties not to participate in class actions. Challenges to such provisions produced conflicting responses in the courts. The Supreme Court ultimately weighed in in two important decisions, presented below. These decisions represent continued expansion of the Court-made notion of a body of federal substantive law governing the enforcement of arbitration agreements under the FAA.

The Supreme Court's treatment of class action waivers and arbitration was presaged by its decision in *Stolt-Nielsen S.A. v. AnimalFeeds International*, 559 U.S. 662 (2010). In that case, the Court overturned a Second Circuit order upholding an arbitration tribunal's determination in favor of classwide arbitration. Justice Alito was joined by Justices Kennedy, Roberts, Scalia, and Thomas in an opinion that shunned the rationale of the Court's earlier plurality opinion in *Green Tree Financial Corp. v. Bazzle, supra,* which had characterized the question of whether class arbitration is appropriate as a matter of "procedure" growing out of the dispute. Instead, the majority grounded its decision on Supreme Court "precedents [under the FAA] emphasizing the consensual basis of arbitration." It explained that "[w]hile the interpretation of an arbitration agreement is generally a matter of state law . . . the FAA imposes certain rules of fundamental importance, including the basic precept that arbitration 'is a matter of consent, not coercion.'" The contractual foundation of arbitration facilitates party choices—including "who will resolve specific disputes," and "*with whom* they choose to arbitrate." Here, where the parties' agreement was silent as to the issue of class action arbitration—and, indeed, had stipulated that there was "no agreement" on the matter—there could be no basis upon which to authorize class arbitration. Explained the Court majority:

> [T]he differences between bilateral and class-action arbitration are
> too great for arbitrators to presume, consistent with their limited pow-
> ers under the FAA, that the parties' mere silence on the issue of class-
> action arbitration constitutes consent to resolve their disputes in class
> proceedings.

Such a result could not be inferred "solely from the fact of the parties' agreement
to arbitrate" because class action arbitration "changes the nature of arbitration" in
various ways: (1) the arbitrator is charged with resolving not just a single dispute,
"but instead resolves many disputes between hundreds or . . . thousands of parties";
(2) the "presumption of privacy and confidentiality" is lost; (3) the arbitrator's
award "adjudicates the rights of absent parties"; and (4) the commercial stakes are
particularly significant, as in class action litigation. Thus, the majority concluded
that, *as a matter of federal law*, there can be no class action arbitration when the
parties have stipulated there is "no agreement" on the matter. The arbitrators had
therefore exceeded their authority.

AT&T Mobility LLC v. Concepcion

563 U.S. 333 (2011)

[Customers (the Concepcions) brought a putative class action against AT&T
Mobility (AT&T), a mobile telephone service provider, alleging that AT&T had
engaged in false advertising and fraud by charging its customers sales tax on the
full retail value of a "free" phone. The contract between the Concepcions and
AT&T provided for arbitration of all disputes between the parties but required
that claims be brought in the parties' "individual capacity, and not as a plaintiff or
class member in any purported class or representative proceeding." The agreement
authorized AT&T to make unilateral amendments, which it did to the arbitration
provision on several occasions.

In the wake of various court rulings denying enforceability to class action
waiver provisions and certain other terms under California law, AT&T substantially
revised its arbitration agreement to include, among other things, the following
provisions:

1. If the arbitrator issues an award in favor of a California customer that is
    greater than "[AT&T]'s last written settlement offer made before an arbi-
    trator was selected but less than $7,500, [AT&T] will pay the customer
    $7,500 rather than the smaller arbitral award."
2. If the arbitrator awards a customer more than [AT&T]'s last written set-
    tlement offer, then "[AT&T] will . . . pay [the customer's] attorney, if any,
    twice the amount of attorneys' fees, and reimburse any expenses, that
    [the customer's] attorney reasonably accrues for investigating, preparing,
    and pursuing [his] claim in arbitration."

AT&T filed a motion to compel the Concepcions to arbitrate as individuals
under the modified arbitration agreement. The district court denied AT&T's
motion in reliance on the three-part test established by the California Supreme
Court in *Discover Bank v. Superior Court*, 113 P.3d 1100 (Cal. 2005), for the

purpose of determining whether a class action waiver in a consumer contract was unconscionable:

> (1) whether the agreement is a consumer contract of adhesion drafted by a party of superior bargaining power; (2) whether the agreement occurs in a setting in which disputes between the contracting parties predictably involve small amounts of damages; and (3) whether it is alleged that the party with the superior bargaining power has carried out a scheme to deliberately cheat large numbers of consumers out of individually small sums of money.

The court held that each limb of the *Discover Bank* test was established and the arbitration agreement was unconscionable because it was unclear that the incentives provided by AT&T were an adequate substitute for classwide proceedings. AT&T appealed to the Ninth Circuit, which unanimously affirmed the district court's decision. It also held that the FAA did not preempt the *Discover Bank* rule because the rule was simply "a refinement of the unconscionability analysis applicable to contracts generally in California."

On appeal, the U.S. Supreme Court reversed and remanded the Ninth Circuit decision on the basis that Section 2 of the FAA preempts the *Discover Bank* rule.]

Justice SCALIA delivered the opinion of the Court, in which ROBERTS, C.J., and KENNEDY, THOMAS, and ALITO, JJ., joined.

. . . Under California law, courts may refuse to enforce any contract found "to have been unconscionable at the time it was made," or may "limit the application of any unconscionable clause." Cal. Civ. Code Ann. §1670.5(a) (West 1985). A finding of unconscionability requires "a 'procedural' and a 'substantive' element, the former focusing on 'oppression' or 'surprise' due to unequal bargaining power, the latter on 'overly harsh' or 'one-sided' results." *Armendariz v. Foundation Health [Psychcare] Servs., Inc.*, 24 Cal. 4th 83, 114, 99 Cal. Rptr. 2d 745 (2000); accord, *Discover Bank*, 36 Cal. 4th, at 159-161, 30 Cal. Rptr. 3d 76.

In *Discover Bank*, the California Supreme Court applied this framework to class-action waivers in arbitration agreements. . . . California courts have frequently applied this rule to find arbitration agreements unconscionable.

When state law prohibits outright the arbitration of a particular type of claim, the analysis is straightforward: The conflicting rule is displaced by the FAA. *Preston v. Ferrer*, 552 U.S. 346, 353 (2008). But the inquiry becomes more complex when a doctrine normally thought to be generally applicable, such as duress or, as relevant here, unconscionability, is alleged to have been applied in a fashion that disfavors arbitration. In *Perry v. Thomas*, 482 U.S. 483 (1987), for example, we noted that the FAA's preemptive effect might extend even to grounds traditionally thought to exist " 'at law or in equity for the revocation of any contract.' " Id., at 492, n. 9 (emphasis deleted). We said that a court may not "rely on the uniqueness of an agreement to arbitrate as a basis for a state-law holding that enforcement would be unconscionable, for this would enable the court to effect what . . . the state legislature cannot." Id., at 493, n. 9.

An obvious illustration of this point would be a case finding unconscionable or unenforceable as against public policy consumer arbitration agreements that fail to provide for judicially monitored discovery. . . .

. . . The same argument might apply to a rule classifying as unconscionable arbitration agreements that fail to abide by the Federal Rules of Evidence, or that disallow an ultimate disposition by a jury (perhaps termed "a panel of twelve lay arbitrators" to help avoid preemption). Such examples are not fanciful, since the judicial hostility towards arbitration that prompted the FAA had manifested itself in "a great variety" of "devices and formulas" declaring arbitration against public policy. *Robert Lawrence Co. v. Devonshire Fabrics, Inc.*, 271 F.2d 402, 406 (C.A.2 1959). And although these statistics are not definitive, it is worth noting that California's courts have been more likely to hold contracts to arbitrate unconscionable than other contracts. . . .

. . . We do not agree that rules requiring judicially monitored discovery or adherence to the Federal Rules of Evidence are "a far cry from this case." . . . The overarching purpose of the FAA, evident in the text of §§2, 3, and 4, is to ensure the enforcement of arbitration agreements according to their terms so as to facilitate streamlined proceedings. Requiring the availability of classwide arbitration interferes with fundamental attributes of arbitration and thus creates a scheme inconsistent with the FAA. . . .

The point of affording parties discretion in designing arbitration processes is to allow for efficient, streamlined procedures tailored to the type of dispute. It can be specified, for example, that the decision-maker be a specialist in the relevant field, or that proceedings be kept confidential to protect trade secrets. And the informality of arbitral proceedings is itself desirable, reducing the cost and increasing the speed of dispute resolution. . . .

California's *Discover Bank* rule . . . interferes with arbitration. Although the rule does not require classwide arbitration, it allows any party to a consumer contract to demand it *ex post*. The rule is limited to adhesion contracts, *Discover Bank*, 36 Cal. 4th, at 162-163, but the times in which consumer contracts were anything other than adhesive are long past. *Carbajal v. H & R Block Tax Servs., Inc.*, 372 F.3d 903, 906 (7th Cir. 2004); see also *Hill v. Gateway 2000, Inc.*, 105 F.3d 1147, 1149 (C.A.7 1997). The rule also requires that damages be predictably small, and that the consumer allege a scheme to cheat consumers. *Discover Bank*, supra, at 162-163. The former requirement, however, is toothless and malleable (the Ninth Circuit has held that damages of $4,000 are sufficiently small, see *Oestreicher v. Alienware Corp.*, 322 Fed. Appx. 489, 492 (2009) (unpublished)), and the latter has no limiting effect, as all that is required is an allegation. Consumers remain free to bring and resolve their disputes on a bilateral basis under *Discover Bank*, and some may well do so; but there is little incentive for lawyers to arbitrate on behalf of individuals when they may do so for a class and reap far higher fees in the process. And faced with inevitable class arbitration, companies would have less incentive to continue resolving potentially duplicative claims on an individual basis.

Although we have had little occasion to examine classwide arbitration, our decision in *Stolt-Nielsen* is instructive. In that case we held that an arbitration panel exceeded its power under §10(a)(4) of the FAA by imposing class procedures based on policy judgments rather than the arbitration agreement itself or some background principle of contract law that would affect its interpretation. . . . We then held that the agreement at issue, which was silent on the question of class procedures, could not be interpreted to allow them because the "changes brought about by the shift from bilateral arbitration to class-action arbitration" are "fundamental."

. . . This is obvious as a structural matter: Classwide arbitration includes absent parties, necessitating additional and different procedures and involving higher stakes. Confidentiality becomes more difficult. And while it is theoretically possible to select an arbitrator with some expertise relevant to the class-certification question, arbitrators are not generally knowledgeable in the often-dominant procedural aspects of certification, such as the protection of absent parties. The conclusion follows that class arbitration, to the extent it is manufactured by *Discover Bank* rather than consensual, is inconsistent with the FAA.

First, the switch from bilateral to class arbitration sacrifices the principal advantage of arbitration—its informality—and makes the process slower, more costly, and more likely to generate procedural morass than final judgment. . . .

Second, class arbitration requires procedural formality. The AAA's rules governing class arbitrations mimic the Federal Rules of Civil Procedure for class litigation. Compare AAA, Supplementary Rules for Class Arbitrations (effective Oct. 8, 2003), online at http://www.adr.org/ sp.asp? id=21936, with Fed. Rule Civ. Proc. 23. And while parties can alter those procedures by contract, an alternative is not obvious. If procedures are too informal, absent class members would not be bound by the arbitration. . . .

We find it unlikely that in passing the FAA Congress meant to leave the disposition of these procedural requirements to an arbitrator. Indeed, class arbitration was not even envisioned by Congress when it passed the FAA in 1925; as the California Supreme Court admitted in *Discover Bank*, class arbitration is a "relatively recent development." 36 Cal. 4th, at 163, 30 Cal. Rptr. 3d 76. And it is at the very least odd to think that an arbitrator would be entrusted with ensuring that third parties' due process rights are satisfied.

Third, class arbitration greatly increases risks to defendants. Informal procedures do of course have a cost: The absence of multilayered review makes it more likely that errors will go uncorrected. Defendants are willing to accept the costs of these errors in arbitration, since their impact is limited to the size of individual disputes, and presumably outweighed by savings from avoiding the courts. But when damages allegedly owed to tens of thousands of potential claimants are aggregated and decided at once, the risk of an error will often become unacceptable. . . .

Arbitration is poorly suited to the higher stakes of class litigation. In litigation, a defendant may appeal a certification decision on an interlocutory basis and, if unsuccessful, may appeal from a final judgment as well. Questions of law are reviewed *de novo* and questions of fact for clear error. In contrast, 9 U.S.C. §10 allows a court to vacate an arbitral award only where the award "was procured by corruption, fraud, or undue means"; "there was evident partiality or corruption in the arbitrators"; "the arbitrators were guilty of misconduct in refusing to postpone the hearing . . . or in refusing to hear evidence pertinent and material to the controversy[,] or of any other misbehavior by which the rights of any party have been prejudiced"; or if the "arbitrators exceeded their powers, or so imperfectly executed them that a mutual, final, and definite award . . . was not made." The AAA rules do authorize judicial review of certification decisions, but this review is unlikely to have much effect given these limitations; review under §10 focuses on misconduct rather than mistake. And parties may not contractually expand the grounds or nature of judicial review. *Hall Street Assocs.[, L.L.C. v. Mattel, Inc.*, 552

U.S., 576 578 (2008)]. We find it hard to believe that defendants would bet the company with no effective means of review, and even harder to believe that Congress would have intended to allow state courts to force such a decision.

The Concepcions contend that because parties may and sometimes do agree to aggregation, class procedures are not necessarily incompatible with arbitration. . . . But what the parties . . . would have agreed to is not arbitration as envisioned by the FAA, lacks its benefits, and therefore may not be required by state law.

The dissent claims that class proceedings are necessary to prosecute small-dollar claims that might otherwise slip through the legal system. See post, at 9. But States cannot require a procedure that is inconsistent with the FAA, even if it is desirable for unrelated reasons. Moreover, the claim here was most unlikely to go unresolved. . . . Indeed, the District Court concluded that the Concepcions were better off under their arbitration agreement with AT & T than they would have been as participants in a class action, which "could take months, if not years, and which may merely yield an opportunity to submit a claim for recovery of a small percentage of a few dollars." [Citation omitted.]

Because it "stands as an obstacle to the accomplishment and execution of the full purposes and objectives of Congress," *Hines v. Davidowitz*, 312 U.S. 52, 67 (1941), California's *Discover Bank* rule is preempted by the FAA. The judgment of the Ninth Circuit is reversed, and the case is remanded for further proceedings consistent with this opinion. *It is so ordered.*

[Justice THOMAS concurred on the basis that "the FAA requires that an agreement to arbitrate be enforced unless a party successfully challenges the formation of the arbitration agreement."]

Justice BREYER, with whom Justice GINSBURG, Justice SOTOMAYOR, and Justice KAGAN join, dissenting.

The [FAA] says that an arbitration agreement "shall be valid, irrevocable, and enforceable, *save upon such grounds as exist at law or in equity for the revocation of any contract.*" 9 U.S.C. §2 (emphasis added). California law sets forth certain circumstances in which "class action waivers" in any contract are unenforceable. In my view, this rule of state law is consistent with the federal Act's language and primary objective. It does not "stan[d] as an obstacle" to the Act's "accomplishment and execution." . . . And the Court is wrong to hold that the federal Act pre-empts the rule of state law. . . .

The *Discover Bank* rule is consistent with the federal Act's language. It "applies equally to class action litigation waivers in contracts without arbitration agreements as it does to class arbitration waivers in contracts with such agreements." . . . Linguistically speaking, it falls directly within the scope of the Act's exception permitting courts to refuse to enforce arbitration agreements on grounds that exist "for the revocation of *any* contract." 9 U.S.C. §2 (emphasis added). The majority agrees. . . .

The *Discover Bank* rule is also consistent with the basic "purpose behind" the Act. . . . The Act sought to eliminate that hostility by placing agreements to arbitrate "*upon the same footing as other contracts.*" *Scherk v. Alberto-Culver Co.*, 417 U.S. 506, 511 (1974) (quoting H.R. Rep. No. 96, at 2; emphasis added). . . .

The majority's contrary view (that *Discover Bank* stands as an "obstacle" to the accomplishment of the federal law's objective . . .) rests primarily upon its claims that the *Discover Bank* rule increases the complexity of arbitration procedures, thereby discouraging parties from entering into arbitration agreements, and to that extent discriminating in practice against arbitration. These claims are not well founded.

. . . Indeed, the AAA has told us that it has found class arbitration to be "a fair, balanced, and efficient means of resolving class disputes." Brief for AAA as Amicus Curiae in Stolt-Nielsen S.A. v. AnimalFeeds Int'l Corp., O.T. 2009, No. 08-1198, p. 25 (hereinafter AAA *Amicus* Brief). And unlike the majority's examples, the *Discover Bank* rule imposes equivalent limitations on litigation; hence it cannot fairly be characterized as a targeted attack on arbitration.

Where does the majority get its contrary idea — that individual, rather than class, arbitration is a "fundamental attribut[e]" of arbitration? . . .

When Congress enacted the Act, arbitration procedures had not yet been fully developed. Insofar as Congress considered detailed forms of arbitration at all, it may well have thought that arbitration would be used primarily where merchants sought to resolve disputes of fact, not law, under the customs of their industries, where the parties possessed roughly equivalent bargaining power. . . . This last mentioned feature of the history — roughly equivalent bargaining power — suggests, if anything, that California's statute is consistent with, and indeed may help to further, the objectives that Congress had in mind. . . .

Why would a typical defendant (say, a business) prefer a judicial class action to class arbitration? AAA statistics "suggest that class arbitration proceedings take more time than the average commercial arbitration, but may take *less time* than the average class action in court." AAA Amicus Brief 24 (emphasis added). Data from California courts confirm that class arbitrations can take considerably less time than in-court proceedings in which class certification is sought. . . . And a single class proceeding is surely more efficient than thousands of separate proceedings for identical claims. Thus, if speedy resolution of disputes were all that mattered, then the *Discover Bank* rule would reinforce, not obstruct, that objective of the Act.

The majority's related claim that the *Discover Bank* rule will discourage the use of arbitration because "[a]rbitration is poorly suited to . . . higher stakes" lacks empirical support. . . .

. . . California is free to define unconscionability as it sees fit, and its common law is of no federal concern so long as the State does not adopt a special rule that disfavors arbitration. Cf. *Doctor's Associates, supra,* at 687. . . .

. . . If California had applied its law of duress to void an arbitration agreement, would it matter if the procedures in the coerced agreement were efficient?

Regardless, the majority highlights the disadvantages of class arbitrations, as it sees them . . . referring to the "greatly increase[d] risks to defendants"; the "chance of a devastating loss" pressuring defendants "into settling questionable claims"). But class proceedings have countervailing advantages. In general, agreements that forbid the consolidation of claims can lead small-dollar claimants to abandon their claims rather than to litigate. I suspect that it is true even here, for as the Court of Appeals recognized, AT & T can avoid the $7,500 payout (the payout that supposedly makes the Concepcions' arbitration worthwhile) simply by paying the claim's face value, such that "the maximum gain to a customer for the hassle of arbitrating a $30.22 dispute is still just $30.22." *Laster v. AT & T Mobility LLC*, 584 F.3d 849, 855, 856 (C.A.9 2009).

. . . In California's perfectly rational view, nonclass arbitration over such sums will also sometimes have the effect of depriving claimants of their claims (say, for example, where claiming the $30.22 were to involve filling out many forms that require technical legal knowledge or waiting at great length while a call is placed on hold). . . .

Finally, the majority can find no meaningful support for its views in this Court's precedent. The federal Act has been in force for nearly a century. We have decided dozens of cases about its requirements. We have reached results that authorize complex arbitration procedures. E.g., *Mitsubishi Motors*, 473 U.S., at 629 (antitrust claims arising in international transaction are arbitrable). We have upheld nondiscriminatory state laws that slow down arbitration proceedings. E.g., *Volt Information Sciences*, 489 U.S., at 477-479 (California law staying arbitration proceedings until completion of related litigation is not pre-empted). But we have not, to my knowledge, applied the Act to strike down a state statute that treats arbitrations on par with judicial and administrative proceedings. Cf. *Preston*, 552 U.S., at 355-356, 128 S. Ct. 978 (Act pre-empts state law that vests primary jurisdiction in state administrative board).

At the same time, we have repeatedly referred to the Act's basic objective as assuring that courts treat arbitration agreements "like all other contracts." *Buckeye Check Cashing, Inc. v. Cardegna*, 546 U.S. 440, 447 . . . (2006). See also, e.g., *Vaden v. Discover Bank*, 556 129 S. Ct. 1262, 1273-1274 (2009); . . . *Allied-Bruce Terminix Cos. v. Dobson*, 513 U.S. 265, 281 (1995); *Rodriguez de Quijas v. Shearson/American Express, Inc.*, 490 U.S. 477, 483-484 (1989); *Perry v. Thomas*, 482 U.S. 483, 492-493, n. 9 (1987); *Mitsubishi Motors, supra*, at 627, 105 S. Ct. 3346. And we have recognized that "[t]o immunize an arbitration agreement from judicial challenge" on grounds applicable to all other contracts "would be to elevate it over other forms of contract." *Prima Paint Corp. v. Flood & Conklin Mfg. Co.*, 388 U.S. 395, 404, n. 12 (1967); see also *Marchant v. Mead-Morrison Mfg. Co.*, 252 N.Y. 284, 299, 169 N.E. 386, 391 (1929) (Cardozo, C.J.) ("Courts are not at liberty to shirk the process of [contractual] construction under the empire of a belief that arbitration is beneficent any more than they may shirk it if their belief happens to be the contrary"); *Cohen & Dayton*, 12 Va. L. Rev., at 276 (the Act "is no infringement upon the right of each State to decide for itself what contracts shall or shall not exist under its laws").

These cases do not concern the merits and demerits of class actions; they concern equal treatment of arbitration contracts and other contracts. . . .

By using the words "save upon such grounds as exist at law or in equity for the revocation of any contract," Congress retained for the States an important role incident to agreements to arbitrate. 9 U.S.C. §2. Through those words Congress reiterated a basic federal idea that has long informed the nature of this Nation's laws. . . . Here, recognition of that federalist ideal, embodied in specific language in this particular statute, should lead us to uphold California's law, not to strike it down. . . .

QUESTIONS

9. Did the *Concepcion* majority ground its decision on the presence of an incentive scheme like the one developed by AT&T as a "substitute" for class actions? Put another way, after *Concepcion*, does a company planning to put a class action waiver in an arbitration agreement need to go to the trouble AT&T did in crafting a set of alternative incentives? Most court decisions following *Concepcion* enforced class action waivers in the absence of AT&T-like provisions. *See, e.g., Kilgore v. KeyBank, N.A.*, 673 F.3d 947, 960 (9th Cir. 2012); *Litman v. Cellco P'ship*, 655 F.3d 225 (3d Cir. 2011), *cert. denied*, 132 S. Ct. 1046 (2012); *Homa v. American Express Co.*, 2012 WL 3594231 (3d Cir. 2012); *Pendergast v. Sprint Nextel Corp.*, 691 F.3d 1224 (11th Cir. 2012).

10. Uber drivers have also tried to escape class action waivers. In *Mohamed v. Uber Technologies*, 848 F.3d 1201, 1208 (9th Cir. 2016), the Court of Appeals reversed a district court finding that delegation clauses in arbitration agreements with Uber drivers were unconscionable. The court found that the questions relating to the validity of the arbitration provision were for an arbitrator, and that the plaintiffs had not shown the delegation clause itself was unenforceable. In this case, the two plaintiffs were Uber drivers who had to sign new contracts on the Uber app before they were able to sign in and start working. The updated agreements stated that disputes were governed by California law, and precluded class proceedings of any kind. Nonetheless, there was an option to opt out of the arbitration agreement within 30 days, which the plaintiffs did not take. What role do you think that the "opt-out" provision had on the enforceability of the agreement? Does it make sense to have the arbitrator decide the question of unconscionability per the delegation clause based on prior cases discussed above? Similar cases have been decided with similar results. In *O'Connor v. Uber Technologies, Inc.*, current and former Uber drivers again filed several class actions alleging that Uber violated federal and state statutes by misclassifying them as independent contractors. Citing *Mohamed v. Uber Technologies*, the Ninth Circuit reversed the district court's class certification of Uber drivers and held the arbitration agreement was enforceable.

11. Are class action waivers enforceable in contracts that do not have arbitration clauses? Does it make sense to hinge the availability of class action on the presence of an arbitration provision in a contract?

American Express Co. v. Italian Colors Restaurant

570 U.S. 228 (2013)

[On June 20, 2013, in an opinion authored by Justice Scalia, the U.S. Supreme Court overturned the decision of the Second Circuit Court of Appeals in *American Express Co. v. Italian Colors Restaurant*. The Court (5-3, with Justice Kagan writing the dissent, and Justice Sotomayor recusing herself from participation in consideration or decision of the case) held that "[t]he FAA does not permit courts to invalidate a contractual waiver of class arbitration on the ground that the plaintiff's cost of individually arbitrating a federal statutory claim exceeds the potential recovery."

The case arose out of an agreement between American Express and a subsidiary (collectively, AmEx) and merchants who accept American Express cards; the agreement required all disputes to be resolved by arbitration and provides that there "shall be no right or authority for any Claims to be arbitrated on a class action basis."

The merchants filed a class action, claiming that AmEx violated §1 of the Sherman Act and seeking treble damages for the class under §4 of the Clayton Act. They alleged that AmEx used its monopoly power to force merchants to accept cards at rates about 30 percent higher than fees for other cards. AmEx moved to compel individual arbitration under the FAA, but the merchants countered that the cost of expert analysis necessary to prove the antitrust claims would greatly exceed the maximum recovery for an individual plaintiff. The federal district court granted the AmEx motion and dismissed the lawsuits.

In *In re Am. Express Merchants' Litig.*, 554 F.2d 300 (2d Cir. 2009) (*AmEx I*), the Second Circuit reversed and remanded, finding that the class action waiver could not be enforced in an antitrust action because to do so would grant AmEx de facto immunity from antitrust liability by removing the merchants' only reasonably feasible means of recovery. On these grounds, the court concluded that the arbitration agreement was unenforceable.

The Supreme Court granted certiorari and, in *Am. Express Co. v. Italian Colors Rest.*, 559 U.S. 1103 (2010), vacated the judgment and remanded for further consideration in light of the Court's holding in *Stolt-Nielsen S.A. v. AnimalFeeds Int'l Corp.*, 559 U.S. 662 (2010). In *American Express Co. Merchants' Litig.*, 634 F.2d 187, 200 (2d Cir. 2011) (*AmEx 2*), the Second Circuit reaffirmed its decision, concluding that the enforcement of the class action waiver would bar the merchants from pursuing their statutory claims because the cost of the plaintiffs' individually arbitrating their dispute with AmEx would be prohibitive and deprive the plaintiffs of statutory protections of the antitrust laws.

In the wake of the Supreme Court's decision in *AT&T Mobility LLC v. Concepcion*, 563 U.S. 333 (2011), AmEx sought to reverse the Second Circuit's holding in *AmEx II*. In *In re Am. Express Merchants' Litig.*, 667 F.3d 204 (2d Cir. 2012) (*AmEx III*), the Second Circuit continued to stand its ground. It concluded that the Supreme Court's jurisprudence supported the principle that parties cannot be forced to arbitrate disputes by class arbitration unless parties agree to do so, but did not require that all class action waivers be deemed per se enforceable. The court distinguished *AT&T Mobility* on the basis that it involved federal preemption of state law, whereas the present case dealt with the vindication of rights under a federal statutory scheme. The Second Circuit concluded that the Supreme Court had not overturned *Mitsubishi v. Soler Chrysler Plymouth*, which stood for the proposition that arbitration must be an effective vehicle for vindicating statutory rights. Moreover, the Court's decision in *Green Tree Financial Corp.-Alabama v. Randolph* stated that a party may avoid an arbitration agreement on the ground that arbitration would be prohibitively expensive, if the party fulfills the burden of showing the likelihood of incurring such costs. The court observed that other circuit courts permitted plaintiffs to challenge class action waivers on the grounds that prose-cuting such claims on an individual basis would be a cost-prohibitive method of enforcing a statutory right. Here, evidence presented by the plaintiffs showed that the cost of merchants' individually arbitrating their dispute with AmEx would be prohibitive, effectively depriving the plaintiffs of the statutory protections of the antitrust laws. Therefore, the arbitration provision was unenforceable. The Second Circuit denied a rehearing en banc with five judges dissenting and the Supreme Court granted certiorari.]

Justice SCALIA delivered the opinion of the Court, in which ROBERTS, C.J., and KENNEDY, THOMAS, and ALITO, JJ., joined.

. . . Congress enacted the FAA in response to widespread judicial hostility to arbitration. See *AT&T Mobility*, supra, 131 S. Ct., at 1745. . . .

. . . [Section 2 of the FAA] reflects the overarching principle that arbitration is a matter of contract. See *Rent-A-Center, West, Inc. v. Jackson*, 561 U.S. ___, ___, 130 S. Ct. 2772, 2776 (2010). And consistent with that [section], courts must "rigor-ously enforce" arbitration agreements according to their terms, *Dean Witter Reynolds Inc. v. Byrd*, 470 U.S. 213, 221 (1985), including terms that "specify with whom [the parties] choose to arbitrate their disputes," *Stolt-Nielsen*, supra, at 683, 130 S. Ct. 1758, and "the rules under which that arbitration will be conducted," *Volt Informa-tion Sciences, Inc. v. Board of Trustees of Leland Stanford Junior Univ.*, 489 U.S. 468, 479 (1989). That holds true for claims that allege a violation of a federal statute, unless the FAA's mandate has been " 'overridden by a contrary congressional command.' " *CompuCredit Corp. v. Greenwood*, 565 U.S. ___, ___, 132 S. Ct. 665, 668-669 (2012) (quoting *Shearson/American Express Inc. v. McMahon*, 482 U.S. 220, 226 (1987)).

No contrary congressional command requires us to reject the waiver of class arbitration here. Respondents argue that requiring them to litigate their claims individually—as they contracted to do—would contravene the policies of the anti-trust laws. But the antitrust laws do not guarantee an affordable procedural path to the vindication of every claim. Congress has taken some measures to facilitate the litigation of antitrust claims—for example, it enacted a multiplied-damages remedy. . . . In enacting such measures, Congress has told us that it is willing to go, in certain respects, beyond the normal limits of law in advancing its goals of deterring and remedying unlawful trade practice. But to say that Congress must have intended whatever departures from those normal limits advance antitrust goals is simply irrational. "[N]o legislation pursues its purposes at all costs." *Rodri-guez v. United States*, 480 U.S. 522, 525-526 (1987) (per curiam).

The antitrust laws do not "evinc[e] an intention to preclude a waiver" of class-action procedure. *Mitsubishi Motors Corp. v. Soler Chrysler-Plymouth, Inc.*, 473 U.S. 614, 628 (1985). The Sherman and Clayton Acts make no mention of class actions. In fact, they were enacted decades before the advent of Federal Rule of Civil Proce-dure 23, which was "designed to allow an exception to the usual rule that litiga-tion is conducted by and on behalf of the individual named parties only." *Califano v. Yamasaki*, 442 U.S. 682, 700-701 (1979). The parties here agreed to arbitrate pur-suant to that "usual rule," and it would be remarkable for a court to erase that expectation.

Nor does congressional approval of Rule 23 establish an entitlement to class proceedings for the vindication of statutory rights. . . .

Our finding of no "contrary congressional command" does not end the case. Respondents invoke a judge-made exception to the FAA which, they say, serves to harmonize competing federal policies by allowing courts to invalidate agreements that prevent the "effective vindication" of a federal statutory right. Enforcing the waiver of class arbitration bars effective vindication, respondents contend, because they have no economic incentive to pursue their antitrust claims individually in arbitration.

The "effective vindication" exception to which respondents allude originated as dictum in *Mitsubishi Motors*, where we expressed a willingness to invalidate, on "public policy" grounds, arbitration agreements that "operat[e] . . . as a prospective waiver of a party's *right to pursue* statutory remedies." 473 U.S., at 637, n. 19 (emphasis added). Dismissing concerns that the arbitral forum was inadequate, we said that "so long as the prospective litigant effectively may vindicate its statutory cause of action in the arbitral forum, the statute will continue to serve both its remedial and deterrent function." *Id.*, at 637, 105 S. Ct. 3346. Subsequent cases have similarly asserted the existence of an "effective vindication" exception, see, e.g., *14 Penn Plaza LLC v. Pyett*, 556 U.S. 247, 273-274 (2009); *Gilmer v. Interstate/Johnson Lane Corp.*, 500 U.S. 20, 28 (1991), but have similarly declined to apply it to invalidate the arbitration agreement at issue.

And we do so again here. . . . [The exception] would certainly cover a provision in an arbitration agreement forbidding the assertion of certain statutory rights. And it would perhaps cover filing and administrative fees attached to arbitration that are so high as to make access to the forum impracticable. See *Green Tree Financial Corp.-Ala. v. Randolph*, 531 U.S. 79, 90 (2000) ("It may well be that the existence of large arbitration costs could preclude a litigant . . . from effectively vindicating her federal statutory rights"). But the fact that it is not worth the expense involved in proving a statutory remedy does not constitute the elimination of the right to pursue that remedy. See 681 F.3d, at 147 (Jacobs, C.J., dissenting from denial of rehearing en banc). The class-action waiver merely limits arbitration to the two contracting parties. It no more eliminates those parties' right to pursue their statutory remedy than did federal law before its adoption of the class action for legal relief in 1938, see Fed. Rule Civ. Proc. 23, 28 U.S.C., p. 864 (1938 ed., Supp V); 7A C. Wright, A. Miller, & M. Kane, Federal Practice and Procedure §1752, p. 18 (3d ed. 2005). . . .

. . . [O]ur decision in *AT&T Mobility* all but resolves this case. There we invalidated a law conditioning enforcement of arbitration on the availability of class procedure because that law "interfere[d] with fundamental attributes of arbitration." 563 U.S., at ___, 131 S. Ct., at 1748. "[T]he switch from bilateral to class arbitration," we said, "sacrifices the principal advantage of arbitration — its informality — and makes the process slower, more costly, and more likely to generate procedural morass than final judgment." Id., at ___, 131 S. Ct., at 1751. We specifically rejected the argument that class arbitration was necessary to prosecute claims "that might otherwise slip through the legal system." Id., at ___, 131 S. Ct., at 1753.

The regime established by the Court of Appeals' decision would require — before a plaintiff can be held to contractually agreed bilateral arbitration — that a federal court determine (and the parties litigate) the legal requirements for success on the merits claim-by-claim and theory-by-theory, the evidence necessary to meet those requirements, the cost of developing that evidence, and the damages that would be recovered in the event of success. Such a preliminary litigating hurdle would undoubtedly destroy the prospect of speedy resolution that arbitration in general and bilateral arbitration in particular was meant to secure. The FAA does not sanction such a judicially created superstructure.

The judgment of the Court of Appeals is reversed. *It is so ordered.*

Justice THOMAS, concurring.

I join the Court's opinion in full. I write separately to note that the result here is also required by the plain meaning of the [FAA]. In *AT&T Mobility LLC v. Concepcion*, 563 U.S. ___, 131 S. Ct. 1740 (2011), I explained that "the FAA requires that an agreement to arbitrate be enforced unless a party successfully challenges the formation of the arbitration agreement, such as by proving fraud or duress." Id., at ___, 131 S. Ct., at 1753 (concurring opinion). . . . Because Italian Colors has not furnished "grounds . . . for the revocation of any contract," 9 U.S.C. §2, the arbitration agreement must be enforced. . . .

Justice KAGAN, with whom Justice GINSBURG and Justice BREYER join, dissenting.

Here is the nutshell version of this case, unfortunately obscured in the Court's decision. The owner of a small restaurant (Italian Colors) thinks that American Express (Amex) has used its monopoly power to force merchants to accept a form contract violating the antitrust laws. The restaurateur wants to challenge the allegedly unlawful provision (imposing a tying arrangement), but the same contract's arbitration clause prevents him from doing so. That term imposes a variety of procedural bars that would make pursuit of the antitrust claim a fool's errand. So if the arbitration clause is enforceable, Amex has insulated itself from antitrust liability—even if it has in fact violated the law. The monopolist gets to use its monopoly power to insist on a contract effectively depriving its victims of all legal recourse. . . .

That answer is a betrayal of our precedents, and of federal statutes like the antitrust laws. Our decisions have developed a mechanism—called the effective-vindication rule—to prevent arbitration clauses from choking off a plaintiff's ability to enforce congressionally created rights. That doctrine bars applying such a clause when (but only when) it operates to confer immunity from potentially meritorious federal claims. In so doing, the rule reconciles the [FAA] with all the rest of federal law—and indeed, promotes the most fundamental purposes of the FAA itself. As applied here, the rule would ensure that Amex's arbitration clause does not foreclose Italian Colors from vindicating its right to redress antitrust harm.

The majority barely tries to explain why it reaches a contrary result. It notes that we have not decided this exact case before—neglecting that the principle we have established fits this case hand in glove. . . .

Start with an uncontroversial proposition: We would refuse to enforce an exculpatory clause insulating a company from antitrust liability—say, "Merchants may bring no Sherman Act claims"—even if that clause were contained in an arbitration agreement. . . .

If the rule were limited to baldly exculpatory provisions, however, a monopolist could devise numerous ways around it. Consider several alternatives that a party drafting an arbitration agreement could adopt to avoid antitrust liability, each of which would have the identical effect. On the front end: The agreement might set outlandish filing fees or establish an absurd (e.g., one-day) statute of limitations, thus preventing a claimant from gaining access to the arbitral forum. On the back end: The agreement might remove the arbitrator's authority to grant meaningful relief, so that a judgment gets the claimant nothing worthwhile. And in the middle: The agreement might block the claimant from presenting the kind of proof that is necessary to establish the defendant's liability—say, by prohibiting any economic testimony (good luck proving an antitrust claim without that!). Or else the agreement might appoint as an arbitrator an obviously biased person—say, the CEO of Amex. The possibilities are endless—all less direct than an express exculpatory clause, but no less fatal. So the rule against prospective waivers of federal rights can work only if it applies not just to a contract clause explicitly barring a claim, but to others that operate to do so.

And sure enough, our cases establish this proposition: An arbitration clause will not be enforced if it prevents the effective vindication of federal statutory rights, however it achieves that result. The rule originated in *Mitsubishi*, where we held that claims brought under the Sherman Act and other federal laws are generally subject to arbitration. 473 U.S., at 628. By agreeing to arbitrate such a claim, we explained, "a party does not forgo the substantive rights afforded by the statute; it only submits to their resolution in an arbitral, rather than a judicial, forum." Ibid. But crucial to our decision was a limiting principle, designed to safeguard federal rights: An arbitration clause will be enforced only "so long as the prospective litigant effectively may vindicate its statutory cause of action in the arbitral forum." Id., at 637. If an arbitration provision "operated . . . as a prospective waiver of a party's right to pursue statutory remedies," we emphasized, we would "condemn[]" it. Id., at 637, n. 19. Similarly, we stated that such a clause should be "set [] aside" if "proceedings in the contractual forum will be so gravely difficult" that the claimant "will for all practical purposes be deprived of his day in court." Id., at 632 (internal quotation marks omitted). And in the decades since *Mitsubishi*, we have repeated its admonition time and again, instructing courts not to enforce an arbitration agreement that effectively (even if not explicitly) forecloses a plaintiff from remedying the violation of a federal statutory right. See *Gilmer v. Interstate/Johnson Lane Corp.*, 500 U.S. 20, 28 (1991); *Vimar Seguros y Reaseguros, S.A. v. M/V Sky Reefer*, 515 U.S. 528, 540 (1995); *14 Penn Plaza*, 556 U.S., at 266, 273-274.

Our decision in *Green Tree Financial Corp.-Ala. v. Randolph*, 531 U.S. 79 (2000), confirmed that this principle applies when an agreement thwarts federal law by making arbitration prohibitively expensive. . . .

. . . So down one road: More arbitration, better enforcement of federal statutes. And down the other: Less arbitration, poorer enforcement of federal statutes. . . .

An arbitration agreement could manage such a mismatch in many ways, but Amex's disdains them all. As the Court makes clear, the contract expressly prohibits class arbitration. But that is only part of the problem. The agreement also disallows any kind of joinder or consolidation of claims or parties. And more: Its confidentiality provision prevents Italian Colors from informally arranging with other merchants to produce a common expert report. And still more: The agreement precludes any shifting of costs to Amex, even if Italian Colors prevails. And beyond all that: Amex refused to enter into any stipulations that would obviate or mitigate the need for the economic analysis. In short, the agreement as applied in this case cuts off not just class arbitration, but any avenue for sharing, shifting, or shrinking necessary costs. Amex has put Italian Colors to this choice: Spend way, way, way more money than your claim is worth, or relinquish your Sherman Act rights. . . .

. . . Our effective-vindication rule comes into play only when the FAA is alleged to conflict with another federal law, like the Sherman Act here. In that all-federal context, one law does not automatically bow to the other, and the effective-vindication rule serves as a way to reconcile any tension between them. Again, then, AT&T Mobility had no occasion to address the issue in this case. The relevant decisions are instead *Mitsubishi* and *Randolph.*

. . . [T]he Court does not consider that Amex's agreement bars not just class actions, but "other forms of cost-sharing . . . that could provide effective vindication." . . .

. . . The FAA conceived of arbitration as a "method of *resolving* disputes" — a way of using tailored and streamlined procedures to facilitate redress of injuries. *Rodriguez de Quijas,* 490 U.S., at 481 (emphasis added). In the hands of today's majority, arbitration threatens to become more nearly the opposite — a mechanism easily made to block the vindication of meritorious federal claims and insulate wrongdoers from liability. . . .

QUESTIONS

12. If their contract contains a class action waiver, are there any remaining options for collective action by or on behalf of consumers or employees? As mentioned in Chapter 7, the Supreme Court in *Epic Sys. Corp. v. Lewis,* 138 S. Ct. 1612, 1632 (2018), held that arbitration agreements calling for individualized proceedings are enforceable per not only the FAA, but also the Fair Labor Standards Act (FLSA) and National Labor Relations Act (NLRA). It thus endorsed "pre-dispute" arbitration clauses, even when they would arguably hinder collective action under labor laws.[17] Does this make sense under labor law, or should collective action rights under §7 of the NLRA prevent such use of arbitration clauses to cut off collective proceedings?

13. Another case dealing with questions around class proceedings in employment cases is *Lamps Plus, Inc. v. Varela,* 139 S. Ct. 1407, 1412 (2019). In that case, the question was whether a court could order classwide, rather than individualized, arbitration proceedings when the arbitration agreement was ambiguous about whether class arbitration was available. The Supreme Court held that the arbitration agreement's ambiguity on the subject did not provide sufficient basis for compelling classwide arbitration. This was consistent with the Court's prior ruling in *Stolt-Nielsen* that silence on the subject is not sufficient to provide basis for an arbitrator to order class proceedings. Chief Justice Roberts, writing for the five-member majority, reasoned that under the FAA, an ambiguous agreement cannot provide a contractual basis for concluding that the parties

agreed to classwide arbitration because individualized and classwide arbitration are so different — and classwide arbitration sacrifices the informality, speed, and low cost that are the primary benefits of arbitration.[18] Four Justices dissented.

Do these opinions say anything about class action waivers? Should class action waivers be enforceable even where there is no arbitration clause? Why or why not?

14. The California courts and legislature have continued with efforts to limit the enforcement of arbitration agreements in adhesion contracts. Consider the California Private Attorneys General Act of 2004 and the decision in *Iskanian v. CLS Transportation, Los Angeles LLC*, 327 P.3d 129 (Cal. 2014) (waiver of employees' right to representative action under California Private Attorneys General Act (PAGA) violated public policy; FAA does not preempt state law as to unenforceability of waivers of PAGA rights), but also note *Langston v. 20/20 Cos., Inc.*, 2014 WL 5335734 (C.D. Cal. 2014) (enforcing prohibition in Mutual Arbitration Agreement in multiple contracts of consolidation of claims into class or representative actions, and requiring all claims to be individually arbitrated).

The U.S. Supreme Court is poised to weigh in on this issue in *Moriana v. Viking River Cruises, Inc.*, No. B297327, 2020 WL 5584508 (Cal. Ct. App. Sept. 18, 2020), review denied (Dec. 9, 2020), *cert. granted*, 142 S. Ct. 734 (2021). In this case, the plaintiff sued her former employer, Viking River Cruises, Inc. (Viking), seeking civil penalties under PAGA. *Moriana v. Viking River Cruises, Inc.*, No. B297327, 2020 WL 5584508 *1 (Cal. Ct. App. Sept. 18, 2020), review denied (Dec. 9, 2020), *cert. granted*, 142 S. Ct. 734 (2021). Viking moved to compel plaintiff's PAGA claims to arbitration, per the terms of her employment agreement, including a delegation provision, which gave the arbitrator the authority to resolve disputes over the terms of the employment agreement. Viking argued that Epic Systems overruled the California Supreme Court decision in *Iskanian v. CLS Transportation Los Angeles, LLC*. The court held that arbitration agreements precluding PAGA claims cannot be enforced because such claims are brought by individuals or classes on behalf of the state and the state did not agree to arbitrate such claims when the employment agreement was formed. The Supreme Court granted cert to decide the preemption issue. SCOTUS had not decided the issue as of the publication of this book.

15. In *Abernathy v. DoorDash, Inc.*, 438 F. Supp. 3d 1062 (N.D. Cal. 2020), a federal district court ordered the online delivery company to individually arbitrate claims filed by more than 5,000 delivery drivers fighting for overtime pay and minimum wages on the basis that DoorDash misclassified them as independent contractors. At the conclusion of the decision, the court stated:

> For decades, the employer-side bar and their employer clients have forced arbitration clauses upon workers, thus taking away their right to go to court, and forced class-action waivers upon

them too, thus taking away their ability to join collectively to vindicate common rights. The employer-side bar has succeeded in
the United States Supreme Court to sustain such provisions. The
irony, in this case, is that the workers wish to enforce the very
provisions forced on them by seeking, even if by the thousands,
individual arbitrations, the remnant of procedural rights left to
them. The employer here, DoorDash, faced with having to actually honor its side of the bargain, now blanches at the cost of the
filing fees it agreed to pay in the arbitration clause. No doubt,
DoorDash never expected that so many would actually seek
arbitration. Instead, in irony upon irony, DoorDash now wishes
to resort to a classwide lawsuit, the very device it denied to the
workers, to avoid its duty to arbitrate. This hypocrisy will not be
blessed, at least by this order.

Id. at 1067-1068.

16. The U.S. Supreme Court is also poised to address "waiver" and what is
    sufficient to waive one's right to arbitrate. The question for cert. asks
    whether an arbitration-specific requirement that the proponent of a
    contractual waiver defense prove prejudice violates the FAA rules that
    lower courts must "place arbitration agreements on an equal footing
    with other contracts." *AT&T Mobility LLC v. Concepcion*, 563 U.S. 333,
    339 (2011). The focus is going to be on whether there is a prejudice
    requirement that must be met in order to prove the waiver of a right to
    arbitrate as part of a contract agreement. *Morgan v. Sundance, Inc.*, 992
    F.3d 711 (8th Cir.), *cert. granted*, 142 S. Ct. 482, 211 L. Ed. 2d 292 (2021).
    In this case, Morgan filed suit against Sundance, Inc. for violation of the
    Fair Labor Standards Act (FLSA). *Morgan v. Sundance, Inc.*, 992 F.3d 711,
    713 (8th Cir.), *cert. granted*, 142 S. Ct. 482, 211 L. Ed. 2d 292 (2021).
    Morgan claimed Sundance failed to pay her, and other similarly situated
    employees, for overtime. Sundance moved to dismiss the complaint,
    arguing under the first-to-file rule that a similar lawsuit was pending
    before a Michigan federal court, which barred this lawsuit. The district
    court denied the motion to dismiss four months later. *Id.* Sundance then
    answered Morgan's complaint but did not mention its right to arbitrate
    the claims. A settlement mediation with the Michigan plaintiffs, Morgan,
    and Sundance followed. *Id.* The Michigan case was resolved, but Mor-
    gan's case moved forward. Then Sundance moved to compel arbitration,
    eight months after the initial complaint was filed. The Eighth Circuit was
    asked whether Sundance waived its right to arbitration by acting incon-
    sistently with its right to arbitrate, and if so, whether the inconsistent
    action prejudiced the plaintiff. The court held that waiver only applies
    where actions inconsistent with one's right to arbitrate created prejudice
    for the other party. Here, the court said that there was no prejudice, thus
    allowing arbitration to proceed. SCOTUS had not decided the issue as of
    the time of this book's publication.

Endnotes

1. Alaska Stat. Ann. §§09.43.010-180 (2020); Ariz. Rev. Stat. §§12-1501-1518 (2020); Ark. Code Ann. §§16-108-201-230 (2020); Colo. Rev. Stat. §§13-22-201-230 (2020); Conn. Gen. Stat. Ann. §§52-408-424 (2020); D.C. Code §§16-4401-4432 (2020); Fla. Stat. §§682.01-.22 (2020); Haw. Rev. Stat. §§658a-1-29 (2020); Kan. Stat. Ann. §5-422-453 (2020); Mich. Comp. Laws §§691.1681-1713 (2020); Minn. Stat. Ann. §§572.08-.30 (2020); Nev. Rev. Stat. §38.206-.248 (2020); N.J. Stat. Ann. §§2a:23b-1-32 (2020); N.M. Stat. Ann. 1978, §44-7a-1-32 (2020); N.C. Gen. Stat. §§1-569.1-.31 (2020); N.D. Cent. Code §§32-29.3-01-29 (2020); Okla. Stat. tit. 12, §§1851-1881 (2020); Or. Rev. Stat. §§36.600-740 (2020); 42 Pa. Cons. Stat. Ann. §§7321.1-31 (2020); Utah Code §§78b-1-101-131 (2020); Wash. Rev. Code §§7.04a.010-903 (2020); W. Va. Code §§55-10-1-33 (2020).
2. HB 59, 191st Leg. (Mass. 2019); HB 288, 2019-2020 Leg. Sess. (Vt. 2019).
3. Stipanowich, Thomas J. (2010) *Arbitration: The "New Litigation,"* 2010 U. Ill. L. Rev. 1.
4. Folberg, Jay H. (2003) *Arbitration Ethics — Is California the Future?*, 18 Ohio St. J. on Disp. Resol. 343.
5. Stipanowich, Thomas J., *supra* note 3.
6. Kent, Jamie. (2004) *The Debate in California over and Implications of New Ethical Standards for Arbitrator Disclosure: Are the Changes Valid or Appropriate?*, 17 Geo. J. Legal Ethics 903.
7. Gaillard, Emmanuel. (2008) *International Arbitration Law.*
8. H. R. 1374, Mar. 7, 2017. https://www.congress.gov/bill/115th-congress/house-bill/1374/text. All information about the AFA of 2017 is found at the aforementioned URL.
9. S.630, Feb. 28, 2019, https://www.congress.gov/bill/116th-congress/senate-bill/630/text.
10. This would be §1036(A)(b)(1) of the Act if it were passed.
11. §1036(A)(b)(2).
12. H. R. 1423 Sept. 24, 2019, https://www.congress.gov/bill/116th-congress/house-bill/1423/text.
13. §402(b)(1).
14. §402(b)(2).
15. Stipanowich, Thomas J. (2012) *The Third Arbitration Trilogy:* Stolt-Nielsen, Rent-a-Center, Concepcion *and the Future of American Arbitration*, 22 Am. Rev. Int'l Arb. 323.
16. *See id.*
17. 138 S. Ct. at 1616–1632. There were three cases involved. In the first of the consolidated cases, an employee brought a class action against an employer, alleging that he violated the FLSA and Wisconsin law, and the Court of Appeals for the Seventh Circuit affirmed an order denying the employer's motion to dismiss and compel individual arbitration. In the second case, employees brought similar class action claims against an employer under the FLSA and California law, and the Court of Appeals for the Ninth Circuit reversed an order granting the employer's motion to compel individual arbitration. In the third case, the employer filed a petition for a review

of the National Labor Relation Board's finding that it was unlawful for the employer to require employees to sign an agreement waiving their right to pursue class and collective actions. The Court of Appeals for the Fifth Circuit held that the employer's arbitration agreement compelling individual arbitration was fair. The Supreme Court reversed and remanded the two cases that ruled for the employees, and affirmed the case upholding the individualized arbitration agreements.

18. *Id.* An important principle of the FAA is that parties must consent to arbitration, and silence is not enough. Ambiguity should be treated the same way because it also does not provide a sufficient basis to conclude that the parties consented to classwide arbitration.

MIXING MODES: MULTI-DOOR PROGRAMS, STEPPED DISPUTE RESOLUTION, AND HYBRID PROCESSES

A. MIXING MODES: THE BIG PICTURE

The prior chapters of this book have been devoted to forms of arbitration, with occasional references to other modes of dispute resolution—notably, negotiation and mediation. Often, however, dispute resolution involves a "mixing of modes," comprising multiple processes that employ various strategies aimed at negotiated settlement before, during, or after litigation or arbitration.[1] Much as drivers on a multi-lane highway shift from lane to lane as circumstances require in the course of reaching their destination, parties and counsel may use a variety of diverse tools or approaches in order to promote their varied priorities in resolving conflict.[2] These priorities include earlier, more efficient dispute resolution, more satisfying outcomes, improving or maintaining critical relationships, and higher rates of compliance and enforceability.

As discussed below, state and federal courts in the United States have developed a variety of programs to promote pretrial settlement with the help of mediators or other third-party neutrals. Given the strong prevalence of negotiated settlement, often through mediation and other ADR options, the process of resolving disputes in litigation may be more accurately characterized as "liti-gotiation."[3]

As explored in earlier chapters, business disputes and other conflicts between contracting parties may be resolved against the backdrop of agreements for binding arbitration. Here, too, there are always opportunities for informal settlement prior to, during, or after adjudication. Rates of settlement in cases referred to arbitration have been increasing in the United States,[4] and a recent study of four major case types of international commercial arbitration revealed rates of settlement or withdrawal ranging from 40 percent (construction disputes) to nearly 90 percent (hospitality and travel disputes). It is no coincidence that in the United States and internationally, contractual dispute resolution provisions often call for parties to negotiate and/or mediate prior to arbitration, and parties often mediate at various points during the course of arbitration.

In this chapter, we will explore a number of questions that have emerged as lawyers and clients have gained experience with mixed-mode dispute resolution:

- What kinds of processes may be appropriate to facilitate informal settlement prior to or during the course of adjudication?
- What dispute resolution options, including tiered or stepped approaches, are being used in the resolution of contract disputes?
- May business relationships benefit from "real-time" approaches to avoiding and managing disputes?
- Is it ever appropriate for a mediator to "change hats" and arbitrate, or for an arbitrator to shift to the role of mediator, in the course of resolving a dispute?

B.   COURT-CONNECTED DISPUTE RESOLUTION PROGRAMS

Mixed-mode dispute resolution has been a feature of the American public justice system since the late 1970s in the wake of the 1976 Pound Conference, at which leaders of the bench and bar sounded a call for more appropriate, less costly alternatives to traditional litigation. Supreme Court Chief Justice Warren Burger spoke of the "need for systematic anticipation" in the justice system, encouraging a move away from the strictures and inefficiencies of traditional process models in favor of more efficient and expeditious procedures more appropriately tailored to the real needs of parties in conflict.[5] Harvard Professor Frank Sander proposed a "multi-door courthouse" that incorporated three concepts: (1) a choice of several discrete approaches to conflict resolution; (2) a mechanism for channeling disputes into specific processes; and (3) sufficient information about a given dispute to facilitate a rational pairing of problem and process (or, as Sander later said, "fitting the form to the fuss").[6]

The Pound Conference served as a wake-up call for federal and state court programs. In subsequent decades, the judiciary came to acknowledge the value of innovative court-connected programs—a development that became a primary wellspring of a Quiet Revolution in dispute resolution. A number of federal and state court programs in the United States and abroad have attempted to provide a smorgasbord of ADR choices for parties. However, for a variety of reasons most court programs have tended to emphasize only one or two processes. Although mediation is by far the most widely employed element of court-connected ADR,[7] some other processes have been utilized. The full dispute resolution spectrum is graphically presented and discussed in Chapter 1. Some court programs have even moved online, as discussed further in the next chapter.

Advisory or Nonbinding Arbitration.   A number of federal and state court programs include forms of nonbinding or advisory arbitration, reference to which is made in Chapter 1. Such processes, in which one or three arbitrators hear abbreviated adversarial presentations by each side and then issue a nonbinding decision (award), share some of the features of court trial. However, witnesses may or may not be called, and documentary evidence may be limited. Moreover, either party may reject the arbitration award and request a trial de novo in court. Most nonbinding arbitration programs are voluntary, but those in which participation is mandatory provide exclusions for cases involving violations of constitutional rights or damage claims in excess of a specified dollar amount, and permit parties to seek exemption from the referral to arbitration.

Early Neutral Evaluation.   As described in a Guide published by the Federal Judicial Center:

> Early neutral evaluation (ENE) is a nonbinding process designed to improve case planning and settlement prospects by giving litigants an early advisory evaluation of the case. . . .
>
> In ENE, a neutral evaluator, usually a private attorney with expertise in the subject matter of the dispute, holds a confidential session with the parties and counsel early in the litigation—generally before much discovery has taken place—to hear both sides of the case. The evaluator then helps the parties clarify issues and evidence, identifies strengths and weaknesses of the parties' positions, and gives the parties a nonbinding assessment of the values or merits of the case. Depending on the goals of the program, the evaluator also may mediate settlement discussions or offer case management assistance, such as developing a discovery plan.
>
> The process was originally designed to improve attorneys' pretrial practices and knowledge of their cases by forcing them and their clients to conduct core investigative and analytical work early, to communicate directly across party lines, to expose each side to the other's case, and to consider the wisdom of early settlement.[8]

Former federal judge-magistrate Wayne Brazil has urged lawyers to consider the benefits of ENE for certain types of disputes. ENE can be particularly beneficial when disputes appear to revolve around disagreements over legal issues and a neutral expert's viewpoint can be valuable. Judge Brazil suggests that ENE can also be useful when extensive group sessions to evaluate the merits would be effective, rather than mediation's oft-used "shuttle diplomacy."[9]

Summary Jury Trial.   Summary jury trial is a nonbinding process aimed at promoting settlement in cases on the eve of trial. A judge presides over an abbreviated hearing before an advisory jury; the parties' counsel present summarized evidence and arguments, generally without calling witnesses but relying instead on the submission of exhibits. The jury then deliberates and delivers an advisory verdict, which may help trigger informal settlement. Summary jury trial was much discussed in the 1980s, when federal district court judge Thomas Lambros first promoted its use. Perhaps because it is relatively cumbersome and does not offer all the potential benefits of mediation or ENE, it has not been widely used.

Mini-Trial.   Mini-trial is private process that is in some respects analogous to summary jury trial. Counsel for the parties present shortened versions of their cases to party representatives who have settlement authority. The hearing is informal, with few or no witnesses and with relaxed procedures, and is typically presided over by a neutral. After the hearing, the client representatives meet, with or without the neutral presider, to discuss the possibility of a negotiated settlement.

Special Masters.   One of the most potentially promising evocations of the spirit of Professor Sander's vision for dynamic programs to tailor dispute resolution processes to specific disputes are court programs in which magistrates or special masters are given wide discretion as process architects, case managers, and settlement facilitators,[10] complementing the role of judges. There have been growing calls for more expansive reliance on special masters where the additional cost to the parties occasioned by their appointment would be more than counterbalanced by savings in procedural efficiency and economy. Although special masters have traditionally been appointed on an ad hoc basis in exceptional cases by courts under Federal Rule of Civil Procedure 53 and corresponding state rules, in January 2019 the American Bar Association House of Delegates adopted the ABA Guidelines for the Appointment and Use of Special Masters in Federal and State Civil Litigation. It also proposed that federal Bankruptcy Rule 9031 be amended to permit courts responsible for cases under the Bankruptcy Code to use special masters as in other federal cases. Among other things, the Guidelines provide:

> (1) Courts and parties should consider using a special master "not only after special issues have developed, but at the outset of litigation."
>
> (2) Courts considering the appointment of a special master should weigh potential benefits such reduced litigant costs against the cost of a special master's services.
>
> (3) Special masters can undertake many management, adjudicative, facilitative, advisory, information gathering, or liaison functions, including:
>
> - discovery oversight and management,
> - coordination of cases in multiple jurisdictions;
> - facilitating resolution of disputes;
> - pretrial case management;
> - providing technical expertise;
> - conducting or reviewing auditing or accounting;
> - conducting privilege reviews and other activities in order to buffer courts;
> - conducting trials or mini-trials upon the consent of the parties;
> - settlement administration;
> - claims administration; and
> - receivership and real property inspection.

QUESTIONS

1. *Use and Timing of Court-Connected Mediation.* As noted above, mediation is the most frequently employed element in court-connected ADR, but there may be considerable variance in the timing of mediation during litigation. Depending on the circumstances (including party

preferences and court practices), it might occur at any of the following points: (a) soon after the filing of a complaint; (b) prior to or after a motion; (c) during or at the end of discovery; (d) after trial and before a court decision. What circumstances might enhance the possibility of a successful mediation at an early stage of litigation? What factors might represent obstacles to early settlement?

2. *Mini-Trials.* Mini-trials have been criticized on the ground that they encourage parties to entrench their positions by developing a "best case" presentation, and usually require the investment of much greater resources than negotiation or mediation. The process also requires litigators to "show their cards," in contrast to mediation where a lawyer can release information as deemed appropriate under the circumstances. However, it appears that they are still employed on occasion. When might a mini-trial format be most likely to be deemed appropriate?

3. *Expanded Use of Special Masters.* Advocates for using special masters more regularly to assist in managing pretrial process and promoting settlement argue that amendments to court procedures are not enough to effectively promote appropriate efficiency and economy in litigation, and that there is need for active oversight and supervision by an independent third party. Do you agree?[11]

4. *Expedited Jury Trials.* Some state and federal courts, by rule or pursuant to statute, have encouraged the use of short (usually no more than one day) trials in which the parties can stipulate to certain modifications of trial procedure. In California, these include reduced juries, limits on monetary outcomes, applicable rules of evidence, use of evidentiary summaries, and most anything else that can be agreed upon, provided the parties waive the right to appeal and certain post-trial motions. Though some elements of an expedited jury trial are mandatory, the parties can negotiate and modify most of the procedures to make them fit their needs and how much they want to spend to get a binding decision. Most importantly, they are encouraged, but not required, to reach a "high/low agreement" that cannot be disclosed to the jury but that assures the plaintiff a minimum recovery and the defendant a payment ceiling, regardless of the judgment. These trial stipulations can be negotiated at the end of a mediation in which a settlement was not reached. This way even a "failed" mediation can result in a more economic trial.[12]

5. *A Creative Alternative?* One federal judge, frustrated by certain parties who regularly enlisted the court's time and resources in pretrial disputes in a particular case, ordered "a new form of alternative dispute resolution." The judge instructed the parties and counsel to meet at a certain place and time and engage in one game of "rock, paper, scissors." The court ruled that the winner of this engagement would be entitled to select the deposition location! *Avista Mgmt., Inc. v. Wausau Underwriters Ins. Co.,* Case No. 6:05-cv-1430-Orl-31JGG (M.D. Fla. June 6, 2006). Perhaps this example of protracted (and expensive) pretrial skirmishes illustrates why courts have increasingly turned to court-annexed ADR to move civil suits along more expeditiously.

C. CONTRACT-BASED DISPUTE RESOLUTION

1. A Spectrum of Process Options

Processes for managing conflict and resolving disputes in the course of
court proceedings may engage private parties as users and service providers. On
the other hand, private dispute resolution very often happens pursuant to private
agreements made before or after disputes arise. Provisions for conflict resolution
may be found in all kinds of contracts, and vary considerably in format. Contract-
based dispute resolution gives parties the opportunity to tailor approaches to their
own particular circumstances, needs, and priorities.[13]

Mediation and Arbitration.   Disputants in the private sector use a wide variety of
dispute resolution processes. Studies of dispute resolution practices and perspectives among Fortune 1,000 corporations offered important insights into private sector trends.[14] The responses from the most recent survey confirmed that corporate
experience with mediation was virtually universal, with 98 percent of respondents
indicating that their company had used mediation at least once in the prior three
years. A large majority of companies, 83 percent, reported at least one recent experience with arbitration, although the overall frequency of use of arbitration had
actually declined in recent years for most categories of disputes in the corporate
experience.

Early Case Assessment, Early Neutral Evaluation, Fact-Finding, and Mini-Trial.   Two-
thirds of responding Fortune 1,000 companies had used some form of early case
assessment, or "ECA," which comprises a range of approaches, including early neutral evaluation, to analyze disputes systematically and formulate strategies to limit
their cost and disruptive impact. Many employed fact-finding, a process in which
parties present or submit one or more factual aspects of a dispute to a neutral third
party who issues a report setting forth findings, either as a free-standing settlement
technique or in support of mediation or other processes.

Dispute Resolution Involving Both Mediation and Arbitration.   Half of corporate
respondents claimed recent experience with "mediation-arbitration," a term that,
although ambiguous, is most likely to mean any situation in which the parties use
mediation alongside (that is, prior to, during, or after) the arbitration process, and
(normally) with separate neutrals acting as mediator and arbitrator. It is possible
that at least some of these experiences involved using mediation and arbitration
pursuant to a "stepped" or "tiered" dispute resolution agreement in which disputes
are submitted to mediation, and, if not resolved, go to arbitration. Such provisions
are discussed below.

International Dispute Resolution.   Although the Fortune 1,000 survey includes
many companies doing business in different parts of the world, it is important
to understand that practices and perspectives on dispute resolution vary greatly
among countries. Meanwhile, mediation appears to be gradually gaining acceptance as a tool for international resolution of commercial disputes. Recently, proponents of mediation secured passage of the Singapore Convention, intended to
provide a mechanism for international recognition and enforcement of mediated

agreements—an analog to the role played by the New York Convention in the realm of binding arbitration.[15] Mediation provisions now appear in many international contracts, sometimes as a part of multi-step or multi-tier dispute resolution provisions along with arbitration, and in some investment treaties. When respondents to an online survey associated with a series of conferences at more than 30 sites around the world were asked to identify what makes up the effective dispute resolution processes, the most popular answer was "combining adjudicative and non-adjudicative processes (e.g. arbitration/litigation with mediation/conciliation)."[16]

2. Stepped or Tiered Dispute Resolution

In the United States, prototypes of tiered dispute resolution developed in labor, construction, and mercantile settings. More than three decades ago, provisions for tiered (stepped) dispute resolution with mediation as a preliminary stage began to appear in standard form construction contracts. Today, multi-tier dispute resolution processes comprising multiple separate approaches to resolving relational conflict in sequence (such as, for example, negotiation, mediation, and arbitration) are frequently found in various kinds of commercial contracts as well as employment contracts.[17]

Some years ago, a group of experienced commercial advocates and arbitrators convened by CPR began a book of guidelines on binding arbitration of business disputes by advising parties that "[m]ost disputes are best resolved privately and by agreement" and that principals should be engaged in efforts to informally negotiate disputes, first directly and then, if necessary, with the help of a mediator or evaluator. Only after these steps should the parties resort to arbitration. Even then, however, "the door to settlement should remain open; arbitrators should encourage the parties to discuss settlement and, if appropriate, to employ a mediator."[18]

Perceived Benefits of Stepped Processes. The CPR Guidelines envision a multi-step "funneling" mechanism for dispute resolution that accommodates the varied priorities of businesses. Business goals for dispute resolution might include a degree of control over the resolution, an efficient and economical path to resolution, privacy and confidentiality, and/or a result that is perceived as fair or advantageous, all of which are often effectively realized through direct negotiations. By avoiding the rancor and "spiraling adversarialism" that is sometimes a byproduct of adjudication, negotiating an early settlement may produce more satisfactory results while enabling parties to maintain or restore relationships. A negotiated settlement may permit parties to promote their business interests through integrative terms and "in-kind" trade-offs that could not be obtained through litigation or arbitration. Early settlement gives parties the opportunity to air their differences and explore solutions in private, avoiding the publicity and visibility that may accompany public litigation (or in some cases, arbitration). Finally, research has shown that negotiated settlements are likely to be more sustainable and complied with voluntarily than decisions by third-party arbitrators or judges.

If unaided efforts to negotiate are unsuccessful, a mediator at the bargaining table may provide important value as referee, an agent of reality, and a creative advisor. Mediators are often especially attuned to the opportunities in relational disputes to employ interest-based cooperative approaches, "expanding the pie" through trade-offs and non-monetary integrative terms, and perhaps even repairing or improving a relationship. In addition to helping resolve commercial disputes earlier and/or more effectively, they may assist parties in developing a customized process for resolving their disputes, predict the potential consequences if the issues in dispute are adjudicated in court or in arbitration, and provide other value. In response to an informal survey, a D.C.-area mediator who had conducted hundreds of commercial mediations indicated that, in his experience, pre-adjudication mediation was a highly efficient and effective way of settling disputes. Where cases did not settle outright, mediation helped to "sharpen the issues" for resolution.

From the early days of the modern era of dispute resolution, it was suggested that contractual provisions for negotiation or mediation of disputes, like court directives to mediate, were necessary to obviate the need for a party to propose negotiation or mediation — actions that might be viewed as reflecting doubts about the strength of the party's own case.

Should mediation also end in impasse and the parties move on to arbitration, procedures are more rigorously formal, adversarial, lawyer-driven, and extended in duration; they may or may not be confidential. Control over the outcome is then given over to the arbitrators — preferably experts — whose decision is likely to be final. And whatever one may say about the ability of arbitrators to fashion remedies appropriate to the circumstances, the practical reality is that commercial arbitrators tend to adhere to the safe ground of recognized judicial remedies rather than exercise creativity at the risk of extended judicial review and possible vacatur. Therefore, while binding arbitration may be perceived as preferable to litigation for business parties, the latter's interests are usually best served by arriving at a negotiated settlement. See Chapter 4.

Besides creating early opportunities for reflection and discussion that might act as a "safety valve" for companies facing what could become a protracted legal fight, pre-dispute procedures give parties the opportunity to cooperatively develop templates tailored to their own specific circumstances and priorities.

Concerns About Pre-Dispute Provisions for Stepped Dispute Resolution.   However, opinion among lawyers and other dispute resolution professionals is far from unanimous regarding contractual stepped dispute resolution provisions. Experienced commercial lawyers and dispute resolution professionals embrace sharply conflicting perspectives regarding the utility of such arrangements.

Critiques of contractual commitments to negotiate or mediate disputes in advance of arbitration or litigation often begin with the observation that, given the obvious benefits of negotiated settlement in business disputes and the pervasive use of mediation, parties and counsel will employ these processes anyway at the appropriate time, in the appropriate circumstances, without the need for pre-dispute contractual mandates.

Second, it is argued, negotiation and mediation are most likely to be effective if parties participate willingly. If parties are only at the settlement table to comply with contractual requirements, such preliminaries may do nothing more than delay the start of adjudication. Moreover, contractual arrangements for stepped negotiations may be too cumbersome and produce unintended consequences. For example, although stepped processes calling for negotiations moving up successive rungs of the corporate ladder are sometimes employed in construction claims resolution procedures, some longtime mediators complain that in some cases such procedures may prevent timely solutions and increase costs, or even cause project managers to feel disempowered.

Third, critics of contractual dispute resolution provisions sometimes contend that the decision to come to the bargaining table or to employ a mediator, and the timing of such decisions, hinge on specific circumstances that may not become apparent until disputes arise or thereafter. Although most commercial disputes are likely to be settled through negotiation at some point, some argue that negotiation and mediation may not be fruitful in advance of adjudication. The optimal moment for informal settlement, some argue, tends to occur at some point during the adjudicative process after they have garnered sufficient information about the case and their chances in adjudication.

Yet another set of concerns respecting pre-dispute agreements to negotiate or mediate involves issues of enforcement. Parties who deliberately employ such provisions may be focused primarily on the utility of platforms for informal bargaining and not on what happens if one or both parties do not follow the prescribed steps. In the latter case, however, the provisions themselves may become the nub of controversy and fodder for judicial intervention, with potential delay or disruption of the dispute resolution process.

Developing Effective Stepped Dispute Resolution Provisions.   Although tiered or stepped dispute resolution provisions are frequently employed in commercial contracts, such options are often embraced without much forethought regarding their operation and enforcement. Effective choice making is rendered more difficult by uncertainties associated with judicial handling of agreements to negotiate or mediate as well as the inherent complexities of multi-step arrangements.[19]

Conscientious drafters will want to focus on the basic functionality of the multi-tier dispute resolution system — that is, to tailor a process that effectively serves the goals and intent of the parties. They should ask key questions, including, "Who should be at the settlement table, and for how long?" "Might there be multiple levels of negotiation?" "Should there be mediation or other third-party intervention at some point?" "What triggers the move from one step to another?" "If we speak of 'good faith' participation, what do we mean?"

However the tiered process is configured, it should offer users a clear and cohesive administrative platform for dispute resolution. The creative urge to develop customized multi-step dispute resolution processes must be tempered with care, since one-off provisions sometimes lead to collateral conflict. Terminology should be used consistently at all stages, and the beginning and end of each stage or steps should be clearly defined. The problem with lack of crystal clarity is exemplified by *Fluor Enterprises Inc. v. Solutia Inc.*,[20] in which questions regarding the "commencement" of mediation in a contractual provision for tiered dispute resolution resulted in competing motions for summary judgment and judicial parsing of the agreement and incorporated terms. Parties should also ensure that they clearly comply with their planned process, such as formally requesting mediation,[21] or take other necessary steps to implement the plan.

Models for multi-tier dispute resolution clauses in commercial contracts may be found in CPR's detailed Master Guide, guidelines published by leading institutional providers of commercial dispute resolution services, and other sources for practitioners.

NOTES AND QUESTIONS

6. *Should Stepped Dispute Resolution Provisions Provide a "Nudge" or a Mandate?* Assuming parties want contractual provisions for negotiation and/or for mediation, should participation be a requirement that is enforceable by a court? If so, should negotiation or mediation be a condition precedent to further steps such as arbitration or litigation? Again, opinions vary. Parties may include contractual provisions for negotiation or mediation without much concern for their legal enforceability. After all, in many cases parties pursue negotiation and/or mediation (with or without contractual requirements) and reach a settlement without resorting to adjudication or, alternatively, move to the final (adjudication) stage without bickering over procedures. Nevertheless, parties are advised to consider enforcement issues if they are concerned that they may require judicial assistance in compelling an involved party to come to the negotiating table. At the same time, they should be aware that provisions to negotiate or mediate disputes prior to adjudication are a double-edged sword, as a claimant's failure to formally comply with such provisions may be used by the defendant to postpone or even derail adjudication.[22]

7. *Mediators and Process Issues; Guided Choice.* Although discussions of the roles of mediators often focus on the resolution of substantive disputes, many experienced mediators bring their skills to bear on process management—not just in regard to the mediation process, but also with respect to alternative process options that may be necessary or appropriate steps in the final resolution of disputes.[23] In this way, mediators sometimes help "set the stage" for adjudication of a dispute, by working with parties to tailor procedures for arbitration or litigation.

This may take a variety of forms. Where mediation fails to resolve some or all of the issues in dispute, for example, a mediator is sometimes able to facilitate an agreement on appropriate arbitration procedures or assist the parties in selecting the arbitrators. In other situations, parties retain mediators for the sole purpose of facilitating the tailoring of an appropriate dispute resolution process. An example of the latter is "Guided Choice":

> Guided Choice is a mediation process in which a mediator is appointed to initially focus on process issues to help the parties identify and address proactively potential impediments to settlement. Mediation confidentiality is a powerful tool to help the parties safely explore ways of setting up a cheaper, faster and better process to explore and address those impediments. Although this person works essentially as a mediator, in Guided Choice the

> mediator does not focus initially on settling the case. Instead, the mediator works with the parties to first facilitate a discussion on procedural and potential impasse issues, and help them analyze the causes of the dispute and determine their information needs for settlement.[24]
>
> 8. *Mediation During Arbitration.* As discussed earlier, opportunities for negotiation or mediation are by no means limited to a period of weeks or months before adjudication. Consideration might be given to whether, instead of (or in addition to) being a preliminary step to adjudication, mediation might be employed concurrently with arbitration.[25] Mediation frequently occurs after the filing of an arbitration demand, at some point during the pre-hearing process, or even during hearings. Sometimes there will be multiple efforts to mediate during the course of resolving a dispute, perhaps with different mediators. See Chapter 4.J, "Arbitration and Settlement."
>
> 9. *"Mediator-in-Reserve."* JAMS has promoted the concept of a "Mediator-in-Reserve." (*See* http://www.jamsadr.com/mediator-in-reserve-policy/.) Under the procedure, the parties pre-select a mediator at the beginning of an arbitration. The mediator is only used, however, if at some point during or at the conclusion of arbitration both parties decide to try settling the matter through mediation. Appointing a mediator ahead of time enables them to move quickly and efficiently if they decide to mediate.

COMMENT: REAL-TIME RELATIONAL CONFLICT MANAGEMENT

"Real-time" strategies for relationships involve active intervention to address issues or resolve conflict in its early stages. The "intervener" is a person—often, but not always, independent of those in the relationship—with appropriate authority and skills to bring things to a successful and early resolution. The intervener's authority derives from his or her personal reputation or notability, position, experience in a profession or field, or proven skills as a facilitator or problem solver.[26]

Successful real-time approaches may accomplish a variety of objectives, including addressing specific issues or concerns raised by a party, avoiding conflict, improving communications, or resolving disputes quickly and cost-effectively. They may also avoid lengthy adjudication and related costs. Real-time intervention thus helps to support or reinforce contractual relationships, or "relational systems" such as trade and professional associations. One way or another, such strategies are designed to work in harmony with the pace and rhythm of the relationship, and to meet the ongoing needs of parties for an early decision, guidance, or facilitation. In this way, real-time approaches differ dramatically from litigation, "mainstream" binding arbitration, or even some lawyer-driven mediation processes that ignore relational concerns and work against relationships.

Real-Time Conflict Management in the Workplace.   In the United States, real-time approaches are most fully developed in the non-unionized employment arena. A variety of factors including a more mobile and educated workforce, increasing emphasis on individual rights and greater expectations for fairness and happiness, corporate emphasis on cost control, improved employee relations, organizational health, and equal opportunity imperatives played a part in the evolution of a spectrum of internal and external "appropriate dispute resolution" approaches. A number of companies have developed multi-pronged, integrated conflict management systems, sometimes with input from the employee stakeholders. Although they vary considerably in detail, these systems typically include both "problem-solving" approaches that focus on the interests of disputants as well as "justice" options that address rights and obligations. The former afford employees avenues outside the formal grievance process in which problems and concerns may be addressed constructively. While it may be appropriate for an aggrieved employee or manager to resort to multiple processes *seriatum*, some systems provide flexibility in the choice of processes and the order in which they are used. The more sophisticated programs tend to offer "access points" for people of varied ethnicity and gender. An organizational ombudsperson may be employed to serve in a neutral capacity outside the usual management structures to address any workplace concern. Conflict management is sometimes centered not in the department of human resources and the legal department, but "embedded" in the corporate culture through line managers who understand it is their job to avoid unnecessary problems through effective communication and active listening. Companies employing integrated programs tend to report that the great majority of workplace issues and disputes are resolved by informal means; relatively few matters end up being adjudicated.

Real-Time Conflict Management in Health Care.   Kaiser Permanente's Health-Care Ombudsman/Mediator (HCOM) program is a flexible and informal approach aimed at early, straightforward, and informal resolution of conflicts and challenging circumstances in the health care setting. Thousands of issues have been managed at point-of-care by a cadre of trained HCOM facilitators, producing early settlements, reduced claims and, apparently, greater levels of satisfaction for patients and medical care providers. Although the HCOM program has proven very successful at Kaiser, it remains exceptional among health care organizations. To the extent that HCOM programs require greater transparency, more rigorous monitoring, open reporting, and a commitment to systems improvement, they may be incompatible with the culture of defensiveness and the litigation mindset prevailing in many companies. The program has been described as a cultural shift from "deny and defend" to a more compassionate and honest response when unexpected adverse outcomes occur, including making apologies for mistakes by caregivers. This allows for open communication between patients and providers, acknowledgment of what happened, and enhancement of patient safety through an organizational commitment to quality improvements in health care delivery. As with any provider-sponsored system, it is reasonable to inquire whether the rights and interests of patients (including impartial and independent intervention, appropriate confidentiality, and informed consent) are and will be effectively served. In concept, however, the HCOM program seems to offer a desirable template for engendering integrative solutions to problems in the patient/provider relationship.

Real-Time Conflict Management on Construction Projects.   Construction projects have also proven fertile ground for the use of real-time approaches to minimizing and managing relational conflict. Historically, jobsite conflict management involved early decision making by project architects and/or engineers. Given the potential conflicts of interest on the part of owner-employed design profession-als, however, new forms of expert evaluation involving independent third parties were developed—the most prominent being dispute review boards (DRBs). DRBs evolved as a short, sharp method for independent expert evaluation of disputes on infrastructure projects and large engineered jobs.[27] The concept involved the establishment of a standing panel of construction and engineering experts to peri-odically convene on site to review and render summary nonbinding opinions on disputes regarding subsurface conditions and other issues. The idea was that the standing and expertise of the decision makers would stimulate a quick settlement of the dispute, avoid prolonged conflict, and obviate the need for traditional bind-ing arbitration or litigation. DRBs achieved an extraordinary level of success, both in terms of the number of claims apparently settled after a DRB hearing and the prophylactic effect on disputes of the very presence in place of a DRB. Although there is little quantitative evidence actually linking DRBs to lower project costs and fewer delays and disruptions,[28] industry perceptions of the DRBs tend to be posi-tive; a number of public contracting authorities are convinced of their value and committed to their use.[29] DRBs were even utilized on the nation's largest construc-tion project, the Boston Central Artery/Tunnel Project, for which standing panels were established for all contracts over $20 million.[30] The "Big Dig" offers a caution-ary tale, however: Due to the sheer volume and complexity of disputes and claims, disputes over entitlement were not concluded in "real time" but left to be resolved at the end of each contract; ultimately, the backlog of claims had to be resolved through a "retrofitted" program of negotiation and mediation.[31]

The DRB's British analog was "statutory adjudication."[32] The procedure, which was established as a required method for resolving various project payment dis-putes by the Housing Grants, Construction and Regeneration Act 1996,[33] consisted of a very short review and decision-making process by a private neutral. Given the temporal limitations, adjudication was necessarily "rough" justice; one English QC suggested that the result might be "little more than a gut reaction" to the dispute.[34] Under the law, the adjudicator's determination was only preliminarily binding, and the dispute could later be taken to binding arbitration or litigation. It appears that the great majority of adjudication decisions are accepted by the losing parties with-out further procedures.[35]

Today, DRBs or Dispute Adjudication Boards (DABs) (which render decisions that are binding unless and until they are reversed by arbitration or litigation) are being used on major projects around the globe. International financial institutions are now mandating the use of the process on large infrastructure projects,[36] and they are provided for in leading standard international construction contracts.[37]

Less well known is the work of "standing mediators," who routinely facilitate discussion and the resolution of issues as they develop on a project. By resolving conflicts before parties "lawyer up" and move into litigation mode, real-time medi-ation can maximize the efficiency and cost-effectiveness of dispute resolution.[38] Although this form of mediation appears not to have seen extensive use, the appointment of a standing dispute resolution professional to mediate issues as they arise during the course of a construction project can be of value in keeping the job on track and helping to limit the number of claims that must be subjected to more formal and expensive dispute resolution procedures.[39]

Occasionally, owners of construction projects have opted for sophisticated custom-designed systems for managing conflict on the job.[40] A model for effective real-time conflict management on construction projects was pioneered by Intel Corporation. Responding to concerns about the duration, cost, and unpredictability of litigation and the limitations of lawyer-driven mediation, Intel augmented the company's traditional stepped dispute resolution system for construction disputes with a custom program for dispute prevention.[41] At the heart of Intel's program is a third-party neutral who is engaged by the owner and general contractor at the beginning of a construction project. Having extensive professional construction expertise and conflict resolution training or experience, as well as communication soft skills, the neutral earns the trust of key members of the construction team. During monthly visits to the jobsite, the neutral assesses job progress and risks, and meets with a senior risk management team appointed by the owner and contractor to survey and evaluate project risks. The team consults with the neutral on appropriate options for addressing developing concerns, including coaching or advisory efforts aimed at dispute prevention as well as more formal dispute resolution roles. At the time of this writing, Intel's conflict management program had been successful in avoiding formal legal disputes on the projects it has been employed on, representing more than $5 billion in construction.

PROBLEM 1

Your client, Walt E. Wally Enterprises, is planning a $2-billion expansion of its WallyWonderWorld in Southern California. The project will include a major resort and "Fun-Sation Station" complex and a state-of-the-art transportation infrastructure comprising more than 200 miles of "Wallyways" both above and below the ground. The client is willing to devote resources to developing a mechanism for proactive management of conflict through early engagement and intervention by one or more third-party facilitators or decision makers, and seeks your guidance. Questions that might be addressed include the following:

1. Should we discuss employment of a multi-step dispute resolution provision in the contract? What "steps" should be included?
2. Would some form of real-time dispute resolution be appropriate?

D. HYBRID PROCESSES: SINGLE NEUTRAL MED-ARB, ARB-MED, AND ARB-MED-ARB

The material in this section is drawn in large part from Stipanowich, Thomas J. (2021), *Arbitration, Mediation and Mixed Modes: Seeking Workable Solutions and Common Ground on Med-Arb, Arb-Med and Settlement-Oriented Activities by Arbitrators*, 26 Harv. Neg. L. Rev. 265 (2021).

PROBLEM 2

You are a sole arbitrator appointed jointly by the parties engaged in a long-term joint venture who, two years into the relationship, found themselves in a dispute over distribution of profits from the joint venture as well as performance-related issues. You worked with the parties to set up an expedited process for arbitration, and set aside ten consecutive days for hearings. In the middle of hearings, the nation was caught in the grip of a pandemic, and the government issued an order directing everyone to shelter in place. Arbitration hearings were put off for six months. Now, counsel for the parties jointly approach you and tell you that the parties were both in financial difficulty as a result of the pandemic. They are now very hopeful that they can pursue a negotiated settlement and ask if you would be willing to help out by "putting on your mediator's hat." They explain that they both believe this is the best approach, since it would not be practical to bring another mediator up to speed given the costs, and they have faith in your ability and fairness.

1. How will you respond to their request? Is this an invitation you are willing to consider? What factors might affect your willingness to switch roles here?
2. Assuming you are willing to consider the invitation, how would you proceed? What concerns might there be about switching neutral roles, and how might they be effectively addressed here?

1. Neutrals in Dual Roles

Imagine you are the sole arbitrator in a commercial dispute and have an experience like the scenario in Problem 2. Would you agree to "switch hats," and, if so, under what conditions? That problem, based on a real-life scenario, illustrates the questions that are pondered by arbitrators and mediators who are asked to "switch hats" during the course of resolving a dispute.

How dispute resolution professionals, commercial advocates and counsel, and business parties respond to these questions varies depending on circumstances, personal preferences, culture, and legal tradition. While in China and some other countries mixed roles are broadly accepted, some other countries have statutes regulating or even prohibiting single-neutral "med-arb." In the United States, lawyers, arbitrators, and mediators tend to be conventionally skeptical about a neutral changing roles during the course of resolving disputes, for reasons discussed below. There are, nevertheless, situations in which experienced parties choose to have one person take on both roles. Some experienced neutrals have made dual-role approaches part of their "brand."

2. Dual-Role Formats

In the current environment of commercial dispute resolution, many professional arbitrators have also developed skills and experience as mediators; similarly, commercial advocates have garnered experience with mediation as well as arbitration. Hence, it should not be surprising that a significant percentage of practicing neutrals have had experiences playing dual roles in the course of resolving disputes. These arrangements generally fall within one of the following categories: med-arb, arb-med, and arb-med-arb.

As used here, "med-arb" refers to a consensual dispute resolution process in which a neutral first attempts to mediate the dispute and, if mediation is unsuccessful in fully resolving the dispute, switches to the role of arbitrator in order to render a binding decision (award), fully and finally addressing the issues in dispute. Resort to med-arb may be stimulated by a variety of factors, including changed or special circumstances or the desire to promote efficiency and economy. On the other hand, the notion of a neutral arbitrating after having mediated raises a variety of concerns in many quarters, most of which are triggered by a neutral's ex parte communications with parties (caucuses) during the mediation phase. See "Concerns About Mixed Roles" below.

"Arb-med" refers to a consensual dispute resolution process in which an appointed arbitrator takes on the role of mediator of substantive disputes at some point during the arbitration process.[42] This kind of transition does not ordinarily raise many of the concerns associated with med-arb. Moreover, should mediation resolve the dispute, it may be possible to convert the settlement agreement into a consent arbitration award. If, on the other hand, mediation is unsuccessful in fully resolving the dispute, there will be an issue regarding next steps. If the parties agree that the arbitrator-turned-mediator will revert to the role of arbitrator in order to render a binding decision ("arb-med-arb"), the concerns associated with med-arb may come into play.

3. Concerns About Mixed Roles

Many lawyers and dispute resolution professionals eschew process options involving mixed roles for neutrals. Most of the key concerns associated with dual roles are centered on med-arb, and specifically on mediators who engage in private ex parte caucuses with individual parties and then switch to the role of arbitrator.[43]

Incompatibility of Mediative and Arbitral Roles. The mediative and arbitral roles are often seen as diametrically opposed. Conventionally, the arbitrator's interaction with the parties is largely, or wholly, confined to adversary hearings in which parties present evidence and contest opposing evidence before the arbitrator, who is charged with adjudicating the dispute; ex parte communications between arbitrators and parties are generally strictly limited. Mediation, on the other hand, may entail extensive ex parte communications between the mediator and individual parties in the form of separate, private caucuses involving confidential communications—all with the goal of helping the mediator facilitate a consensual resolution of the dispute. Moreover, experience and competence as a mediator does not automatically qualify an individual to perform the role of arbitrator. Some excellent mediators may not have the temperament, managerial skills, or procedural knowledge to be effective arbitrators; similarly, many arbitrators lack the ability to be effective mediators. There are also issues of personal preference or philosophy; many mediators avoid arbitrating due to lack of interest, concerns about its impact on their mediation practice, or discomfort with an adjudicative role. Mixed roles present unique challenges even for neutrals experienced in both arbitration and mediation.

Concerns About Party Autonomy.   Some fear that the "big stick" wielded by a mediator who is expected to arbitrate a dispute if mediation fails to achieve settlement will undermine party self-determination and prevent a negotiated settlement from truly representing the will of the parties. This fear is particularly acute concerning situations in which the neutral "telegraphs" a personal perspective on the issues. Awareness of such dynamics, however, may cause neutrals to avoid or tread very lightly with respect to evaluation in the course of settlement discussions. Similar concerns may arise if an agreement by disputing parties to have their neutral switch roles appears to be driven by the neutral.

Less Candid Communications; Increased Incentive to "Spin" the Mediator.   Parties who know a mediator reserves the arbitral role should mediation fail may be less forthcoming in their discussions with the mediator, thereby compromising the ability of the mediator to serve the parties effectively. Moreover, parties and counsel may feel incentivized to manipulate the mediator in ways favorable toward their positions, with both sides putting on a performance of sorts to shape the neutral's view in an attempt to increase their chances of prevailing when he or she becomes the arbitrator—the ultimate decision maker.

Due Process Concerns.   Mediation frequently involves extensive confidential ex parte communications between the mediator and individual parties. If mediation is unsuccessful, there is always the possibility that the mediator-turned-arbitrator's view of the issues has been affected by information shared in ex parte discussions. This may include information that is not directly relevant to the issues contested in arbitration and has never been tested by cross-examination or rebuttal in the arbitration hearing—but which nevertheless colors a neutral's view of the parties or their positions on the issues in conflict. How, some might ask, can a mediator-turned-arbitrator purge his mind of acts and positions learned in confidence, and what is to prevent the neutral from relying on information vouchsafed confidentially in mediation in making an award? And how, if at all, might a party not privy to the confidential communication effectively respond and counteract its potential impact?

Expectations Raised by Mediator Communications, Evaluation.   Although critiques of med-arb nearly always focus on what parties share with mediators in private caucuses, little emphasis has been placed on concerns relating to what mediators communicate to the parties—or how what mediators say and do is perceived by the parties. Communications between mediators and parties tend to be exceptionally free-flowing, and may include vague or ambiguous statements. What a mediator thinks (s)he said and what a party thinks they heard may be very different. These dynamics are of particular concern in regard to case evaluations. A mediator's guarded evaluation of elements of a case or prediction of what might happen in arbitration could be interpreted or remembered as setting a floor of expectations for an award they might make at the conclusion of arbitration hearings. In other words, communications made by the mediator during mediation, including case evaluations or predictions offered during caucus, may raise one or both parties' specific expectations regarding a future award by the mediator-turned-arbitrator, thus creating the potential for anger and frustration if the anticipated result does not occur.

Potential Defenses to Arbitration Award.   The perceived fundamental dichotomy between mediation and arbitration—their diametrically opposite orientations toward ex parte discussions—may give rise to procedural grounds for motions to disqualify an arbitrator or overturn arbitration awards. Parties who want a neutral to serve in mixed roles must be very clear about the resolution of the foregoing issues and should address pertinent waiver issues (such as parties' waiver of the right to challenge any resulting arbitration award on grounds of ex parte contact). These issues are of greatest concern in the international sphere, since some countries place limits on med-arb.

4.   Why Switch Hats?

Recent studies indicate that today many neutrals do "switch hats" from time to time, and some have established such services as a valuable component of their toolbox and a part of their professional brand. In 2001, a commission sponsored by the New York–based CPR Institute for Dispute Resolution first propounded guidance for business parties considering med-arb and arb-med.[44] Although the commission recognized that mixed-role processes might prove beneficial in some cases, the emphasis was on the various risks and how they might be addressed. Twenty years later, the experience of neutrals who have since developed a specialization in mixed roles reinforces the notion that such roles can be embraced, if done selectively and carefully.[45] Several rationales are offered in support of this view:

The Dangers of Mixed Roles Are Overstated.   Some neutrals who have had a number of experiences with dual roles believe that the concerns about situations where mediators are exposed to problematic confidential information in caucus are overblown, in part because relatively few cases fail to settle in mediation and end up in arbitration. Neutral Martin Weisman states:

> Of approximately twelve. . . [med-arb] cases in which I have served as the neutral in the past few years, only two have gone to the arbitration stage. All these cases were complex commercial disputes involving a variety of issues. In the two matters that did go to arbitration, the number of issues arbitrated was significantly reduced as a result of agreements obtained during the mediation stage.[46]

A Switch of Hats May Be the Appropriate Response to Special Circumstances.   There may be strong reasons for the parties to have a neutral "switch hats," including changed circumstances. As some neutrals' experiences reveal, employing separate individuals to mediate and arbitrate a dispute may not always be practical or preferable. As New York neutral Richard Silberberg puts it:

> In each instance [where I participated in arb-med], the parties had one or more compelling reasons, some of a highly personal nature, why they

wanted me to switch hats and mediate. . . . In each instance, the designation of a different neutral to mediate the dispute would not have accommodated or been responsive to the stated concerns that motivated the parties to ask me to switch hats.[47]

Mixed Roles May Enhance Creativity and Effective Problem Solving.   One neutral who regularly engages in dual roles explains:

> I have embraced [mixed roles] because I view myself, above all else, as a "problem solver," rather than just an arbitrator and a mediator, and because I think being an effective problem solver requires exercising some creativity and involves taking some risk. I strongly believe that mixed mode dispute resolution is the wave of the future of our field.[48]

Mixed Roles May Be Effective Ways of Serving Key Interests.   Prioritizing negotiated or mediated settlement discussions may afford parties the opportunity to craft integrative solutions that better achieve business priorities. As many skilled mediators know, even if facilitated discussions do not lead directly to resolution of substantive disputes, the mediation process may permit the structuring of customized approaches that lead to a final resolution, including refined formats for binding arbitration. The prospect of a quicker and more efficient process combined with the opportunity to structure business solutions or customized processes for final resolution augurs well for the maintenance or improvement of underlying relationships.

Having a single neutral serve in both roles (or having an arbitrator engage in settlement discussions) permits the parties to avoid having to educate two separate neutrals, with attendant savings of time and cost.[49] There may be circumstances, for example, where both parties regard the need for a final resolution as paramount. In such situations, having their mediator transition to an arbitral role, or vice versa, may be viewed as the simplest and best way of meeting their mutual needs. This is most likely to be true in circumstances in which an arbitrator has heard much of the evidence and is well acquainted with the issues in dispute, and may be able to shift to a mediator role immediately, with none of the delays and costs associated with engaging another mediator. The rationale for having an arbitrator engage with the parties in settlement discussions was eloquently put forward by David Rivkin in the course of promoting a "Town Elder" model for international arbitration[50] — a vision that hearkens back to the "original conception of arbitration. . . two business people taking their dispute to a wise business person who they both trusted. . . and then asking the arbitrator to provide them with the best solution to their dispute." The latter would include circumstances in which "each side has a problem proving an important part of its case; when there is a clear middle ground that is beneficial to both sides; or when a written award may cause difficulty for both sides, not matter who wins."

Med-arb (or arb-med-arb) also offers parties the prospect of a final resolution if mediation fails to achieve informal settlement. Moreover, it is sometimes said that if the parties are aware that their mediator will render a final and binding decision in the absence of a settlement, they may feel additional pressure to settle their dispute in mediation. In other words, the mediator's ultimate arbitral authority functions as a "big stick" to settle the case, which starkly emphasizes the opportunity to reach a mutually acceptable resolution and avoid the risks of a third-party decision. Indeed, at least one study indicates that med-arb with a single neutral may promote more problem solving, reduce hostility and competitiveness between parties, and lead to more concessions.[51]

Mixed Roles Leverage (and Depend on) Strong Rapport and Trust.   A mediator who has won the confidence and trust of the parties may be viewed as the ideal third party to adjudicate the dispute if the parties are unable to reach a negotiated settlement. For similar reasons, parties may look to an arbitrator to take on the role of mediator if there is reason to believe a dispute may be resolved amicably before the conclusion of arbitration. In addition to being a convenient choice, the sitting arbitrator may also have extensive familiarity with the issues and the evidence. Having had an opportunity to observe the arbitrator manage arbitration proceedings, including supervising aspects of the pre-hearing process and hearings, the parties may have developed a level of rapport with and trust in that person. This may permit them to feel comfortable with that person playing a more direct role in negotiations, including perhaps their offering of preliminary views or serving as a facilitator/mediator going forward.

Mixed Roles May Set the Stage for a Consent Arbitration Award.   Arbitrating parties may see special benefits in informally settling disputes prior to the rendition of an award so that the settlement may be incorporated in a "consent" arbitration award, thus laying the groundwork for enhanced enforcement.[52] Having the arbitrator play a more direct role in negotiated settlement is one way of increasing the likelihood that a settlement will occur, with the added benefit that the arbitrator who is being asked to issue the consent award may be more familiar with the details of and circumstances surrounding the settlement.

All that said, engaging with mixed roles is not for everyone, and certainly not for beginners. It requires deliberate planning, a seasoned neutral who enjoys the trust of the parties, good judgment, educated consent, and careful contractual drafting. As explained above, mediator evaluations and the handling of confidential communications in ex parte "caucuses" are areas of particular concern that require thoughtful handling. In the international commercial realm, moreover, the picture is further complicated by national or regional variations in attitudes and practices, discussed in Section D.5.

NOTES AND QUESTIONS

10. *Arbitrating Disputes Under a Mediated Settlement Agreement.* Because settlements often involve complex terms, including restructured relationships, and because mediation often ends with the parties signing brief "term sheets" that outline the points of agreement, the eventual drafting of complex settlement documents may be left to the parties' counsel. In such situations, disputants may worry about the other side's good faith in carrying out their deal, or fear that they will fall into new conflicts as a repaired relationship goes forward. A mechanism that resolves such concerns can provide a crucial assurance of certainty and security about implementation of potential settlements. After helping to facilitate a

settlement, therefore, mediators are sometimes asked to be named as arbitrators in the agreement to resolve any disputes with regard to the mediated terms of settlement. Parties may find especially attractive the idea that any dispute over implementation will be decided by someone they have come to know and trust, and who presumably knows better than any outsider what they intended to achieve by their agreement. However, even a post-agreement change of hats may involve problems. *See, e.g., Morgan Phillips v. JAMS/Endispute,* 140 Cal. App. 4th 795 (2006) (neutral who had mediated a settlement agreement under which he agreed to arbitrate future disputes was sued when a dispute arose and he withdrew as arbitrator).

11. *Eleventh-Hour Arb-Med (Arbitrator Mediates After Completing Award).* Occasionally, arbitration parties opt for a variation of arb-med in which the neutral first conducts an arbitration hearing and makes an award, but does not reveal the contents to the parties. She then mediates the dispute. The arbitration award is not revealed unless the mediation fails to produce an agreement. The approach is sometime touted as a "solution" to the perceived drawbacks of problems of med-arb or arb-med-arb. The arbitrator has no ex parte communications until after deciding the award. The parties each have additional information gleaned from the arbitration, providing a common basis for settlement discussions. The gap between their assessments of the case value may also be narrowed by the experience of arbitrating, although even at the end of the arbitration hearing, they can only make a guess about the award. In the shadow of the unannounced arbitration determination, the parties can still retain control of the outcome in the mediation phase and can shape a resolution that best meets their needs rather than being required to accept an imposed result from the arbitrator.

On the other hand, eleventh-hour settlement lacks many of the benefits of an earlier resolution. The parties have already gone to considerable time, trouble, and expense preparing for and conducting adjudication. From a psychological point of view, moreover, one wonders if parties who have just endured a complete adjudicative process in which they played adversary roles will be attuned to engage in bargaining — especially the collaborative kind. Also, unless the arbitrator is in a position to finalize an award immediately upon the close of hearings, mediation might have to await the completion of the award. Finally, one wonders about the expectations of an arbitrator-turned-mediator in such a situation: Although it is doubtful that many have experiences with this kind of procedure, one would think that the parties would be scrutinizing the neutral's words, facial expressions, tone, etc. for any hint of how they ruled. However, resort to a process of this kind may make sense where the parties are both very concerned about the risks associated with the arbitration award, or where they have come belatedly to the mutual realization that a negotiated resolution may permit the crafting of arrangements beyond the rather limited remedial scope of arbitral awards.

PROBLEM 3

Efforts to structure a suitable, workable, and enforceable ADR agreement are sometimes undermined by a lack of precision. Such an issue may be particularly acute when a single individual is assigned multiple roles, or where the neutral's role may be characterized in more than one way.

These concerns are illustrated by *Ex parte Industrial Technologies*, 707 So. 2d 234 (Ala. 1997), a case in which a bank filed suit on a promissory note, and the defendants counterclaimed for conversion of certain equipment taken by the bank during collection efforts. Prior to trial, the parties agreed to refer the matter to out-of-court process (described as "mediation or arbitration") with a retired circuit judge, Snodgrass, as "mediator/arbitrator." After a period of settlement negotiations supervised by Judge Snodgrass, the parties announced their "stipulation of agreement" acknowledging the conversion of the equipment, calling for appraisers to determine the fair market value of the detained property, and calling for Snodgrass to determine the interest factor to be used in computing the rental value of the property during the detention period. Snodgrass subsequently issued an "order" directing the bank to pay both rental value during the detention and the value of the equipment at the time of detention, less salvage value at the time of return. The defendants/counterclaimants sought to enforce the outcome, which they termed a "binding arbitration order," but the bank responded that the proceeding was merely mediation without binding results. The Alabama Supreme Court determined that both the parties' agreement and the subsequent process were fatally flawed. First of all, it was impossible to determine the precise character of the process agreed to by the parties, but rather only that the parties apparently intended for the judge to determine damages based on a mutually agreeable formula. Unfortunately, the court concluded, there was never a meeting of the minds as to whether Snodgrass was empowered to award damages over and above the rental value. While the participants had the opportunity to overcome the lack of precision in tailoring the original ADR agreement during the subsequent negotiation and drafting of the "stipulation of agreement," they instead merely exacerbated their earlier mistakes.

Imagine you are legal counsel for the borrower in the above case, and you have another opportunity to "get it right" with the dispute resolution agreement. What changes should be made?

PROBLEM 4

You are a dispute resolution professional in private practice. Lawyers for a fast-food franchisor and franchisee in a dispute over claims that each one violated provisions of their franchise agreement have approached you to conduct a dispute resolution process under the following terms, to which they have agreed:

Mediation and Arbitration Agreement

_____, plaintiff, and _____, defendant, agree to resolve the dispute pending between them, and any issues arising from or related to that dispute, with _____ as the Neutral.

Mediation Process

Representatives of the parties with full settlement authority will attend the mediation. The parties will follow the recommendations of the Neutral regarding the agenda most likely to resolve the dispute. [The balance of this section tracks the first example of a mediation agreement in the Web Appendix. You may assume that the language here outlines a typical mediation process.]

Arbitration Process

The parties, after consultation with their counsel, agree that if they do not reach agreement through mediation at the scheduled mediation session, the Neutral shall make a "final settlement proposal" and will identify it using those words. Unless all of the parties accept the Neutral's final settlement proposal by the time deadline set by the Neutral, then the final settlement proposal shall become a binding arbitration award under the Federal Arbitration Act (FAA).

The parties mutually agree to waive their right to seek vacatur of the award under the FAA, and any other rights of appeal, with the purpose that the Neutral shall be the final and sole judge of their dispute. It is their intent that the Neutral's final settlement proposal or the parties' agreed outcome, as the case may be, shall become an arbitration award that may not be appealed by any party and that may be entered as a final judgment in the State Superior Court without any further proceedings thereon. . . .

1. What are the advantages and disadvantages of this procedure?
2. What concerns, if any, would you share about the procedure? What suggestions might you make for modifications? (In the course of thinking about your answer, you may want to consult the Guidelines set out in Section D.6 below.)

5. Varying Cultural and Legal Traditions

There are no generally accepted standards for mixed neutral roles in international practice. Such developments are hampered by disparities in how different cultures and legal traditions define "mediation" (or "conciliation") and "arbitration," and their perceptions of the roles of mediators or arbitrators — often reflecting the realities of different public justice systems. In some jurisdictions, mediators engage in a wide spectrum of activities in the course of facilitating negotiations, while in others mediators are prohibited or strongly discouraged from engaging in arbitration or case evaluation.

In some countries, it is common for arbitrators to play an active role in setting the stage for settlement. In Germany and Switzerland, for example, arbitrators frequently offer preliminary views regarding issues in dispute and may even engage in discussions aimed at amicable settlement. In China, Japan, and some other Asian countries, there are cultural predispositions to the notion of arbitrators facilitating settlement. Scott Donahey, a neutral with substantial international experience, notes that "[i]n various Asian countries, there is a profound societal and philosophical preference for agreed solutions."[53] He explains that "Asian cultures frequently seek a 'harmonious' solution, one which tends to preserve the relationship, rather than one which, while arguably factually and legally 'correct,' may severely damage the relationship of the parties involved."

> Where the Westerner will segregate the function of facilitator from that of decision-maker, the Asian will make no clear distinction. The Westerner seeks an arbiter that is unconnected to the parties to the dispute, one whose mind has not been predisposed by previous knowledge of the dispute or the facts which underlie it, a judge who is prepared to "let the chips fall where they may." On the other hand, many Asians seek a moderator who is familiar with the parties and their dispute, who will not only end their state of disputation but assist the parties in reaching an agreed solution, or, failing that, will find a position which will not only be one that terminates their dispute, but one that will allow the parties to resume their relationship with as little loss of "face" as possible. Thus, the distinction between the function of the arbitrator and that of the conciliator is blurred. . . .
>
> The traditional Western view is that the conciliation process should be separate from the arbitration process and that the same persons who act as conciliators should not act as arbitrators in the same dispute. . . . However, the traditional Western view is changing, largely due to the influence of Asian cultures. . . . A combined conciliation and arbitration process offers significant advantages in reaching an agreed settlement and in preserving existing commercial relations between the parties.

Some of these perspectives and practices have influenced recommendations issued by a CEDR Commission in 2009 and the more recent Rules on the Efficient Conduct of Proceedings in International Arbitration ("Prague Rules"). This chapter will conclude with a summary of recent efforts to develop international guidelines for practices involving mixed neutral roles.

PROBLEM 5

ExGen Corporation, a major multinational corporation, filed suit in federal court against Herupa, Inc., a Japanese supplier of components for ExGen's new manufacturing process, alleging $8 million in damages resulting from delays in the delivery of components. Liability was not contested, but there was a dispute as to damages. When discovery was nearly concluded and the parties were on the verge of going to trial, they were persuaded by the court to mediate the dispute.

You are selected to be the mediator. After two lengthy days of negotiating, including extensive ex parte discussions with both parties, you have engendered some movement on both sides. The parties are still about $1.8 million apart — ExGen demands $4.8 million and Herupa is offering $3.0 million. There does not appear to be an opportunity for avoiding impasse by expanding the pie through collateral business arrangements or other accommodations.

1. Faced with the possibility that there will be no settlement, you are considering a recommendation to the parties to submit the dispute to an abbreviated "baseball arbitration" process in which the arbitrator picks between the final numbers. How might you suggest the process be structured? (Note: You may find it useful to consult the Guidelines in Section D.6 in thinking about your response to this question and those that follow.)

2. Suppose you go ahead and invite the parties to discuss whether or not to use this process and jointly advise you as to their mutual decision. You are somewhat surprised when the parties' attorneys notify you that they have agreed to such a process, and want *you* to be the arbitrator. What will you do?

3. What if the parties also tell you that after discussing the matter, they want you to decide the case without a hearing, but on the basis of memoranda that each party will submit to you in confidence?

4. Assume that as mediator you have resolved some but not all the issues in a complex commercial dispute between ExGen and Herupa. The parties indicate that they desire to arbitrate, but have as yet reached no agreement on the nature of the agreement or the selection of arbitrators. Can you help design an arbitration process, including how the arbitrator(s) will be selected?

6. Emerging Guidelines for Mixed-Mode Practice and Dual Roles

The International Task Force on Mixed Mode Dispute Resolution was established as a cooperative effort of the International Mediation Institute, the College of Commercial Arbitrators, and the Straus Institute for Dispute Resolution for the purpose of developing clear, effective international guidance regarding various forms of interplay between adjudicative processes and settlement-oriented functions for business parties, their legal counsel, and neutrals. Drawing on collective experience, the work of previous study groups, and the reflective observations of scholars and practitioners from around the world, the Task Force is in the process of developing new *Practice Guidelines for Situations in Which a Mediator Changes Roles to Function as an Arbitrator, or an Arbitrator Performs the Functions of a Mediator.* Key elements of the current working draft are briefly summarized here.

(1) *Need for Careful, Informed, Independent Reflection by Parties and Counsel.* Any decision by parties to employ neutrals in dual roles (med-arb, arb-med, or

arb-med-arb) or to have an arbitrator engage directly in helping facilitate settlement should be the product of careful, informed, and independent reflection and discussion by the parties. At some point it will be critical for the parties to engage the neutral(s) in the discussion to receive their input and to ensure their comfort with and commitment to the process. Indeed, the parties' faith and trust in the ability of a neutral to "thread the needle" of a dual role may be the single most critical element in submitting to such arrangements.

(2) *Ensuring Parties' Mutual Understandings Regarding Roles of Mediator and Arbitrator.* Given the diversity in perspectives and practice in different parts of the world, it is critical for participants in international dispute resolution—parties, counsel, and dispute resolution professionals—to anticipate that there may be different expectations among parties from different cultures and legal traditions, and to take responsibility for ensuring mutual understanding and true meeting of the minds regarding the roles and functions of mediators and arbitrators.

(3) *Neutral's Competency, Availability, Independence, and Impartiality.* A mediator should be authorized to shift to the role of arbitrator in the course of resolving a dispute, or vice versa, only if the parties are confident of the neutral's fitness for both roles. The qualifications for the roles are significantly different. Moreover, since the standards of impartiality and independence are higher, it may not be possible for a neutral to effectively shift to the role of arbitrator after having served as mediator.

(4) *An Agreement in Writing.* Any ex ante arrangement regarding mixed neutral roles or an ad hoc agreement regarding switching roles should be integrated in a written contract. Among other things, the agreement should include a clear demarcation of the respective phases or stages of the process, using clear and concise language to separately identify and delimit mediation and arbitration. The agreement should avoid conflating roles (such as "mediator/arbitrator" or "binding mediator") and be precise in describing how and when an arbitrator shifts to the role of mediator, or vice versa.

(5) *The Agreement Should Include Some Form of Waiver.* A provision to the effect that the neutral's participation in prior settlement discussions as well as their exposure to ex parte communication will not be asserted by any party as grounds for challenging the appointment of the neutral as arbitrator or any arbitration award rendered by the neutral.

(6) *Key Process Options.* If, prior to the commencement of mediation, the parties are considering med-arb or arb-med-arb, any of the following process options may be explored and discussed between the parties and by the parties with a prospective mediator. Such provisions should be incorporated in the parties' written agreement. Perhaps the two most consequential choices to be made by the parties are (1) the scope of the neutral's role as mediator/facilitator of settlement—that is, whether the neutral will engage in case evaluation or offer proposals for settlement; and (2) whether settlement discussions should include private caucus sessions with individual parties.

If a mediator is expected to switch to an arbitral role if settlement is not achieved, there is always the possibility of avoiding private caucuses and conducting the entire mediation process in joint session—an approach some neutrals have successfully employed to settle disputes, thus avoiding arbitration. If, as is often the case, the participants prefer to use private caucuses during the mediation phase, a number of process options are available, including the following:

- An agreement that if med-arb proceeds to arbitration, the neutral arbitration award must be dependent solely on evidence and arguments presented during arbitration proceedings, and not on any other communications or information conveyed during mediation.
- An agreement that the parties consent to med-arb with full awareness that information received in ex parte caucuses in the mediation phase may be taken into account by the mediator turned arbitrator in formulating their arbitration award.
- A requirement that, at the conclusion of mediation and before arbitration, the neutral shall disclose to the parties as much of the confidential information they received (or provided) during the mediation as they consider material to the arbitration proceedings.
- An agreement that at the conclusion of mediation and before arbitration, the parties will confer regarding the continued service of neutral.
- A requirement for separate written consent by the parties to have the neutral arbitrate after the conclusion of mediation, or an agreement that either party may opt out of the process at that stage.
- An agreement permitting neutrals to recuse themselves at the conclusion of mediation.

(7) *Variations on Med-Arb.* Even where mediation is not successful in resolving all substantive issues in dispute, mediators may be able to help set the stage for a dispute resolution process, including facilitating arbitration procedures that are customized to more effectively suit the circumstances and serve the needs of the parties.

One variant of med-arb is Mediation and Last-Offer-Arbitration (MEDALOA), in which traditional mediation is followed by a process in which each party submits a written final or "last offer" to the neutral. As arbitrator, the neutral proceeds to pick the last offer they consider most equitable, or most appropriate under the standards established by the parties. Although this process sometimes occurs during mediation, it may be agreed to beforehand.

(8) *Considerations for Parties Contemplating Arb-Med.* An individual appointed as arbitrator may agree to switch to the role of mediator at some point in the arbitration process. The switch is likely to be prompted by the parties' belief that with the help of the neutral, a negotiated settlement is achievable. An added advantage is that the neutral's initial arbitral appointment will facilitate the conversion of any mediated settlement agreement into a consent arbitration award. Of course, any arrangement struck by the parties should address what happens if mediation fails to fully resolve disputes.

On occasion, it is agreed that an arbitrator will take on the role of mediator after rendering a final award but prior to its publication. (Accounts of such proceedings describe a process in which the completed award is placed, unopened in a sealed envelope, on the table in full view of the parties.) Such an approach may have appeal for parties who are anxious about the risks of defaulting to a third-party decision and may overcome the concerns that ex parte communication received during the mediation would influence the arbitration award. Moreover, in their role as a mediator, the neutral has the benefit of full information regarding the dispute and the strengths and weaknesses of the parties' cases.

(9) *Med-Arb, Arb-Med-Arb with a Tribunal.* Although engaging an entire tribunal in the mediation phase of med-arb is likely to be cumbersome, two options are readily apparent: having the chair of the arbitration panel act as a mediator, or, alternatively engaging the two wing arbitrators as co-mediators. A variant of the latter approach might involve each wing arbitrator being authorized to meet separately (caucus) with the party that appointed them during the course of mediation. The downside of this approach would be to reinforce concerns about the independence and impartiality of the respective wing arbitrators. An alternative would be to have wing arbitrators caucus with the party that did *not* appoint them.

Endnotes

1. Stipanowich, Thomas J. & Fraser, Veronique. (2017) *The International Task Force on Mixed Mode Dispute Resolution: Exploring the Interplay Between Mediation, Evaluation and Arbitration,* 40 Fordham Int'l L.J. 839.

2. Stipanowich, Thomas J. (2021) *Arbitration, Mediation and Mixed Modes: Seeking Workable Solutions and Common Ground on Med-Arb, Arb-Med and Settlement-Oriented Activities by Arbitrators,* 26 Harv. Neg. L. Rev. (forthcoming).

3. Galanter, Marc. (1983) *Reading the Landscape of Disputes: What We Know and Don't Know (And Think We Know) About Our Allegedly Contentious and Litigious Society,* 31 UCLA L. Rev. 4, 5, 12-16.

4. Stipanowich, Thomas J. & Ulrich, Zachary P. (2014) *Commercial Arbitration and Settlement: Empirical Insights into the Roles Arbitrators Play,* 6 Y.B. on Arbitration & Mediation 1.

5. Stipanowich, Thomas J. (2017) *Living the Dream of ADR: Reflections on Four Decades of the Quiet Revolution in Dispute Resolution (Symposium Keynote),* 18 Cardozo J. Conflict Resol. 513, 514-515.

6. Stipanowich, Thomas J. (1998) *The Multi-Door Contract and Other Possibilities,* 13 Ohio St. J. on Disp. Resol. 303-304.

7. Niemic, Robert J. et al. (2001) *Descriptions of the Principal Court-Based ADR Processes,* in Guide to Judicial Management of Cases in ADR (Federal Judicial Center).

8. *Id.*

9. Brazil, Wayne. (2009) (For an empirical analysis of ENE results, see Brazil, Wayne, *Early Neutral Evaluation,* ABA, 2012; For an empirical analysis of ENE results, see Rosenberg and Folberg, 46 Stanford Law Review 1487, Alternative Dispute Resolution: An Empirical Analysis,1994).

10. Stipanowich, Thomas J., *supra* note 6.

11. *See* Hirsh, Merril et al. (2016) *Special Masters: A Different Answer to a Perennial Problem,* Judges J. 26 (Spring 2016).

12. *See* Cal. Civ. Proc. §630.01-.12; Rule 3.1547(a)(2) (USDCNDC General Order No. 64).

13. Stipanowich, Thomas J., *supra* note 6.

14. Stipanowich, Thomas J. & Lamare, Ryan. (2014) *Living with ADR: Evolving Perceptions and Use of Mediation, Arbitration and Conflict Management in Fortune 1,000 Corporations,* 19 Harv. Negot. L. Rev. 1.

15. United Nations Convention on International Settlement Agreements Resulting from Mediation (2018) (the "Singapore Convention on Mediation") (New York).

16. Stipanowich, Thomas J., *supra* note 2.

17. Stipanowich, Thomas J. (2021) *Multi-Tier Dispute Resolution Processes in the United States,* Chapter 11, *Multi-Tier Approaches to the Resolution of International Disputes: A Global and Comparative Study* (Anselmo Reyes & Gu Weixia, eds.).

18. *See* CPR Commission on the Future of Arbitration, Commercial Arbitration at Its Best: Successful Strategies for Business Users 5-6 (2001) (Thomas J. Stipanowich & Peter H. Kaskell, eds.).

19. *See* Nolan-Haley, Jacqueline. (2012) *Mediation: The "New Arbitration,"* 17 Harv. Negot. L. Rev. 61, 87.

20. 147 F. Supp. 2d 648 (S.D. Tex. 2001).

21. *See Tattoo Art* (n 78) 647; *MB America, Inc. v. Alaska Pac. Leasing Co.,* 367 P.3d 1286, 1289-1291 (Nev. 2016).

22. *See, e.g., Sor Tech, LLC v. MWR Life, LLC,* 2019 U.S. Dist. LEXIS 146817, 2019 WL 4060350, at *13 (S.D. Cal. 2019).

23. *See supra* note 18, at 18-20.

24. Lurie, Paul M. & Lack, Jeremy. (2014) *Guided Choice Dispute Resolution Processes: Reducing the Time and Expense to Settlement,* 8 Disp. Resol. Int'l 167, 175-177.

25. *See,* e.g., American Arbitration Association, *Commercial Arbitration Rules and Mediation Procedures,* www.adr.org/sites/default/files/CommercialRules_Web.pdf, accessed Aug. 29, 2020, stating that "[s]ubject to the right of any party to opt out, in cases where a claim or counterclaim exceeds $75,000, the rules provide that the parties shall mediate their dispute upon the administration of the arbitration or at any time when the arbitration is pending."

26. Stipanowich, Thomas J. (2007) *Real-Time Strategies for Relational Conflict,* IBA Legal Prac. Div. Mediation Newsl. (July), at 6.

27. Stipanowich, Thomas. J., *supra* note 6, at 360-364.

28. However, a study of 3,000 projects over a ten-year period indicates that projects that used DRBs "faced reduced costs and schedule growth" when compared to non-DRB projects. *See* Agdas, Duzgun & Ellis, Ralph D. (2013) *Analysis of Construction Dispute Review Boards,* 5(3) J. Legal Affairs & Disp. Resol in Eng'g & Constr. 122 (August).

29. *See, e.g.,* 2009 Caltrans DRB-DRA Amended 2006 Specifications. Caltrans' specifications call for a DRB in contracts over $10 million and individual Dispute Resolution Advisors (DRAs) in other projects.

30. Dettman, Kurt L., Harty, Martin & Lewin, Joel. (2010) *Resolving Megaproject Claims: Lessons from Boston's Big Dig*, 30(2) Constr. Law. 5 (Summer).
31. *Id.* at 10.
32. Gaitskell, Robert. (2005) *Trends in Construction Dispute Resolution*, Society of Construction Law Papers No. 129.
33. United Kingdom Statute 1996 c 53 Pt II §108.
34. Tackaberry, John. (2002) *Flexing the Knotted Oak: English Arbitration's Task and Opportunity in the First Decade of the New Century*, Society of Construction Law Papers 3 (May).
35. *Id.* at 11.
36. *See, e.g., EIC Contractor's Guide to the MDB [Multilateral Development Bank] Harmonised Edition (June 2010) of the FIDIC Conditions of Contract for Construction (April 2011)*, 28 Int'l Constr. L. Rev. 439 (2011).
37. Jaeger, Axel-Volkmar & Hök, Götz-Sebastian. (2010) FIDIC—A Guide for Practitioners 396-397.
38. *See* Stipanowich, Thomas J. (2016) *Beyond Getting to Yes: Using Mediator Insights to Facilitate Long-Term Business Relationships*, 34 Alternatives 97 (July/August).
39. *See* Gould, Nicholas et al. (2010) *Mediating Construction Disputes: An Evaluation of Existing Practice* 17 (discussing project mediation in the UK and CEDR's Project Mediation package).
40. Wall, Colin J. (1992) *The Dispute Resolution Adviser in the Construction Industry*, in *Construction Conflict Management and Resolution* (Peter Fenn & Rod Gameson, eds.), at 328.
41. The program was spearheaded by Howard Carsman, manager of construction claims and contracts for Intel Corporation.
42. "Arb-med" or "arb-med-arb" may also be used to refer to multi-step processes in which arbitration and mediation are conducted by different neutrals. *See, e.g.,* Singapore International Arbitration Centre (SIAC) & Singapore International Mediation Centre (SIMC), *SIAC-SIMC Arb-Med-Arb Protocol* (2014).
43. Stipanowich, Thomas J., *supra* note 2.
44. *See supra* note 18, at 22. The sponsoring organization is now known as the International Institute for Conflict Prevention & Resolution.
45. For an extensive exploration of dual-role practices in the United States and internationally, see Stipanowich, Thomas J., *supra* note 2.
46. Weisman, Martin C. (2013) *Med-Arb: The Best of Both Worlds*, 19 Disp. Res. 40.
47. Email from Richard Silberberg, Partner, Dorsey & Whitney, New York, NY to Thomas Stipanowich (June 12, 2020) (on file with author).
48. *Id.*
49. Nigmatullina, Dilyara. (2019) *Combining Mediation and Arbitration in International Commercial Dispute Resolution* 32-34.
50. Rivkin, David W. (2008) *Towards a New Paradigm in International Arbitration: The Town Elder Model Revisited*, 24 Arb. Int'l 375.
51. Nigmatullina, *supra* note 49, at 45.

52. In order to avoid difficulties of enforcement of a consent award where a single neutral plays multiple roles, it is important to ensure that the arbitral tribunal is engaged with respect to an active dispute, which would mean that an arb-med-arb format would be necessary.

53. Donahey, M. Scott (1995) *The Asian Concept of Conciliator/Arbitrator: Is It Translatable to the Western World?*, 50 Disp. Resol. J.

CHAPTER 10

FURTHER DIRECTIONS FOR DISPUTE RESOLUTION

This book has analyzed arbitration from a practice perspective, as well as a legal view. We also noted some possible new directions for the law, including proposed legislation that could preclude enforcement of arbitration clauses in certain contexts. Additionally, the book noted where the Supreme Court may act in the near future—and some of these cases may be decided by the time the book is in publication! Indeed, the legal landscape of arbitration is ever-changing.

In this chapter, however, we go further to connect the arbitration materials with other evolving issues in alternative dispute resolution. We look at important opportunities and challenges confronting lawyers in resolving disputes, managing conflicts, and solving problems, today and in the future. Lawyers can now approach disputes and the litigation experience in new ways, with more satisfactory results for those they represent. As advisors to organizations and individual clients, lawyers are ideally poised to bring about significant positive changes in disputing culture and in the community more broadly.

Whether designing systems to manage conflict, pioneering "upstream" interventions, or working with new technologies, attorneys and conflict resolution professionals today have unprecedented tools for preventing and resolving disputes, as well as facilitating deals and decisions. In this chapter, we introduce three emergent areas of research and practice—dispute systems design, online dispute resolution, and efforts to transform the community—that will shape the course of dispute resolution, now and in the future.

A. DISPUTE SYSTEMS DESIGN

The field of dispute systems design (DSD) arose in response to the increasing demand on the part of organizations and others for more effective institutional approaches to managing conflict and disputes, both proactively and after the fact. The term "dispute systems design" is not widely known, even though the ideas and practices undergirding DSD are well understood in a variety of contexts.

For example, you already know what a "system" is. Generally speaking, a system is a set of steps or processes or modules that are intended to do something. Systems take input (like raw data) and generate output (like results). The way you get food at a fast-food restaurant is an example of a simple system. Customers stand in line, approach the counter, order their food, pay their money, and then wait for their food to be ready. Different restaurants may have variations on this system, like having the customers wait off to the side or giving them a buzzer that lets them know when their food is ready. Moreover, the order-taking system is only one of the systems operating in the fast-food restaurant. Food preparation, facilities management, employee supervision—all of these systems are interlocked processes within the broader system architecture of running a fast-food restaurant.

Likewise, you already know what "design" means. When you design an object, you figure out how it should look or fit together or operate, depending on what you are designing and its purpose. If you are designing a door, you will want to know where and how the door will be used. The front door of a house usually has a knob, for example, but a push bar may make more sense for the door of a classroom. Design considerations and methodologies may vary depending on the situation, but the basic definition of design—figuring out how to make something—remains consistent across contexts.

Finally, some of you may be familiar with the term "system design." At its most basic, system design is simply figuring out how to put together something that does something. For many professionals in different fields, system design is a well-developed set of practices that translate fairly well across substantive areas. Indeed, dispute systems design draws upon these same shared practices.

But what is a dispute system, and what does dispute systems design entail? These topics could fill an entire semester-long class. Let's go through some of the basics.

1.   *What Is a Dispute System?*

In this book, you have been learning about methods or processes for managing disputes. Negotiation, mediation, arbitration, and even litigation are processes that have evolved to handle conflict. We can think about these processes, as well as any other approach for dealing with disputes, as "dispute systems."

Dispute systems range in complexity and scope, and they may vary in terms of formality, structure, resources, authority, and purpose. Some dispute systems are quite simple. A complaint box is an example of a simple dispute system that allows companies to discover problems and deal with upset customers. Other dispute systems are more complex. A truth and reconciliation commission (TRC), for example, is a system intended to restore the social order by allowing people who have been harmed to address those harms (and sometimes the offender) in an open forum.

Dispute systems may be created to respond to an event, like the Victims Compensation Fund in the wake of 9/11; or to manage existing disputes within an organization, like an employee grievance process; or to prevent potentially contentious situations from ripening into disputes, as when companies enter early structured negotiation to clarify provisions within agreements.

In addition, organizations or groups may put together a dispute system to help them manage issues that may arise during a specific project or initiative. For example, the Boston Central Artery/Tunnel Project, better known as the "Big Dig" and one of the nation's largest construction projects, utilized a "real-time" dispute resolution system called the Dispute Review Board (DRB). The DRB consisted of two neutral technical panelists (such as construction engineers with specialties in excavation) and a panel chair with significant dispute resolution experience. Panelists were appointed at project startup, permitting them to become familiar with project personnel, technical aspects, and progress. DRB operating rules minimized formality and attempted to cut out all vestiges of a legal hearing process, such as lawyer argument and examination of witnesses, with the goal of maximizing the flexibility of the panel to control the gathering of information. Once the panel gathered all information, the panelists deliberated and produced a recommendation, complete with supporting rationale, for the project director. DRB systems have often been successful in promoting early and effective dispute resolution.

As you can see from the diagram below, dispute systems include interventions that run along continuums of responsive to proactive, from one-time to ongoing. Responsive systems are intended for disputes that have already arisen, whereas proactive/preventive systems are designed to catch potential conflicts "upstream" and prevent them from ripening into disputes. Ongoing systems handle particular kinds of disputes over an indefinite period of time, while one-time systems are designed to manage or prevent a particular event.

© Jennifer W. Reynolds 2021

Note that although mapping dispute systems in this way may be a helpful learning tool, many dispute systems may fall in different quadrants depending on the purpose and goals of the system. Where might the complaint box fall on this graph, for example? How about the TRC or the DRB?

PROBLEM: THE DUEL

In the 2016 smash musical *Hamilton*, two soldiers (Lawrence and Lee) get into an argument over some negative statements that Lee made about George Washington. They decide to settle their dispute with a duel. Listen to the song "The Ten Duel Commandments" on the Internet. The song outlines the dueling procedure that the men will use. From the lyrics, you should be able to identify why the duel is happening, who is involved and in what capacity, what timing and location constraints exist, and whether there are opportunities for resolving the dispute without using deadly weapons.[1] Is dueling an effective dispute system? Why or why not?[2]

2.   *What Is Dispute Systems Design?*

Dispute systems design (DSD) is an analytical framework and approach for developing processes to manage or prevent disputes. Although DSD is an emergent subdiscipline in alternative dispute resolution, the underlying principles and practices of the field are familiar to anyone who has worked in system design or project management.

Generally speaking, dispute systems designers analyze conflict patterns in an organization, design and develop processes to handle disputes arising from these conflict patterns, and then oversee implementation and evaluation of the new process. Throughout the process, designers work closely with sponsors and clients, along with others who are considered "stakeholders" in the new system. Designers may come from inside or outside the organization, and lawyers commonly serve as designers or participate on design teams.

Dispute systems design, like system design more generally, does not happen in a vacuum. The creation and implementation of a dispute system requires designers to think carefully about the "context and culture" of the system, as Professors Lisa Amsler, Janet Martinez, and Stephanie Smith have pointed out:

> [W]e approach cultural differences through an iceberg metaphor: visible above the water line are behaviors and institutions; immediately below the surface are knowledge structures, values, beliefs, and norms; and deep down are fundamental assumptions. . . . By understanding the disputants' cultural context and perspectives, one can design a strategy or process more attuned to the parties' preferences; the resulting design may help bridge those differences within an organization or a society.[3]

In addition, having an appreciation of context and culture means looking carefully at the existing processes for managing conflict. In a seminal text on designing dispute systems, Professors Stephen Goldberg, Jeanne Brett, and William Ury pointed out that diagnosis is core to systems design:

> Learning what kinds of disputes occur and with whom is the designers' first diagnostic task. . . . If the disputes tend to have a strong emotional element, the design should consider methods to vent emotions. If the disputes involve[e] purely legal or technical issues . . . a low-cost rights procedure may be appropriate. . . . [T]he designers will also focus on the causes of those disputes. Sometimes identifying causes can suggest ways to prevent similar disputes in the future.[4]

Other key considerations when designing a dispute system include the following:

- **Goals.** When creating a dispute system, designers must know what the system is intended to achieve. For example, a company seeking to implement new anti-discrimination procedures may be motivated by a number of goals. They may want to cultivate an equitable and respectful workplace: They may be seeking to reduce liability by identifying and addressing problems before they turn into legal matters. They may want the positive public recognition that comes from having such procedures in place. Knowing these goals will help you figure out what to focus on in your design. Additionally, to the extent that the goals are in conflict, recognizing this conflict early and working with clients to figure out relative priorities will help ensure system success.

- **Sponsorship**. Designers need the support and sponsorship of clients before engaging in the design process. New dispute systems are typically a change to the status quo, and designers will need institutional or sponsor support to make sure that they are able to secure the resources and cooperation necessary to effect those changes. Sometimes the client is also the sponsor of the system, as when the president of an organization hires a designer. Other times the client is not the same person as the sponsor, and the sponsor must be approached separately. If the designer was hired by the general counsel and not the president, for example, the president may need to be brought into the loop as a sponsor of the project. Often written agreements about the purposes and scope of the work, as well as a commitment to providing resources across a specified period of time, are helpful ways to define and secure sponsorship.

- **Resources and logistics**. Questions of resources and logistics (e.g., timing, location, staffing, etc.) are of fundamental importance in developing systems. As software designers say, systems are never cheap, fast, and good—they can only be two of the three. An inexpensive high-quality system will take a long time to develop, and a quick and cheap system probably is not going to be good. Designers must work with sponsors and clients to ensure that the goals of the system are in line with the available resources and feasible as a matter of logistics.

- **Stakeholders**. The stakeholders are all the people who are interested in the system, including the future users of the system and those who will be responsible for implementing and evaluating the system going forward. In addition, there may be multiple other individuals and groups who have some kind of stake in the process and outcome. Consider, for example, the previous example of anti-discrimination procedures—what people other than employees and human resources officers might care about how those procedures are developed and rolled out?

- **Communication**. Finally, designers must pay special attention to keeping stakeholders and other constituencies informed of the process all along the way. Thoughtful communication promotes system buy-in and helps identify obstacles at an early stage. For larger systems, designers may develop a communication strategy that sorts stakeholders into tiers. Each tier will have its own type and frequency of outreach, which will help ensure that people have the information they need when they need it.

QUESTIONS

1. Recently, Facebook created an oversight board to manage concerns regarding the process for "deplatforming" individuals from the mammoth social media site. Who are the stakeholders for such a system? If you were on the board, how would you communicate with these

stakeholders—what kinds of matters would you report, how often, and to whom?

2. After the terrorist attacks of September 11, 2001, mediator Kenneth Feinberg was appointed Special Master of the 9/11 Victims Compensation Fund, a federal compensation fund for victims and their families. In exchange for taking money from the fund, victims and their families agreed not to sue the airlines involved in the tragedy. The fund distributed more than $7 billion to 5,562 people over three years.[5] Robert Ackerman describes the process used in allocating the funds:

> Procedurally, the regulations allowed claimants to choose one of two tracks for consideration of their claims. If a claimant chose Track A, a Claims Evaluator would determine eligibility and the claimant's presumed award in accordance with the regulations within 45 days of filing; thereafter the claimant could either accept the award or request a hearing before the Special Master or his designee. Under Track B, the Claims Evaluator would determine eligibility (again within 45 days); thereafter, eligible claimants would proceed directly to hearing. 28 C.F.R. 104.33 spelled out the procedures to be used at the hearing. Consistent with the statute, claimants could be represented by counsel, present evidence (orally or in writing), and present witnesses (including experts); the Special Master or his designee would be permitted to question witnesses. In short, "the objective of hearings shall be to permit the claimant to present information or evidence that the claimant believes is necessary to a full understanding of the claim." Hearings would, "to the extent practicable, be scheduled at times and in locations convenient to the claimant or his or her representative" and "limited in length to a time period determined by the Special Master or his designee." The Special Master was required to notify the claimant in writing of the amount of the award, but was not obliged to "create or provide any written record of the deliberations that resulted in that determination." Again, consistent with the statute, there would be "no further review or appeal of the Special Master's determination." The process was designed to take no more than 120 days, consistent with 405(b)(3) of the Act.[6]

Media commentators described the scheme for the fund as "about as fair as it could possibly be," "a good start on the road to recovery," "eminently fair," and "offering speedy and rational compensation." Based on what you have read so far about DSD, what might be some of the challenges in developing a dispute system to handle the conflicts coming out of a mass disaster? What kinds of system components might be useful in addressing these challenges?

3. In 1936, surrealist artist Meret Oppenheim covered a teacup and saucer with soft brown fur. This artwork, called "Object" or "Le Déjeuner en

fourrure (Lunch in fur)," is on display at the Museum of Modern Art in New York and may be viewed online.[7] Examine Oppenheim's teacup and saucer. Is it well designed? What would we have to know before we could answer that question definitively?

NOTE: ADR AND POST-SETTLEMENT IMPLEMENTATION

Ken Feinberg has designed more than one dispute system in the wake of a mass disaster. In addition to his work on the 9/11 Victims Compensation Fund, he has been involved with the design and implementation of dispute systems related to the BP Deepwater Horizon tragedy, the Boston Marathon bombing, and the Catholic Church sex abuse scandal. Before becoming involved with these high-profile disasters, Feinberg had already started thinking about how ADR can be productively deployed in these kinds of contexts, with particular focus on how alternative methods may improve post-settlement implementation of agreements:

> What is usually ignored is the role of ADR after the underlying dispute is resolved; all too often there is little or no followup when it comes to the role ADR plays in implementing a settlement, in making sure that the terms and conditions of the settlement are satisfied in an efficient and fair manner.
>
> The role of ADR in post-settlement implementation is most apparent in large class actions involving mass torts, major insurance policy settlements and consumer litigation. In these and other similar complex and protracted litigations, a comprehensive settlement involves literally thousands of individual plaintiff claimants, all demanding their fair share of allocated settlement proceeds. To the public and many ADR commentators, an aggregate settlement has in fact been achieved. But fundamental questions remain: Which claimants will receive the benefits of the comprehensive settlement? How much [will they] receive and based upon what terms and conditions? It is in resolving these questions that ADR plays an additional creative and important role.
>
> First, the ADR neutral may play an important role after a settlement is reached by fashioning an allocation formula for distribution of proceeds to eligible claimants. . . .
>
> Second, even in those cases where comprehensive settlement terms and conditions are negotiated up front by the litigating parties themselves, ADR may still play a critically important role in the settlement's implementation. Mediation or arbitration may become available to those individual claimants who challenge their allocated share of the aggregate award. . . .[8]

> Feinberg points out that ADR provides "one-stop shopping" for litigants, which means that "[n]ot only can ADR be used effectively to help resolve the underlying dispute among the parties, but it also can become a valuable tool in assuring effective implementation of a settlement, maximizing the likelihood that all parties will comply with the deal and will view the settlement as fair, just, and equitable."

3. The Stages of Dispute Systems Design

When you design a system, you are creating something that is supposed to do something. This act of creation sits between two sets of activities. You can think of these activities as falling into the categories of "pre-design" and "post-design."

Pre-Design Activities	Post-Design Activities
Contracting with the client and securing sponsorship (someone with authority)	Testing
	Rolling out a pilot version or beta test
Deciding on vision—what do you want the system to do?	Announcing, communicating
	Making adjustments and fixing problems
Identifying and talking with stakeholders	Evaluating the success of the system
Identifying resources	Training people to use the system
Communicating as appropriate about the plan	Training people to help users
Coming up with project management plan	Managing change resistance
Analyzing what currently exists, if anything, to do what this system will do	
Considering wider context and what challenges and opportunities exist (for example, can you buy the system you need?)	

Pre-design activities fall into two big categories: planning and analysis. Planning activities include contracting with the client; securing sponsorship; deciding on the vision; identifying resources; and coming up with a project management plan. Analysis activities include identifying and talking with stakeholders; communicating as appropriate; analyzing what currently exists; and looking for additional opportunities and challenges as the wider context comes more into view. We think of planning as the first step, particularly because it involves early activities like securing sponsorship. But in reality, planning and analysis often overlap and inform one another.

Post-design activities also fall into two categories: implementation and evaluation. Implementation includes all those activities related to rolling out the newly designed system. These activities include testing, rolling out beta versions, announcing progress, making adjustments and fixing problems, and training people to use or operate the system. Evaluation is the assessment of the system post-rollout, to ensure that it is operating correctly and efficiently, and to make sure that the goals of the system are actually being met. Again, there can be some iteration between the stages, especially if the rollout exposes significant design concerns or there are changes in the plan or resource allocation.

Putting it all together, the design of a dispute system typically unfolds in five stages — and again, these are loosely linear and may involve some overlap and revisiting:

1. **Preparation and planning**. Decide on goals and scope; determine resources; secure the client and sponsor; come up with the project plan.
2. **Analysis**. Analyze what currently exists (strengths and weaknesses) or, if nothing currently exists, figure out what people do in the absence of a system; talk to stakeholders; consider wider context.
3. **Design**. Create a system that addresses the goals, given the resources, and includes the stakeholders in a meaningful way.
4. **Implementation**. Roll out pilot version and "beta test"; deal with any issues and make adjustments.
5. **Evaluation**. Develop metrics that help determine whether the system is meeting its goals and set up mechanisms for ongoing assessment and continuous improvement.

Within these five stages, one of the most important and challenging tasks is to work with stakeholders. Stakeholders are absolutely essential to the success of the project. Their interests and concerns and knowledge guide designers in navigating the culture, diagnosing the issues, and developing a system that is usable, functional, and responsive to system goals. Yet many designers fail to take stakeholder interests properly into account. With this in mind, Professors Amsler, Martinez, and Smith recommend putting together a "stakeholder-driven design team" that uses "participatory and collaborative processes to identify user options, prioritize among user options, and solicit feedback on the draft design."[9]

What does it mean to be a "stakeholder-driven" designer? One possible response comes from Cathy Constantino and Christina Sickles Merchant, two noted systems design experts. They recommend tailoring DSD processes to specific problems and ensuring that disputants have the knowledge and skills to use the processes. According to Constantino and Merchant, dispute systems should be simple, easily accessible, and designed to resolve disputes early and at the lowest bureaucratic level possible. Finally, these experts note that designers should allow disputants to retain maximum control over the dispute resolution method and choice of neutrals, if applicable.[10] In these ways, designers keep user experience at the forefront of the design process.

Another aspect of being "stakeholder-driven" is taking the evaluation stage of design seriously. Because evaluation looks like it takes place after implementation, it can be easy for designers and stakeholders to forget. Yet evaluation activities should start taking place early in the process, as designers identify possible metrics and data gathering strategies. As Professors Amsler, Martinez, and Smith state:

> Evaluation is important in three primary respects. First, evaluation is necessary for system operators to ascertain whether the system is working. Are key stakeholder groups staying out of the system? Are costs significantly exceeding projections? Are neutrals failing to deliver quality services or violating ethics rules? Are users satisfied with the options and services?

Second, ongoing evaluation identifies opportunities for improvement. Third, it is important for users to understand how—and how well—the system operates. Transparency increases credibility and therefore participation, encouraging further feedback from participants.[11]

In evaluating design, there are two different kinds of evaluative criteria to consider: project-specific and design-oriented. Project-specific criteria refer to the purposes of the system: How well is the system delivering on its goals, given the resource allocation and other requirements or constraints? Design-oriented criteria refer to general design principles that apply to all systems: predictability, reliability, accuracy, and efficiency. Furthermore, in systems used by humans (like dispute systems), design criteria include usability, equality, rationality, and dignity.

Arbitration is one possible tool, or mechanism, to include in a system design. However, it is not the only tool. This book has focused on arbitration, but one should always consider the various tools in their dispute resolution toolbox. Furthermore, it may even make sense to "mix and match" as we discussed in the previous chapter. DSD invites creativity and optionality—making it ideal for problem-solving. Indeed, lawyers and dispute resolution professionals should consider all the various tools at their disposal for solving problems.

QUESTIONS

4. Imagine you are designing a new grievance process for your organization. What sort of evaluation metrics might you put into place? How would you gather the data needed for these metrics?

5. Sometimes we make design choices that violate one or more design principles. For example, in police interrogations, the police are allowed to lie. Why do we permit this, as a design matter? What benefit do we believe comes from designing police interrogations in this way? How does this design choice violate one or more of the design principles listed above? How can designers and others balance these trade-offs against one another?

Dispute systems design is a fascinating area of study and practice. You may have the opportunity to take additional courses in this area, or you may find yourself helping a client work through possible design choices around dispute systems in the future. Keep in mind that what you have learned in this class about conflict, negotiation, mediation, and arbitration are some of the most useful building blocks of DSD practice.

B.   TECHNOLOGY AND ONLINE DISPUTE RESOLUTION

Communication is increasingly digital and virtual in every aspect of our lives. The implications of new technology for improving negotiation, as well as for managing and resolving conflict, are immense.

1. Growth of Online Dispute Resolution

As discussed in earlier chapters, the resources of cyberspace can be used to assist traditional face-to-face ADR. For example, there is a smartphone app to help you assess your negotiation style and determine afterwards how you can improve.[12] Another program is designed to help lawyers plan a specific negotiation strategy, including how much to demand or offer at the beginning and at each successive round to reach a target amount. At the same time, technologies like ADRNotable help mediators organize their notes and craft settlement terms. It also helps mediators keep track of time spent in caucus, and assists dispute resolution neutrals in keeping track of billing. Arbitrations have also moved online with the use of video technology, as well as platforms dedicated to secure text-based arbitration.

Nonetheless, ODR programs go beyond facilitating traditional face-to-face arbitration and other ADR Processes. They also can creatively use technology in transformative ways. Developments at the crossroads of technology and dispute resolution have created a new age for ODR that fits within dispute systems design — asking designers to "fit the technology to the fuss." Furthermore, ODR has grown considerably over time to include automated decision making, as well as online negotiation, mediation, arbitration, community courts, and variations thereof. While some debate the definition of ODR, it seems that the field will grow and develop as technology continues to disrupt the field of dispute resolution. Moreover, younger generations who grew up with technology are increasingly embracing ODR due to their comfort with online communications — without the costs or hassles of travel or time away from work.[13]

Accordingly, ODR has gained significant traction in the United States and abroad. ODR is not simply virtual mediation and arbitration using platforms like Zoom. Asynchronous text-based mediation and arbitration is growing in use. CREK is an example of an ODR provider on the market that offers ODR services for a complete range of disputes.[14] Its system "supports all phases of the ODR lifecycle including Diagnosis, Automated Negotiation, Negotiation, Mediation & Evaluation/Adjudication/Arbitration. Its Workflow and Rules Engine, Private & Joint Caucus (Discussions/Chats including Video), Collaborative Editing of Awards and Settlement Agreements, Timeline, Scheduling, and Notes" help parties arrive at a fair resolution. CREK mainly assists asynchronous text-based mediation and arbitration and is available in a variety of languages.[15] This is just one among a growing sea of ODR providers.[16]

Private ODR is not alone. Public systems have grown in importance. This expansion of public ODR has been especially robust in the last five years. In fact, courts have joined the bandwagon by adopting ODR and developing e-courts.[17] Many jurisdictions in the United States are experimenting with ODR, with some launching small claims e-courts seeking to replace in-person hearings.[18] Hundreds of courts now offer online processes for case types ranging from traffic tickets to divorce to debt claims. This could have significant impact on how we view "court ADR" reimagined as "court ODR." This also raises new issues around transparency and what constitutes "access to justice" through the courts.

Moreover, the Covid-19 pandemic has forced dispute resolution professionals to consider how they can fashion means for resolving and preventing disputes without travel or in-person meetings that could be unsafe due to Covid-19. As a result, developers and policymakers are scrambling to utilize technology to improve efficiency and provide business continuity. Mediators and arbitrators have learned to commandeer processes through virtual meetings using technologies such as Zoom, Microsoft Teams, and WhatsApp. This has caused lawyers to learn new skills and consider opportunities and hurdles provided by new technologies. Some have long predicted lawyering's move online, but the Covid-19 pandemic has quickened the pace of new developments.[19]

ODR is not just about efficiency or elimination of costs and difficulties of travel. Instead, technology has opened new virtual doors to the courthouse for those that cannot afford the time and costs of in-person processes. It also provides a "safe space" for individuals who fear the legal system or experience stress in traditional face-to-face processes. Additionally, technology, including artificial intelligence (AI), can be built into ODR programs to foster dispute prevention and problem diagnosis. This can reduce many disputes from escalating into lawsuits. We are even seeing ODR used to resolve blockchain disputes.[20] Furthermore, institutional interest in research and development of best practices around ODR has inspired studies fostered by Pew Charitable Trust (PEW) and the National Center for State Courts (NCSC).[21]

2.   *Growth of OArb*

ODR has certainly entered the arbitration world. Indeed, many of the original ODR platforms used online arbitration (OArb). Here are some examples:

eBay.   eBay is an early example of companies using ODR to promote efficient claims resolution and build goodwill. Indeed, eBay learned that it could retain loyal customers and even inspire them to make more purchases if customers trust that they will get a remedy if a purchase goes awry. Specifically, unhappy buyers can file an online claim in the eBay Resolution Center.[22] This will inform the seller that there has been an issue, which will prompt negotiations between the seller and the buyer. If the buyer is satisfied with the seller's solution, the buyer can close the case. If unsatisfied with the seller's response, or the seller has not responded in three days, the buyer has 21 days to report it to eBay to continue the process. At this point, eBay helps resolve the issue, typically within 48 hours.[23]

NetNeutrals.   Related to eBay is another ODR service, NetNeutrals. This is designed for eBay as an independent feedback review process.[24] It focuses only on questions relating to negative feedback for products sold on eBay. It starts with negotiation and also offers OArb, for a fee, which employs a neutral third party to review the case and determine if clear and convincing evidence exists that a review violates eBay's policies.

Modria.   The creators of eBay's ODR process branched off as Modria, which Tyler Technologies has acquired for resolving disputes online.[25] Modria is a flexible software that allows direct negotiation, and also supports the inclusion of a mediator and/or arbitrator. While OArb is not its main functionality, the program allows for a neutral to make a final determination.[26]

Matterhorn.   Matterhorn is another company that provides ODR, mainly within the courts.[27] Matterhorn can allow for online negotiation, as well as mediation or arbitration. It is capable of handling disputes such as small claims cases, family court compliance, traffic court, civil infractions, and misdemeanours. The software is especially effective for facilitating easy payment of fines, as well as OArb where appropriate.[28]

FairClaims.   FairClaims is an ODR provider that focuses on OArb.[29] The process involves the claimant signing in and providing information about the dispute and the other party. FairClaims facilitates an OArb hearing, where each side has a brief opportunity to state their case, and then the arbitrator will ask specific questions to both sides based on the statements and evidence. At the conclusion of the hearing, the arbitrator may ask for additional evidence from either or both parties, who will then have four days to upload the additional evidence. The arbitrator will render a decision within eight days of the hearing, and if an award of payment is granted, it must be made within 14 days.

FORUM.   Another ODR provider that focuses on OArb is FORUM. This provider specializes in business-to-business, employment, franchise, intellectual property, and domain name dispute resolution.[30] The process again requires the claimant to file a claim using FORUM's online portal.[31] FORUM then appoints an arbitrator or panel of arbitrators who handles scheduling hearings and ultimately makes a binding ruling issuing an award, which can be entered in any court of competent jurisdiction. Preliminary scheduling hearings can be conducted via telephone, online, email, or in person depending on the parties' agreement.[32] Many cases are handled solely on the documents, meaning that the parties do not attend hearings in the case.

ARS.   Another example OArb provider is Arbitration Resolution Services (ARS). This provider offers online arbitration services for both business to individual and business to business disputes.[33] The process is much the same as the prior providers noted, with all documents handled through an online portal.[34] ARS arbitrators usually decide cases on the documents, without a formal hearing.[35] The goal is to further efficiency and fairness in a flexible manner, which is a hallmark of OArb.[36]

Of course, this is only the tip of the iceberg as new platforms come on the scene. The ODR world is continually growing and expanding.

3.   *Ethical Considerations for ODR*

Research around ODR in the United States is ramping up, particularly as we seek to address failures of traditional processes to address access to justice (A2J) shortcomings. As noted earlier, the NCSC and PEW have been researching ODR with an aim toward promotion of new processes that give voice and means to remedies for all individuals regardless of education, income, or other resources.[37] Even before Covid-19, PEW ODR research was underway.[38] PEW stated that its project aims were the following:

- Increase the availability and quality of free online legal tools that help everyone navigate complex problems and connect to resources.

- Develop, promote, and evaluate technologies that improve how people interact with state and local courts.
- Conduct research to identify policies that can improve outcomes for people involved in the civil legal system.
- Build partnerships with the private sector, policymakers, and other stakeholders to advance comprehensive improvement to the civil legal system.

This research includes plans to work with selected group(s) and the NCSC with respect to RFP No. CLSM-2019-01.[39] At the same time, the Pew Charitable Trusts is researching use of emerging technologies, such as natural language processing (NLP), to help people identify their own legal issues.[40]

Moreover, the National Center for Technology and Dispute Resolution (NCTDR)[41] has become foundational in ODR. The field of ODR dates back to 1997 with a grant to Ethan Katsh and Janet Rifkin from the Hewlett Foundation to establish the National Center for Technology and Dispute Resolution. Since then, NCTDR has been in the forefront of advocating and researching ODR, holding an annual International Forum and an online resource called Cyberweek, publishing the *International Journal of Online Dispute Resolution* and the treatise *Online Dispute Resolution: Theory and Practice* (2012 and 2021), conducting experiments such as the eBay pilot study, and fostering the metaphor of the "Fourth Party." The NCTDR's 49 Fellows from around the globe are working transnationally on ODR projects.

The NCTDR also has been a leader in creating Ethical Principles for ODR, which provide ideals or values that are built upon traditional dispute resolution notions but go further to address the incorporation of technology into conflict management. They provide guidance for the development of ethical standards, best practices, certification — and dispute systems design, referenced above. Notably, the Principles are nimble in order to offer ongoing guidance as new technologies emerge. Already, the Principles have served as a stimulus for the development of rules-based ODR standards by the International Center for Online Dispute Resolution (ICODR), which are directly based upon the Principles.[42] The ICODR ODR Standards list is as follows:

- **Accessible**: ODR must be easy for parties to find and participate in and not limit their right to representation. ODR should be available through both mobile and desktop channels, minimize costs to participants, and be easily accessed by people with different physical ability levels.
- **Accountable**: ODR systems must be continuously accountable to the institutions, legal frameworks, and communities that they serve.
- **Competent**: ODR providers must have the relevant expertise in dispute resolution, legal, technical execution, language, and culture required to deliver competent, effective services in their target areas. ODR services must be timely and use participant time efficiently.
- **Confidential**: ODR must maintain the confidentiality of party communications in line with policies that must be made public around (a) who will see what data, and (b) how that data can be used.
- **Equal**: ODR must treat all participants with respect and dignity. ODR should enable often silenced or marginalized voices to be heard, and ensure that offline privileges and disadvantages are not replicated in the ODR process.

- **Fair/Impartial/Neutral**: ODR must treat all parties equally and in line with due process, without bias or benefits for or against individuals, groups, or entities. Conflicts of interest of providers, participants, and system administrators must be disclosed in advance of commencement of ODR services.
- **Legal**: ODR must abide by and uphold the laws in all relevant jurisdictions.
- **Secure**: ODR providers must ensure that data collected and communications between those engaged in ODR is not shared with any unauthorized parties. Users must be informed of any breaches in a timely manner.
- **Transparent**: ODR providers must explicitly disclose in advance (a) the form and enforceability of dispute resolution processes and outcomes, and (b) the risks and benefits of participation. Data in ODR must be gathered, managed, and presented in ways to ensure it is not misrepresented or out of context.

At the same time, the American Bar Association (ABA) has established an ODR Task Force aimed at creating best practices around ODR and making the market more transparent to instill trust in its users. The ODR Task Force in the United States is organized around three main "Working Groups": (1) guidance with respect to best practices, and institutions' involvement in establishing and regulating such practices; (2) guidance with respect to special issues relating to court ODR; and (3) guidance with respect to special issues relating to private ODR. For all these groups, there is an overall interest in exploring how institutions should deal with resistance and facilitate best implementation of ODR. The ABA hopes to work in concert with ICODR and NCTDR so that all three groups can ultimately co-author standards for ODR. This will help with stakeholder building and maximizing impact.

QUESTIONS

6. You are a law clerk for the supreme court of State X (could be any state in the United States), and one of the justices has asked you to offer your thoughts on the efficiency and ethical considerations State X should consider with respect to a proposed ODR program for handling debt collection cases. Specifically, this proposed program would require all parties (debtors and creditors) to file their cases online and seek to first settle the case through online text-based mediation before proceeding to any trial in court. The proposed system would require creditors to pay a small filing fee, which would cover the costs of having online mediators facilitating discussions through a secure portal where parties could exchange correspondence and evidence. What thoughts would you share with the justice regarding this proposed system?

7. The same justice from the supreme court of State X is also on an "Access to Justice Commission" for State X. The state is considering use of a "chatbot" that could answer basic legal questions, or at least provide guidance on next steps for those with legal issues. The idea is to expand access to justice by making this freely available and saving individuals from having to hire attorneys for smaller dollar claims. The chatbot would incorporate AI by deciphering data on prior cases in order to provide predictions

about individuals' cases based on individuals' answers to a few questions. The first "chatbot" would provide guidance to debtors in debt collection cases. What ethical issues come to mind? What would you recommend to the justice regarding this proposal?

4. ODR Education

While law schools have long offered courses in negotiation and dispute resolution to complement traditional civil procedure and trial practice classes, ADR (alternative or appropriate dispute resolution) education is expanding to include ODR. A number of law schools now include modules as well as full courses.[43]

The NCTDR has received information from 14 colleges and universities that offer courses at least 50 percent focused on ODR. These courses in the United States and abroad span ODR law, policy, design, and more. Students in these classes often have the opportunity to use ODR platforms and experience simulations. They also may study technology in the context of system design, and write papers that address best means for using technology to assist in resolving a particular type of dispute.

For example, Professor Schmitz (one of the authors) has taught several versions of "Dispute Resolution in the Digital Age (DRDA)." Two of the versions of DRDA include one for in-person J.D. students, and the other for a fully online LL.M in Dispute Resolution. Other versions are more condensed two-credit versions. All the versions of the course consider technology through the lens of dispute systems design and practice, including simulations using various ODR platforms. The courses also include an examination of ethical dilemmas and completion of a final project proposing a system design for addressing resolution of a chosen area of conflict. Similar ODR courses are offered at Stanford, Pepperdine, Mitchell Hamline, Missouri, The Ohio State, and elsewhere—and are growing with importance as technologies further disrupt what we see as "traditional" ADR processes.

NOTE: DSD AND ODR

In 2020, Professor Amy Schmitz and system designer Heather Schweie Kulp conducted 11 interviews with people of varied demographic backgrounds. Their goal was to learn whether their subjects would find a court-based ODR system valuable, and specifically what they would expect from such a system before being willing to use it. In other words, they were engaged in the analysis stage of dispute systems design, talking with stakeholders (potential users) with an eye toward figuring out what a court-based ODR system might look like. Here are the questions they asked in their interviews:

- What does the phrase "online dispute resolution" bring to mind for you? What would you expect that to look like?
- Imagine yourself in one of the three following situations:
   a.   You have a credit card from a national retailer such as JC Penney or Best Buy. You cannot pay the card balance or even minimum for nine

months, and after attempting to collect, the credit card company files a court case asking a judge to force you to pay.

or

b. You have a small business, and one of your clients has not paid an amount due. You file a court case to ask a judge to force the client to pay.

or

c. You and your former spouse are having regular arguments about when your child should be with you during the summer. You file a court case to determine when the child should be with each parent.

In the scenario,

- Would you rather talk with the other side in online dispute resolution or have a hearing in front of a judge? Why?
- What medium (for example, typed text, audio, video, or forms) would you want to use to talk to the other side?
- What would you think if you were required to use online dispute resolution?
- What would you want to be true of an online dispute resolution system you were required to use?
- What would you not want in an online dispute resolution system you were required to use?
- What would make you stop using an online dispute resolution system?
- What support or assistance would you want in place to use the system?[44]

If you were conducting these interviews, what kind of themes might you expect to see emerging from the responses? How would you answer these questions yourself? Even though the sample size was small, the interviewers gathered useful data around varying definitions of ODR, expectations of assistance, expectations of security, and access and competencies. Read their full report in *Dispute Resolution Magazine*, Volume 26 (2020).

C. TRANSFORMING THE COMMUNITY

Lawyers who focus on dispute resolution often have the skills and outlook that make it easier to facilitate broader social changes. If you have studied how and why conflict might manifest as disputes, if you can see how relationships and identity can affect judgment and decision making, if you have learned the basic elements of dispute processing and system design — you are well positioned to make a positive difference in your workplace and your community. Put another way, the ADR mindset tends to focus on solving problems and restoring relationships, and many scholars and practitioners are thinking about how to bring that mindset to some of the most difficult and intractable challenges of our time.

In this section, we consider some recent trends in alternative practice around human rights, access to justice, and activism. The "new lawyer," as Julie Macfarlane has written, must be able to "modify and evolve their professional role consistent with changes in their professional environment."[45] We maintain that the new lawyer must also consider her professional identity in the context of her political and social environments as well, crafting a practice that is in harmony with personal values, professional goals, and community well-being.

1. *Human Rights*

For many people, human rights implicate deep, foundational beliefs around the inherent value of every person and the need to recognize and protect core rights and entitlements. Advocates of human rights are often engaged in legal and political campaigns seeking to validate or enshrine these rights and entitlements.

How does ADR fit into this picture? Although the tenets of mediation (informed consent, impartiality, self-determination) seem consistent with human rights, generally speaking it is not immediately obvious how mediation or other dispute resolution skills may be used to promote human rights or address violations of human rights. As clinical professors James Cavallaro and Stephan Sonnenberg point out, human rights and conflict resolution are typically taught in different courses, a separation that persists into practice:

> The division between these fields reflects and amplifies, to a significant degree, the historic tensions between professionals in these fields. Speaking in generalities, these actors have worked separately, frequently believing their approaches to be incompatible. Perhaps the clearest example of the perceived (and often real) tensions between these two fields has been the "peace versus justice" debate. In its simplest, most irreconcilable form, the clash between conflict resolution advocates and rights practitioners posits that situations of conflict can either be managed by accommodating all parties (including rights abusers) or, instead, by advocating justice (that is, investigation, prosecution, and punishment of rights advocates) regardless of the consequences.[46]

As Cavallaro and Sonnenberg indicate, a frequent criticism of ADR is that alternative practices prefer peace to justice — in other words, ADR focuses on managing the presenting conflict with less focus on substantive outcomes.

It is true that an agnostic focus seems at odds with human rights advocacy. Mediators and arbitrators are not advocates. They are neutrals who seek to promote fair and just outcomes through unbiased guidance and objective processes. Even though many have pointed out that pure neutrality is impossible — no one can completely rid themselves of their own perspectives, assumptions, beliefs, and biases — mediators and arbitrators strive for objectivity and even-handedness in their professional work. This is true even when they might normally have sympathy toward the situation of one of the parties or agree with someone on the merits of an issue.

That said, there are increasing calls from some corners of the mediation and arbitration communities for neutrals to take more responsibility for promoting certain substantive goals around human rights and dignity. These calls fall into two camps.

First, there are long-standing concerns around the way disputants (especially more disadvantaged disputants) may find themselves in mediation or arbitration. Even though alternative processes are often billed as consensual, you may end up in mediation or arbitration without actual consent. Court-connected processes may be mandated in some instances or strongly encouraged in others, making it difficult for you to have your "day in court." Similarly, boilerplate agreements to arbitrate may make it hard if not impossible for consumers or employees to seek effective redress from large corporations, especially if they are precluded from joining together as a class. Although this book has been all about the upsides of avoiding litigation and coming to private agreements, we have also recognized that there are cases in which public litigation is an individual and social good. To the extent that mediation or arbitration prevents parties from litigation, we should be concerned about the implications at stake for human dignity and self-autonomy.

Second, many scholars and practitioners have criticized alternative practices as creating false equivalencies, erasing moral culpability, downplaying power disparities, and privileging the status quo. For example, when a mediator mediates a sexual harassment case, the mediator does not pass judgment on either party or set forth ethical principles that will be used to resolve the situation. Rather, the mediator allows both parties to speak and attempts to guide them through an impartial process of exchanging information and proposing possible solutions. But without a greater understanding of the power dynamics and other contextual factors at play, these critics claim, the mediator may be unwittingly perpetuating these disparities and exacerbating the historical or social conflict underlying the dispute.

With this in mind, some ADR practitioners have started adopting new modes of practice that take human rights and anti-racist principles into account. As discussed in Chapter 13, there is increasing interest in applying mediation and mediation techniques to public controversies, civil unrest, and racial injustice.[47] For example, a community dispute resolution center outside of Portland, Oregon, has expanded its mediation training offerings to include sessions focusing on dealing with white supremacy and creating more space for restorative justice. Billing themselves as providing "equity-informed mediation,"[48] the center explicitly recognizes the social and political influences at play in all conflict and disputes and seeks to guide parties to more equity-based assessments and solutions.

QUESTIONS

8. Is an equity-based approach to mediation at odds with the practice's fundamental principles? Why or why not?

9. Professors Cavallaro and Sonnenberg observe that although dispute resolution practitioners have begun incorporating human rights into their practices, human rights advocates have been less sanguine about adopting dispute resolution methods. What benefits do you see for human rights advocates in becoming more effective at dispute resolution? Are there any risks you would be concerned about?

NOTE: ACCESS TO JUSTICE

If human rights are the "what" and "why," access to justice is the "how." Access to justice in the ADR context refers to how well dispute resolution processes provide disadvantaged individuals and communities with the ability to be heard and obtain redress. This includes means for obtaining redress for injuries or defending themselves in situations that typically involve inequitable distributions of resources or power. How can alternative approaches improve access to justice? One possibility is that alternative processes provide an avenue toward resolution that the legal system does not or cannot otherwise provide. Consider the following analysis by Professor Jacqueline Nolan-Haley, writing in the context of international dispute resolution:

> Article 33(1) of the United Nations ("U.N.") Charter identifies several processes for the peaceful resolution of disputes, including negotiation, mediation, conciliation, and arbitration. These are what we understand today as standard alternative dispute resolution ("ADR") processes. The four core ADR processes are promoted as vehicles for enhancing access to justice in legal systems that are often inaccessible to the general population. ADR is offered as a complement to court systems, and there is no end to the promises it offers. In Uganda, for example, ADR has been romanticized as a fix for broken legal systems and a tool to help individual citizens achieve access to justice. Court-connected mediation in Ghana, revered as almost divine intervention, has been credited with "reuniting families, repairing marriages, saving children and securing their future."
>
> To the extent that the term ADR has become synonymous with access to justice, there has been, in effect, a merger of ADR and access to justice. Multiple countries with different legal infrastructures and regulatory frameworks claim that ADR is an "access-to-justice" provider. Countries differ in the manner in which they accept the legitimacy of ADR as a means of providing access to justice. In some Latin American countries with weak judicial systems, ADR, particularly mediation, is considered not merely as a complement to achieving access to justice through the court system, but a substitute for it. There has been widespread acceptance of court-connected ADR in the U.S., while Russian citizens resist ADR innovations in their judicial system.

Professor Nolan-Haley points out that merely setting up alternative processes in lieu of more formal legal procedures does not automatically provide access to justice for disputants. What considerations might be relevant in determining whether an ADR process provides genuine access to justice?

2. Activism

Today, ADR is mainstream in law and business. Mediation and arbitration are well-established processes inside and outside courts, and negotiation is often the way that litigation is resolved and transactions are made. For this reason, many people argue that the "A" in ADR (alternative) is no longer applicable.

It is worth remembering, however, that ADR was not always as common as it is now. In the 1960s and 1970s, ADR proponents truly were alternative, working outside the mainstream to find new and better ways for community members to have access to holistic, sensible, participatory, and representative dispute resolution processes. These early proponents were ADR activists in the sense that they were seeking extralegal approaches to handling disputes that also would empower individuals and transform society.[49] In many ways, alternative dispute resolution—with its focus on party autonomy and dignity—developed as an activist response to a civil justice system that was seen as impersonal, rigid, inaccessible, and unfairly biased against disadvantaged or marginalized people.[50]

That said, as the legal system has become more dependent on negotiation, mediation, and arbitration, ADR has become more institutionalized and professionalized, focusing more on the efficient resolution of disputes than on innovative value-creating solutions or the transformation of people and communities. Yet many in ADR still feel a pull toward the activist roots of the field, and there has been growing interest of late in thinking about ADR skills and processes within the context of activism and social justice.

We have already discussed how some mediators and others have been moving toward incorporating values around human rights into their work. In addition, there are opportunities for negotiators and system designers to consider how to bring their skillsets to assist activists. For example, Professor Jen Reynolds has argued for thinking about the cross-applicability of activism and dispute systems design (DSD), identifying two benefits from thinking about them together:

> First, systems design thinking may help analysts, activists, and others better describe what activists do. More precise language describing what activists do might, in turn, help better delineate the markers and contours of social activism and thus make it easier to understand how social activism compares and interacts with other institutions and dynamics. Additionally, such language (and accompanying frameworks) may make it easier for activists to organize themselves and what they are already doing more sensibly and strategically. For example, when approaching potential allies, activists who are proficient systems designers may have an easier time identifying stakeholder interests, developing agreements around support, and coordinating the involvement of outsiders.
>
> Second, and related to this latter point, systems design thinking may help identify potential areas of growth and capacity-building for activists. Mapping activities within a system can make it easier to see what is working well, what is working poorly and what is entirely missing. Note that many activists already undertake these kinds of organizational self-analyses, and indeed much activist literature contains information about strategies and campaigns that is entirely consistent with the precepts of DSD. Thinking about activism and system design together does not reveal new and never-before-considered directions, but instead serves as an important reminder of, and possible framework for, developing the multiple competencies that successful activists need to be effective.

In other words, there are natural synergies in the work of activists, negotiators, and designers—all people who are seeking to make (or sometimes resist) a change. Of course, an increasing focus on activism may pull ADR theorists and practitioners away from some of the pillars of ADR practice. Figuring out how to manage this tension productively is a central challenge for the field.

QUESTIONS

10. Two law students recently published a report called "Power, Protest, and Political Change."[51] The goal of their report was to "consolidate the wisdom from activists all over the world" on negotiation, within the greater context of their knowledge around dispute resolution, negotiation, and community organizing. In a similar vein, Professor Reynolds has proposed having law school courses and clinics that bring together students and outside activists to learn about collaboration, negotiation, systems design, and other approaches to managing conflict and implementing change. What might be the benefits of creating more "mixed" audiences for law classes?

11. Imagine that an activist group comes to you for advice. The city has recently stepped up its efforts to prevent people from living in tents along the side of the road or under overpasses. The activists are concerned that these unhoused people have nowhere to go and these evictions are disruptive and harmful. Do you think that the ADR skills and processes you have learned might be helpful in advising the activists? Based on your work in this class, how might you put together a plan for handling this issue?

12. As we have mentioned throughout this book, one of the most important new arenas for ADR is the criminal context. Plea bargaining, problem-solving courts, restorative justice, and victim-offender mediation are just some of the criminal justice processes to which many ADR scholars and practitioners have begun turning their attention. From what you have learned so far, what might be some of the potential benefits of applying an ADR perspective to the criminal context?

D. CONCLUSION

We conclude this book with some observations about the importance of conflict management, especially as part of a larger problem-solving mindset that recognizes a lawyer's responsibility in helping clients resolve disputes. Abraham Lincoln, while practicing law in the 1850s, had these words for his colleagues at the bar:

> Discourage litigation. Persuade your neighbors to compromise whenever you can. Point out to them how the nominal winner is often a real loser, in fees, expenses, and waste of time. As a peacemaker the lawyer has a superior opportunity of being a good man. There will still be business enough.[52]

The revolution in the management and resolution of conflict that inspired the writing of this book continues apace. It has become increasingly important for lawyers to provide their clients with an expanding range of tools for managing and resolving disputes, based on an appreciation of their appropriate uses and limitations. This is true for attorneys who advise or advocate on behalf of businesses and government institutions as well as lawyers who represent employees, consumers, and those who are injured.

We hope this book has provided you with the understanding of process choices that is essential to modern law practice. If we have not led you to all the answers, we hope we have equipped you to ask the right questions and imparted the knowledge, as well as introduced the skills, to help you resolve your clients' disputes.

Endnotes

1. These mechanisms for returning participants to negotiation before they have to engage in a win-lose contest are sometimes called "loop-back procedures." Goldberg, Stephen, Brett, Jeanne & Ury, William. (1997) *Designing an Effective Dispute System.*

2. This problem was inspired by Professor Jill Gross. Gross, Jill. (2019) *Dispute Resolution Themes in "Hamilton: An American Musical,"* Disp. Resol. Mag. 30.

3. Amsler, Lisa, Martinez, Janet & Smith, Stephanie. (2016) *Guiding Principles and Analytic Framework for Dispute Systems Design.*

4. Goldberg, Stephen, Brett, Jeanne & Ury, William, *supra* note 1.

5. Feinberg, Kenneth R. (2005) *What Is Life Worth?*

6. Ackerman, Robert. (2005) *The September 11th Victim Compensation Fund: An Effective Administrative Response to National Tragedy,* 10 Harv. Negot. L. Rev. 135.

7. https://www.moma.org/learn/moma_learning/meret-oppenheim-object-paris-1936/.

8. Feinberg, Kenneth R. (2001) *One-Stop Shopping: Using ADR to Resolve Disputes and Implement a Settlement,* 19 Alternatives 59.

9. Amsler, Lisa, Martinez, Janet & Smith, Stephanie, *supra* note 3.

10. Constantino, Cathy & Sickles Merchant, Christina. (1996) *Designing Conflict Management Systems.*

11. Amsler, Lisa, Martinez, Janet & Smith, Stephanie, *supra* note 3. These experts have recently published a notable new book refining and explicating their theories and methods. *See* Amsler, Lisa, Martinez, Janet & Smith, Stephanie. (2020) *Dispute System Design.*

12. See, for example, the *Negotiation 360* app at https://negotiation-360.com/.

13. Schmitz, Amy J. & Colin Rule, The New Handshake: Online Dispute Resolution and the Future of Consumer Protection (American Bar Association Section on Dispute Resolution 2017). *See also* Katsh, Ethan & Rabinovich-Einy, Orna. (2017) *Digital Justice: Technology and the Internet of Disputes.*

14. Crek, https://www.crekodr.com/.

15. Interview with Chittu Nagarajan, Founder of CREK, at The Arbitration Conversation Episode 50: Chittu Nagarajan, Founder and CEO of CREKODR.com, https://www.youtube.com/watch?v=AUX2PLuyjaQ.

16. Schmitz, Amy J. & Martinez, Janet. (2020) *ODR Providers Operating in the U.S., in Online Dispute Resolution: Theory and Practice: A Treatise on Technology and Dispute Resolution* (Mohamed S. Abdel Wahab, Ethan Katsh & Daniel Rainey, eds.).

17. Schmitz, Amy J. (2019) *Expanding Access to Remedies Through E-Court Initiatives*, 67 Buff. L. Rev. 101.

18. Paul Embley, NCSC, *Presentation at the First Int'l Forum on Online Courts*, U.S. Courts and Online Dispute Resolution 13 (Dec. 3, 2018), https://assets.publishing.service.gov.uk/government/uploads/system/uploads/attachment_data/file/761379/US.pdf; *Utah Courts Recent Press Notifications*, Utah Courts (Aug. 13, 2020), http://www.utcourts.gov/utc/news/2020/08/13/to-tackle-the-unmet-legal-needs-crisis-utah-supreme-court-unanimously-endorses-a-pilot-program-to-assess-changes-to-the-governance-of-the-practice-of-law/.

19. Susskind, Richard. (2013) *Tomorrow's Lawyers: An Introduction to Your Future.*

20. Schmitz, Amy J. & Rule, Colin. (2019) *Online Dispute Resolution for Smart Contracts*, 2019 J. Disp. Resol. 203.

21. Schmitz, Amy J. (2020) *Measuring "Access to Justice" in the Rush to Digitize*, 88 Fordham L. Rev. 2381.

22. *Using the Resolution Center as a Buyer*, eBay, https://www.ebay.com/help/buying/resolving-issues-sellers/using-resolution-center-buyer?id=4636&st=3&pos=2&query=Using%20the%20Resolution%20Center%20as%20a%20buyer&intent=dispute%20resolution&lucenceai=lucenceai (last visited Mar. 1, 2020).

23. *Ask eBay to Step in and Help for Buyers*, eBay, https://www.ebay.com/help/buying/returns-refunds/ask-ebay-step-help-buyers?id=4701 (last visited Mar. 1, 2020).

24. *About Us: An Innovative Approach to Dispute Resolution*, NetNeutrals, https://netneutrals.com/About-Us (last visited June 5, 2020).

25. *Modria,* Tyler Technologies, https://www.tylertech.com/products/Modria (last visited June 5, 2020).

26. *Integrated Software for Courts & Justice Agencies*, Tyler Technologies, https://www.tylertech.com/solutions/courts-public-safety/courts-justice#DisputeResolution (last visited June 5, 2020).

27. *What Is Matterhorn*, Matterhorn, https://getmatterhorn.com/tour/what-is-matterhorn/ (last visited June 6, 2020).

28. *What Is Matterhorn*, Matterhorn, https://getmatterhorn.com/odr-solutions/ (last visited June 6, 2020).

29. *How It Works*, FairClaims, https://www.fairclaims.com/how_it_works (last visited June 6, 2020).

30. *About Us,* FORUM, https://www.adrforum.com/about (last visited June 6, 2020).

31. *Business to Business Arbitration*, FORUM, https://www.adrforum.com/arbitration/b2b (last visited June 6, 2020). Employment and intellectual property arbitration seem to be handled through a very similar set of rules and procedures.

32. *Code of Procedure for Resolving Business-To-Business Disputes*, FORUM, https://www.adrforum.com/assets/resources/Arbitration/Rules/Forum.B2B_Rules.v2.3.pdf (last visited June 29, 2020).

33. *Alternative Dispute Resolution Through Online Arbitration and Mediation*, Arbitration Resolution Services, https://www.arbresolutions.com/about/ (last visited June 6, 2020).

34. *How It Works*, Arbitration Resolution Services, https://www.arbresolutions.com/how-it-works/ (last visited June 6, 2020).

35. *Rules & Regulations Business to Business Program*, Arbitration Resolution Services, https://www.arbresolutions.com/rules-regulations-business-to-business-program/ (last visited June 29, 2020).

36. *Rules & Regulations Business to Business Program*, Arbitration Resolution Services, https://www.arbresolutions.com/rules-regulations-business-to-business-program/ (last visited June 29, 2020); *Rules & Regulations Business to Individuals Program*, Arbitration Resolution Services, https://www.arbresolutions.com/rules-regulations-businesses-to-individualsprogram/ (last visited June 29, 2020).

37. *Online Dispute Resolution Faces Major Challenges*, Artificial Lawyer, Mar. 19, 2019, at https://www.artificiallawyer.com/2019/03/19/online-dispute-resolution-faces-major-challenges-survey/ (last visited May 10, 2019).

38. The Pew Charitable Trusts, Civil Legal System Modernization, at https://www.pewtrusts.org/en/projects/civil-legal-system-modernization (last visited June 29, 2019).

39. *Outcome Evaluation for Online Dispute Resolution in State Courts*, May 31, 2019 (as amended), at https://www.pewtrusts.org/-/media/assets/2019/04/2019-clsm-rfp-01-amended.pdf (last visited June 29, 2019).

40. Rickard, Erika. (2019) *How Artifical Intelligence Could Improve Access to Legal Information*, Pew, at https://www.pewtrusts.org/en/research-and-analysis/articles/2019/01/24/how-artificial-intelligence-could-improve-access-to-legal-information (last visited Jan. 28, 2019).

41. *International Journal of Online Dispute Resolution*, http://odr.info/ethics-and-odr/; Wing, Leah. (2016). *Ethical Principles for Online Dispute Resolution: A GPS Device for the Field*, 3 Int'l J. Online Disp. Resol. 1.

42. *International Council for Online Dispute Resolution*, at http://icodr.org/index.php/standards/ (last visited Jan. 1, 2020).

43. Schools that have posted their courses with the National Center for Technology and Dispute Resolution include Creighton University, Dominican University, Mitchell Hamline School of Law, Nova Southeastern Florida, Pepperdine School of Law, Santa Clara University, Southern Methodist University, Stanford Law School, University of Massachusetts Amherst, and University of Missouri School of Law (Columbia).

44. Kulp, Heather & Schmitz, Amy J. (2020) *Real Feedback from Real People: Emphasizing User-Centric Designs for Court ODR*, 26 No. 2 Disp. Resol. Mag. 6.

45. Macfarlane, Julie. (2009) *The New Lawyer*.

46. Sonnenberg, Stephan & Cavallaro, James L. (2012) *Name, Shame, and Then Build Consensus? Bringing Conflict Resolution Skills to Human Rights*, 39 Wash. U. J.L. Pol'y 257.

47. Rogers, Nancy H. et al. (2016) *Planning in Advance for Civil Unrest: A Role for Mediation-Wise Attorneys*, Disp. Resol. Mag. 11 (Summer 2016). *See also* Froehlich, William et al. (2020) *Sharing Dispute Resolution Practices with Leaders of a Divided Community or Campus: Strategies for Two Crucial Conversations*, 35 Ohio St. J. on Disp. Resol. 5.

48. https://resolutionsnorthwest.org/services/.

49. Harrington, Christine B. & Merry, Sally E. (1988) *Ideological Production: The Making of Community Mediation*, 22 Law & Soc'y Rev. 709-736.

50. Reynolds, Jennifer W. (2018) *The A Is for Activism*, in *The Negotiator's Desk Reference* (Schneider & Honeyman, eds.).

51. Davies, Brooke & Oyolu, Daniel. (2020) *Power, Protest, and Political Change*, at https://hnmcp.law.harvard.edu/power-protest-and-political-change/.

52. Stipanowich, Thomas J. (2010) *Lincoln's Lessons for Lawyers*, Disp. Res. Mag. 18.